KU-535-229

ORKNEY AND
SHETLAND ISLANDS

0 kilometres   75

0 miles   50

THE HIGHLANDS
AND ISLANDS

GLASGOW
Pages 94–109

CENTRAL
SCOTLAND

GLASGOW   EDINBURGH

SOUTHERN
SCOTLAND

EDINBURGH
Pages 52–79

EYEWITNESS TRAVEL GUIDES

SCOTLAND

EYEWITNESS TRAVEL GUIDES

SCOTLAND

Main Contributors: JULIET CLOUGH, KEITH DAVIDSON,
SANDIE RANDALL & ALASTAIR SCOTT

LONDON, NEW YORK,
MELBOURNE, MUNICH AND DELHI
www.dk.com

PROJECT EDITOR Rosalyn Thiro
ART EDITOR Marisa Renzullo
EDITORS Felicity Crowe, Emily Green
DESIGNER Paul Jackson

MANAGING EDITORS Fay Franklin, Louise Bostock Lang
MANAGING ART EDITOR Annette Jacobs
SENIOR EDITOR Helen Townsend
EDITORIAL DIRECTOR Vivien Crump
ART DIRECTOR Gillian Allan
PUBLISHER Douglas Amrine

PICTURE RESEARCH Brigitte Arora
DTP DESIGNERS Maite Lantaron, Lee Redmond

CONTRIBUTORS
Juliet Clough, Keith Davidson, Alan Freeman,
Sandie Randall, Alastair Scott, Roger Smith

MAPS
Ben Bowles, Rob Clynes
(Colourmap Scanning, London)

PHOTOGRAPHERS
Joe Cornish, Paul Harris, Stephen Whitehorn

ILLUSTRATORS
Richard Bonson, Gary Cross, Jared Gilby, Paul Guest,
Kevin Jones Associates, Claire Littlejohn,
Chris Orr & Associates, Ann Winterbotham

Printed and bound in China by L. Rex Printing Co., Ltd
First published in Great Britain in 1999
by Dorling Kindersley Limited
80 Strand, London WC2R 0RL
Reprinted with revisions 2000, 2001, 2002, 2004, 2006

Copyright 1999, 2006 © Dorling Kindersley Limited, London
A Penguin Company

ALL RIGHTS RESERVED. NO PART OF THIS PUBLICATION MAY BE
REPRODUCED, STORED IN A RETRIEVAL SYSTEM, OR TRANSMITTED IN ANY
FORM OR BY ANY MEANS, ELECTRONIC, MECHANICAL, PHOTOCOPYING,
RECORDING OR OTHERWISE, WITHOUT THE PRIOR WRITTEN PERMISSION
OF THE COPYRIGHT OWNER.

A CIP CATALOGUE RECORD IS AVAILABLE FROM THE BRITISH LIBRARY.
ISBN 1 4053 11924
ISBN 978 1405 3119 22

**The information in this
Dorling Kindersley Travel Guide is checked regularly.**
Every effort has been made to ensure that this book is as up-to-date
as possible at the time of going to press. Some details, however,
such as telephone numbers, opening hours, prices, gallery hanging
arrangements and travel information, are liable to change. The
publishers cannot accept responsibility for any consequences arising
from the use of this book, nor for any material on third party
websites, and cannot guarantee that any website address in this
book will be a suitable source of travel information. We value the
views and suggestions of our readers highly. Please write to:
Publisher, DK Eyewitness Travel Guides,
Dorling Kindersley, 80 Strand, London, Great Britain WC2R 0RL.

The dramatic, sunlit ruins of Tantallon Ca[stle]

CONTENTS

INTRODUCING SCOTLAND

PUTTING SCOTLAND ON THE MAP *8*

A PORTRAIT OF SCOTLAND *10*

SCOTLAND THROUGH THE YEAR *36*

THE HISTORY OF SCOTLAND *40*

Mary, Queen of Scots (1542–87)
of the House of Stuart

SCOTLAND REGION BY REGION

SCOTLAND AT A GLANCE *50*

◁ The tranquil river, lush greenery and snowy peaks of Glencoe in the Highlands

the southeast coast

EDINBURGH 52

SOUTHERN SCOTLAND
80

GLASGOW 94

Detail of the decorated vaulting in
Roslin Chapel, in the Pentland Hills

CENTRAL SCOTLAND
110

THE HIGHLANDS AND
ISLANDS 126

TRAVELLERS'
NEEDS

WHERE TO STAY 164

WHERE TO EAT 174

SPECIAL INTERESTS
AND OUTDOOR
ACTIVITIES 184

Skirlie – a traditional Scottish dish
of oatmeal, onions and thyme

SURVIVAL GUIDE

PRACTICAL
INFORMATION 198

TRAVEL INFORMATION
208

GENERAL INDEX 216

Royal Scots Greys Memorial to the
Scottish soldiers of the Boer War

ACKNOWLEDGMENTS
223

GLOSSARY OF GAELIC
TERMS 224

ROAD MAP OF
SCOTLAND
Inside back cover

Walkers enjoying a glorious
summer's day in Glen Etive

Edinburgh Castle on its volcanic
rock above the city centre

INTRODUCING
SCOTLAND

PUTTING SCOTLAND ON THE MAP 8-9
A PORTRAIT OF SCOTLAND 10-35
SCOTLAND THROUGH THE YEAR 36-39
THE HISTORY OF SCOTLAND 40-47

Putting Scotland on the Map

S EPARATED FROM CONTINENTAL EUROPE by the
North Sea, Scotland forms the northern
part of Great Britain. It is a mountainous,
sparsely populated land. The highest
peak is Ben Nevis, at 1,344 m (4,406 ft).
The coastline is also ringed by hundreds of islands; at the farthest
extreme Shetland lies just six
degrees south of the Arctic Circle.
Edinburgh is the historic capital,
and Glasgow is the largest city
with a population of 569,000.
The country has good road,
rail and ferry connections.

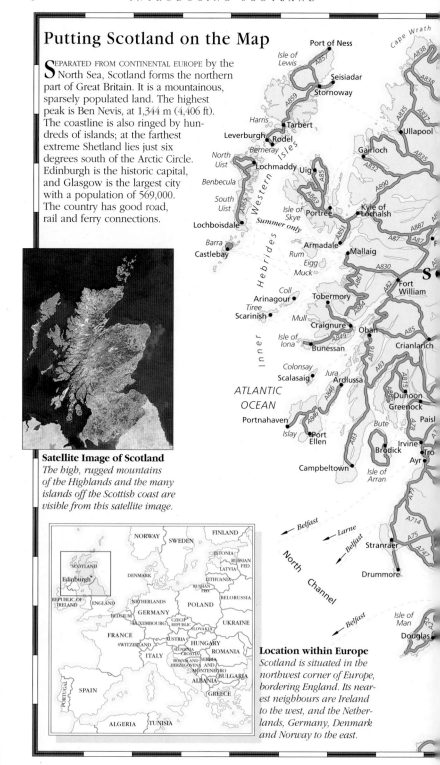

Satellite Image of Scotland
*The high, rugged mountains
of the Highlands and the many
islands off the Scottish coast are
visible from this satellite image.*

Location within Europe
*Scotland is situated in the
northwest corner of Europe,
bordering England. Its nearest neighbours are Ireland
to the west, and the Nether-
lands, Germany, Denmark
and Norway to the east.*

ORKNEY AND SHETLAND ISLANDS

Shetland Islands

Unst
Yell
Mainland Brae
Walls
Foula
Lerwick
Passenger only

Passenger only

Fair Isle

Westray
Mainland Sanday
Stromness Stronsay
Kirkwall
Orkney Islands
Hoy

Scrabster
Thurso
Wick

Aberdeen
Aberdeen

0 kilometres 50
0 miles 50

Scrabster
Thurso
Wick
Helmsdale

Elgin
Fraserburgh
Inverness
Peterhead

Braemar
Aberdeen
Dee

SCOTLAND

Pitlochry
Montrose
Forfar
Arbroath
Perth
Dundee
St Andrews

Stirling
Kirkcaldy
Dunfermline
Rosyth
EDINBURGH
Glasgow
East Kilbride
Peebles
Galashiels
Berwick-upon-Tweed

Hawick
Jedburgh
Alnwick

Dumfries
Hexham
Newcastle Upon Tyne
Castle Douglas
Carlisle
ENGLAND
Sunderland

Cockermouth
Penrith
Whitehaven
Keswick

Kendal

Barrow-in-Furness
Heysham
Lancaster

Kirkwall
Lerwick
Zeebrugge
Stavanger Bergen

NORTH SEA
NORTH SEA

KEY TO MAP

Motorway (highway)
Major road
Ferry route
National border

0 kilometres 50
0 miles 50

MILEAGE CHART

LONDON

111 / 179	*BIRMINGHAM*						
150 / 241	102 / 164	*CARDIFF*					
74 / 119	185 / 298	228 / 367	*DOVER*				
372 / 599	290 / 467	373 / 600	442 / 711	*EDINBURGH*			
389 / 626	292 / 470	374 / 602	466 / 750	45 / 72	*GLASGOW*		
529 / 851	448 / 721	530 / 853	600 / 965	158 / 254	167 / 269	*INVERNESS*	
184 / 296	81 / 130	173 / 278	257 / 414	213 / 343	214 / 344	371 / 597	*MANCHESTER*

10 = Distance in miles
10 = Distance in kilometres

A PORTRAIT OF SCOTLAND

WITH SUCH A DISTINCTIVE *national dress, drink, bagpipe music, landscape and folklore, Scotland has shaped an identity recognizable the world over. It is a land of astonishing contrasts and possesses a magical quality, whether seen shrouded in mist or rising majestic above the mirror of a loch.*

In a straight line from the far south to the far north, the Scottish mainland reaches about 440 km (275 miles), yet its coastline stretches nearly 10,000 km (6,200 miles). There are 787 major islands, almost all lying off the northern or western coasts. The topography is generally extremely mountainous with wild heather moorlands in the north and west, pine forests mixed with quality pasture in the middle, fertile farmland in the east and, in the south, the rounded, grass-covered hills of the Lowlands. Picturesque lochs and rivers are scattered throughout. Most of Scotland's five million people live

Red deer in the Highlands

in the country's Central Belt. The Scots cherish the differences that set them apart from the English, and cling tenaciously to the distinctions that differentiate them region by region – their customs, dialects and the Gaelic language. It is perhaps more by their differences than similarities that the Scots can be defined but, for all that, they are immensely proud of their nation and its separate institutions, such as education and law. The Scots can be dour but equally they can flash with inspiration. They delight in self-deprecating humour and continue to honour their tradition of hospitality.

A view from Edinburgh Castle over the rooftops of the capital to Calton Hill

◁ Isolated dwellings set among the lofty mountains on Skye, the largest island of the Inner Hebrides

POLITICS AND THE ECONOMY

Ever since the Treaty of Union in 1707, which combined the parliaments of Scotland and England into one governing body convening in Westminster (London), Scotland has felt estranged from the mechanisms of government, and short-changed by the small allocation of time given to Scottish affairs. Today, all the major political parties of the UK find support in Scotland. The Scottish National Party, which campaigns for complete independence, has gained in popularity. In 1997 the Scots voted for the re-establishment of a Scottish parliament, which began in 1999. This parliament has a wide-ranging administrative role, though major financial controls and decisions of national interest are retained by Westminster.

A hammer-thrower at the Braemar Games

Scotland's economy has fluctuated in the last 100 years. It has had to fight back from the demise of its heavy industries – shipbuilding, coal mining and steel production. Today, the major contributors to the economy are North Sea oil, tourism and services, aided by a wide spectrum of light industries. Chief among these is the manufacture of electronic components and microchips, contributing to the sobriquet of a "Silicon Glen", but this industry, which employs many people, has become shaky in response to the global market.

The Viking fire festival, *Up Helly Aa*, in Shetland

Whisky production is a leading revenue earner for the Exchequer (treasury department), although it employs few people. Agriculture retains its importance but has become beleaguered by disastrous markets. Fishing also remains an important industry, yet there is increasing competition for dwindling stocks. Scotland's level of unemployment is on a par with the UK, though there are worse-off areas, such as the Western Isles where it reaches 15 per cent.

SOCIETY

The Scots are a gregarious people and enjoy company, whether this be in a small group at a Highland *ceilidh* (literally, a "visit"), a crowded bar, or as part of the colourful, and usually peaceful, Saturday armies of football (soccer) fans. Sometimes they have to travel far to find company; the Highland region has a population density of eight people per square kilometre (20 per sq mile), and the lack of public transport means a car is vital.

Edinburgh bagpiper

Church attendance is in decline in all but the Gaelic-speaking areas, where Sundays are observed as days of rest. In most towns, and all cities, a full range of leisure activities and entertainment runs into the wee hours, but in rural areas opening hours are shorter, and restaurants may stop serving early.

Scotland is renowned as the home of golf, but football is without doubt the national passion, and England the favourite opponent. Other popular sports include hill-walking, skiing, rugby, shinty and curling. There are also annual Highland Games – great gatherings of whisky, music, craft stalls and tests of stamina and strength (*see p29*).

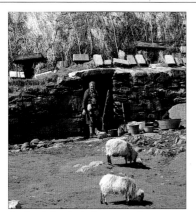

Small-scale farming in the Western Isles

many smaller festivals. The Scottish film industry is booming, following the success of *Trainspotting* (1996). The musical scene has also been enjoying a time of vibrancy, ranging from opera, Gaelic song, *pibroch* (the classical music of the bagpipes) to such varied international bands as Snow Patrol, Texas, Travis and the revived Wet Wet Wet. Traditional music has experienced a renaissance over the last decade using rhythms and instruments from around the world. With an estimated four Scots living abroad for every one living in the homeland, this influence is not surprising. Bands like Salsa Celtica combine Scottish folk and jazz with Latin American influences to great effect. In dance, on offer are the varied delights of Scottish country, Highland and *ceilidh* dancing and step dancing, a tradition reintroduced from Cape Breton. Although only about 50,000 people speak Gaelic, the language has been boosted by increased funding for Gaelic radio and television programmes. Literature has a strong following, too, with no shortage of respected Scottish authors and poets *(see pp24–5)*.

Yet for all their love of sports, the Scots are an unhealthy race. Their appetite for red meat and greasy fish and chips contributes to a high incidence of heart problems, and they have the highest consumption of alcohol and tobacco in the UK.

CULTURE AND THE ARTS

Scotland offers an excellent programme of the performing arts, subsidized generously by the Scottish Arts Council. The Edinburgh Festival and Fringe *(see pp 78–9)* is the largest celebration of its kind in the world, and there are

Edinburgh's Festival Fringe Office detail

The blue waters of Loch Achray in the heart of the Trossachs, north of Glasgow

The Geology of Scotland

SCOTLAND IS A GEOLOGIST'S PLAYGROUND, with rocks displaying three billion years of geological time. Starting with the hard granitic gneiss in the Western Isles, which was formed before life developed on earth, the rocks tell a story of lava flows, eras of mountain-building, numerous ice ages and even a time when the land was separated from England by the ancient Iapetus Ocean. Four major fault and thrust lines, running across Scotland from north-east to southwest, define the main geological zones.

FAULT AND THRUST LINES

–– Moine Thrust

–– Great Glen Fault *(see pp148–9)*

–– Highland Boundary Fault

–– Southern Uplands Fault

The gabbro *(dark rock) of the Cuillin Hills on Skye was created by subterranean magma in the Tertiary period, a time when the dinosaurs had died out and mammals were flourishing.*

CHANGING EARTH

Scotland · Equator
Iapetus Ocean
· England

☐ Ancient landmass

About 500 million years ago
Scotland was part of a landmass that included North America, while England was part of Gondwana. After 75 million years of continental breakup and drift, the two countries "collided", not far from the modern political boundary.

Scandinavia
Scotland

☐ Glaciation in the last Ice Age

··· Present-day national boundaries

The last Ice Age, which ended 10,000 years ago, was the most recent chapter in Scotland's geological history when, like Scandinavia, it became glaciated.

Rock layers in a stepped effect

The action of sea tides and waves continually erodes the existing coastline.

Plateau-topped hills on the island are the exposed remains of a basalt lava flow.

Lewisian gneiss *is one of earth's oldest substances, created in the lower crust three billion years ago and later thrust up and exposed. Hard, infertile and grey, it forms low plateaus filled with thousands of small lochs in the Western Isles.*

U-shaped valleys in the Highlands are a legacy of the last Ice Age. The weight and movements of glaciers broke off spurs, deepening and rounding out the existing river valleys.

Quartzite peaks soar above a base of sandstone in parts of the Torridon range. The quartzite can be mistaken for snow from a distance.

Freshwater loch

Deep sea loch

The basalt columns of the Isle of Staffa (see p133) were formed 60 million years ago. A flow of lava cooled slowly, contracting and fracturing in a distinctive hexagonal pattern similar to the Giant's Causeway in Ireland.

The Highland Boundary Fault runs from Stonehaven, on the east coast, to Arran on the west as an obvious line of hills.

Serpentine

Old lava flow

TYPICAL FEATURES

This cross-section is an idealized representation (not to scale) of some of the distinctive geology of the Highlands and islands of northwest Scotland. The tortuously indented coastline of this part of the country is a result of high precipitation in the area during the last Ice Age which heavily eroded the layers of ancient rocks, leaving a beautiful and contrasting landscape of boulder-strewn glens and deep lochs.

Devonian sandstone is prevalent in the Orkney Islands (see p158). In places, the sea has eroded the horizontally layered rock into spectacular cliffs and stacks, as with the 137-m (450-ft) Old Man of Hoy.

The Landscape and Wildlife of Scotland

SCOTLAND IS A LAND OF CONTRASTS, from the austere majesty of the mountains to the subtle undulations of the Lowland valleys, and from dramatic coastal cliffs to dense forests. It is in the wilds of the Highlands and islands that you are most likely to encounter Scotland's wealth of wildlife. Many once prolific species are slowly dying out; preserving them and their habitats is now paramount.

A tiny goldcrest

NATIVE ANIMALS

There are no large or dangerous wild animals in Scotland, but there are a few which are rarely found living wild elsewhere in the British Isles. Shetland ponies and Highland cattle, by their names alone, are instantly associated with Scotland, and you are unlikely to see a golden eagle or red deer outside of the Scottish Highlands.

COASTAL

The immense, windswept coastline of Scotland provides some of the best chances to view the country's wildlife. Islands such as Skye *(see pp152–3)*, pictured above, sustain myriad nesting seabirds, including puffins, guillemots and kittiwakes, while the Bass Rock, off the east coast near North Berwick, has a breeding colony of gannets. The Scottish coast is also home to seals, whales and dolphins.

Puffin

Grey seals *have long inhabited the rocky Scottish coasts, such as in Shetland or in North Rona, and are easily spotted.*

Kittiwakes, *with their white and grey plumage, are widespread along the Scottish cliffs, from St Abb's Head on the east coast to Handa Island off the northwest coast (see p157).*

LOCHS AND RIVERS

Scotland has an abundance of sea lochs, fresh water lochs and rivers, enabling a wide range of animal and insect life to flourish. Sea lochs, such as those shown above on the western isle of North Uist, may contain wild salmon and otters, although the latter are more likely to be spotted at a manmade sanctuary, such as the one at Kylerhea on Skye. Many Scottish rivers, the Tay being just one example, provide a wonderful opportunity for fishermen to catch salmon and trout.

Dragonfly

Wild otters *breed along many parts of Scotland's coast and in its sea lochs. Unlike their Asian cousins, they have webbed feet with which they catch and eat their prey.*

Salmon *swim into Scotland's lochs and rivers every year to breed. They travel miles upstream and up steep waterfalls in order to spawn.*

Shetland ponies are indigenous to the windswept, northerly isles of the same name, but can also be found on the mainland. The ponies are small, with thick, wiry coats.

Highland cattle, bred in Scotland since the 1500s, are recognizable by their long horns and shaggy coats.

The golden eagle is one of Scotland's most enduring emblems. Found at high altitudes, this majestic bird takes its prey in one silent swoop.

MOUNTAIN AND MOORLAND

The hills and mountains of Scotland are a refuge for rare arctic and alpine plants, while heather and grasses flourish on the moorlands and Lowlands. This contrast of landscapes can be seen right across the Scottish Highlands and islands, as shown here on Mull. Birds of prey, such as eagles and kestrels, favour this terrain; red deer graze on the bleak moorland.

Kestrel

WOODLAND AND FOREST

Some of Scotland's forests form part of a protected Forest Park. Woodland refuges, such as the one in the Borders shown above, are home to red squirrels and goldcrests, while pine martens and wildcats favour the rockier terrain of the Highland forests. Birch and oak woods are dotted around the country.

Pine marten

Sheep roam freely on the moorland and hills of Scotland, but they are usally marked so they can be identified by the farmer.

Red deer are the most common deer in Europe and can often be sighted in the Highlands of Scotland. Their signature coats are at their most vibrant in summer. The stags shed their antlers in spring.

Wildcats can still be found in forest areas, but their numbers are dwindling. A stocky body, thick fur and short, blunt tail distinguish them from a domestic cat.

Red squirrels are far rarer than their grey counterparts, but they share the same bushy tail for agility and communication, and sharp, hooked claws for a sure grip on trees.

Evolution of the Scottish Castle

FEW SIGHTS CAN MATCH the romance of a Scottish castle set upon a small island in the middle of a quiet loch. These formidable retreats, often in remote settings, were built all over the Highlands, where incursions and strife between the clans were common. From the earliest Pictish *brochs* (Iron Age stone towers) and Norman-influenced motte and bailey castles, the distinctively Scottish tower-house evolved, first appearing in the 14th century. By the mid-17th century fashion had become more important than defence, and there followed a period in which numerous huge Scottish palaces were built.

Detail of the Baroque façade, Drumlanrig

MOTTE AND BAILEY

These castles first appeared in the 12th century. They stood atop two adjacent mounds enclosed by a wall, or palisade, and defensive ditches. The higher mound, or motte, was the most strongly defended as it held the keep and chief's house. The lower bailey was where the common people lived.

The keep contained the chief's house, lookout and main defence.

Duffus Castle, Morayshire

Duffus Castle (c.1150) was atypically made of stone rather than wood. Its fine defensive position dominates the surrounding flatlands north of Elgin.

The Motte of earth or rock was sometimes partially man-made.

The Bailey enclosed dwellings and storehouses.

EARLY TOWER-HOUSE

Designed to deter local attacks rather than a major assault, the first tower-houses appeared in the 13th century, and their design lived on for 400 years. They were built initially on a rectangular plan, with a single tower divided into three or four floors. The walls were unadorned, with few windows. Defensive structures were on top, and extra space was made by building adjoining towers. Extensions were vertical, to minimize the area open to attack.

Crenellated parapet for sentries

Claypotts Castle (c.1570), with uniquely projecting garrets above its towers

Braemar Castle (c.1630), a conglomeration of extended towers

Neidpath Castle, standing upon a steep rocky crag above the River Tweed, is an L-shaped tower-house dating from the late 14th century. Once a stronghold for Charles II, its walls still bear damage from a siege conducted by Oliver Cromwell.

Featureless, straight walls contain arrow slits for windows.

LATER TOWER-HOUSE

Though the requirements of defence were being replaced by those of comfort, the style of the early tower-house remained popular. By the 17th century wings for accommodation were being added around the original tower (often creating a courtyard). The battlements and turrets were kept more for decorative than defensive reasons.

Drum Castle, near Aberdeen, a 13th-century keep with a mansion house extension from 1619

The priest's room has secret access.

Original 15th-century tower-house

This round angle tower contains a stairway.

Sixteenth-century horizontal extension

Traquair House (see p87), by the Tweed, is the oldest continuously inhabited house in Scotland. The largely unadorned, roughcast exterior dates from the 16th century, when a series of extensions were built around the original 15th-century tower-house.

Decorative, corbelled turret

Blair Castle *(see p139)*, incorporating a medieval tower

CLASSICAL PALACE

By the 18th century the defensive imperative had passed and castles were built in the manner of country houses, rejecting the vertical tower-house in favour of a horizontal plan (though the building of imitation fortified buildings continued into the 19th century with the mock-Baronial trend). Outside influences came from all over Europe, including Renaissance and Gothic revivals, and echoes of French châteaux.

Dunrobin Castle (c.1840), Sutherland

Larger windows are due to a lesser need for defence.

Balustrades replace defensive battlements.

Decorative cupola

Drumlanrig Castle (see p88) was built in the 17th century and has traditional Scots aspects as well as Renaissance features, such as the decorated stairway and façade.

Renaissance-style colonnade

Baroque horseshoe stairway

Scottish Gardens

SCOTLAND HAS A GREAT number of diverse and beautiful gardens. Some are renowned for their layout, such as Pitmedden, or for particular plants. Rhododendrons flourish in Scotland's acidic, peaty soil, and the Royal Botanic Garden in Edinburgh is famous for its spectacular, colourful display. Some gardens have a striking backdrop of lakes or mountains, while others form the grounds of a stately home. Gulf Stream gardens like Inverewe offer visitors a rare chance to view exotic, subtropical flora at a northern latitude. The gardens shown here are some of Scotland's finest.

Inverewe Garden (see p156) *is renowned for its lush, exotic, subtropical flora. Ferns, lilies, giant forget-me-nots and rare palms are just some of the 2,500 species that thrive in the mild climate.*

Crarae Gardens (see p130) *are sited on a slope overlooking Loch Fyne, surrounded by mature woodland. There are many walks, all designed to cross a picturesque burn at the centre. The gardens are riotous with spectacular rhododendrons in spring and ablaze with golden and russet leaves during the autumn.*

The Botanic Gardens, Glasgow (see p103), *have a wonderful collection of orchids, begonias and cacti. Kibble Palace, a domed, iron conservatory, houses tropical tree ferns from around the world.*

Logan Botanic Garden is an outpost of the Royal Botanic Garden in Edinburgh. The garden is divided into two main areas – a walled garden with cabbage palms, and a woodland area. The Gulf Stream enables subtropical plants to grow here.

Inverewe Garden

Angus' Garden

Crarae Gardens

Arduaine Garden

Younger Botanic Garden

Botanic Garden Glasgow

Logan Botanic Garden

THE RHODODENDRON

These examples illustrate three of the 900 rhododendron varieties. The first is tropical, grown under glass in Scotland; the second is evergreen; the third is an azalea, which used to be considered a separate species. Rhododendrons also fall into scaly-leaved and non-scaly groups.

Macgregoriae

Augustini

Medway

Drummond Castle Gardens are laid out as a large boxwood parterre in the shape of a St Andrew's Cross. Yellow and red roses and antirrhinums provide the colour, and a sundial forms the centrepiece.

THE GULF STREAM

The west coast of Scotland is the surprising location for a number of gardens where tropical and subtropical plants bloom. Although on the same latitude as Siberia, this area of Scotland lies in the path of a warm water current from the Atlantic. Inverewe is the most famous of the Gulf Stream gardens, with plants from South America, South Africa and the South Pacific. Other gardens include Achamore on the Isle of Gigha and Logan Botanic Garden near Stranraer.

Tree ferns warmed by the Gulf Stream, Logan Botanic Garden

Pitmedden Garden •

Crathes Gardens •

Drummond
Castle
Gardens
•

• Royal Botanic
Garden, Edinburgh

• Kailzie Gardens

Dawyck   Priorwood
Botanic Gardens
Garden

0 kilometres   50

0 miles   50

Pitmedden Garden was created in 1675 and later restored to its full glory as a formal garden by the National Trust for Scotland. Split into two levels, it has four parterres, two gazebos, box hedges and a splendid fountain at its centre.

Crathes Gardens' topiary and scented borders are centred around the beautiful tower house, Crathes Castle (see p145). There are eight different themed gardens, such as the Golden Garden designed in the style of Gertrude Jekyll.

Dawyck Botanic Garden is another branch of Edinburgh's Royal Botanic Garden, and specializes in rare trees, such as the Dawyck Beech, flowering shrubs and blankets of narcissi.

The Royal Botanic Garden, Edinburgh (see p68), is internationally renowned as a base for scientific research. With almost 17,000 species, the garden has a marvellous range of plants. Exotic plants are found in the many glasshouses, and the grounds are enhanced by beautifully maintained lawns.

Great Scottish Inventions

Marmalade

DESPITE ITS RELATIVELY small size and population, Scotland has produced a remarkable number of inventors over the centuries. The late 1700s and 1800s were years of such intense creativity that they became known as the Period of Scottish Enlightenment. Many technological, medicinal and mechanical breakthroughs were made at this time, including the invention of the steam engine, the bicycle, antiseptic and the telephone. Out of the country's factories, universities and laboratories came a breed of men who were intrepid and forward-thinking. Their revolutionary ideas and experiments produced inventions that have shaped our modern, progressive society.

Logarithm tables *(1594) were devised by John Napier as a practical way of multiplying and dividing large numbers. Though easy to use, the tables took 20 years to create.*

Continous electric light *(1834) was invented by James Bowman Lindsay using galvanic cells in a revolutionary design.*

Parallel motion operated all the valves in time.

A flywheel stored energy so that the engine ran smoothly.

The pneumatic tyre/tire *(John Dunlop, 1887), was originally patented by RW Thomson and then developed by Dunlop for use on bicycles and, later, cars.*

Piston rod

Golf clubs *were originally wooden and hand-crafted by carpenters such as Old Tom Morris. By 1890, aluminium-headed clubs had been introduced.*

The rotative steam engine *(James Watt, 1782) was a refinement of the existing steam engine. This new model soon became the driving force behind the Industrial Revolution in Britain, powering all manner of machinery. Watt's success led to his name being given to the modern unit of power.*

The bicycle *(Kirkpatrick Macmillan, 1839) was originally known as a velocipede, and it was not until the 1860s that bicycles began to be manufactured and sold in significantly large quantities.*

Colour photography *(1861) was developed by the Scottish physicist, James C Maxwell. The first to experiment with three-colour photography, he photographed this tartan ribbon using coloured water as a filter.*

Spray nozzle

Steam generator

Antiseptic *(Joseph Lister, 1865) in the form of carbolic acid was a most important breakthrough in surgery. Lister discovered that, applied to wounds and sprayed around the theatre, the acid helped to prevent germs and infection.*

Carbolic acid reservoir

The thermos flask *(Sir James Dewar, 1892) was first designed as a vacuum for storing low-temperature gases. The flask was later mass produced as the thermos, for maintaining the temperature of hot and cold drinks.*

The telephone *(Alexander Graham Bell, 1876) was the scientific breakthrough that revolutionized the way the world communicated, introducing the transmission of sound by electricity.*

Penicillin *(Alexander Fleming, 1928) is a discovery that has changed the face of medicine. Fleming's brainchild was the first antibiotic drug to treat diseases, and by 1940 it was being used to save the lives of wounded soldiers.*

The radar receiver *(Robert Watson-Watt, 1935) was in use long before World War II, since Watson-Watt's team had built the first working radar defence system by 1935. Radar is an acronym for "radio detection and ranging".*

The first television *(John Logie Baird, 1926), or "televisor", was black and white, and unable to produce sound and pictures together, but it was nevertheless hailed as a monumental invention. In 1928, Baird demonstrated the possibilities of creating colour images.*

Dolly the cloned sheep *was developed in 1996 by a team of scientists at Edinburgh's Roslin Institute. Dolly, the first successful clone of an adult animal in the world, gave birth in 1998.*

Writers and Intellectuals

FROM MEDIEVAL POETS through Robert Burns to Irvine Welsh, writers in the three literary languages of Scotland – Scots, English and Gaelic – have created a body of literature expressing both their place in the European mainstream and the diversity within Scotland. In 1999 a new parliament was established in Scotland, three centuries after the dissolution of the last one. Political devolution follows three decades of ferment in which literature has reached new heights of success.

Robert Burns encircled by images of his literary creations

THE GOLDEN AGE BEFORE ENLIGHTENMENT

OFTEN REGARDED as the golden age of Scottish literature, the century leading up to the Reformation of 1560 showed strong links with the Continent and a rich tradition of poetry, culminating in the achievements of William Dunbar and Robert Henryson. John Barbour established the mythic heroism of the national hero in *The Bruce* (c.1375). Other early works were James I's *Kingis Quair* (c.1424) and Blind Harry's *Wallace* (c.1478).

Philosopher David Hume

Dunbar was to pre-eminence for his polished art, from *Lament for the Makars* (1508), an elegy to poets, to his insult poetry known as "flyting". Henryson's work has insight, as in *The Testament of Cresseid* (c.1480), which tells the legend from the woman's point of view. Gavin Douglas translated Virgil's *Aeneid* into Scots in 1513. The golden age ended with Sir David Lindsay's much revived play, *A Satire of the Three Estates*, in 1540. The ballad tradition continues to influence Scottish literature.

ENLIGHTENMENT AND ROMANTICISM

THE INTELLECTUAL TRIUMPHS of the Enlightenment in Scotland were fuelled by the expanding educational system.

Among the great thinkers of the time were Adam Smith (1723–90), who theorized on political economy, and Adam Ferguson (1723–1816), who founded modern sociology. Other prominent figures were William Robertson (1721–93) and David Hume (1711–76), both of whom helped to define modern history. Hume's greatest legacy was in philosophy – his rigorous empiricism offended Christian orthodoxy and foretold crises of faith versus scientific knowledge. James Macpherson published the *Ossian Chronicles* in 1760, supposedly the documentation of his discovery of an old Celtic tradition in the Hebrides. This fictional work tapped a nostalgia for ancient civilizations and, allied to fears about progress, Romanticism was born. Allan Ramsay wrote poems in Scots, as did the tragic Robert Fergusson, who died in poverty aged 25.

The country's most fêted literary figure, Robert Burns (1759–96), was a man of his time. His "heaven-taught ploughman" persona fitted fashion but belied a sound education. His works ranged from love lyrics to savage satire (*Holy Willie's Prayer*), nationalism to radical ideals (*A Man's a Man for a' That*).

THE 19TH CENTURY

DESPITE THE importance of Edinburgh in British culture, it was the pattern of leaving Scotland to achieve fame in London, initiated in the mid-18th century by James Boswell and Tobias Smollett, that would predominate in the Victorian decades.

The poetry of Walter Scott (1771–1832) enjoyed phenomenal success. His novels, especially *Waverley* (1814), rose to greater glory. Francis Jeffrey's Whig-orientated *Edinburgh Review* led opinion, challenged by *Blackwood's* Tory alternative. James Hogg published by the latter work before writing his startling,

Map of Robert Louis Stevenson's Treasure Island, based on an island in the Firth of Forth

gothic *Private Memoirs and Confessions of a Justified Sinner* (1824). Following Susan Ferrier and John Galt, standards were modest, despite the prodigious career of Margaret Oliphant. Thomas Carlyle noted the provinciality of Edinburgh in the 1830s.

A later response to anxieties of the age came from Robert Louis Stevenson (1850–94) in *Dr Jekyll and Mr Hyde*. This contrasted with the sentimentality of home-spun or so-called kailyard (literally "cabbage patch") fiction, led by JM Barrie and SR Crockett. Barrie's dramas often catered for bourgeois tastes, as did the *Sherlock Holmes* stories of Arthur Conan Doyle (1859–1930), which endure today.

Arthur Conan Doyle's sleuth, Sherlock Holmes, in *The Graphic* (1901)

***Rob Roy* film poster (1995), from Walter Scott's novel of 1817**

EARLY 20TH-CENTURY RENAISSANCE

GEORGE DOUGLAS BROWN'S fierce anti-kailyard novel, *The House with the Green Shutters* (1901), opened the century and serious art was reborn. Hugh MacDiarmid's poetry in the 1920s carried literature into the stream of modernism. *A Drunk Man Looks at the Thistle* (1926) combines disparate Scottish dialects with political and social commentary in one of the century's great symbolist works. Edwin Muir also won international acclaim. Successors included Sidney Goodsir

Smith and William Soutar. Fiction reached epic and innovative proportions with Neil Gunn (*Butcher's Broom*, 1933) and Lewis Grassic Gibbon (*A Scots Quair*, 1932–4). Others included Willa Muir, Nan Shepherd and Fionn MacColla. John Buchan attempted serious work and popular thrillers. Nationalist impetus was dissipated by the rise of fascism, and new directions were sought after World War II.

POST-1945

SORLEY MACLEAN wrote in his native Gaelic of the ancient Highland culture's plight. Norman MacCaig began a career characterized by metaphysical whimsy, and George Bruce and Robert Garioch evoked the strictures of nature and social class.

Edwin Morgan has celebrated art and modernity (*Sonnets from Scotland*, 1984), Liz Lochhead continues to produce fresh drama and poetry and Jackie Kay explores the experience of being a black Scottish citizen. While James Bridie, Bill Bryden and John Byrne made an impact in the theatre, Muriel Spark rose to international acclaim

for her blackly comic novels (*The Prime of Miss Jean Brodie*, 1961). Urban realism developed quietly before William MacIlvanney's breakthrough with *The Big Man* (1985).

Following Alasdair Gray's bizarre *Lanark* (1981), a powerful wave propelled fiction into the highly productive present, in which Iain Banks remains a bestseller (*The Crow Road*, 1992). Tom Leonard's poems initiated a tradition using urban demotic speech. James Kelman elevated this to new levels, winning the Booker Prize for *How Late it Was, How Late* (1994).

Irvine Welsh's portrayal of drug culture is now world famous, though the energy and profundity of *Trainspotting* (1993) is absent from its successors. The private dramas articulated in AL Kennedy's stories are poignant and mysterious (*So I am Glad*, 1995), while Ian Rankin's Edinburgh based crime thrillers receive international acclaim (*Black & Blue*, 1997).

Poster for the film version of Irvine Welsh's novel

Clans and Tartans

THE CLAN SYSTEM, by which Highland society was
divided into tribal groups led by autocratic chiefs,
can be traced to the 12th century, when clans were
already known to wear the chequered wool cloth
later called tartan. All members of the clan
bore the name of their chief, but not all
were related by blood. Though they had
noble codes of hospitality, the clansmen
had to be warriors to protect their herds, as
can be seen from their mottoes. After the
Battle of Culloden *(see p146)*, all the clan
lands were forfeited to the Crown, and the
wearing of tartan was
banned for nearly
100 years.

The Mackays, also
known as the Clan
Morgan, won lasting
renown during the
Thirty Years War.

The MacLeods are
of Norse heritage.
The clan chief
still lives in
Dunvegan
Castle, Skye.

The MacDonalds
were the most power-
ful of all the clans,
holding the title of
Lords of the Isles.

The Mackenzies
received much of
the lands of Kintail
(see p151) *from
David II in 1362.*

CLAN CHIEF

The chief was the clan's patriarch, judge
and leader in war, commanding absolute
loyalty from his clansmen who gave military service in return for his protection.
The chief sum-
moned his clan
to do battle by
sending a run-
ner across his
land bearing a
burning
cross.

Bonnet
with eagle
feathers,
clan crest
and plant
badge.

Dirk

Sporran,
or pouch,
made of
badger's
skin.

**Feileadh-
mor,** or
"great plaid"
(the early
kilt), wrap-
ped around
waist and
shoulder.

**Basket-
hilted
sword**

The Campbells
were a widely
feared clan who
fought the Jacobites
in 1746 (see p147).

The Black Watch, raised in 1729
to keep peace in the Highlands, was
one of the Highland regiments in
which the wearing of tartan survived. After 1746, civilians were
punished by exile for up to seven
years for wearing tartan.

The Sinclairs *came from France in the 11th century and became Earls of Caithness in 1455.*

The Frasers *came over to Britain from France with William the Conqueror and his followers in 1066.*

George IV, *dressed as a Highlander, visited Edinburgh in 1822, the year of the tartan revival. Many tartan "setts" (patterns) date from this time, as the original ones were lost.*

The Gordons *were famously good soldiers; the clan motto was "by courage, not by craft".*

The Stuarts *were Scotland's royal dynasty. Their motto was "no one harms me with impunity".*

The Douglas *clan was prominent in Scottish history, though its origin is unknown.*

CLAN TERRITORIES

The territories of 10 major clans are marked here with their clan crests and tartan. The patterns shown are modern versions of original tartan designs.

PLANT BADGES

Each clan had a plant associated with its territory. It was worn on the bonnet, especially on the day of battle.

Scots pine was worn by the MacGregors of Argyll.

Rowan berries were worn by the Clan Malcolm.

Ivy was worn by the Clan Gordon of Aberdeenshire.

Spear thistle, now a national symbol, was a Stuart badge.

Cotton grass was worn by the Clan Henderson.

HIGHLAND CLANS TODAY

Once the daily dress of the clansmen, the kilt continues to be a symbol of national pride. The one-piece *feileadh-mor* has been replaced by the *feileadh-beag*, or "small plaid", made from approximately 7 m (23 ft) of material with a double apron fastened at the front with a silver pin. Though they exist now only in name, the clans are still a strong source of pride for Scots, and many still live in areas traditionally belonging to their clans. Many visitors to Britain can trace their Scots ancestry back to the Highlands.

Modern Highland formal dress

Highland Music and Games

THE HIGHLANDS AND ISLANDS of Scotland have been the focus of Gaelic culture for hundreds of years. Although the language itself is little spoken today, the legacy of the Gaelic lifestyle lives on in the music and activities of the people. The bagpipes, a traditional Highland instrument, are an important part of Scotland's identity around the world, and the Highland Games are an amalgamation of the Gaelic customs of music, dancing and contests of strength.

Pibroch is the classical music of the piping world. Played by solo pipers, these slow, melancholy tunes produce a haunting sound that is easier on the ear than the almost discordant sound a group of bagpipers makes.

The blow-pipe is used to inflate the bag by blowing air, as continuously as possible, into the pipe's mouthpiece.

A piper's hat is made traditionally from ostrich feathers.

The chanter pipe has eight finger-holes, used to play the melody.

The drones, or "borduns", are the three pipes that give the pitch. They are pitched on a fixed note, one bass and the other two higher, each at intervals of a fifth.

The bag, made from animal hide, is inflated by air from the blow-pipe; the air is then expelled under pressure applied by the piper's elbow.

THE BAGPIPES

Bagpipes have been the traditional sound of the Highlands for many centuries and are thought to have been introduced to Britain by the Romans. After the Battle of Culloden in 1746 they were banned for 11 years, along with Highland dress, for inspiring the Highlanders to rebel against English rule. The pipes have now become one of the most recognized emblems of Scotland.

TRADITIONAL GAELIC MUSIC

Music has always featured strongly in the Highlands' Gaelic communities. Solo instruments include the harp and accordion, and *ceilidh* bands are still common.

Accordions have accompanied ceilidhs *ever since the dances began in the crofting communities of the Scottish Highlands and islands.*

Ceilidh bands *are an alternative to the solo accordion as accompaniment for the modern* ceilidh *(a Gaelic word for "visit"). The band's instruments usually include fiddles, accordions and penny whistles.*

The harp *is Irish in origin but was introduced to Scotland in the 1800s. The "clarsach", as it is known, has enjoyed a revival in recent years.*

HIGHLAND GAMES AND ACTIVITIES

As well as music, the Highlands of Scotland are famous for their Games. The first Games took place many hundreds of years ago, and may have served a military purpose by allowing clan chiefs to choose the strongest men from those competing in contests of strength. Highland Games are held annually at Braemar *(see p38)*, as well as at Oban and Dunoon, among others. Another activity in the Highlands is the re-enactment of past battles and rebellions.

Re-enacting Highland battles *is popular with modern-day clansmen to commemorate their forefathers' fight for freedom. The above occasion was the 250th anniversary of the Battle of Culloden, where over 2,000 Highland warriors died.*

The Highland Games (or Gatherings) *as they are played today date from the 1820s. The most common contests and events are tossing the caber, weight shifting, piping, singing, dancing and throwing the hammer. The result is a cacophony of sound and activity, which can be overwhelming to a first-time spectator.*

Tossing the caber *is one of the most famous Highland sports, and requires strength and skill. The athlete must run with the tree trunk and toss it so that it flips over 180° and lands vertically, straight ahead.*

Throwing the hammer *involves revolving on the spot to gather speed, while swinging the hammer (a weight on the end of a long pole) around the head, before launching it across the field. The winner is the contestant whose hammer reaches the furthest distance.*

Weight shifting *is a severe test of strength and stamina. Here, the man stands with his back to a bar, over which he must throw the huge weight. The bar is raised after each successful attempt, until only one person is left in the competition.*

Highland dancing *is an important part of the Games, and the dances often have symbolic meanings – for instance the circle in a reel represents the circle of life. In the sword dance, the feet skip nimbly over the swords without touching them.*

Scotch Whisky

WHISKY IS TO THE SCOTS what champagne is to the French, and a visit to Scotland would not be complete without sampling this fiery, heart-warming spirit. All malt whiskies are produced using much the same process, but the environment, maturity and storage of the whisky have such a strong bearing on its character that every one is a different experience. There is no "best" malt whisky – some are suited to drinking at bedtime, others as an aperitif. All the distilleries named below produce highly rated Single Malt Scotch Whiskies, a title that is revered by true whisky connoisseurs.

A 1920s steam wagon transporting The Glenlivet to the nearby railways

Talisker *is an individualistic malt with an extremely hot, peppery, powerful flavour that is guaranteed to warm the toes.*

Glenmorangie *is the biggest selling single malt in Scotland, with a light, flowery taste and strong perfume.*

Lochnagar *is reputed to have been a favourite with Queen Victoria, who visited this distillery located near Balmoral. This is a sweet whisky with overtones of sherry.*

Lagavulin *is a classic Islay whisky with a dry, smoky palate. Islay is thought to be the best of the whisky-producing islands.*

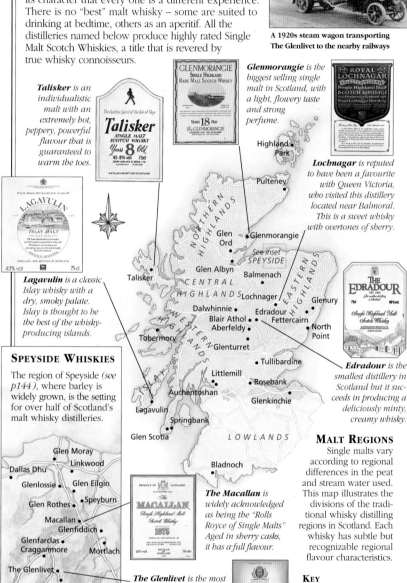

SPEYSIDE WHISKIES

The region of Speyside (*see p144*), where barley is widely grown, is the setting for over half of Scotland's malt whisky distilleries.

Edradour *is the smallest distillery in Scotland but it succeeds in producing a deliciously minty, creamy whisky.*

MALT REGIONS

Single malts vary according to regional differences in the peat and stream water used. This map illustrates the divisions of the traditional whisky distilling regions in Scotland. Each whisky has subtle but recognizable regional flavour characteristics.

The Macallan *is widely acknowledged as being the "Rolls Royce of Single Malts" Aged in sherry casks, it has a full flavour.*

The Glenlivet *is the most famous of the Speyside malts, distilled since 1880.*

KEY

• Single malt distilleries

How Whisky is Made

Traditionally made from just barley, yeast and stream water, Scottish whisky (from the Gaelic *usquebaugh*, or the "water of life") takes a little over three weeks to produce, though it must be given at least three years to mature. Maturation usually takes place in oak casks, often in barrels previously used for sherry. The art of blending was pioneered in Edinburgh in the 1860s.

Barley grass

1 Malting is the first stage. Barley grain is soaked in water and spread on the malting floor. With regular turning the grain germinates, producing a "green malt". Germination stimulates the production of enzymes which turn the starches into fermentable sugars.

2 Drying of the barley halts germination after 12 days of malting. This is done over a peat fire in a pagoda-shaped malt-kiln. The peat-smoke gives flavour to the malt and eventually to the mature whisky. The malt is gleaned of germinated roots and then milled.

3 Mashing of the ground malt, or "grist", occurs in a large vat or "mash tun", which holds a vast quantity of hot water. The malt is soaked and begins to dissolve, producing a sugary solution called "wort", which is then extracted for fermentation.

4 Fermentation occurs when yeast is added to the cooled wort in wooden vats, or "washbacks". The mixture is stirred for hours as the yeast turns the sugar into alcohol, producing a clear liquid called "wash".

5 Distillation involves boiling the wash twice so that the alcohol vaporizes and condenses. In copper "pot stills", the wash is distilled – first in the "wash still", then in the "spirit still". Now purified, with an alcohol content of 57 per cent, the result is young whisky.

6 Maturation is the final process. The whisky mellows in oak casks for a legal minimum of three years. Premium brands give the whisky a 10- to 15-year maturation, though some are given up to 50 years.

Traditional drinking vessels, or *quaichs*, made of silver

Blended whiskies are made from a mixture of up to 50 different single malts.

Single malts are made in one distillery, from pure barley malt that is never blended.

Scottish Food and Drink

T HE SCOTTISH LARDER is generous in meat and fish, which are usually served simply, without heavy sauces. Grouse, venison, Aberdeen Angus beef, salmon, trout and Scotland's many cheeses are all highly regarded. The country's cold, wet climate and shallow soil have proved better suited to growing oats than wheat. Oats are still present in traditional Scottish foods such as porridge and oatcakes (as opposed to wheat-based bread) and, of course, the haggis.

Porridge

Toasted bread

Roast grouse with crispy bacon on top

Fried bread-crumbs

Green beans

Rowan jelly

Bread sauce

Game chips

Kippers *are fresh herring, split down the back, then salted and cured by smoking over a fire. They are often eaten at breakfast with toast.*

Grouse *is one of the best known game birds, and a young bird is delicious when roasted. The meat should be served with game chips (thinly sliced, deep-fried potatoes), home-made bread sauce and vegetables.*

Scotch broth *is a light, thin soup based on neck or shoulder of mutton or beef, to which pearl barley and vegetables, such as carrots and leeks, are added.*

Cock-a-leekie soup *is a famous Scottish dish, consisting of pieces of chicken, leeks, rice and prunes, simmered together in the stock from the cooked chicken.*

Cullen skink *is a delicious soup made from smoked, or "finnan", haddock, milk and mashed potato. It originates from the village of Cullen, on the Moray Firth.*

THE HAGGIS

Haggis is undoubtedly the most famous of all Scottish dishes. It can be counted alongside the tartan kilt and the bagpipes as one of the most recognized symbols of Scotland. It is on Burns Night, 25 January, that the haggis is particularly celebrated. The poet Robert Burns *(see p89)*

wrote an address to this extraordinary pudding and it is now the custom to read the poem aloud, while plunging a knife into the haggis at the appropriate moment. Haggis contains spiced sheep's innards and oatmeal and is eaten with "neeps" (turnips) and potato.

Aberdeen Angus steak *is a favourite with all meat-eating Scots and is best served medium-rare with a mushroom and wine sauce, chunky chips (French fries) and mixed vegetables.*

Venison *should be hung for ten days before being seasoned with mixed spices, wine and vinegar, then roasted and cut into collops (slices).*

Stovies, *a mixture of onions and potatoes, were traditionally cooked with dripping (fat) from the Sunday joint.*

Skirlie *is a mixture of oatmeal and onions; it is usually flavoured with thyme, a herb that grows wild in Scotland.*

Poached salmon *tastes best when cooked whole in a bouillon of water, wine and vegetables, during which its deep red flesh turns a delicate pink. Salmon is caught in Scotland's east coast rivers.*

Criffel · Lanark blue · Oatcakes · Isle of Mull · Seater's Orkney · Crannog

Scottish cheeses *are among the finest in Europe. The many varieties range from hard, cheddar-like varieties to soft and creamy cheeses, or those flavoured with herbs and garlic. Eat them with traditional oatcake crackers.*

Scotch pancakes *are a wonderful teatime treat. They are best served warm, with plenty of butter and a homemade fruit jam, honey or golden syrup.*

Butterscotch tart, *a delicious pastry-based dessert, has a rich butterscotch filling and a topping of fluffy meringue. This is for the sweet-toothed only.*

Orange marmalade · Grapefruit and ginger marmalade

Marmalade *was created in Dundee in the 1700s when grocer James Keiller was landed with a large cargo of unsaleable, bitter Seville oranges. His wife, Janet, made them part of a preserve that now appears on breakfast tables worldwide.*

Dundee cake

Crabbie's ginger wine · Glayva liqueur · A pint of bitter · A pint of lager · Irn-bru soda drink

Dundee cake and shortbread *are two classic Scottish delicacies. The cake is rich and sweet, made with dried fruits and spices and topped with almonds. Shortbread often accompanies a cup of tea*

Drinks *available in Scotland cover the usual gamut of wines, beers, spirits, liqueurs and soft drinks. A pint of bitter, or "heavy", is a popular drink in Scottish bars, and there are many whisky-based liqueurs, such as Glayva. Irn-bru is refreshing and non-alcoholic.*

Touring Scotland by Car

THE TEN ROUTES marked on this map are excellent examples of the options open to motorists touring Scotland. Some routes are circular, using a major city as a base; some can be combined into longer itineraries. Main roads are few and far between in the Highlands, but driving conditions are generally good, and traffic is light outside the peak July and August holiday period. The driving times given in the key assume normal conditions without lengthy stops. Further information about road travel is on pages 214–15.

The far northwest can be visited in a circular tour starting at Braemore Junction, near Ullapool, heading west on a series of single-track roads past tiny crofting settlements and some of the oldest rocks in Britain. The route rejoins the two-lane road near Unapool.

From Kyle of Lochalsh, this route along the west coast encompasses the magnificent mountains and coastline of Wester Ross, taking in Loch Carron, Torridon, Loch Maree, Gairloch and Inverewe Gardens.

KEY TO TOURING ROUTES

The Border Abbeys & Scott's View
195 km (120 miles), 3–4 hours

Walter Scott's Country
185 km (115 miles), 3–4 hours

Fife Fishing Villages & St Andrews
195 km (120 miles), 3–4 hours

Eastern Grampians & Royal Deeside
180 km (110 miles), 4 hours

High Mountains of Breadalbane
180 km (110 miles), 4 hours

Loch Lomond & the Trossachs
225 km (140 miles), 5 hours

Inveraray & the Mountains of Lorne
225 km (140 miles), 4 hours

Glencoe & the Road to the Isles
160 km (100 miles), 3 hours

Sea Lochs of the West Coast
195 km (120 miles), 4 hours

The Far Northwest
160 km (100 miles), 3–4 hours

Loch Lomond is the first point of interest on a tour of Inveraray and the Mountains of Lorne. After Tarbet is a pass known as "The Rest and Be Thankful", then a drive to the 18th-century town of Inveraray (see p130), and on past Kilchurn Castle.

The Road to the Isles (see pp136–7) begins in Crianlarich, then crosses desolate Rannoch Moor to Glencoe (see p134) and past Fort William. The rugged scenery shown here is near the end of the tour route.

0 kilometres 50
0 miles 50

Unapool, Lochinver, Ullapool, Poolewe, Gairloch, Braem, Torridon, Shieldaig, Achnashe, Kyle of Lochalsh, Mallaig, Fort Willia, Crianlar, Inveraray, Tarbe

TIPS FOR DRIVERS

Hazards Watch out for sharp bends and animals on the roads in the Highlands. The sudden noise of jets above the glens can also startle drivers. Minor roads are often single track. Snowfall may result in road closures.
Fuel Fill up your car with fuel in towns, as there are few filling stations in rural areas.

Passing through Royal Deeside in the eastern Grampians, this route links Perth with Aberdeen, crossing a 700-m (2,000-ft) pass before descending to Balmoral Castle. The stretch from Braemar is on pages 144–5.

St Andrews (see p123) and the historic fishing villages of East Fife can be reached from Edinburgh over the Forth Bridge, and back via the hunting palace of the Stuart kings at Falkland (see p124).

A tour of Walter Scott's Country takes in the River Tweed Valley, with its attractive hills, market towns and an arboretum at Dawyck.

Melrose Abbey is one of the highlights of a tour taking in attractive Border towns, the famous Border Abbeys and Scott's View – one of the finest viewpoints in southern Scotland. More details of part of this tour are on page 85.

Stirling, with its castle, is the base from which to explore the high mountains of Breadalbane. The route passes through Callander, past Rob Roy's grave and Loch Earn. It then climbs over a mountain pass down to Glen Lyon, one of the most beautiful glens, and on through Crieff.

From Glasgow, this route includes Loch Lomond, Lochearnhead and Balquhidder. Just north of Callander, it turns west into the Trossachs. Heading back via Drymen, there is access to Loch Lomond.

SCOTLAND THROUGH THE YEAR

OST VISITORS come to Scotland between May and August when they enjoy the best weather, long hours of daylight and the chance to sample world-class events such as the Edinburgh International Festival or the Glasgow International Jazz Festival. The countryside lures tourists and Scots alike, and at the height of summer it gets very busy in areas such as Loch Ness (monster spotting) or Royal

Poster for the Edinburgh Fringe

Deeside (site of Balmoral Castle, the British Royal Family's Scottish residence). Out of season, a good winter snowfall in the Highlands provides an opportunity for snowboarding or skiing. Edingurgh's organized celebration at New Year – known locally as Hogmanay – has seen a rise in visitor numbers in late December. During most weeks of the year, but especially during the summer, a festival is held somewhere across the country.

Full colours of gorse in springtime

SPRING

THE SNOW clears off the mountains after April, the salmon swim up the rivers and the country prepares for visitors. There are some excellent festivals and a series of important sporting events. British Summer Time, when the clocks go forward one hour, starts at the end of March.

MARCH

Cairngorm Snow Festival *(third weekend)*, Aviemore. Daytime events at the Cairngorm ski area and evening street parades in Aviemore.

APRIL

Puppet and Animation Festival *(first 2 weeks)*, workshops and displays at 70 venues nationwide, based in Edinburgh.
International Science Festival *(two weeks, early Apr)*, Edinburgh. World's largest science festival, hosted in various venues.
Scottish Grand National *(mid-Apr)*, Ayr Racecourse. Scotland's top steeplechase event.
The Melrose Sevens *(mid-Apr or early May)*, Melrose, Borders. International seven-a-side rugby union event.
Glasgow Art Fair *(late Apr)*. Commercial art show in

various galleries; the main pavilion is in George Square.
Shetland Folk Festival *(late Apr)*. Traditional Scottish music in an island setting.
Beltane *(30 Apr)*, Calton Hill, Edinburgh. Pagan celebration to welcome start of summer.
Scottish Rugby Union Cup Final *(30 Apr)*, Murrayfield Stadium, Edinburgh. Scotland's showpiece club rugby event.

MAY

Scottish Cup Final *(mid-May)*, Hampden Park, Glasgow. Scottish football's showpiece club event.
International Children's Festival *(fourth week)*, Edinburgh. Performing arts event.
Wigtown Book Fair *(21-22)*, Wigtown, Dumfries & Galloway. Scotland's National Book Town plays host to book lovers and collectors.

An inter-Scotland rugby match at Murrayfield Stadium, Edinburgh

AVERAGE DAILY HOURS OF SUNSHINE

Hours

Jan Feb Mar Apr May Jun Jul Aug Sep Oct Nov Dec

Sunshine Chart
Although Scotland is not in any way synonymous with sunshine, its summers are marked by very long hours of daylight, due to the country's northerly latitude. Thus there is a relatively high proportion of hours of sunshine between the months of May and July.

SUMMER

THIS IS THE BUSIEST TIME of year. Many towns and villages stage their own version of the Highland Games, at varying scales. Days are long – in Shetland there is no proper night at midsummer, while even the south sees sunrise around 4:30am, sunset around 10pm.

The traditional event of tossing the caber at the Highland Games

JUNE

Hawick Common Riding *(early Jun)*. Patrolling district boundaries on horseback.
RSAC Scottish Rally *(mid-Jun)*, Dumfries & Galloway. Major motor sport event.
Glasgow International Jazz Festival *(17-26)*. Various venues across the city.
St Magnus Festival *(third week)*, Orkney. Arts event.
The Longest Day *(late Jun)*. No formal celebration, but many people see in the longest day on hilltops such as Arthur's Seat in Edinburgh.

Royal Highland Show *(late Jun)*, Ingliston, Edinburgh. Agricultural and food fair.
Traditional Boats Festival *(last weekend)*, Portsoy harbour, Banffshire. Scotland's fisheries heritage on display.

JULY

Game Conservancy Scottish Fair *(first weekend)*, Scone Palace, Perth. Major shooting and fishing event.
T in the Park *(second weekend)*, Balado, Fife. Scotland's biggest rock festival.
The Barclays Scottish Open *(mid-Jul)*, Alexandria. Fixture on European golf tour.

AUGUST

Traquair Fair *(first weekend)*, Innerleithen, Borders. Folk music, theatre and market stalls at a country house.
Eyemouth Maritime Festival *(12-15)*, Berwickshire. Music, crafts and seafood.
Edinburgh Festival *(various dates in Aug)*. "The

Grouse shooting on the "Glorious Twelfth" of August

Festival" comprises an international arts festival, an extensive fringe festival and other events dedicated to film, television, books, jazz and blues music *(see pp78–9)*.
Edinburgh Military Tattoo *(throughout Aug)*. Martial music and displays on Edinburgh Castle Esplanade.
Glorious Twelfth *(12 Aug)*. Grouse shooting season opens.
World Pipe Band Championships *(mid-Aug)*, Glasgow Green. Bagpipe music competition with some Highland Games events.
Great Scottish Run *(third Sun)*, Glasgow. A half-marathon for all to enter.

Drums and marching at the Edinburgh Military Tattoo in August

AVERAGE MONTHLY RAINFALL (EDINBURGH)

mm / Inches

100 / 4
80 / 3
60 / 2
40 / 1
20
0 / 0

Jan Feb Mar Apr May Jun Jul Aug Sep Oct Nov Dec

Rainfall Chart
The east coast has a consistently lower rainfall in comparison with the rest of the country. The Northern Isles, Inner and Outer Hebrides (Western Isles) and Western Highlands are likely to have three times as much precipitation as Edinburgh, Fife or Tayside.

The soft colours of autumn in Tayside

AUTUMN

CATCH A FINE DAY in the countryside and the autumn colours can be spectacular. Scotland may be beginnning to wind down after the summer, but there are still some attractions to be found for the attentive visitor. Schools have a week's holiday in October, which was traditionally a break to allow the children to work on the potato harvest.

SEPTEMBER

Ben Nevis Hill Race *(first Sat)*, Fort William. Annual race up and down the highest mountain in Britain.
Braemar Gathering *(first weekend)*, Braemar, Aberdeenshire. One of the country's leading Highland Games *(see p29)* with members of the Royal Family usually in attendance.
Leuchars Air Show *(mid-Sep)*, RAF Leuchars, Fife. Airshow with flying displays and other attractions.
Ayr Gold Cup *(mid-Sep)*, Ayr Racecourse. Prestigious flat-race for horses.
Open Doors Day *(last Sat)*, Edinburgh. Organized by the Cockburn Association, a number of the city's finest private buildings are opened to the public. Contact the Association for details (0131 557 8686).
Hairth O' Knokrach Festival *(mid-Sep)*, weekend of live Celtic, World and Roots music, song and dance at Craigshiels meadow in the Forest of Ae, Galloway Forest Park. Fire spectaculars, workshops and stalls.

Shot-putting at Braemar

OCTOBER

Highland Feast *(first week)*, the Highland's largest food festival with events throughout the region.
Royal National Mod *(second week)*, venue changes yearly. Performing arts competition promoting Gaelic language and Gaelic culture in general.

NOVEMBER

St Andrew's Week *(last week)*. Various venues in St Andrews host ceilidh evenings and festivals of Scottish food and drink.
St Andrew's Night *(30 Nov)*. National day of Scotland's patron saint. Many private and society dinners.

PUBLIC HOLIDAYS

These public holidays are observed throughout Scotland. Some local authorities declare extra holidays that apply only to their own areas.

New Year *(1–2 Jan)*. Two days in Scotland, compared with just the one day in England.
Good Friday *(late Mar or early Apr)*. Easter Monday is not an official holiday in Scotland.
May Day *(first Monday in May)*.
Spring Bank Holiday *(last Monday in May)*.
Summer Bank Holiday *(first Monday in August)*.
Christmas Day *(25 Dec)*.
Boxing Day *(26 Dec)*.

AVERAGE MONTHLY TEMPERATURE (EDINBURGH)

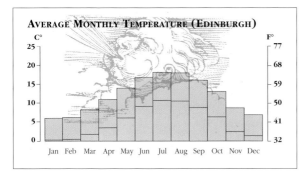

Temperature Chart
This bar chart illustrates the average minimum and maximum monthly temperatures recorded in Edinburgh. The west of Scotland tends to be warmer than the east, while the Highlands can be arctic-like, with heavy snowfalls during the winter.

WINTER

THIS IS A SEASON of short days and cold weather, but Christmas and New Year celebrations provide a welcome antidote. Haggis sales peak in late January with Burns Night parties. This quiet period is probably the best time of year to visit Scotland's museums and galleries.

DECEMBER

Edinburgh's Hogmanay
(late Dec into early Jan).
World's biggest New Year celebration. Several days of events, including processions and street theatre, in the capital. The centrepiece is a vast street party on 31 December.

Edinburgh's Royal Mile overflowing with Hogmanay revellers

JANUARY

The Ba' Game *(1 Jan)*,
Kirkwall, Orkney Isles. A centuries-old tradition to welcome the New Year involving the young men of Kirkwall playing a ball game on the town's streets.

Celtic Connections *(second half of month)*, Glasgow. Two weeks of music and *ceilidhs* on a Celtic theme, held in various venues.

Burns Night *(25 Jan)*. Scotland celebrates the birth of its national poet with readings and "Burns Suppers". Haggis, potatoes, turnips and whisky are on the menu.

Up Helly Aa *(last Tue)*, Lerwick, Shetland Isles. Midwinter fire festival.

FEBRUARY

Inverness Music Festival *(last week)*, Inverness. A week of classical and traditional music and dance.

Walker surveying the winter landscape in the Mamores in the Scottish Highlands

THE HISTORY OF SCOTLAND

*S*COTLAND HAS BEEN TORN APART *by religion and internal politics, coveted by a richer and more powerful neighbour and wooed and punished for 400 years as the vital partner in the power struggles between England, France and Spain. She has risen and fallen through the ages, acquiring romance from tragedy, producing genius out of poverty and demonstrating an irrepressible spirit.*

"They spend all their time in wars, and when there is no war, they fight one another" is a description of the Scots written in about 1500. For the visitor, the chief delight in this turbulent history is that so much is still tangible and visible.

The earliest settlers in the country are believed to have been Celtic-Iberians, who worked their way north along the coast from the Mediterranean, and arrived in Scotland about 8,000 years ago. Around 2000 BC their descendants erected majestic standing stones, which are found all over the country. The layout of those at Callanish in the Western Isles shows an advanced knowledge of astronomy. These people also built underground round-houses and an abundance of forts, indicating that they were no strangers to invasion and warfare.

In AD 82 the Romans penetrated deep into "Caledonia", as they called the country, and Tacitus recorded victories against the Picts (the "painted people") and other tribes. Yet the

An elaborately carved Pictish stone at Aberlemno, Angus

Romans never conquered Caledonia because their resources were stretched too thin. Instead, they built Hadrian's Wall from Wallsend on the east coast to Bowness-on-Solway in the west, and later the Antonine Wall, a shorter wall further north, thereby endeavouring to shut out the Caledonians. Despite the country's relative isolation from the rest of Britain, however, it is believed that the original form of the Scottish kilt derived from the Roman tunic, or toga.

By AD 400 the Romans had abandoned their northern outposts, and Scotland was divided between four races, each with its own king. These were the predominant Picts, the Britons and Angles in the south, and the smallest group – the Scots – who originally came from Ireland and occupied the southwest of the country.

In the late 4th century AD a Scot, St Ninian, travelled to Rome and, upon his return, built a church at Whithorn, thereby introducing Christianity to "Dalriada", the Kingdom of the Scots.

TIMELINE

Skara Brae

4000 BC	2500 BC	1000 BC		AD 500
3100 BC Skara Brae settlement on Orkney buried by a storm	**2900–2600 BC** Callanish standing stones and others erected, showing advanced astronomical knowledge			**AD 400** Romans abandon Caledonian outposts. Picts, Scots, Britons and Angles have separate kingdoms

300 BC Iron Age begins; weapons are improved

AD 82–4 Romans invade but do not conquer "Caledonia"

AD 121 Hadrian's Wall built

Roman coin

◁ **Return of Mary, Queen of Scots to Edinburgh** in 1561, by James Drummond (1816–77)

CHRISTIANITY AND UNIFICATION

Christianity remained in an isolated pocket centred around Whithorn on the Solway Coast, until the great warrior-missionary, St Columba, arrived from Ireland and established his monastery on the small Hebridean island of Iona in 563. Fired by his zeal, the new religion spread rapidly. By 800, Iona had achieved widespread influence, and Columban missionaries worked all over Europe. The Celtic Church developed along monastic lines and remained predominantly reclusive by nature, dedicating itself to worship and scholarship. Among its surviving works of art is the famous *Book of Kells*. This lavish, illuminated 8th- to 9th-century manuscript is thought to have been started on Iona, and later moved to Ireland for safe-keeping.

An illustrated page from the ornate *Book of Kells*, now kept in Trinity College, Dublin

The consolidation of a common religion helped to ease the merging of tribes. In 843 the Picts and Scots united under Kenneth MacAlpin. Curiously, the once-mighty Picts were the ones to lose their identity. They remain a mystery, except for their exquisite stone carvings depicting interwoven patterns, warriors and a wondrous mythology.

A long era of terrible Viking raids began in 890, resulting in the Norse occupation of the Western Isles for 370 years, and Shetland and Orkney for almost 600 years. The Norse threat possibly encouraged the Britons to join "Scotia", and in 1018 the Angles were defeated. Scotland became one united kingdom for the first time.

Viking axe

FEUDALISM AND THE CLANS

Under the powerful influence of Margaret, the English wife of Malcolm III (1057–93), a radical shift occurred during the king's reign away from the Gaelic-speaking culture of most of Scotland to the English-speaking culture of the south. This divide was widened under "good king" David I (1124–53). Under his reign Royal Burghs were created – towns built on the king's land and given special trading privileges in exchange for annual payments to him. He also introduced a national system of justice and weights and measures and, in the Lowlands, a feudal system based on Anglo-Norman lines.

Power devolved through an introduced aristocracy, largely French-speaking, and a structure bonded through land tenure. David I tried to impose this system in the north, but the region remained out of his control and, indeed, had its own "kings" –

TIMELINE

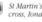

St Martin's cross, Iona

563 Columba founds a monastery on Iona and spreads Christianity, easing the merging of tribes

1018 King Malcolm of Scotia defeats the Angles. His grandson, Duncan, unites the country of Scotia, excluding the Norse-held islands

600	700	800	900	1000

685 The Pictish King Bruide defeats the Angles of Northumbria at Forfar in Angus

843 Picts and Scots are united under Kenneth MacAlpin. Picts subsequently become lost to obscurity

890 Northern and Western Isles occupied by the Norsemen

the Lords of the Isles. In the Highlands a different social structure based on kinship – that of families, or clans – had evolved. The chief was a patriarch who held land, not privately, but on behalf of his people. It was an inheritable position, but the chief remained accountable to the clan and could be removed by common consent, unlike the feudal landlords whose power was vested through legal title to the land. This subtle but fundamental difference was mirrored on a national level – in England, the monarch was the King of England; in Scotland, he was known as the King of Scots.

The lion of Scotland, dating from 1222

THE WARS OF INDEPENDENCE AND THE BATTLE OF BANNOCKBURN

In 1222 the lion of Scotland's coat of arms first appeared on the great seal of Alexander II. This was during a relatively peaceful interlude among frequent periods of turmoil when it seemed that Scotland was in danger of breaking apart.

When Alexander III's infant daughter died in 1290, there was no heir to the throne. Edward I of England installed a puppet king and, in 1296, led a devastating invasion that carried off the Stone of Destiny – the Scots' coronation throne – and earned him the title "Hammer of the Scots". Scotland was crushed and, but for one man, lost. William Wallace rose and led a revolt that rekindled hope until his capture and execution six years later. His cause was taken up by Robert the Bruce who, against all odds, won support and raised an army that changed the course of history by winning a decisive victory over the English at the Battle of Bannockburn, near Stirling, on 23 June 1314.

Confronted by the largest English army to cross the border, the Scots were outnumbered three to one, and their arms were inferior. Yet Bruce had chosen his ground and his strategy carefully and, despite the enemy's skilful bowmen and heavy cavalry, the Scots soon gained the victory they needed so badly. Scotland had won back her independence, but it was not until 1329 that her sovereign status was recognized and secured by a Papal bull (six days after Bruce had died). Even so, the wars with England would continue for another 300 years.

Robert the Bruce in combat at the Battle of Bannockburn (1314)

1124–53 David I imposes Norman feudal system. A clan system prevails in Highlands	1296 Edward I takes Stone of Destiny from Scone Abbey to Westminster	1320 Declaration of Arbroath sent to the Pope – an eloquent appeal for recognition of Scottish independence and sovereignty
1100	**1200**	**1300**	**1400**

Edward I (1239–1307)

1154 Loss of "southern counties" to England

1263 Western Isles won back from Norse

1314 Robert the Bruce defeats the English at Bannockburn

1328–9 Independence and sovereignty affirmed by Treaty with England and Papal bull

1326 Meeting of first Scottish Parliament

THE STUARTS

In 1371 began the long dynasty of the House of Stuart, a family distinguished by intelligence and flair but prone to tragedy. James I introduced wide legal reforms and approved the first university. James III won Orkney and Shetland from King Christian of Denmark and Norway through marriage to his daughter. James IV ended his illustrious reign with uncharacteristic misjudgement at the Battle of Flodden, in which 10,000 Scots died. But the most famous of the Stuarts was Mary, Queen of Scots (1542–87) who acceded to the throne as an infant.

Raised in France, Mary was beautiful, clever, gentle and spirited, but her reign was destined to be difficult. She was a Catholic in a country changing to Protestantism, and a threat to her cousin, Elizabeth I, whose claim to the English throne was precarious. Had Mary married wisely she might have ruled successfully, but her husbands alienated her potential supporters.

Mary returned to Scotland aged 18, already a widow and Dowager Queen of France, and spent just six turbulent years as Scotland's queen. She married again and following the public scandal of her secretary's murder by her second husband and his subsequent murder, she married for a third time. However, her choice, was unacceptable to both the public and the church. She was deposed and held captive, making a daring escape from an island castle to England, only to be imprisoned there for 18 years and then finally executed on the orders of her cousin, Elizabeth.

Woodcut of Protestant martyr George Wishart being burned at the stake in 1546

Mary, Queen of Scots, of the House of Stuart

THE REFORMATION

Until Mary's reign, Scotland's national religion, like the rest of Europe, was the Church of Rome. It had become extremely rich and powerful and, in many ways, self-serving and divorced from the people. When Martin Luther sparked the Reformation in Germany in 1517, the ripples of Protestantism spread. In Scotland the most vociferous leader was the firebrand preacher John Knox (see p58), who fearlessly denounced Mary.

There followed a long period of religious tension and strife. At first the main contentions were between Roman Catholics and Protestants. As Catholicism was purged, albeit with revivals and impregnable strongholds in the Highlands and islands, the conflicts shifted to Presbyterians versus Episcopalians. The differences lay in the structures of the churches and in their forms of worship. The feuds blazed and spluttered for 150 years.

TIMELINE

Flodden field banner

1603 Union of the Crowns. James VI of Scotland becomes James I of England and moves to London

1559 John Knox leads Reformation in Scotland

1450   1500   1550   1600

1472 Orkney and Shetland come under Scottish rule

1513 10,000 Scots die in Battle of Flodden

1587 Mary executed on the orders of Elizabeth I

1488–1513 James IV's strong leadership. Edinburgh becomes capital

1542–67 Reign of Mary, Queen of Scots

James VI (1566–1625)

UNION WITH ENGLAND

Mary's son, James VI, had reigned for 36 years when he became heir to the English throne. In 1603 he moved his court to London (taking his golf clubs), thus removing the monarchy from a permanent presence in Scotland for good. Scotland still retained its own parliament but found it increasingly difficult to trade in the face of restrictive English laws. In 1698 it tried to break the English monopoly on foreign trade by starting its own colony in Panama, a scheme that failed and brought financial ruin.

Protestant preacher John Knox

The first proposal to unite the two parliaments received a hostile reception from the public. Yet influential Scots saw union as a means of securing equal trading rights. The English saw it as a means of securing the Protestant line of succession to the throne, for by now the deposed Stuarts were threatening to reinstate the Catholic line. James VII was deposed in 1689 and fled to France. In 1707 the Act of Union was passed and the Scottish Parliament was dissolved.

BONNIE PRINCE CHARLIE AND THE JACOBITES

In 1745 James VII's grandson, Prince Charles Edward Stuart, secretly entered Scotland, landing on the west Highland coast with seven men and a promise of French military support, which never materialized. His call to arms to overthrow the

Articles of Union between England and Scotland, signed 22 July 1706 and accepted in 1707

Hanoverian usurper, George II, drew a poor response and only a few Highland chiefs offered support. From this dismal start his campaign achieved remarkable success, but indecisive leadership weakened the side.

The rebel army came within 200 km (125 miles) of London, throwing the city into panic, before losing heart and retreating. At Culloden, near Inverness, the Hanoverian army (which included many Scots, for this was not an issue of nationalism) defeated the Jacobites on a snowy 16 April 1746. The cause was lost. Bonnie Prince Charlie became a fugitive hotly pursued for six months, but despite a £30,000 reward on his head he was never betrayed.

Feather-capped Scottish Jacobites being attacked by Royalists at Glen Shiel in the Highlands, 1719

MacDonald shield

1642 Civil war in England	**1692** Massacre of Glencoe – a Campbell-led force murders its hosts, the MacDonalds, as an official punitive example		**1745–6** Jacobite rising. Bonnie Prince Charlie tries to recover throne, but loses the Battle of Culloden and flees

1650	1700	1750

1746 Abolition of Feudal Jurisdictions

1689 James VII loses throne as he tries to restore Catholicism

1726 Roadbuilding under General Wade

1698 First Darien (Panama) Expedition to found a trading colony. Bank of Scotland established

1706–7 Union of Parliaments. Scottish Parliament dissolved

Cogs   Piston

Boiler

James Watt's steam engine, which shifted the source of industrial power from water to steam

THE AFTERMATH OF CULLODEN AND THE CLEARANCES

Culloden was the turning point in Highland history, such was the severity of the oppressive measures following the battle. An Act was passed banning the wearing of tartan, the playing of pipes and the carrying of arms. The ties of kinship between chief and people were severed, and a way of life was extinguished. From then on chiefs assumed the roles of feudal landlords, and the land, once held for the people, became their private property. When sheep were found to thrive profitably on the land, the people became a hindrance and, as a result, were removed.

The evictions, or so-called Clearances, began in the 1760s. Some were achieved quite peacefully through financial incentives, but increasingly they were enforced through violence and burning, the most notorious taking place on the Duke of Sutherland's estate in 1814.

In the 1860s, by which time Queen Victoria had made the Highlands popular and sporting estates all the rage for hunting deer, the inland glens were as empty as they are today.

INDUSTRIALIZATION AND THE SCOTTISH ENLIGHTENMENT

While the Highlands were emptying, parts of southern Scotland were booming. For a large part of the 18th century Glasgow's tobacco lords operated a lucrative stranglehold on the European market, and linen, cotton and coal in their turn became important national industries.

The Industrial Revolution, made possible by Scotsman James Watt's revolutionary contribution to the steam engine, brought wealth to the nation (yet at the expense of health and social conditions) and turned Glasgow into the "Workshop of the Empire" – a reputation it retained until the demise of its famous shipbuilding industry in the 20th century.

A flowering of original thinkers also emerged in Scotland in the 18th century *(see pp24–5)*, most notably

Shipbuilding factory in Clydeside, now closed

TIMELINE

1769 James Watt patents his steam engine

1832 Sir Walter Scott buried at Dryburgh Abbey

Early telephone

1886 Crofters Ac[t] provides secure tenure and fair rents

1814 "The Year of Burning" of the Sutherland Clearances

1775	1800	1825		1875

1786 Robert Burns publishes *Poems, Chiefly in the Scots Dialect*

1840 Glasgow's population reaches 200,000 as its shipbuilding and cotton industries flourish

1848 Queen Victoria uses Balmoral as a retreat, and Scottish culture becomes fashionable with the English

1876 Alexander Graham Bell patents the first working telephone the philosopher David Hume, economist Adam Smith and the "Bard of Humanity", Robert Burns.

In the 19th century, Scotland's architecture led the way in Europe, as epitomized by the development of Edinburgh's New Town (see pp64–5). This bold plan to create a residential centre away from the congested Old Town was begun in 1770, and the design was greatly expanded in 1822 to produce a model of elegance that is outstanding to this day. Among the more famous of those who have occupied these classic Georgian houses was Sir Walter Scott, one of the world's earliest best-selling novelists.

In this same period, known as the Scottish Enlightenment, Thomas Telford excelled in engineering and, ever increasingly, Scots were finding fame and fortune abroad by exploring and developing foreign lands.

A North Sea oil rig, providing prosperity in the late 20th century

The Scottish National Party, founded in 1934, is seen by many as too extremist, and its popularity has fluctuated. The exploration of North Sea oil since the late 1960s boosted Scotland's economy and its ability to self govern. In 1997 the Labour government held a referendum in which, by a large majority, the Scots voted for the re-establishment of a Scottish Parliament in 1999.

Although its tax-raising powers are restrained, the new Scottish Parliament has devolved authority over health, education, local government, social work, housing, economic development, transport, law, home affairs, environment, agriculture, forestry, fishing, sport and the arts. For many Scots it is seen as heralding a new beginning with a renewed pride and strength in their culture, identity and heritage.

THE PROCESS OF DEVOLUTION

For a long time, following the Act of Union, it was clear that England and Scotland were never intended to be equal. The political centre moved to Westminster and accordingly forced any Scot with a talent or aptitude for politics to leave Scotland. This, and an imbalance in the system weighted in favour of English affairs, caused a general feeling of apathy and impotence to take root in the Scottish psyche. Various reforms adjusted the imbalance, but the sense of political estrangement continued to fester.

SNP demonstrations in 1997, encouraging voters to say "Yes" to Scottish devolution

				1996 Stone of	1999 Scottish
1888 Scottish Labour Party founded by James Keir Hardie	1920s Hugh Mac-Diarmid reinstates Scots as literary language	1967 North Sea oil exploration begins		Destiny (see p60) returns to Scotland	Parliament re-established

1945 Alexander Fleming wins Nobel Prize

1900	1925	1950	1975	2000

1914–18 4,000 Scots die in World War I	1934 Scottish National Party founded		

1931 Economic slump – 65 per cent unemployment in Clyde shipyards

Stone of Destiny

SCOTLAND REGION BY REGION

SCOTLAND AT A GLANCE 50-51
EDINBURGH 52-79
SOUTHERN SCOTLAND 80-93
GLASGOW 94-109
CENTRAL SCOTLAND 110-125
THE HIGHLANDS AND ISLANDS 126-161

Scotland at a Glance

STRETCHING FROM the rich farmlands of the
Borders to a chain of isles only a few degrees
south of the Arctic Circle, the Scottish landscape
has a diversity without parallel in Britain. The cities
of Glasgow and Edinburgh bustle with people and
offer numerous attractions. The northeast is an
area rich in wildlife, and as you travel northwest, the land becomes more mountainous
and its archaeological treasures more numerous. In the far northwest, in the Western
Isles, Scotland's earliest relics stand upon
some of the oldest rock on earth.

Western Isles

The Isle of Skye (see pp152–3),
*renowned for its
dramatic scenery,
has one of Scotland's
most striking coast-
lines. On the east
coast, a stream
plunges over Kilt
Rock, a cliff of
hexagonal basalt
columns named
after its likeness to
an item of Scottish
national dress.*

THE HIGHLAND
AND ISLANDS
(see pp126–61

The Trossachs (see pp116–17) *are a beautiful range
of hills straddling the border between the Highlands
and the Lowlands. At their heart, the forested slopes of
Ben Venue rise above the still
waters of Loch Achray.*

Strathclyde

GLASG
(see pp94–

Culzean Castle (see pp92–3)
*stands on a cliff's edge on the
Firth of Clyde, amid an extensive
country park. One of the jewels of
southern Scotland, Culzean is a
magnificent showcase of work by
the Scottish-born architect,
Robert Adam (1728–92).*

◁ **Loch Lomond in the Highlands**

Shetland
Islands

Orkney
Islands

Highland

Grampian

Tayside

Central

NTRAL SCOTLAND
(see pp110–25)

Lothian   **EDINBURGH**
(see pp52–79)

SOUTHERN SCOTLAND
(see pp80–93)

Borders

Dumfries
&
Galloway

The Cairngorms (see pp140–41) *cover an area prized for its beauty and diversity of wildlife, though there are also many historical relics to be found, such as this early 18th-century arch at Carrbridge.*

Royal Deeside (see pp144–5) *in the Grampians has been associated with British royalty since Queen Victoria bought Balmoral Castle in 1852.*

Edinburgh (see pp52–79) *is the capital of Scotland. Between its medieval castle and The Palace of Holyroodhouse stretches the Royal Mile. Here, the historic sights range from the old Scottish Parliament buildings to the house of John Knox. By contrast, Georgian terraces predominate in the New Town.*

The Burrell Collection (see pp104–5), *on the southern outskirts of Glasgow, is a museum of some of the city's greatest art treasures. It is housed in a spacious, glass building opened in 1983.*

0 kilometres   50

0 miles   50

EDINBURGH

THE HISTORIC STATUS *of Edinburgh, the capital of Scotland, is beyond question, with ancient buildings scattered across the city, and the seat of Scotland's new parliament lying close to the royal residence of The Palace of Holyroodhouse. The range of historical and artistic attractions draws visitors from all over the world.*

Castle Rock in Edinburgh has been occupied since around 1,000 BC in the Bronze Age, which is no surprise given its strategic views over the Firth of Forth. The Castle itself houses the city's oldest building, St Margaret's Chapel, dating from the 11th century. A few years later, Margaret's son, King David I, founded Holyrood Abbey a mile to the east. The town that grew along the route between these buildings, the "Royal Mile", became a popular residence of kings, although not until the reign of James IV (1488–1513) did Edinburgh gain the status of Scotland's capital. James built The Palace of Holyroodhouse as a royal residence in 1498 and made the city an administrative centre.

Overcrowding made the Old Town a dirty and difficult place to live, and threw rich and poor together. The construction of a Georgian New Town to the north in the late 1700s gave the wealthy an escape route, but even today Edinburgh has a reputation for social extremes. It has major law courts, is second only to London as a financial centre in the British Isles and houses the new Scottish parliament. Bankers and lawyers form the city's establishment, and the most ambitious architectural developments of recent years have been for financial sector companies. Yet outlying housing estates, built in the years following World War II, still have echoes of the Old Town poverty.

Edinburgh is best known today for being a major tourist centre. There are wonderful museums and galleries to visit, and the city enjoys a widely renowned nightlife. At the height of the International Festival, in August, it is estimated that the population actually doubles from 400,000 to 800,000.

A juggler performing at the annual arts extravaganza, the Edinburgh Festival

◁ The Grassmarket area of the city, dominated by the imposing edifice of Edinburgh Castle

Exploring Edinburgh

THE CENTRE OF EDINBURGH is divided neatly in half by Princes Street, the principal shopping area. To the south lies the Old Town, site of the ancient city, which grew along the route of the Royal Mile, from the Castle Rock in the west to The Palace of Holyroodhouse in the east. At the end of the 18th century, building for the New Town started to the north of Princes Street. The area is still viewed today as a world-class example of Georgian urban architecture, with its elegant façades and broad streets. Princes Street has lots to offer, including shopping, art galleries, the towering Scott Monument and the landmark Balmoral Hotel clock tower, as well as the city's main train station, Waverley.

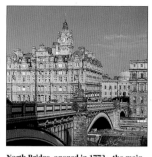

North Bridge, opened in 1772 – the main route connecting the Old and New Towns

Edinburgh Castle's Royal Scots soldiers

GETTING AROUND

Central Edinburgh is compact, so walking is an excellent way to explore the centre. Other options include a comprehensive bus service and a multitude of black taxis. Avoid exploring the centre by car, because the streets tend to be congested with traffic, and parking may be difficult. Car use has been actively discouraged by the local authority in recent years. On main routes special lanes are provided for buses, taxis and bicycles, and in the suburbs there is also a good network of bicycle paths.

SIGHTS AT A GLANCE

Historic Areas, Streets and Buildings
Edinburgh Castle pp60–61 ❷
The Exchange ❸
Greyfriars Kirk ❹
New Scottish Parliament ❸
New Town pp64–5 ❾
The Palace of
   Holyroodhouse ⓫
The Royal Mile pp56–9 ❶

Monuments
Scott Monument ❼

Landmarks
Calton Hill ❿
Holyrood Park and
   Arthur's Seat ⓮

Museums, Galleries and Exhibitions
National Gallery of Scotland ❻
Our Dynamic Earth ⓬
The Royal Museum and
   Museum of Scotland ❺
Scottish National Portrait
   Gallery ❽

KEY

▨	Street-by-street map *see pp64–5*
▨	Royal Mile
▨	Major sight
▨	Place of interest
🚌	Bus station
🚉	Train station
P	Parking
ℹ	Tourist information
✉	Post office
➕	Hospital
✚	Church

SEE ALSO

• *Where to Stay* pp166–7
• *Where to Eat* pp176–8

0 metres   300
0 yards   300

The Royal Mile ●

T HE ROYAL MILE is a stretch of four ancient streets (from Castlehill to Canongate) which formed the main thoroughfare of medieval Edinburgh, linking the castle to The Palace of Holyroodhouse. Confined by the city wall, the "Old Town" grew upwards, with some tenements climbing to 20 floors. It is still possible, among the 66 alleys and closes off the main street, to sense Edinburgh's medieval past.

Eagle sign outside Gladstone's Land

LOCATOR MAP

Gladstone's Land is a preserved 17th-century merchant's house.

Scotch Whisky Heritage Centre introduces visitors to Scotland's national drink.

The Camera Obscura contains an observatory from which to view the city.

Edinburgh Castle ←   CASTLEHILL   LAWNMARKET

Lady Stair's House
This 17th-century house is now a museum of the lives and works of writers Burns, Scott and Stevenson.

The Hub is the headquarters of the Edinburgh Festival.

🎦 Camera Obscura
📞 *(0131) 226 3709.* ⭘ *daily.* 📷 ✉
The lower floors of this building date from the early 17th century and were once the home of the Laird of Cockpen. In 1852, Maria Short added the upper floor, the viewing terrace and the Camera Obscura – a large pinhole camera that pictures life in the city centre as it happens. A marvel at the time, it remains one of Edinburgh's most popular attractions.

🎦 Gladstone's Land
(NTS) 477B Lawnmarket. 📞 *(0131) 226 5856.* ⭘ *Apr–Oct: 10am–5pm Mon–Sat, 2–5pm Sun.* 📷
This 17th-century merchant's house has been carefully restored. It provides a window on life in a typical Old Town house before over-crowding drove the rich inhabitants north-west to the ever-expanding Georgian New Town. "Lands", as they were then known, were tall, narrow buildings erected on small plots of land. The six-floor house that is Gladstone's Land was named after Thomas Gledstanes, the merchant who built it in 1617. The house still has the original arcade booths on the street façade as well as a painted ceiling.

Although the house is extravagantly furnished, it also contains items, such as wooden overshoes that had to be worn in the dirty streets, which serve as a reminder of the less salubrious features that were part of the old city.

A chest in the beautiful Painted Chamber is said to have been given by a Dutch sea captain to a Scottish merchant who saved him from a shipwreck. A similar house, named Morocco's Land (*see p59*), can be found further to the east, on Canongate.

The bedroom of Gladstone's Land

The Signet Library has one of the city's most lavish interiors. Visits can be made following a written application.

St Giles Cathedral contains the beautiful Thistle Chapel, with a bagpiping angel on its arched entrance.

The City Chambers were designed by John Adam in the 1750s.

The Heart of Midlothian is an arrangement of granite cobblestones on the former site of the city jail.

BANK STREET

HIGH STREET

GEORGE IV BRIDGE

Royal Museum
of Scotland,
Greyfriars Bobby

Charles II statue is a tribute to the 17th-century monarch who defeated the Covenanters at the Battle of Bothwell Brig in 1679.

Parliament House was built in 1639. The Scottish parliament convened here from 1640 until its dissolution in 1707, after the Union of Parliaments.

Rib-vaulting in the Thistle Chapel, St Giles Cathedral

🏛 Writers' Museum

Lady Stair's Close. ☎ (0131) 529 4901. ◯ Mon–Sat. This fine old town mansion was built in 1622. In the 1720s it was acquired by Elizabeth Dowager Countess of Stair, and has since been called Lady Stair's House. Its official title reflects its role as a museum of memorabilia from Robert Burns, Sir Walter Scott and Robert Louis Stevenson.

⛪ Parliament House

Parliament Sq, High St. ☎ (0131) 225 2595. ◯ Mon–Fri. ♿ limited. This majestic, Italianate building was constructed in the 1630s for the Scottish Parliament. Parliament House has been home to the Court of Session and the High Court since the Union of Parliaments (see p45) in 1707. It is well worth seeing, as much for the spectacle of its many gowned

and wigged advocates as for the beautiful stained-glass window in the Great Hall, commemorating the inauguration of the Court of Session by King James V in 1532.

⛪ St Giles Cathedral

Royal Mile. ☎ (0131) 225 9442. ◯ 9am–7pm Mon–Sat, 1–5pm Sun. Properly known as the High Kirk (church) of Edinburgh, it is ironic that St Giles is popularly known as a cathedral. Though it was twice the seat of a bishop in the 17th century, it was from here that John Knox directed the Scottish Reformation, with its emphasis on individual worship freed from the authority of bishops. A tablet marks the place

where Jenny Geddes, a local market stallholder, scored a victory for the Covenanters in 1637 by hurling her stool at a preacher who was reading from an English prayer book.

The Gothic exterior of the cathedral is dominated by a 15th-century tower, the only part to escape heavy renovation in the 19th century. Inside, the impressive Thistle Chapel, with its rib-vaulted ceiling and carved heraldic canopies can be seen. The chapel honours the knights, past and present, of the Most Ancient and Most Noble Order of the Thistle. The carved royal pew in the Preston Aisle is used by Queen Elizabeth II when staying in Edinburgh.

**Bagpiping angel
from the entrance
of the cathedral**

Exploring Further Down the Royal Mile

THE SECTION of the Royal Mile from High Street to Canongate passes two monuments to the Reformation: John Knox's house and the Tron Kirk. The Canongate was once an independent district, owned by the canons of the Abbey of Holyrood, and sections of its south side have been restored. Beyond Morocco's Land, the road stretches for the final half-mile (800 m) to The Palace of Holyroodhouse.

LOCATOR MAP

HIGH STREET

SOUTH BRIDGE STREET

The Mercat Cross marks the city centre. It was here that Bonnie Prince Charlie *(see p153)* was proclaimed king in 1745.

The Tron Kirk
was built in 1630 for the Presbyterians who left St Giles Cathedral when it came under the control of the Bishop of Edinburgh.

🕮 John Knox's House

45 High St. 📞 *(0131) 556 9579.* 🕐 *10am–4:30pm Mon–Sat.* ♿ *limited.* 🎦 📷 *by appointment.*

As a leader of the Protestant Reformation and minister at St Giles, John Knox (1513–72) was one of the most important figures in 16th-century Scotland. Ordained as a priest in 1536, Knox later became convinced of the need for religious change. He took part in the Protestant occupation of St Andrews Castle in 1547 and served two years as a galley slave in the French navy as punishment. On release, Knox went to London and Geneva to espouse the Protestant cause, returning to Edinburgh in 1559. The townhouse on the Royal Mile that bears his name dates from 1450 and it was here that he spent the last few months of his life. It is one of the few structures from this period that survive today. Displays tell the story of Knox's life in the context of the political and religious upheavals of his time.

🏛 Museum of Childhood

42 High St. 📞 *(0131) 529 4142.* 🕐 *Mon–Sat (Sun during Edinburgh Festival).* ♿ *limited.* 🌐 *www.cec.org.uk*

This museum is not merely a toy collection but an insight into childhood, with all its joys and trials. Founded in 1955 by a city councillor, Patrick Murray (who claimed to eat children for breakfast), it was the world's first museum of childhood. The collection includes medicines, school books and old-fashioned toys. With its nickelodeon and antique slot machines, this has been called the world's noisiest museum.

🏛 Canongate Tolbooth: The People's Story Museum

163 Canongate. 📞 *(0131) 529 4057.* 🕐 *10am–5pm Mon–Sat (Sun during Edinburgh Festival).*

Edinburgh's social history museum is housed in the Canongate Tolbooth, dating

An 1880 automaton of the Man on the Moon, Museum of Childhood

John Knox's House

Dating from 1450, the oldest house in the city was the home of the preacher John Knox during the 1560s. He is said to have died in an upstairs room. It contains relics of his life.

Morocco's Land is a reproduction of a 17th-century tenement house. It takes its name from the statue of a Moor which adorns the entrance.

→ **Museum of Edinburgh**
Canongate Tolbooth

CANONGATE

Museum of Childhood

Though created as a museum for adults by a city councillor who was known to dislike children, this lively musem now attracts flocks of young visitors.

MUSEUM OF CHILDHOOD

Moubray House was to be the signing place of the Act of Union in 1707, until a mob forced the authorities to retreat to another venue.

from 1591. With its distinctive clock tower, this was the focal point for life in the Burgh of Canongate. Until the mid-19th century it contained law courts, a jail and the meeting place for the burgh council. It has been a museum since 1954.

Focusing on the lives of ordinary citizens from the late 18th century to the present, it covers subjects such as public health, recreation, trade unions and work. The riots, disease and poverty of the 19th century are also covered, and with subjects as diverse as wartime, football and punk rock, this collection gives a valuable insight into life in Edinburgh.

A prison cell in the Canongate Tolbooth: The People's Story Museum

LIFE BELOW THE OLD TOWN

Until the 18th century most residents of Edinburgh lived along and beneath the Royal Mile and Cowgate. The old abandoned cellars and basements, which lacked any proper water supply, daylight or ventilation, were once centres of domestic life and industry. Under these conditions, cholera, typhus and smallpox were common. Mary King's Close, under the City Chambers, is one of the most famous of these areas – its inhabitants were all killed by the plague around 1645.

In 2003 many of these closes were opened up for the first time and guided visits are now possible through The Real Mary King's Close (0870) 243 0160.

🏛 The Museum of Edinburgh

142–146 Canongate. **☎** (0131) 529 4143. **◯** 10am–5pm Mon–Sat (Sun during Aug).

Huntly House was built in the early 16th century and damaged in the English raid on Edinburgh in 1544. First used as a family townhouse, it was later divided into apartments but by the 19th century it was little more than a slum. In 1924 the local authority bought the property and opened the museum in 1932. The collection includes exhibits such as Neolithic axe heads, Roman coins, military artifacts and glassware. A section is also dedicated to Field Marshal Earl Haig, Commander-in-Chief of the British Army during World War I.

Edinburgh Castle ❷

S TANDING UPON the basalt core of an extinct volcano, Edinburgh Castle is an assemblage of buildings dating from the 12th to the 20th century, reflecting its changing role as fortress, royal palace, military garrison and state prison. Though there is evidence of Bronze Age occupation of the site, the original fortress was built by the 6th-century Northumbrian king, Edwin, from whom the city takes its name. The castle was a favourite royal residence until the Union of the Crowns *(see p45)* in 1603, after which the king resided in England. After the Union of Parliaments in 1707, the Scottish regalia were walled up in the Palace for over a hundred years. The Palace is now the zealous possessor of the so-called Stone of Destiny, a relic of ancient Scottish kings which was seized by the English and not returned to Scotland until 1996.

Beam support in the Great Hall

Scottish Crown
Now on display in the palace, the Crown was restyled by James V of Scotland in 1540.

Military Prison

Governor's House
Complete with Flemish-style crow-stepped gables, this building was constructed for the governor in 1742 and now serves as the Officers' Mess for the castle garrison.

Vaults
This French graffiti, dating from 1780, recalls the many prisoners who were held in the vaults during the wars with France in the 18th and 19th centuries.

MONS MEG

Positioned outside St Margaret's Chapel, this siege gun (or *bombard*) was made in Belgium in 1449 for the Duke of Burgundy, who gave it to his nephew, James II of Scotland. It was used by James against the Douglas family in their stronghold of Threave Castle *(see p89)* on the Dee in 1455, and later by James IV against Norham Castle in England. After exploding during a salute to the Duke of York in 1682, it was kept in the Tower of London until it was returned to Edinburgh in 1829, at Sir Walter Scott's request.

STAR SIGHTS
★ **Great Hall**
★ **Palace**

VISITORS' CHECKLIST

Castle Hill. 🕿 (0131) 225 9846.
🕐 Apr–Oct: 9:30am–6pm daily;
Nov–Mar: 9:30am–5pm daily
(last admission: 45 mins before
closing). ♿ ⬛ 📷 🎁 🍴 ⬜
ⓦ www.historic-scotland.gov.uk

Argyle Battery
*These battlements offer a panoramic
view north over Princes Street to the
city's New Town, the Firth of Forth
and Fife.*

★ Palace
*Mary, Queen of
Scots, gave birth to
James VI in this
15th-century palace,
where the Stone of
Destiny and Crown
Jewels are displayed.*

Entrance

**Royal
Mile**

The Esplanade is the
location of the Military
Tattoo *(see p79).*

**The Half Moon
Battery** was built in
the 1570s as a plat-
form for the artillery
defending the eastern
wing of the castle.

St Margaret's Chapel
*This stained glass
window depicts Malcolm
III's saintly queen, to
whom the chapel is
dedicated. Probably built
by her son, David I, in
the early 12th century,
the chapel is the castle's
oldest existing building.*

★ Great Hall
*With its restored open-timber
roof, the hall dates from the
15th century and was the
meeting place of the Scottish
Parliament until 1639.*

The Standard Life Building, at the heart of the city's financial centre

The Exchange ❸

Lothian Rd, West Approach Rd and Morrison St.

LOCATED WEST of Lothian Road, The Exchange is the most important recent development in central Edinburgh. The once unsightly area was rejuvenated when Festival Square and the Sheraton Grand Hotel were built in 1985. Three years later the local authority published a plan to promote the area as a financial centre. In 1991 investment management firm Baillie Gifford opened Rutland Court on West Approach Road. The ambitious **Edinburgh International Conference Centre**, on Morrison Street, was designed by Terry Farrell and opened in 1995. There has been a fever of construction work ever since. Standard Life opened a new headquarters on Lothian Road in 1997, which has some fine artistic features, and in 1998 Scottish Widows opened a bold new building.

🄷 Edinburgh International Conference Centre
🄲 *(0131) 300 3000.* &
🅆 *www.eicc.co.uk*

Greyfriars Kirk ❹

Greyfriars Place. 🄲 *(0131) 226 5429.*
🄾 *Easter–Oct: Mon–Sat; Nov–Mar: Thu.* & ✓

GREYFRIARS KIRK occupies a key role in the history of Scotland, as this is where the National Covenant was signed in 1638, marking the Protestant stand against the imposition of an episcopal church by King Charles I. Greyfriars was then a relatively new structure, having been completed in 1620 on the site of a Franciscan friary.

Throughout the 17th century, during years of bloodshed and religious persecution, the kirkyard was used as a mass grave for executed Covenanters. The kirk also served as a prison for Covenanter forces captured after the 1679 Battle of Bothwell Brig. The Martyrs' Monument is a sobering reminder of those times. The original kirk building was severely damaged by fire in 1845 and substantially rebuilt. Greyfriars is best known for its association with a dog, Bobby, who lived by his master's grave from 1858 to 1872. Bobby's statue stands outside Greyfriars Kirk.

A tribute to Greyfriars Bobby

Royal Museum and Museum of Scotland ❺

Chambers St. 🄲 *(0131) 247 4422.* 🄾
10am–5pm Mon–Sat, 8pm Tue, noon–5pm Sun. 🄫 & ✓
🅆 *www.nms.ac.uk*

STANDING SIDE BY SIDE on Chambers Street, these two buildings could not be more different from one another. The older of the museums, the **Royal Museum**, is a great Victorian palace of self improvement. Designed by Captain Francis Fowke of the Royal Engineers, the building was completed in 1888. Although it started life as an industrial museum, over time its collection was developed to include an eclectic assortment of exhibits, ranging from stuffed animals to ethnographic and technological items. These are all displayed in rooms leading off the large and impressive central hall.

There was, however, no room available to display Scotland's impressive array of antiquities. As a result, they were crammed into inadequate spaces in the National Portrait Gallery in Queen Street, or were hidden away altogether and put into storage. As far back as the 1950s, recommendations were made that a new facility be built to house the nation's historical treasures. The government did not commit funding to the project until as recently as 1989. Work on a site next door to the Royal Museum on Chambers Street started in 1993, and the building took five years to complete. The result was the **Museum of Scotland**, a contemporary flourish of confident design by architects Gordon Benson and Alan Forsyth, which opened to the public in December 1998.

Described as one of the most important buildings erected in Scotland in the second half of the 20th century, the museum tells the story of the country, starting with its geology and natural history. It then moves through to the early peoples of Scotland, the centuries when Scotland was a kingdom in its

The 9th-century Monymusk Reliquary on display at Edinburgh's Museum of Scotland

own right, and then on to later industrial developments. Some stunning items are on show, including St Fillan's Crozier, which was said to have been carried at the head of the Scottish army at Bannockburn in 1314. The Monymusk Reliquary is also on display. Dated to around AD 800, it was a receptacle for the remains of the Christian missionary, St Columba *(see p42)*.

National Gallery of Scotland **6**

The Mound. ☎ *(0131) 624 6200.* ◯ *10am–5pm Mon–Sat, Sun pm.* ♿ ☑ ⓦ www.nationalgalleries.org

O NE OF SCOTLAND'S finest art galleries, the National Gallery of Scotland is worth visiting for its 15th- to 19th-century British and European paintings alone, though plenty more can be found to delight the enthusiastic art-lover.

Some of the highlights among the Scottish works exhibited are the society portraits by Allan Ramsay and Henry Raebum, including the latter's *Reverend Robert Walker Skating on Duddingston Loch*, thought to date from the beginning of the 19th century.

Rev Robert Walker Skating on Duddingston Loch

The collection of early German pieces contains Gerard David's almost comic-strip treatment of the *Three Legends of St Nicholas*, from around the beginning of the 16th century. Works by Raphael, Titian and Tintoretto accompany other southern European paintings, including Velazquez's *An Old Woman Cooking Eggs*, from 1620.

There is an entire room devoted to *The Seven Sacraments* by Nicholas Poussin, dating from around 1640. Flemish painters represented include Rembrandt, Van Dyck and Rubens, while among the British offerings are important works by Ramsay, Reynolds and Gainsborough.

Scott Monument **7**

Princes Street Gardens East. ◯ *9am–6pm Mon-Sat, 10am-6pm Sun.* ♿

S IR WALTER SCOTT (1771–1832) is one of the most important figures in the history of Scottish literature *(see p86)*. Born in Edinburgh, Scott initially pursued a legal career but he soon turned to writing full time as his ballads and historical novels began to bring him success. His works looked back to a time of adventure, honour and chivalry, and did much to promote this image of Scotland abroad.

In addition to being a celebrated novelist, Sir Walter was also a major public figure – he organized the visit of King George IV to Edinburgh in 1822. After Scott's death in 1832, the Monument was constructed on the south side of Princes Street as a tribute to his life and work. This great Gothic tower was designed by George Meikle Kemp and reaches a height of 61 m (200 ft). It was completed in 1840, and includes a statue of Sir Walter at its base, sculpted by Sir John Steell. Inside the huge structure, 287 steps give access to the topmost platform. The rewards for those keen enough to climb up are excellent views around the city centre and across the Forth to Fife.

The imposing Gothic heights of the Scott Monument on Princes Street

Scottish National Portrait Gallery **8**

1 Queen St ☎ *(0131) 556 8921.* ◯ *10am–5pm Mon–Sun, 10am–7pm Thu.* ♿ ⓦ www.nationalgalleries.org

A N INFORMATIVE exhibition on the royal house of Stuart is just one of the attractions at the Scottish National Portrait Gallery. The displays detail the history of 12 generations of Stuarts, from the time of Robert the Bruce to Queen Anne. Memorabilia include Mary, Queen of Scots' jewellery and a silver travelling canteen left by Bonnie Prince Charlie *(see p153)* at the Battle of Culloden. The upper gallery has a number of portraits of famous Scots, including a picture of Robert Burns.

Van Dyck's *Princess Elizabeth and Princess Anne*, National Portrait Gallery

Street-by-Street: New Town ❾

Albert Monument, Charlotte Square

T HE FIRST PHASE of Edinburgh's "New Town" was built in the 18th century, to relieve the congested and unsanitary conditions of the medieval old town. Charlotte Square at the western end formed the climax of this initial phase, and its new architectural concepts were to influence all subsequent phases. Of these, the most magnificent is the Moray Estate, where a linked series of very large houses forms a crescent, an oval and a twelve-sided circus. The walk shown here explores this area of monumental Georgian town planning.

Moray Place
The crowning glory of the Moray Estate, this circus consists of a series of immense houses and apartments, many still inhabited.

The Water of Leith is a small river running through a delightful gorge below Dean Bridge. There is a riverside walkway to Stockbridge.

Dean Bridge
This was built in 1829 to the design of Thomas Telford. It gives views down to the Water of Leith and upstream to the weirs and old mill buildings of Dean Village.

Ainslie Place, an oval pattern of town houses, forms the core of the Moray Estate, linking Randolph Crescent and Moray Place.

STAR SIGHTS

★ **Charlotte Square**

★ **The Georgian House**

NEW TOWN ARCHITECTS

The driving force behind the creation of the New Town was George Drummond (1687–1766), the city's Provost, or Mayor. James Craig (1744–95) won the overall design competition in 1766. Robert Adam (1728–92) introduced classical ornamentation to Charlotte Square. Robert Reid (1774–1856) designed Heriot Row and Great King Street, and William Playfair (1790–1857) designed Royal Circus. The monumental development of the Moray Estate was the work of James Gillespie Graham (1776–1855).

Robert Adam

No. 14 was the residence of judge and diarist Lord Cockburn from 1813 to 1843.

0 metres   100
0 yards   100

KEY

--- Suggested route

★ **The Georgian House**
No. 7 is owned by the National Trust for Scotland and is open to the public. It has been repainted in its original colours and furnished with appropriate antiques, and is a testament to the lifestyle of the upper sector of 18th-century Edinburgh society.

LOCATOR MAP
See Edinburgh Map pp54–5

Bute House is the official residence of the First Minister of the Scottish Parliament.

★ **Charlotte Square**
The square was built between 1792 and 1811 to provide a series of lavish town houses for the most successful city merchants. Most of the buildings are now used as offices.

No. 39 Castle Street was the home of the writer Sir Walter Scott *(see p86).*

Princes Street Gardens
Princes Street was part of the initial building phase of the New Town. The north side is lined with shops; the gardens to the south lie below the castle.

No. 9 was the home of surgeon Joseph Lister *(see p23)* from 1870 to 1877. He developed methods of preventing infection both during and after surgery.

West Register House was originally St George's Church, designed by Robert Adam.

A view from Edinburgh Castle across the towers and spires of the city to Calton Hill in the distance

Calton Hill ❿

City centre east, via Waterloo Pl.

CALTON HILL, at the east end of Edinburgh's most memorable and baffling landmarks – a half-finished Parthenon. Conceived as the National Monument to the dead of the Napoleonic Wars, building began in 1822 but funds ran out and it was never finished. Public shame over its condition has given way to affection, as attitudes have softened over the last 170 years or so.

Fortunately, the nearby tower commemorating the British victory at Trafalgar was completed, in 1816. Named the **Nelson Monument**, the

tower is designed to resemble a telescope standing on its end. It provides a fine vantage point from which to admire the views of Edinburgh and the surrounding area.

The Classical theme continues on top of Calton Hill with the old **City Observatory**, designed by William Playfair in 1818 and based on Athens' Tower of the Winds. The public can attend free lectures here arranged by the Astronomical Society of Edinburgh. Tours are by previous arrangement only.

Another Classical building, the **Royal High School**, was created during the 1820s on the Regent Road side of Calton Hill. It was designed by Thomas Hamilton, with the Temple of Theseus at Athens in mind. Often cited as a possible home for a Scottish parliament, the building was the focus for the Vigil for Scottish Democracy, which campaigned from 1992 to 1997 for self government. A discreet cairn marking this effort stands a little way east of the National Monument on Calton Hill. The cairn contains several "gift" stones, including one from Auschwitz in memory of a Scottish missionary who died there.

The final resting place of Thomas Hamilton is the **Old Calton Cemetery**, south of

Waterloo Place, which he shares with philosopher David Hume and other celebrated Edinburgh residents.

🏛 **Nelson Monument**
☎ *(0131) 556 2716.* ⭕ *Mon–Sat (Apr–Sep: Mon pm only).* 📷
🏛 **City Observatory**
Calton Hill. ☎ *(0131) 556 4365.* ⭕ *by arrangement only.* 📷

The grand façade of The Palace of Holyroodhouse, renovated in the 17th century following a fire

The Palace of Holyroodhouse ⓫

East end of the Royal Mile. **Palace** ☎ *(0131) 556 1096.* ⭕ *9:30–4:30pm daily.* **Queen's Gallery** ☎ *(0131) 556 1096.* ⭕ *9:30–4:30pm daily* 📷

KNOWN TODAY AS Queen Elizabeth II's official Scottish residence, The Palace of Holyroodhouse was built by James IV in the grounds of an abbey in 1498. It was later the home of James V and his wife, Mary of Guise, and was remodelled in the 1670s for Charles II. The Royal Apartments (including the Throne Room and Royal Dining Room) are used for investitures and

City Observatory, Calton Hill, based on Classical Greek architecture

for banquets whenever the Queen visits the palace. A chamber in the so-called James V tower is famously associated with the unhappy reign of Mary, Queen of Scots (see p44). It was probably in this room, in 1566, that Mary saw the murder of her trusted Italian secretary, David Rizzio, authorized by her jealous husband, Lord Darnley. She was six months pregnant when she witnessed the murder, during which Rizzio's body was pierced "with fifty-six wounds".

In the early stages of the Jacobite uprising of 1745 (see p45), the last of the pretenders to the British throne, Charles Edward Stuart (Bonnie Prince Charlie) held court at Holyroodhouse, dazzling Edinburgh society with his magnificent parties.

James V's arms, Holyroodhouse

The new **Queen's Gallery** displays works from the Royal Collection.

Our Dynamic Earth ⓬

Holyrood Road. 📞 (0131) 550 7800. 🕐 Apr–Oct: 10am–5pm daily; Nov–Mar: Wed–Sun. 🖼 📷 ♿ �🌐 www.dynamicearth.co.uk

OUR DYNAMIC EARTH is a permanent exhibition about the planet. Visitors are taken on a journey from the earth's volcanic beginnings to the first appearance of life. Further displays concentrate on the world's climatic zones and dramatic natural phenomena such as tidal waves and earthquakes. State-of-the-art lighting and interactive techniques produce the special effects for 90 minutes of learning and entertainment.

The exhibition building is fronted by a 1,000-seat stone amphitheatre designed by Sir Michael Hopkins, and it incorporates a translucent tented roof. Situated beneath Salisbury Crags, the modern lines of Our Dynamic Earth contrast sharply with the natural landscape.

New Scottish Parliament ⓭

Holyrood. 📞 0131 348 5200. 📷 ♿ �🌐 www.scottish.parliament.uk

FOLLOWING DECADES of Scottish calls for more political self-determination, a referendum in 1997 on the issue of whether or not to have a Scottish parliament, with some powers devolving from the UK parliament in London, resulted in a majority "yes" vote (see p47). Designed by the late Enric Miralles, well known for his work on buildings at the 1992 Barcelona Olympics, the new parliament building was opened in October 2004 by Queen Elizabeth II. Despite its controversial xxxx million cost, the parliament has been hailed as one of the most spectacular and architecturally exciting new public buildings in the United Kingdom.

Holyrood Park and Arthur's Seat ⓮

Main access via Holyrood Park Rd, Holyrood Rd and Meadowbank Terrace.

HOLYROOD PARK, adjacent to The Palace of Holyroodhouse, covers over 260 hectares (640 acres) of varying terrain, topped by a rugged 250-m (820-ft) hill.

Known as Arthur's Seat, the hill is actually a volcano that has been extinct for 350 million years. The area has been a royal hunting ground since at least the time of King David I, who died in 1153, and a royal park since the 16th century.

The name Holyrood, which means "holy cross", comes from an episode in the life of David I when, in 1128, he was knocked from his horse by a stag while out hunting. Legend has it that a cross appeared miraculously in his hands to ward off the animal and, in thanksgiving, the king founded the Abbey of the Holy Cross, Holyrood Abbey. The name Arthur's Seat is probably a corruption of Archer's Seat, a more prosaic explanation for the name than any link with the legendary King Arthur.

The park has three small lochs. St Margaret's near the Palace is the most romantic, with its resident swans and position under the ruins of St Anthony's Chapel. Dunsapie Loch is the highest, sitting 112 m (367 ft) above sea level under Arthur's Seat. Duddingston Loch, on the south side of the park, is home to a large number of wildfowl.

The **Salisbury Crags** are among the park's most striking features. Their dramatic profile, along with that of Arthur's Seat, can be seen from many kilometres away. The Crags form a parabola of red cliffs that sweep round and up from Holyrood Palace, above a steep supporting hillside. A rough track, called the Radical Road, follows their base.

Arthur's Seat and the Salisbury Crags, looming above the city

Further Afield

A LTHOUGH INEXTRICABLY linked to the rest of Edinburgh, the inhabitants of Leith insist that they do not live in the city itself. More than just a docks area, Leith has plenty of attractions for the visitor. Close by is the magnificent Royal Botanic Garden. Dean Village offers riverside walks, galleries and antique shops. To the west of the city are the historic Hopetoun House and Linlithgow Palace, to the east is Haddington and a dramatic coastline.

10km = 6miles

KEY

▦	Urban area
✈	Airport
▣	Train station
—	Intercity train line
▭	Motorway (highway)
▭	Major road
═	Minor road

SIGHTS AT A GLANCE

Dean Village ❸
East Lothian Coast ❽
Forth Bridges ❹
Haddington ❼
Hopetoun House ❺
Leith ❷
Linlithgow Palace ❻
Royal Botanic Garden ❶

A specimen from the Palm House in the city's Royal Botanic Garden

Royal Botanic Garden ❶

Inverleith Row. ☎ (0131) 552 7171. ▭ ○ Apr–Sep: 10am–7pm daily; Mar, Oct: 10am–6pm; Nov–Feb: 10am–4pm ⬤ ⬤ ⓦ www.rbge.org.uk

T HIS MAGNIFICENT garden lies a short way to the north of the New Town, across the Water of Leith (a river that runs from the Pentland Hills down through Edinburgh and into the Firth of Forth at Leith). The garden is a descendant of a Physic Garden near Holyroodhouse that was created by two doctors in 1670. It was moved to its present location in 1820, and since then has been progressively enlarged and developed. Public access is from the east (well served by buses) and from the west (offering better car parking). The garden benefits from a hill site, giving southerly views across the city.

There is a rock garden in the southeast corner and an indoor exhibition and interpretation display in the northeast corner. There are also extensive greenhouses in traditional and modern architectural styles, offering fascinating hideaways on rainy days. Be sure not to miss the alpine display to the northwest of the greenhouses, or the beautiful and fragrant rhododendron walk.

Leith ❷

Northeast of the city centre, linked by Leith Walk.

L EITH IS A HISTORIC port that has traded for centuries with Scandinavia, the Baltic and Holland, and has always been the port for Edinburgh. It was incorporated into the city in 1920, and now forms a northeastern suburb.

The medieval core of narrow streets and quays includes a number of historic warehouses and merchants' houses dating from the 13th and 14th centuries. There was a great expansion of the docks in the 19th century, and many port buildings date from this period.

Shipbuilding and port activities have diminished, but there has been a renaissance in recent years in the form of conversions of warehouse buildings to offices, residences and, most notably, restaurants. The Shore and Dock Place now has Edinburgh's most dense concentration of seafood bistros and varied restaurants (see pp177–8).

The tourist attractions have been further boosted by the presence of the former British **Royal Yacht Britannia**, which is on display in Leith's new Ocean Terminal.

⚓ Royal Yacht Britannia

Ocean Terminal, Leith Docks. ☎ (0131) 555 8800. ○ daily. ▨ ⬤ ⓦ www.royalyachtbritannia.co.uk

The British Royal Yacht Britannia, berthed at Leith's Ocean Terminal

Leger's *The Team at Rest* (1950), Scottish National Gallery of Modern Art

Dean Village ❸

Northwest of the city centre.

THIS INTERESTING area lies in the valley of the Water of Leith, just a few minutes' walk northwest from Charlotte Square *(see map p54)*. A series of water mills along the river have been replaced by attractive buildings of all periods.

Access to Dean Village can be gained by walking down Bell's Brae from Randolph Crescent. A riverside walk threads its way between the historic buildings, crossing the river on a series of footbridges. Upstream from Dean Village the riverside walk leads in a few minutes to a footbridge and a flight of steps giving access to the **Scottish Gallery of Modern Art and Dean Gallery**. The main access for vehicles, and less energetic pedestrians, is on Belford Road.

Downstream from Dean Village, the riverside walkway passes under the magnificent high level bridge designed by Thomas Telford. It then passes St Bernard's Well before arriving in the urban village of

Stockbridge. Both antiques and curio shops can be found on the south side of the river in St Stephen Street. The riverside walk continues northeast, close to the Royal Botanic Garden. The city centre is a short walk away, via Royal Circus and Howe Street.

🏛 **Scottish Gallery of Modern Art & Dean Gallery**
Belford Road. 🄲 *(0131) 624 6200.*
🄾 *daily.* special exhibitions only.
♿ 🅦 www.nationalgalleries.org

17th-century stone houses on the historic Bell's Brae

Forth Bridges ❹

Lothian. 🚇 🅿 *Dalmeny, Inverkeithing.*

THE SMALL TOWN of South Queensferry is dominated by the two great bridges that span 1.5 km (1 mile) across the River Forth to the town of Inverkeithing. The spectacular rail bridge, the first major steel-built bridge in the world, was opened in 1890 and remains one of the greatest engineering achievements of the late Victorian era. Its massive cantilevered sections are held together by more than eight million rivets, and the painted area adds up to some 55 ha (135 acres). The saying "it's like painting the Forth Bridge" has become a byword for non-stop, repetitive endeavour.

The neighbouring road bridge was the largest suspension bridge outside the US when it was opened in 1964. The two bridges make an impressive contrast, best seen from the promenade at South Queensferry. The town got its name from Queen Margaret *(see p61)*, who reigned with her husband, King Malcolm III, in the 11th century. She used the ferry here on her frequent journeys between Edinburgh and her home, the royal palace at Dunfermline in Fife *(see p124)*. From Queensferry you can take a boat trip down the River Forth to visit the tranquil island of Inchcolm with its exceptionally well-preserved 12th-century abbey.

The huge, cantilevered Forth Rail Bridge, seen from South Queensferry

Hopetoun House ❺

West Lothian. 🅒 (0131) 331 2451.
�(Dalmeny then taxi. ◯ mid–Apr–
Sep: 10am–5:30pm daily. 🖼 🅑 🗐
🆆 www.hopetounhouse.com

A N EXTENSIVE PARKLAND by the
Firth of Forth, designed
in the style of Versailles, is the
setting for one of Scotland's
finest stately homes. The original house was completed in
1707 and later absorbed into
William Adam's grand
extension. The dignified,
horseshoe-shaped plan and
lavish interior represent Neo-
Classical 18th-century architecture at its best. The red and
yellow state drawing rooms,
with their Rococo plasterwork
and ornate mantelpieces, are
particularly impressive. The
present Marquess of Linlithgow
is a descendant of the first
Earl of Hopetoun, for whom
the house was originally built.

**A wooden panel above the main
stairs depicting Hopetoun House**

Linlithgow Palace ❻

Kirk Gate, Linlithgow, West Lothian.
🅒 (01506) 842896. �(🅟 ◯
Apr–Sep: 9:30am–5:45pm daily;
Oct–Mar: 9:30am–3:45pm daily. 🖼
🅑 limited.

S TANDING ON THE edge of
Linlithgow Loch, the former
royal palace of Linlithgow is
now one of the country's most
visited ruins. It dates back
largely to the building com-

Ornate fountain in the ruins of Linlithgow Palace

missioned by James I in 1425,
following a fire the previous
year, though some sections date
from the 14th century. The vast
scale of the building is demonstrated by the 28-m (94-ft) long
Great Hall, with its huge fireplace and windows. The restored fountain in the courtyard
was a wedding present in 1538
from James V to his wife, Mary
of Guise. His daughter, Mary,
Queen of Scots (see p44), was
born at Linlithgow in 1542.
   The adjacent Church of St
Michael is Scotland's largest pre-
Reformation church and a fine
example of the Scottish Decorated style. Consecrated in the
13th century, the church was
damaged by the fire of 1424.

Haddington ❼

East Lothian. 🛈 Edinburgh & Lothians
(0845) 225 5121.

T HIS ATTRACTIVE county town
is situated about 24 km
(15 miles) east of Edinburgh.
It was destroyed on various
occasions during the Wars of
Independence in the 13th–14th

centuries, and
again in the 16th
century. The
agricultural revo-
lution brought
great prosperity,
giving Hadding-
ton many historic
houses, chur-
ches, and other
public buildings.
A programme of
restoration has
helped the town
to retain its cha-
racter. The River
Tyne encloses
the town, and
there are attractive riverside
walks and parkland. ("A walk
around Haddington" guide is
available from newsagents.)
The parish church of St Mary's,
southeast of the centre, dates
from 1462 and is one of the
largest in the area. Parts of
the church have been rebuilt
in recent years, having been
destroyed in the siege of 1548.
A short way south of the
town lies **Lennoxlove House**,
with its ancient tower house.

🏛 **Lennoxlove House**
🅒 (01620) 823720. ◯ Easter–Oct:
pm only Wed–Thu & Sat–Sun. 🖼

East Lothian Coast ❽

🛈 Edinburgh & Lothians (0845) 225
5121. 🆆 www.visitscotland.com

S TRETCHING EAST from Mussel-
burgh for some 65 km (40
miles), the coast of East Lothian
offers many opportunities for
beach activities, windsurfing,
golf, viewing seabirds and
coastal walks. The coastline is
a pleasant mixture of beaches,

The historic and tranquil town of Haddington on the River Tyne

low cliffs, woodland, golf courses and some farmland. Although the A198 and A1 are adjacent to the coast for only short distances, they give easy access to a series of public car parks (a small charge is made in summer), close to the shore. Among these visitor points is Gullane, perhaps the best beach for seaside activities. Yellowcraig, near Dirleton, is another lovely bay, lying

Tantallon Castle, looking out to the North Sea

about 400 m (440 yds) from the car park. Limetree Walk, near Tyninghame, has the long, east-facing beach of Ravensheugh Sands (a ten-minute walk along a woodland track). Belhaven Bay, just west of Dunbar, is a large beach providing walks along the estuary of the River Tyne. Barns Ness, east of Dunbar, offers a geological nature trail and an impressive lighthouse. Skateraw Harbour is an attractive small bay, despite the presence of Torness nuclear power station to the east. Finally, there is another delightful beach to be found at Seacliff, reached by a private toll road that leaves the A198 about 3 km (2 miles) east of North Berwick. This sheltered bay has spectacular views of the Bass Rock, home to one of the largest gannet (a type of marine bird) colonies in Britain. The rock itself can be seen at close quarters by taking the boat trip from North Berwick harbour (summer only). At the town's **Scottish Seabird Centre** it is possible to control cameras on the rock and on the Island of Fidra, for live coverage of the birdlife without disturbing it. Also of interest along this coastline are **Dirleton Castle** and **Tantallon Castle**, perched on a cliff top near Seacliff beach. There is a small industrial museum at Prestonpans. North Berwick and Dunbar are towns worthy of a visit.

Scottish Seabird Centre
(01620) 890202. ☐ daily.
W www.seabird.org
Dirleton Castle
(01620) 850330. ☐ daily.
Tantallon Castle
(01620) 892727. ☐ 9:30am–4:30pm Sat–Wed ☐ Thu, Fri.

EAST LOTHIAN COASTAL WALK

For a very attractive longer coast walk, there is easy public access along the footpath from Gullane Bay to North Berwick. The path follows the coastline, crossing grassy heathland between the alternating sandy bays and low rocky headlands, with views of the coast of Fife to the north. There are small islands along the way. The last part of the walk into North Berwick has wonderful views east to the white slopes of the Bass Rock.

TIPS FOR WALKERS

Starting point: Gullane Bay.
Finishing point: North Berwick.
Length: 10 km (6 miles); 3 hours.
Getting there: by car; a bus service between Edinburgh and North Berwick gives access to both ends.
Level: easy (one steep section).

Dirleton

North Berwick

Gullane Bay

Muirfield

Gullane

KEY

0 kilometres 2
0 miles 1

☐ Urban area
-- Route

▬▬ Major road
═ Minor road
╫╫╫ Train line
☼ Viewpoint
P Parking

SHOPPING IN EDINBURGH

DESPITE THE GROWTH of new out-of-town malls, Princes Street remains one of the top 12 retail centres in the British Isles. With the ancient Castle rising above the gardens along the street's south side, it is a unique and picturesque place to shop. Although many familiar chain stores can be found here, the capital also boasts its very own

Colourful Wemyssware china

department store, Jenners, a marvellous institution that has been in business for over 150 years. But there are shopping attractions away from Princes Street, too, including Scotland's best delicatessen (Valvona & Crolla), several excellent wine merchants, a selection of Highland clothing outfitters and an appealing collection of specialist stores.

DEPARTMENT STORES

PRINCES STREET has several good department stores, with **House of Fraser** at the west end being one of the best. Located opposite the Scott Monument, is **Jenners**. Founded on a different site in the late 1830s, it has gained a reputation as Edinburgh's top store. During the Christmas season it is famed for its central atrium housing a Christmas tree. **John Lewis**, belonging to a nationwide chain of stores, is in a contemporary building of architectural interest on Leith Street. The famous **Harvey Nichols** can also be found in the capital.

CLOTHING

DESIGNER LABELS FOR men and women can be found in both Jenners and House of Fraser *(see Department Stores)*. **Corniche** on Jeffrey Street offers more interesting and

Traditional Highland dress and accessories, for sale on the Royal Mile

exciting women's fashion by designers such as Jean-Paul Gaultier and Vivienne Westwood, while **Jane Davidson** is home to a more traditional, chic look. George Street contains a number of women's stores, including **Phase Eight** and **Escada**. **Cruise** has separate shops for men and women. Men can also go to **Thomas Pink**, and **Austin Reed** for smart suits and shirts. The **Schuh** chain has fashionable footwear for men and women. Several shops on the Royal Mile, including **Ragamuffin**, sell interesting knitwear. The Royal Mile also boasts Highland outfitters offering made-to-measure kilts; **Hector Russell** is one of the best. **Kinloch Anderson** in Leith is also a leading example, and the shop has a small display on the history of tartan. Outdoor equipment and water-proof clothing can be found at leading supplier **Graham Tiso**.

FOOD AND DRINK

EDINBURGH HAS A reputation as Scotland's top city for eating out, and it matches this status on the shopping front with some very good food stores. **Valvona & Crolla**, a family-run delicatessen trading since the 1930s, is acknowledged as one of the best of its kind in the UK, let alone Scotland, and stocks good breads and an award-winning Italian wine selection. The **Peckham's** chain is present here, while **Glass & Thompson** is a good deli serving the New Town. Celebrated cheesemonger **Iain Mellis** started his business in Edinburgh, **MacSweens** are master haggis makers, and **Real Foods** is one of Scotland's longest-established wholefood stores.

Specialist wine merchants include **Peter Green** and **Cockburns of Leith**, as well as chains such as **Oddbins**, while **Cadenheads** supplies rare whiskies. **Justerini & Brooks** is the most distinguished wine and spirit

Princes Street from the top of Calton Hill

merchant in the city centre and **The Wine Basket** has an extensive range of beers from small independent breweries.

BOOKS AND NEWSPAPERS

THE CITY'S BOOK TRADE is dominated by the high street **Waterstone's** chain, with two branches in Princes Street (the west end branch has a fine coffee shop). A third branch of Waterstone's is found on George Street nearby. **Ottakar's** is also well represented with a branch on George Street and another at Cameron Toll. **The International Newsagents** on the High Street has a good selection of foreign newspapers and magazines.

ART, DESIGN AND ANTIQUES

ORIGINAL ART WORKS are on sale at a variety of galleries in the city. **The Scottish Gallery** in the New Town has everything from jewellery for under £100, to pieces by well-known Scottish artists sold at £10,000 or more. The prices at the **Printmakers Workshop** are more affordable, with an innovative range of limited-edition prints for sale, and the **Collective Gallery** offers experimental works. **Inhouse** has some remarkable designer furniture. Browsers looking for antiques should try Victoria Street, St Stephen's Street, the Grassmarket and Causeway-side. For large-scale fixtures

and fittings, the **Edinburgh Architectural Salvage Yard** sells everything from Victorian baths to staircases and doors.

Intricately patterned Edinburgh Crystal, a popular souvenir

DIRECTORY

DEPARTMENT STORES

Harvey Nichols
30–34 St Andrew's Sq,
EH2 2AD
(0131) 524 8388.

House of Fraser
145 Princes St, EH2 4YZ.
(0131) 225 2472.

Jenners
48 Princes St, EH2 2YJ.
(0131) 225 2442.

John Lewis
69 St James Centre,
EH1 3SP.
(0131) 556 9121.

CLOTHING

Austin Reed
39 George St, EH2 2HN.
(0131) 225 6703.

Corniche
2 Jeffrey St, EH1 1DT.
(0131) 556 3707.

Cruise (men)
80 George St, EH2 3DF.
(0131) 226 3524.

Cruise (women)
31 Castle St, EH2 3DN.
(0131) 220 4441.

Escada
35a George St, EH2 2HN.
(0131) 225 9885.

Graham Tiso
41 Commercial St, EH6 6JD.
(0131) 554 9101.

Hector Russell
137–141 High St,
EH1 1SG.
(0131) 558 1254.

Jane Davidson
52 Thistle St, EH2 1EN.
(0131) 225 3280.

Kinloch Anderson
Commercial St, EH6 6EY.
(0131) 555 1390.

Phase Eight
47b George St,
EH2 2HT.
(0131) 226 4009.

Ragamuffin
278 Canongate, EH8 8AA.
(0131) 557 6007.

Schuh
6a Frederick St, EH2 2HB.
(0131) 220 0290.

Thomas Pink
32a Castle St, EH2 3HT.
(0131) 225 4264.

FOOD AND DRINK

Cadenheads
172 Canongate,
EH8 8BN.
(0131) 556 5864.

Cockburns of Leith
7 Devon Place, EH12 5HJ.
(0131) 337 6005.

Glass & Thompson
2 Dundas St, EH3 6HZ.
(0131) 557 0909.

Iain Mellis
30a Victoria St, EH1 2JW.
(0131) 226 6215.

Justerini & Brooks
14a Coates Cres, EH3 7AF.
(0131) 226 4202.

MacSweens
Dryden Rd, Bilston Glen,
Loanhead, EH20 9LZ.
(0131) 440 2555.

Oddbins
37b George St, EH2 2HN.
(0131) 220 3488.

Peckham's
155 Bruntsfield Place,
EH10 4DG.
(0131) 229 7054.

Peter Green
37a/b Warrander Park Rd,
EH9 1HJ.
(0131) 229 5925.

Real Foods
37 Broughton St, EH1 3JU.
(0131) 557 1911.

Valvona & Crolla
19 Elm Row, EH7 4AA.
(0131) 556 6066.

The Wine Basket
144 Dundas St, EH3 5DQ.
(0131) 557 2530.

BOOKS AND NEWSAGENTS

The International Newsagents
351 High St, EH1 1PW.
(0131) 225 4827.

Ottakar's
57 George St, EH2 2JQ.
(0131) 225 4495.

Waterstone's
128 Princes St, EH2 4AD.
(0131) 226 2666.

ART, DESIGN AND ANTIQUES

Collective Gallery
28 Cockburn St, EH1 1NY.
(0131) 220 1260.

Edinburgh Architectural Salvage Yard
31 West Bowling Green
St, EH6 5NX.
(0131) 554 7077.

Inhouse
28 Howe St, EH3 6TG.
(0131) 225 2888.

Printmakers Workshop
23 Union St, EH1 3LR.
(0131) 557 2479.

The Scottish Gallery
16 Dundas St, EH3 6HZ.
(0131) 558 1200.

What to Buy

Scottish blend tobacco

SCOTLAND OFFERS A WIDE RANGE of goods and souvenirs to tempt its visitors. Most food and drink items can be found in Edinburgh's food stores and off-licences (liquor stores that also stock tobacco). A number of specialist shops in the city sell more unusual Scottish crafts and products, from handcrafted jewellery to clothing, such as tartan kilts and knitwear. Certain areas of Scotland specialize in particular crafts – Orkney is famed for its jewellery, Caithness and Edinburgh for their beautifully engraved glassware.

Caithness glass paperweight   **Edinburgh glass goblet**

Scottish glass is beautifully decorated. The Caithness glass factories in Oban, Perth and Wick offer tours to show how delicate patterns are engraved.

Amethyst brooch   **Celtic brooch**

Celtic earrings

Scottish jewellery reflects either the area in which it was made, a culture (such as Celtic) or an artistic movement such as Art Nouveau. The unbroken, intricate patterns and knotwork in the jewellery pictured above symbolize the wish for eternal life.

Dagger ("sgian dubh")

Sporran   Belt

Classic Scottish kilt

Tartan tie and scarf

Stag horn is carved into all manner of objects, both functional, as with this ashtray, and decorative.

Scottish tartan originally existed in the form of large woollen shawls (or plaids) worn by Highlanders in the 15th and 16th centuries. Today, "tartan" refers to the distinctive patterns woven into woolen cloth. Some of these patterns are based on the designs of centuries past. Tartan is used in the making of kilts and many other items.

Scottish textiles vary greatly, but the most distinctive include chunky woollens from the islands; smart tweeds, such as Harris tweed with its fine-toothed check; softest cashmere, used to make sweaters, cardigans and scarves; and fluffy sheepskin rugs.

Cable-knit sweater

Tweed jacket

PACKAGED FOODS

Food is a popular and accessible form of souvenir or gift to purchase during a visit to Scotland. Teatime is a favourite meal with the Scottish, offering such treats as Dundee cake, butter shortbread, Abernethy biscuits, Scotch pancakes and parlies (ginger cookies). Oatcakes are the traditional accompaniment to cheese in Scotland, although they also complement pâté and sweet toppings such as jam or honey. They are also delicious toasted and served with plenty of butter.

Vegetarian haggis   **Original haggis**

Haggis, the most famous of Scottish foods (see p32), traditionally consists of sheep's offal and oatmeal. It is now also available in vegetarian, venison and whisky-laced varieties.

Traditional pure butter shortbread   **Oatcakes**

Scotch Abernethy biscuits

Dairy vanilla fudge   **LochRanza whisky fudge**

Fudge is an extremely sweet confectionary made almost entirely of sugar and condensed milk. There are many different flavours, from vanilla to rum and raisin, walnut, chocolate and whisky.

BOTTLED DRINKS

Home to a large number of distilleries and breweries, Scotland is perhaps associated most with its alcoholic beverages. There is certainly a good range on sale, including locally brewed beers and ales, many varieties of Scotch whisky (see pp30–31) and an assortment of spirits and liqueurs, such as Drambuie and Glayva. But Scotland is also famed for its mountain spring water, which is sold still, fizzy (carbonated) or flavoured with fruits such as peach or melon.

Historic Scottish ales

Beers and ales figure prominently in the drink produced in Scotland. Traditionally served by the pint in pubs, they can also be purchased in bottles. Alternative choices include fruit ales and heather ales, brewed using ancient Highland recipes.

Caledonian spring water

Whisky is undoubtedly the most famous of all Scottish spirits. There are a huge number of whiskies from which to choose, each with a unique taste (see pp30–31). Drambuie is a variation on a theme, being a whisky-based, herb flavoured liqueur.

Drambuie   **Glenfiddich**   **LochRanza**   **Glen Ord**   **Bell's**

ENTERTAINMENT IN EDINBURGH

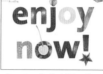

A LTHOUGH MOST people associate entertainment in Edinburgh with the festivals that take place in August, the city also benefits from its status as the Scottish capital by acting as a centre for drama, dance and music. The Filmhouse is an important venue on the arthouse cinema circuit and some argue that Edinburgh's nightclubs are as

A postcard advertising the Edinburgh Festival

good as those in Glasgow these days. Many bars offer an excellent range of Scotch whiskies and cask ales, while the expansion of the café-bar scene in the last few years means it is now possible to find a decent cup of coffee later on in the evening. Edinburgh is home to Scotland's national rugby union stadium, Murrayfield, host to international matches.

ENTERTAINMENT GUIDES

T HE TWICE MONTHLY arts and entertainments magazine, *The List*, covers all events in both Edinburgh and Glasgow.

THEATRE AND DANCE

E DINBURGH'S POPULIST **The King's Theatre** hosts pantomimes and performances by touring companies. It is run by the same organization that manages Edinburgh Festival Theatre *(see Classical Music and Opera)*, which dominates in ballet and contemporary dance, although there are children's shows and music hall-style performances there too. **Edinburgh Playhouse** often has runs of internationally successful musicals, such as "Mama Mia" and "Chicago", while **The Traverse** is home to more experimental work and has helped launch the careers of young Scottish playwrights. **The Royal Lyceum** tends to

The ornate, colourful interior of The King's Theatre, opened in 1906

Edinburgh Festival Theatre, venue for dance, classical music and opera

opt for a more classical repertory with well-known plays and adaptations, but sometimes showcases new work too. Edinburgh University's theatre company stages shows at **Bedlam**, while both **Theatre Workshop** and **St Bride's** present innovative productions.

CLASSICAL MUSIC AND OPERA

V ISITS FROM the Glasgow-based Scottish Opera and the Royal Scottish National Orchestra are hosted at the impressive, glass-fronted **Edinburgh Festival Theatre** which opened in 1994. Edinburgh is the home of the internationally acclaimed Scottish Chamber Orchestra, which stages performances at **The Queen's Hall**. Smaller venues throughout the city also host recitals, including Edinburgh University's **Reid Concert Hall** and **St Cecilia's Hall**. **St Giles Cathedral** hosts classical concerts by small groups, such as string quartets.

Logo for the annual Film Festival

ROCK, JAZZ AND WORLD MUSIC

F OR MAJOR ROCK concerts by bands such as REM or U2, Murrayfield Stadium *(see Sports)* is called into use from time to time. Edinburgh Playhouse *(see Theatre and Dance)* has also played host to major pop stars. Edinburgh has an eclectic nightclub scene, and intimate sessions – including jazz and world music – often take place at clubs *(see Café-bars, Bars and Clubs)*. The Queen's Hall *(see Classical Music and Opera)* also hosts smaller shows. Folk and jazz musicians appear at the **Tron Ceilidh House** and **Henry's Jazz Bar**, respectively.

Some Edinburgh pubs have resident folk musicians and jazz bands – check *The List* magazine for details. **The Assembly Rooms** hosts regular *ceilidhs* (traditional Highland dance evenings).

CINEMA

E DINBURGH, LIKE every other major city, has seen a move to multiplex cinemas. However, the **UGC**, **UGI** and **Odeon Multiplex** are all quite far from the centre. Only a few minutes from Princes Street is the **OMNI** leisure centre with a 12-screen cinema village. **The Dominion** is an old-fashioned, family-run affair, while **The Cameo** offers late-night shows and offbeat modern classics. **The Filmhouse** is the arthouse movie theatre for the city, and centre for the International Film Festival.

Opening ceremony of a Five Nations rugby union match at Murrayfield

SPORTS

THE IMPRESSIVE **Murrayfield Stadium** is the national centre for Scottish rugby and international matches are played from late January to March. There are two association football (soccer) sides, **Heart of Midlothian** in the west and **Hibernian** in Leith. **Meadowbank Stadium and Sports Centre** hosts league basketball and a range of athletics events throughout the summer.

CAFÉ-BARS, BARS AND CLUBS

CAFÉ-BARS have become a common sight in Edinburgh, and Broughton Street is an obvious centre. Some are associated more with nightlife, including **Assembly**, **Indigo Yard**, **Po-Na-Na** and **The City Café**. Good examples of more traditional Edinburgh bars are **The Café Royal**, **Bennet's**, **The Cumberland** or **The Bow Bar**. All serve good cask ales, many brewed in Scotland, and an extensive selection of single malt Scotch whiskies. Some of the city's acclaimed club venues, which also host live bands from time to time, are **The Bongo Club**, **The Liquid Room** and **The Venue**.

DIRECTORY

THEATRE AND DANCE

Bedlam
11b Bristow Place, EH1 1E2.
☎ *(0131) 225 9893.*

Edinburgh Playhouse
18–22 Greenside Place, EH1 3AA.
☎ *(08/0) 6063424.*

The King's Theatre
2 Leven St, EH3 9LQ.
☎ *(0131) 529 6000.*

The Royal Lyceum
30b Grindlay St, EH3 9AX.
☎ *(0131) 248 4800.*

St Bride's
10 Orwell Terrace, EH11 2DZ.
☎ *(0131) 346 1405.*

Theatre Workshop
34 Hamilton Place, EH3 5AX.
☎ *(0131) 226 5425.*

The Traverse
10 Cambridge St, EH1 2ED.
☎ *(0131) 228 1404.*

CLASSICAL MUSIC AND OPERA

Edinburgh Festival Theatre
13-29 Nicolson St, EH8 9FT.
☎ *(0131) 529 6000.*

The Queen's Hall
Clerk St, EH8 9JG.
☎ *(0131) 668 2019.*

Reid Concert Hall
Bristo Sq, EH8 9AL.
☎ *(0131) 650 4367.*

St Cecilia's Hall
Niddry St, EH1 1LJ.
☎ *(0131) 650 2805.*

St Giles Cathedral
High St, EH1 1RE.
☎ *(0131) 225 9442.*

ROCK, JAZZ AND WORLD MUSIC

Assembly Rooms
54 George St, EH2 2LR.
☎ *(0131) 220 4349.*

Henry's Jazz Bar
8–16a Morrison St, EH3 8BJ.
☎ *(0131) 221 1288.*

Tron Ceilidh House
9 Hunter Sq, EH1 1QW.
☎ *(0131) 226 0931.*

CINEMA

The Cameo
38 Home St, EH3 9LZ.
☎ *(0131) 228 4141.*

The Dominion
18 Newbattle Terrace, EH10 4RT.
☎ *(0131) 447 4771.*

The Filmhouse
88 Lothian Rd, EH3 9BZ.
☎ *(0131) 228 2688.*

Odeon Multiplex
120 Wester Hailes Rd, EH14 1SW.
☎ *(0131) 453 1569.*

OMNI Edinburgh
Greenside Place, EH1 3BN.
☎ *(0131) 524 7772.*

UCI
Fort Kinnaird, Newcraighall, EH15 3RD.
☎ *(0131) 669 0777.*

UGC
Fountain Park, EH11 1AF.
☎ *(0131) 228 8788.*

SPORTS

Heart of Midlothian
Tynecastle Stadium, Gorgie Rd, EH11 2NL.
☎ *(0131) 200 7200.*

Hibernian Football Club Ltd
12 Albion Place, EH7 5QG.
☎ *(0131) 661 2159.*

Meadowbank Stadium and Sports Centre
139 London Rd, EH7 6AE.
☎ *(0131) 661 5351.*

Murrayfield Stadium
Murrayfield, EH12 5PJ.
☎ *(0131) 346 5000.*

CAFÉ-BARS, BARS AND CLUBS

Bennet's
8 Leven St, EH3 9LG.
☎ *(0131) 229 5143.*

The Bongo Club
37 Holyrood Rd, EH8 8BA.
☎ *(0131) 558 7604.*

The Bow Bar
80 West Bow, EH1 2HH.
☎ *(0131) 226 7667.*

The Café Royal
19 W Register St, EH2 2AA.
☎ *(0131) 556 1884.*

The City Café
19 Blair St, EH1 1QR.
☎ *(0131) 220 0127.*

The Cumberland
1–3 Cumberland St, EH3 6RT.
☎ *(0131) 558 3134.*

Assembly
41 Lothian St, EH6 8BR.
☎ *(0131) 220 4288.*

Indigo Yard
7 Charlotte Lane, EH2 4QZ.
☎ *(0131) 220 5603.*

The Liquid Room
9c Victoria St, EH1 2HE.
☎ *(0131) 225 2564.*

Po-Na-Na
43b Frederick St, EH2 1EP.
☎ *(0131) 226 2224.*

The Venue
15–21 Calton Rd, EH8 8DL.
☎ *(0131) 557 3073.*

The Edinburgh Festival

AUGUST IN EDINBURGH means "the Festival". The Edinburgh International Festival is one of the world's premier arts jamborees, covering drama, dance, opera, music and ballet. The more eclectic "Fringe" developed in parallel with the official event, but has now exceeded it in terms of size. Both have been going strong for over 50 years, as has the Edinburgh International Film Festival. The British Army contributes with the Military Tattoo and, more recently, the Edinburgh Book Festival and Jazz & Blues Festival have also been staged in August. A total of half a million people visit these events.

A masked Fringe street performer

calendar of performing arts. It boasts a strong programme of classical music, traditional ballet, contemporary dance, opera and drama, and is held in major venues across the city *(see Directory p77)*.

The grand finale of the International Festival is a breathtaking spectacle, with some 250,000 crowding into the city centre to see a magnificent fireworks display based at the Castle. The lucky few with tickets for the Ross Bandstand in Princes Street Gardens also experience the fireworks concert by the Scottish Chamber Orchestra.

Entrance to the Fringe information office, located on the Royal Mile

EDINBURGH INTERNATIONAL FESTIVAL

AS A CULTURAL antidote to the austerity of post-war Europe, where many cities were devastated and food rationing was common even in the victorious countries, Edinburgh held its first arts festival in 1947. Over the years it grew in scope and prestige, and it is now one of the top events in the world

THE FRINGE

THE FRINGE started with a few performances providing an alternative to the official events of the International Festival, in the first year it was staged. A decade later, coming to Edinburgh to appear "on the Fringe" was an established pastime for amateurs, student drama companies or anyone else. All that was

needed was a space to perform in the city in August. This haphazard approach has long since given way to a more formal one, with an administrative body running the Fringe and, in recent years, a core of professionally-run venues attracting the bulk of the Fringe audiences. The Assembly Rooms in George Street *(see Directory p77)* and the Pleasance Theatre in The Pleasance host shows by television celebrities whose stand-up comedy or cabaret fails to fit the International Festival format.

The original vibrancy of the Fringe still exists, and in church halls and other odd venues across Edinburgh, including the city's streets, Fringe-goers can find everything from musicals performed by school children to experimental adaptations of Kafka's works.

Enjoying the August sun and street entertainment on the Royal Mile

EDINBURGH INTERNATIONAL FILM FESTIVAL

LIKE THE OTHER long established festivals that take place in Edinburgh, the International Film Festival dates from 1947. Although it started with a focus on documentary cinema, it soon began to widen and encompass both arthouse and popular movies.

The Festival invented "the retrospective" as a means of studying a film-maker's work. It has seen premieres by such noted directors as Woody Allen and Steven Spielberg. Since its 1995 relaunch, the

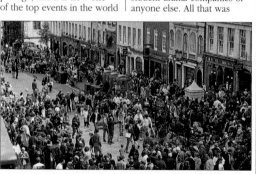

Crowds throng around the colourful Fringe street performers

The Military Tattoo at Edinburgh Castle, with an audience of thousands

Festival has been broken down into four main sections. There is a showcase for young British talent, a world premieres section, a film study category, and a major retrospective.

Although the showings are screened primarily at The Filmhouse on Lothian Road, every city centre cinema now takes part in the festival to some extent *(see Directory p77 for details of all the cinemas).*

EDINBURGH MILITARY TATTOO

THE ENDURING popularity of the Military Tattoo never fails to surprise some people, or to charm others. It has been running since 1950, when the British Army decided to contribute to Edinburgh's August events with displays of martial prowess and music on the picturesque Castle Esplanade.

Temporary stands are built on the Esplanade each summer in preparation for the 200,000 visitors who watch the Tattoo over its three-week run. This enormous spectacle heralds the approach of the other, assorted August arts festivals. Marching bands and musicians from the

A painted street performer showing his skill at staying as still as a statue

armed forces of other countries are invited every year to enhance the show. For many, the highlight of the Tattoo is a solo piper playing a haunting pibroch lament *(see p28)* from the Castle battlements.

A temporary marquee selling books at the Edinburgh Book Festival

EDINBURGH BOOK FESTIVAL

EVERY AUGUST, a mini-village of marquees is erected in the beautiful Georgian surroundings of Charlotte Square Gardens in the city centre. This temporary village plays host to two weeks of book-related events and talks by a variety of writers, from novelists and poets to those who specialize in cook books or children's fiction. Scottish authors are always well represented.

Originally held every other year, the Book Festival became so popular that since 1998 it has been an annual event coinciding with the other festivals.

EDINBURGH JAZZ & BLUES FESTIVAL

FOR AROUND TEN days in early August a selection of international jazz performers comes to Edinburgh to give concerts, accompanied by Scotland's principal jazz musicians.

The HVB and ARE on Clerk Street *(see p76)* are the main centres, although other venues in the city are used. There is also a free, open-air Mardi Gras day in the Grassmarket, in the Old Town, on the opening Saturday. The Blues element of the Festival is held in its own separate venue and is also very successful, attracting many UK and American performers.

DIRECTORY

Edinburgh International Festival
The Hub, Edinburgh's Festival Centre, Castlehill, Royal Mile, EH1 2NE
☎ *(0131) 473 2010.*
ⓦ www.erf.co.uk

The Fringe
The Fringe Office, 180 High St, EH1 1QS.
☎ *(0131) 226 0026.*
ⓦ www.edfringe.com

Edinburgh International Film Festival
88 Lothian Rd, EH3 9BZ.
☎ *(0131) 228 4051.*
ⓦ www.edfilmfest.org.uk

Edinburgh Book Festival
Scottish Book Centre, 137 Dundee St, EH11 1BG.
☎ *(0131) 228 5444.*
ⓦ www.edbookfest.co.uk

Edinburgh Jazz & Blues Festival
Assembly Direct, 89 Giles St, EH6 6BZ.
☎ *(0131) 553 4000.*
☎ Box office: *(0131) 467 5200.*
ⓦ www.jazzmusic.co.uk

Military Tattoo
Edinburgh Tattoo, 32 Market St, EH1 1QB.
☎ *(0131) 225 1188.*
ⓦ www.edintattoo.co.uk

SOUTHERN SCOTLAND

···

*S*OUTHERN SCOTLAND *is a blend of attractive landscapes and historic houses, castles and abbeys. Sadly, many of these ancient buildings exist only in fortified or ruined form due to the frontier wars that dated from the late 13th century. The rounded hills of the Scottish Borders and the more rugged peaks of Dumfries & Galloway bore the brunt of this fierce conflict between Scotland and England.*

In 1296 Scotland committed itself to the Wars of Independence against the English, and it was Southern Scotland that suffered the most. The strife caused by the many battles lasted for three centuries, as first Scottish self-determination, and then alliances with France, led to strained relations between Scotland and its southern neighbour, England. Dryburgh, one of the area's magnificent 12th-century abbeys, was burned twice, first by the English in 1322 and then again in 1544.

The virtual independence of the Borders district brought further conflict. Powerful families had operated under local laws set in place since the mid-12th century, and when Scottish kings were not fighting the English, they led raids into the Border country to try and bring it back under central control.

Over the years, some of the great dramas of Scottish history have been played out in the South. Robert the Bruce's guerrilla army defeated an English force at Glen Trool in 1307, but Flodden, near Coldstream, was the scene of the country's worst military reverse in 1513, when King James IV of Scotland and thousands of his men fell in battle.

Today, the quiet countryside around the Borders market towns, and the beautiful mountain scenery in Dumfries & Galloway, seem to belie such violent history. The area is now known for its manufacturing of textiles and for promoting its literary associations, as Sir Walter Scott lived at Abbotsford, near St Boswells. But it is the ruins of the great Border abbeys, castles and battlegrounds that serve as a reminder of Southern Scotland's turbulent past.

Fishing in the tranquil waters of the River Tweed, which weaves its way through the Border country

◁ The majestic ruins and colourful gardens of Melrose Abbey, one of the four great Border abbeys

Exploring Southern Scotland

SOUTHERN SCOTLAND has a variety of landscapes and small towns of great character, but the region is often overlooked by visitors keen to reach Edinburgh, Glasgow or the Highlands. The hills around Glen Trool in Dumfries & Galloway are beautiful and dramatic while, further east, the Border hills are less rugged but offer some classic panoramas such as Scott's View, near Melrose. The Ayrshire coast has a string of holiday resorts; the Solway Firth coast is fine touring country, quiet and picturesque; and St Abb's Head in the east is one of Scotland's most important wildlife reserves.

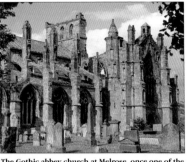

The Gothic abbey church at Melrose, once one of the richest abbeys in Scotland

M8

GLASGOW

HAMILTON

NEW LANARK 11

PENTLAND HILLS 10

BIGGAR

A78

ARDROSSAN

A77

M74

A702

KILMARNOCK

A70

PRESTWICK

A70

AYR

SANQUHAR 12

MOFF

CULZEAN CASTLE 21

DRUMLANRIG CASTLE 13

M76

A713

BURNS HERITAGE TRAIL 15

GALLOWAY FOREST PARK 19

CAERLAVEROCK CASTLE 16

A77

A75

THREAVE CASTLE 14

STRANRAER

THE RHINNS OF GALLOWAY 20

KIRKCUDBRIGHT 17

Solway Firth

WHITHORN 18

0 kilometres 20

0 miles 20

GETTING AROUND

Travelling east to west and vice versa can be problematic as all the main routes run north–south from Edinburgh and Glasgow to England. There are rural bus services but these tend to be infrequent and slow. Rail links down the east coast from Edinburgh, and from Glasgow to Ayrshire, are good, and there is also a train service from Glasgow to Stranraer, the ferry port for Northern Ireland. Exploring scenic areas away from the coasts is best done by car.

KEY

▦	Motorway (highway)
▦	Major road
▦	Scenic route
--	Scenic path
~	River
☀	Viewpoint

EDINBURGH · A1 · **DUNBAR**

ST ABB'S HEAD ❶

Berwick-upon-Tweed, Newcastle upon Tyne

A68 · A7 · A6089 · **COLDSTREAM**

EBLES ❾ ABBOTSFORD HOUSE ❼ MELROSE ABBEY ❻ ❷ **KELSO**

RAQUAIR HOUSE ❽ TOUR OF THE BORDER ABBEYS ❺

SELKIRK EILDON HILLS ❹ ❸

JEDBURGH · **HAWICK** · CHEVIOT HILLS

St Highland Way

LOCKERBIE

Carlisle

Crisp winter day in the Pentland Hills

SIGHTS AT A GLANCE

Abbotsford House ❼
Burns Heritage Trail ❺
Caerlaverock Castle ❻
Culzean Castle pp92–3 ㉑
Drumlanrig Castle ⓭
Eildon Hills ❹
Galloway Forest Park ⓳
Jedburgh ❸
Kelso ❷
Kirkcudbright ⓱
Melrose Abbey ❻
New Lanark ⓫
Peebles ❾

Pentland Hills ❿
St Abb's Head ❶
Sanquhar ⓬
The Rhinns of Galloway ⓴
Threave Castle ⓮
Traquair House ❽
Whithorn ⓲

Tour
Tour of the Border Abbeys ❺

SEE ALSO

• *Where to Stay* pp167–8
• *Where to Eat* p178

The shattered crags and cliffs of St Abb's Head

St Abb's Head ❶

The Scottish Borders. 🚆 Berwick-upon-Tweed. 🚌 from Edinburgh. 📞 (01890) 771443. ◯ Easter–Oct: 10am–5pm daily.

THE JAGGED CLIFFS of St Abb's Head, rising 91 m (300 ft) from the North Sea, offer a spectacular view of thousands of seabirds wheeling and diving below. During the May to June breeding season, this nature reserve becomes an important site for more than 50,000 cliff-nesting sea birds, including fulmars, guillemots, kittiwakes and puffins.

St Abb's village has one of the few unspoiled working harbours on Scotland's east coast. A clifftop trail begins at the visitors' centre, where displays include identification boards and a touch table where young visitors can get to grips with wings and feathers.

Kelso ❷

The Scottish Borders. 🚶 6,035. ⬛ 🛈 The Square (0870) 608 0404. 🌐 www.visitscottishborders.com

KELSO HAS a charming centre, with a cobbled square surrounded by Georgian and Victorian buildings. Nearby **Kelso Race Course** holds regular horse races. The focus of the town, however, is the ruin of the 12th-century **abbey**. This was the oldest and wealthiest of the four Border Abbeys founded by David I, but it suffered from wars with England and was severely

damaged in 1545. **Floors Castle** on the northern edge of Kelso was designed by William Adam in the 1720s, and reworked by William Playfair after 1837.

🅷 **Kelso Race Course**
📞 (01668) 280800. 🏅 ♿
♙ **Floors Castle**
📞 (01573) 223333. ◯ Mar–Oct: daily. 🏅 ♿ 🎫

Jedburgh ❸

The Scottish Borders. 🚶 4,250. ⬛ 🛈 Murray's Green (01835) 863435. 🌐 www.visitscottishborders.com

THE TOWN IS home to the mock-medieval **Jedburgh Castle**. Built in the 1820s, the castle was once the local jail but now serves as a museum with some good displays on the area's history and life in a 19th-century prison.

Built around 1500, **Mary, Queen of Scots' House** is so-called due to a visit by the queen in 1566. The house was converted into a general mu-

Jedburgh's medieval Abbey church at the centre of the attractive town

seum in the 1930s, and in 1987 (on the 400th anniversary of Mary's execution) it became a centre dedicated to telling her life story. Exhibits include a copy of her death mask.

Jedburgh Abbey is one of the great quartet of 12th-century Border Abbeys, along with Dryburgh, Kelso and Melrose. The Abbey church has some interesting features including a rose window.

♙ **Jedburgh Castle**
📞 (01835) 863254. ◯ Easter–Oct: daily (Sun: pm). 🏅
🏛 **Mary, Queen of Scots' House**
📞 (01835) 863331. ◯ Mar–Nov: daily. 🏅
🏰 **Jedburgh Abbey**
📞 (01835) 863925. ◯ daily. 🏅

A picturesque view of the Eildon Hills in late summer sunshine

Eildon Hills ❹

The Scottish Borders. 🚌 🛈 Melrose (0870) 608 0404.

THE THREE PEAKS of the Eildon Hills dominate the central Borders landscape. Mid Hill is the tallest at 422 m (1,385 ft), while North Hill once had a Bronze Age hill fort dating from before 500 BC, and later a Roman fort. In this part of the country the most celebrated name is Sir Walter Scott (see p86), who had a particular affection for these hills. A panorama of the Eildons called **Scott's View** lies just east of Melrose, near Dryburgh Abbey, and this is the best location to see the hills' position as they rise above the Tweed Valley.

Tour of the Border Abbeys ❺

THE SCOTTISH BORDERS are scattered with the ruins of ancient buildings destroyed in conflicts between England and Scotland. Most poignant of all are the Border Abbeys, whose magnificent architecture bears witness to their former spiritual and political power. Founded during the 12th-century reign of David I, the abbeys were destroyed by Henry VIII in 1545. This tour takes in the abbeys and some other sights.

Kelso Abbey ②
The largest of the four Border Abbeys, Kelso was founded in 1128 and took 84 years to complete.

Melrose Abbey ⑥
Once one of the richest abbeys in Scotland, it is here that Robert the Bruce's heart is buried *(see p86)*.

Floors Castle ①
Open from Easter–Oct, the Duke of Roxburgh's 18th-century home is close to the Tweed.

Scott's View ⑤
This was Sir Walter Scott's favourite view of the Borders. During his funeral, the hearse stopped here briefly as Scott had done so often in life.

Dryburgh Abbey ④
Also set on the bank of the Tweed, Dryburgh is considered the most evocative monastic ruin in Scotland. Sir Walter Scott is buried here.

KEY

▰▰▰	Tour route
═══	Other road
☀	Viewpoint

TIPS FOR DRIVERS

Length: 50 km (32 miles).
Stopping-off points: Leave the car at Dryburgh Abbey and take a walk northwards to the foot-bridge over the River Tweed.

0 kilometres   5

0 miles   3

Jedburgh Abbey ③
The abbey was established in 1138, though fragments of 9th-century Celtic stonework survive from an earlier structure. The visitors' centre illustrates the lives of Augustinian monks.

The ruins of Melrose Abbey, viewed from the southwest

Melrose Abbey ❻

Melrose, The Scottish Borders.
📞 (01896) 822562. 🕐 9:30am–
6:30pm daily. 📷 🔥 limited.

THE ROSE-PINK RUINS of this, one of the most beautiful of the Border Abbeys, bear testimony to the devastation of successive English invasions. Built by David I in 1136 for Cistercian monks from Yorkshire, and also to replace a 7th-century monastery, Melrose was repeatedly ransacked by English armies, most notably in 1322 and 1385. The final blow, from which none of the abbeys recovered, came in 1545 when Henry VIII of England implemented his destructive Scottish policy known as the "Rough Wooing". This resulted from the failure of the Scots to ratify a marriage treaty between Henry VIII's son and the infant Mary, Queen of Scots. What remains of the abbey are the outlines of cloisters, the kitchen, monastic buildings and the shell of the abbey church with its soaring east window and profusion of medieval carvings. The rich decorations of the south exterior wall include a gargoyle shaped like a pig playing the bagpipes and several animated figures, including a cook with his ladle.

An embalmed heart, found here in 1920, is probably that of Robert the Bruce, the abbey's chief benefactor, who had decreed that his heart be taken on a crusade to the Holy Land. It was returned to Melrose Abbey after its bearer, Sir James Douglas, was killed in Spain.

Abbotsford House ❼

Galashiels, The Scottish Borders.
📞 (01896) 752043. 🚌 from
Galashiels. 🕐 Jun–Sep: 10am–5pm
daily; mid- Mar–May & Oct: 2–5pm
daily (Sun: pm). 📷 🔥 limited.

FEW HOUSES BEAR the stamp of their creator so intimately as Abbotsford House, the home of Sir Walter Scott for the final 20 years of his life. He bought a farm here in 1811, known as Clarteyhole ("dirty hole" in Borders Scots), though he soon renamed it Abbotsford, in memory of the monks of Melrose Abbey who used to cross the River Tweed nearby. He later demolished the house to make way for the turreted building we see today, its construction funded by the sales of his popular novels.

Scott's library contains more than 9,000 rare books and his collections of historic relics reflect his passion for the heroic past. The walls bristle with an extensive collection of arms and armour, including Rob Roy's broadsword *(see p117)*. Stuart mementoes include one of many crucifixes belonging to Mary, Queen of Scots and a lock of Bonnie Prince Charlie's hair. The surprisingly small study, in which Scott wrote his *Waverley* novels, is open to the public, as is the room in which he died in 1832.

SIR WALTER SCOTT

Sir Walter Scott (1771–1832) was born in Edinburgh and trained as a lawyer. He is best remembered as a major literary figure and champion of Scotland, whose poems and novels (most famously his *Waverley* series) created enduring images of a heroic wilderness filled with the romance of the clans. His orchestration, in 1822, of the state visit of George IV to Edinburgh was an extravaganza of Highland culture that helped establish tartan as the national dress of Scotland. He served as Clerk of the Court in Edinburgh's Parliament House and for 30 years was Sheriff of Selkirk. He loved Central and Southern Scotland, putting the Trossachs *(see pp116–17)* firmly on the map with the publication of the *Lady of the Lake* (1810). His final years were spent writing to pay off a £114,000 debt following the failure of his publisher in 1827. He died with his debts paid, and was buried at Dryburgh Abbey in 1832.

The Great Hall at Abbotsford, adorned with arms and armour

Traquair House ⓫

Peebles, The Scottish Borders. **(**
(01896) 830323. 🚌 *from Peebles.* 🕐
*Apr, May, Sep noon–5pm; Jun, Jul, Aug
10:30am–5pm; Oct 11am–4pm* 📷 **&**
limited. [W] *www.traquair.co.uk*

A S SCOTLAND'S OLDEST continuously inhabited house,
Traquair has deep roots in
Scottish religious and political
history stretching back over
900 years. Evolving from a
fortified tower to a stout-
walled 17th-century
mansion *(see p19)*,
the house was a
Catholic Stuart
stronghold for 500
years. Mary, Queen
of Scots was among
the many monarchs to
have stayed here. Her
crucifix is kept in the
house and her bed
is covered by a
counter-pane that she
made. Family letters
and a collection of
engraved Jacobite
drinking glasses are
among the relics re-
calling the period of
the Highland rebellions.
Following a vow made by the
fifth Earl, Traquair's Bear Gates
(the "Steekit Yetts"), which
closed after Bonnie Prince
Charlie's visit in 1745, will not
reopen until a Stuart reas-
cends the throne. A secret

**Mary's crucifix,
Traquair House**

stairway leads to the Priest's
Room, which, with its clerical
vestments that could be disguised as bedspreads, attests
to the problems faced by
Catholic families until Catholicism was legalized in 1829.

Peebles ⓭

The Scottish Borders. 👥 *8,000.* 🚌
from Galashiels. 🚻 *23 High St (0870)
608 0404.*

T HIS CHARMING BORDERS
town has some fascin-
ating sights, including
the **Tweeddale Museum**
which houses full-scale
plaster casts of part of the
Parthenon Frieze, and casts
of a frieze depicting the
entry of Alexander the Great
into Babylon. Nearby, the
**Scottish Museum of Orna-
mental Plasterwork** is
housed in a quaint work-
shop. The walled **Kailzie
Gardens** attract day-
trippers from Edinburgh.

🏛 **Tweeddale Museum**
(*(01721) 724820.* 🕐
*Easter–Oct: Mon–Sat; Nov–Mar:
Mon–Fri.* 🅿
🏛 **Scottish Museum of
Ornamental Plasterwork**
(*(01721) 720212.* 🕐 *Mon–Fri.*
🌑 *First 2 weeks in Aug.* 📷 **&**
🌼 **Kailzie Gardens**
(*(01721) 720007.* 🕐 *daily.* 📷 📷

Pentland Hills ⓰

The Lothians. 🚊 *Edinburgh, then
bus.* 🚻 *Regional Park Headquarters,
Edinburgh (0131) 445 3383.*

T HE WILDS OF the Pentland
Hills stretch for 26 km
(16 miles) southwest of Edinburgh, and offer some of the
best hill-walking country in
Southern Scotland. Walkers can
saunter along the many signposted footpaths, while the
more adventurous can take
the chairlift at the Hillend dry
ski slope to reach the higher
ground leading to the 493 m
(1,617 ft) hill of Allermuir. Even
more ambitious is the classic
scenic route along the ridge
from Caerketton to West Kip.
To the east of the A703,
in the lee of the Pentlands,
stands the exquisite and
ornate 15th-century **Rosslyn
Chapel**. It was originally
intended as a church, but
after the death of its founder,
William Sinclair, it was used
as a burial ground for his
descendants. The delicately
wreathed Apprentice Pillar
recalls the legend of the
apprentice carver who was
killed by the master stone-
mason in a fit of jealousy at
his pupil's superior skill.

🔓 **Rosslyn Chapel**
(*(0131) 440 2159.* 🕐 *daily.*
📷 **&** [W] *www.rosslynchapel.com*

Details of the highly ornate, decorative carved-stone vaulting in Rosslyn Chapel

The Classical 18th-century tenements of New Lanark on the banks of the Clyde

New Lanark ⓫

Clyde Valley. 🏛 185. 🚌 🚇 Lanark.
ℹ Horsemarket, Ladyacre Rd, Lanark
(01555) 661661.
🅦 www.seeglasgow.com

Sᴵᴛᴜᴀᴛᴇᴅ ʙʏ ᴛʜᴇ beautiful
falls of the River Clyde,
with three separate waterfalls,
the village of New Lanark was
founded in 1785 by the industrial entrepreneur David Dale.
Ideally located alongside the
river for the working of its
water-driven mills, the village
had become the largest producer of cotton in Britain by
1800. Dale and his successor,
and son-in-law, Robert
Owen, were philanthropists
whose reforms demonstrated
that commercial success
need not undermine the
wellbeing of the workforce.
The manufacturing of cotton
continued here until the
late 1960s.
  The **New Millennium
Experience** illustrates New
Lanark's significance as a window on to working life in the
early 19th century.

Eɴᴠɪʀᴏɴs: 24 km (15 miles)
north, the town of Blantyre
has a memorial to the Clyde
Valley's most famous son, the
explorer David Livingstone.

🏛 **New Millennium
Experience**
New Lanark Visitor Centre. 📞
(01555) 661345. 🅾 11am–5pm daily.
📷 🚻 📹 by appointment.

Dᴀᴠɪᴅ Lɪᴠɪɴɢsᴛᴏɴᴇ

Scotland's great missionary
doctor and explorer was
born in Blantyre where he
began working life as a
mill boy at the age of ten.
Livingstone (1813–73)
made three epic journeys
across Africa, from 1840,
promoting "commerce and
Christianity". He became
the first European to see
Victoria Falls, and died in
1873 while searching for
the source of the Nile. His
body is buried in West-
minster Abbey in London.

Sanquhar ⓬

Dumfries & Galloway. 🏛 2,500.
🚌 🚇 ℹ Sanquhar Tolbooth
Museum (01659) 50186.

Nᴏᴡ ᴏғ ᴄʜɪᴇғʟʏ historic
interest, the town of
Sanquhar was famous in the
history of the Covenanters.
In the 1680s, two declarations
opposing the rule of bishops
were pinned to the Mercat
Cross, the site of which is
now marked by a granite
obelisk. The first protest was
led by a local teacher, Richard
Cameron, whose followers
became the Cameronian regiment. The Georgian **Tolbooth**
was designed by architect
William Adam in 1735 and
houses a local interest museum
and tourist centre. The Post
Office, opened in 1763, is the
oldest in Britain, predating
the mail coach service.

Drumlanrig Castle ⓭

Thornhill, Dumfries & Galloway.
ℹ (01848) 331555. 🚌 🚇 Dumfries,
then bus. 🅾 May–Aug: noon–4pm
daily. ⬤ May & Jun: Fri. 📷 🚻

Rɪsɪɴɢ sQᴜᴀʀᴇʟʏ from a grassy
platform, the massive
fortress-palace of **Drumlanrig
Castle** was built from pink
sandstone between 1679 and
1691 on the site of a 15th-
century Douglas stronghold.
The castle's multi-turreted,

**The Baroque front steps and
doorway of Drumlanrig Castle**

formidable exterior conceals a priceless collection of art treasures as well as such Jacobite relics as Bonnie Prince Charlie's camp kettle, sash and money box. Hanging within oak-panelled rooms are paintings by Leonardo da Vinci, Holbein and Rembrandt. The emblem of a crowned and winged heart recalls the famous Douglas ancestor "The Good Sir James", known as "the Black Douglas" in England. Legend has it he bore Robert the Bruce's heart on crusade against the Moors in Spain, to fulfil a vow made by the former king.

The exterior of Burns Cottage, birthplace of Robert Burns

The sturdy island fortress of Threave Castle on the Dee

Threave Castle ⓮

(NTS) Castle Douglas, Dumfries & Galloway. [(01556) 502611. ▓ Dumfries. ◯ Apr–Sep: daily. ▓

A MENACING GIANT of a tower, this 14th-century Black Douglas stronghold on an island in the Dee (accessed by rowing boat) commands the most complete medieval riverside harbour in Scotland. Douglas's struggles against the early Stuart kings culminated in his surrender here after a two-month siege in 1455 – but only after James II had brought the cannon Mons Meg to batter the castle. Threave was finally dismantled after an army of Protestant Covenanters defeated its Catholic defenders in 1640. Only the shell of the kitchen, great hall and domestic levels remain.

Burns Heritage Trail ⓯

South Ayrshire, Dumfries & Galloway. ℹ Dumfries (01387) 253862, Ayr (01292) 678100. ⓦ www.dumfriesandgalloway.co.uk

ROBERT BURNS (1759–96) left behind a remarkable body of work ranging from satirical poetry to tender love songs. His status as national bard is unchallenged and an official Burns Heritage Trail leads visitors around sights in southwest Scotland where he lived.

In Dumfries, the **Robert Burns Centre** focuses on his years in the town, while **Burns House**, where he lived from 1793 to 1796, contains memorabilia. His Greek-style mausoleum can be found in St Michael's Churchyard.

At **Ellisland Farm** on the River Nith there are further displays, with some of Burns' family possessions. Mauchline, some 18 km (11 miles) east of Ayr, has the **Burns House and Museum** in another former residence.

Alloway, just south of Ayr, is the real centre of the Burns Trail. The **Tam O'Shanter Experience** is a contemporary film and video centre based on his poem about witches. **Burns Cottage**, the poet's birthplace, houses memorabilia and a collection of manuscripts. The ruins of Alloway Kirk and the 13th-century Brig o' Doon have the best period atmosphere.

🏛 **Robert Burns Centre**
Mill Rd, Dumfries. [(01387) 264808. ◯ Apr–Sep: 10am–5pm Mon–Sat; 2–5pm Sun.
🏛 **Burns House**
Burns St, Dumfries. [(01387) 255297. ◯ Apr–Sep: 10am–5pm Mon–Sat; 2–5pm Sun.
🏛 **Ellisland Farm**
Holywood Rd, Auldgirth. [(01387) 740426. ◯ Apr–Sep: 10am–5pm Mon–Sat; 2–5pm Sun. ▓ ▓ ▓
🏛 **Burns House and Museum**
Castle St, Mauchline. [(01290) 550045. ◯ 10am–5pm daily. ▓ ▓ limited.
🏛 **Tam O'Shanter Experience**
Murdoch's Lane, Alloway. [(01292) 443700. ◯ 9am–5pm daily. ▓ ▓ ▓ by appointment.
🏛 **Burns Cottage**
Alloway. [(01292) 443700. ⓦ www.robertburns.org ◯ 10am–4pm daily. ▓ ▓

SCOTTISH TEXTILES

Weaving in the Scottish Borders goes back to the Middle Ages, when monks from Flanders established a thriving woollen trade with the Continent. Cotton became an important source of wealth in the Clyde Valley during the 19th century, when handloom weaving was overtaken by power-driven mills. The popular Paisley patterns were based on original Indian designs.

A colourful pattern from Paisley

The moated fairy-tale Caerlaverock Castle with red stone walls

Caerlaverock Castle **16**

Near Dumfries, Dumfries & Galloway.
i (01387) 770244. ☐ 9:30am–6:30pm daily.
W www.historic-scotland.gov.uk

THIS IMPRESSIVE, three-sided, red stone structure, with its distinctive moat, is the finest example of a medieval castle in southwest Scotland. It stands 14 km (9 miles) south of Dumfries, and was built in around 1270.

Caerlaverock came to prominence in 1300, during the Wars of Independence, when it was besieged by Edward I, king of England, setting a precedent for more than three centuries of strife. Surviving chronicles of Edward's adventures describe the castle in much the same form as it stands today, despite being partially demolished and rebuilt on many occasions, due to the clashes between the English and Scottish forces during the 14th and 16th centuries. Throughout these troubled times, Caerlaverock Castle remained the stronghold of the Maxwell family, and the Maxwell crest and motto remain over the door. It was the struggle between Robert Maxwell, who was the first Earl of Nithsdale and a supporter of Charles I, and a Covenanter army that caused the castle's ruin in 1640.

Kirkcudbright **17**

Dumfries & Galloway. 🚶 3,600. 🚉
i Harbour Sq (01557) 330494.
☐ Feb–Oct: daily.

BY THE MOUTH of the River Dee, at the head of Kirkcudbright Bay, this attractive town has an artistic heritage. The Tolbooth, dating from the late 16th century, is now the **Tolbooth Art Centre**, which exhibits work by Kirkcudbright artists from 1880 to the present day. The most celebrated of these artists was Edward Hornel (1864–1933), a friend of the Glasgow Boys, who painted striking images of Japanese women. Some of his work is displayed in his former home, Broughton House, on the High Street.

MacLellan's Castle in the town centre was built in 1582 by the then Provost of Kirkcudbright, while outside, the ruins of Dundrennan Abbey date from the 12th century. Mary, Queen of Scots spent her last night there before fleeing to England in May 1568.

🏛 **Tolbooth Art Centre**
High St. **C** (01557) 331556.
☐ Mon–Sat. 🖼 &
♣ **MacLellan's Castle**
C (01557) 331856. ☐ Mar–Oct:
9:30am–6:30pm daily. 🖼

Whithorn **18**

Dumfries & Galloway. 🚶 1,000.
🚉 Stranraer. 🚉 **i** Dashwood Sq,
Newton Stewart (01671) 402431.
W www.dumfriesandgalloway.co.uk

THE EARLIEST SITE of continuous Christian worship in Scotland, Whithorn (meaning white house) takes its name from the white chapel built by St Ninian in 397. Though nothing remains of the chapel, a guided tour of the archaeological dig reveals evidence of Northumbrian, Viking and Scottish settlements ranging from the 5th to the 19th centuries. **The Whithorn Story** provides audio-visual information on the excavations, and contains a fine collection of ancient carved stones.

🏛 **The Whithorn Story**
45–47 George St. **C** (01988) 500508.
☐ Easter–Oct: 10:30am–5pm. 🖼
🅿 & **W** www.whithorn.com

Galloway Forest Park **19**

Dumfries & Galloway. 🚉 Stranraer.
i Clatteringshaws Visitor Centre
(01644) 420285, Glen Trool Visitor
Centre (01671) 402420, Kirroughtree
Visitor Centre (01671) 402165.
W www.forestry.gov.uk

THIS IS THE WILDEST stretch of country in Southern Scotland, with points of historical interest as well as great beauty.

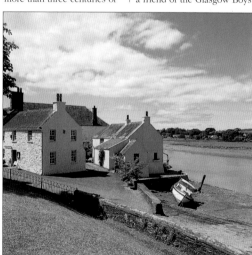

Traditional stone buildings on the shore at Kirkcudbright

Loch Trool, Galloway Forest Park, site of one of Robert the Bruce's victories

The park extends to 670 sq km (260 sq miles) just north of Newton Stewart. The principal focal point is Loch Trool. By Caldons Wood, to the west end of the loch, the Martyrs' Monument marks the spot where six Covenanters were killed at prayer in 1685. Bruce's Stone, above the north shore, commemorates an occasion in 1307 when Robert the Bruce routed English forces. The hills to the north of Loch Trool are a considerable size, and worthy of note. Bennan stands at 562 m (1,844 ft), Benyellary at 719 m (2,359 ft), while Merrick, at 843 m (2,766 ft), is the tallest mountain in Southern Scotland. A round trip from Loch Trool to Merrick's summit and back, via the silver sands of Loch Enoch to the east, is a total of 15 km (9 miles) over rough but very rewarding ground.

The Rhinns of Galloway ⑳

Dumfries & Galloway. 🚆 Stranraer. 🚌 Stranraer, Portpatrick. 🛳 Stranraer. 🛈 28 Harbour St, Stranraer (01776) 702595.

IN THE EXTREME southwest of Scotland, this peninsula is almost separated from the rest of the country by Loch Ryan and Luce Bay. It has a number of attractions, including the **Logan Botanic Garden**, near Port Logan. Established in 1900, subtropical species in the garden benefit from the area's mild climate.

Stranraer on Loch Ryan is the main centre and ferry port for Northern Ireland. The nearby **Portpatrick** is a prettier town, featuring a ruined church dating from 1629 and the remains of 16th-century Dunskey Castle.

🌺 Logan Botanic Garden
Near Port Logan, Stranraer. 🄲 (01776) 860231. ◯ Mar–Oct: daily.

GALLOWAY FOREST PARK WALK

This walk gives a taste of wild hill-country and remote, high-level lochs. Adequate footwear, waterproof clothing and a map are recommended. From the car park, descend towards the house, cross a bridge, and take a path northeast through a field. Follow the valley of the Gairland Burn for about 1.5 km (1 mile) to find Loch Valley. A few minutes further north, the path reaches lonely Loch Neldricken, from where you can return by the same route. This area is a combination of glaciated hills and small hill lochs, set in hollows scraped out by the ice thousands of years ago. If time is short, or the weather poor, there are shorter walks around Loch Trool.

KEY
▪▪ Footpath
= Access road
☼ Viewpoint
🅿 Parking

TIPS FOR WALKERS
Starting point: Bruce's Stone car park, north side of Loch Trool.
Length: 10 km (6 miles).
Getting there: By car: off the A714, about 14 km (9 miles) north of Newton Stewart, along an access road for 8 km (5 miles).

Culzean Castle ㉑

Robert Adam by George Willison

Sᴛᴀɴᴅɪɴɢ ᴏɴ ᴀ ᴄʟɪꜰꜰ'ꜱ ᴇᴅɢᴇ in an extensive parkland estate, the 16th-century keep of Culzean (pronounced Cullayn), home of the Earls of Cassillis, was remodelled between 1777 and 1792 by the Neo-Classical architect Robert Adam. Restored in the 1970s, it is now a major showcase of Adam's later style of work. The grounds became Scotland's first public country park in 1969 and, with farming flourishing alongside ornamental gardens, they reflect both the leisure and everyday activities of life on a great country estate.

View of Culzean Castle (c.1815), by Nasmyth

Lord Cassillis' Rooms contain typical mid-18th-century furnishings, including a gentleman's wardrobe of the 1740s.

A Plan of Culzean Castle

First Floor

- Blue Drawing Room
- Picture Room
- State Bedroom
- Lord Cassillis' Rooms
- Saloon Ante Room
- Dressing Room
- Saloon
- Front Hall
- Eisenhower Presentation
- Entrance
- Shop
- Old Eating Room
- Dining Room
- Ship Model Room
- Armoury
- Benefactor's Room
- Oval Staircase

Ground Floor

The clock tower, fronted by the circular carriageway, was originally the family coach house and stables. The clock was added in the 19th century, and today the buildings are used for residential and educational purposes.

Star Features

★ **Saloon**

★ **Oval Staircase**

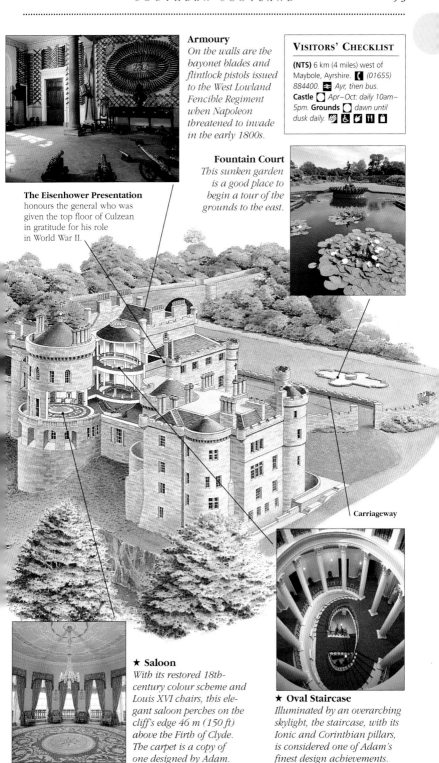

Armoury

On the walls are the bayonet blades and flintlock pistols issued to the West Lowland Fencible Regiment when Napoleon threatened to invade in the early 1800s.

VISITORS' CHECKLIST

(NTS) 6 km (4 miles) west of Maybole, Ayrshire. **C** (01655) 884400. ⬛ *Ayr, then bus.* **Castle** ◯ *Apr–Oct: daily 10am–5pm.* **Grounds** ◯ *dawn until dusk daily.*

Fountain Court

This sunken garden is a good place to begin a tour of the grounds to the east.

The Eisenhower Presentation

honours the general who was given the top floor of Culzean in gratitude for his role in World War II.

Carriageway

★ Saloon

With its restored 18th-century colour scheme and Louis XVI chairs, this elegant saloon perches on the cliff's edge 46 m (150 ft) above the Firth of Clyde. The carpet is a copy of one designed by Adam.

★ Oval Staircase

Illuminated by an overarching skylight, the staircase, with its Ionic and Corinthian pillars, is considered one of Adam's finest design achievements.

GLASGOW

Glasgow displays *audacity in everything, from the profile of its new buildings, such as the titanium clad buildings and tower of the new Science Centre, to the presence of designer clothes shops and the wit of its people. As recently as the 1970s, this was a city with a fading industrial history and little sense of direction, but much has changed since then.*

Glasgow's city centre, on the north bank of the River Clyde, has been occupied since ancient times. The Romans already had a presence in the area some 2,000 years ago, and there was a religious community here from the 6th century. Records show Glasgow's growing importance as a merchant town from the 12th century onwards.

Historic buildings such as Provand's Lordship, a 15th-century townhouse, remind visitors of its pre-industrial roots, but modern Glasgow grew from the riches of the British Empire and the Industrial Revolution. In the 18th century the city imported rum, sugar and tobacco from the colonies, while in the 19th century Glasgow reinvented itself as a cotton manufacturing centre. It then became a site for shipbuilding and for heavy engineering, attracting many incomers from poverty-stricken districts in the Scottish Highlands and islands, and in Ireland, in the process. Between the 1780s and the 1880s the population exploded from around 40,000 to over 500,000. The city boundaries expanded, and, despite an economic slump between the two World Wars, Glasgow clung to its status as an industrial giant until the 1970s, when its traditional skills were no longer needed. This was a bad time, but the city bounced back as European City of Culture in 1990, and UK City of Architecture in 1999. A £500 million project at Glasgow Harbour has begun to reclaim the city's old shipyards and dockland for commercial, residential and leisure usage.

Fashionable brasseries in the rejuvenated Merchant City area of Glasgow

◁ Stained glass by architect and designer Charles Rennie Mackintosh, whose work can be seen all over the city

Exploring Glasgow

Glasgow city centre is a neat grid of streets running east to west and north to south on the north bank of the River Clyde. This small area includes the main train stations, the principal shopping facilities and, at George Square, the tourist information office. Outside the centre, Byres Road to the west of Kelvingrove Park is the focus of the district known as "the West End", with its bars and restaurants near the University. Pollok Country Park, in the southwest, is home to the wonderful Burrell Collection.

Detail of St Mungo Museum's deceptively modern façade

GETTING AROUND

An extensive regional train service links Glasgow with its suburbs. In the city itself there is an underground system that operates daily in a simple loop around the centre, both north and south of the River Clyde. The M8 motorway (highway) cuts through central Glasgow, linking Inverclyde and the airport in the west with Edinburgh in the east. Buses and black cabs are other options.

"SPT" sign outside St. Enoch subway station

SIGHTS AT A GLANCE

Historic Streets and Buildings
George Square ②
Glasgow Cathedral
  and Necropolis ⑤
Pollok House ⑰
Willow Tea Room ⑦

Museums and Galleries
Burrell Collection pp104–5 ⑱
Gallery of Modern Art ①
Glasgow Science Centre ⑩
Hunterian Art Gallery ⑬
Kelvingrove Art Gallery
  and Museum ⑪

Museum of Transport ⑫
People's Palace ⑮
Provand's Lordship ③
St Mungo Museum of
  Religious Life and Art ④
Tenement House ⑨

Parks and Gardens
Botanic Gardens ⑭

Arts Centres
Glasgow School of Art ⑧
House for an Art Lover ⑯
Piping Centre ⑥

Sauchiehall Street, the heart of
the city's busy shopping district

SEE ALSO
• *Where to Stay* pp168–9
• *Where to Eat* pp178–80

KEY
Place of interest
Bus station
Train station
Underground station
Parking
Tourist information
Post office
Hospital
Church

0 metres 300
0 yards 300

OUTSIDE THE CENTRE
CLYDEBANK
Botanic Gardens ⑭
Hunterian Art Gallery ⑬
Museum of Transport ⑫
Kelvingrove Art Gallery and Museum ⑪
SPRINGBURN
GOVAN
IBROX
Glasgow Science Centre ⑩
PAISLEY
House for an Art Lover ⑯
People's Palace ⑮
POLLOKSHIELDS
Glasgow Green
POLLOK-SHAWS
Pollok Park
Pollok House ⑰
Burrell Collection ⑱
Queens Park
GOVANHILL

The imposing City Chambers in George Square, where a statue of Sir Walter Scott stands atop the central column

Gallery of Modern Art ❶

Royal Exchange Sq. 📞 *(0141) 229 1996.* 🕐 *10am–5pm Mon–Wed & Sat, 10am–8pm Thurs, 11am–5pm Fri & Sun.* ♿ ✉ W www.glasgowmuseums.com

ONCE THE HOME of Glasgow's Royal Exchange (the city's centre for trade), this building dates from 1829 and also incorporates a late 18th-century mansion that formerly occupied the site. The local authority took over the Exchange just after World War II, and for many years it served as a library. It finally opened its doors as the Gallery of Modern Art in 1996. One of the largest contemporary art galleries outside London, the GoMA is currently developing a new collection of work by Glasgow based artists. Accordingly, most of the gallery is home to a lively and thought-provoking programme of temporary exhibitions featuring work by Scottish and international artists. Many of these focus on contemporary and social

Ornate tower of the Gallery of Modern Art

issues, often featuring groups that are marginalized in today's society.

George Square ❷

City centre. **City Chambers** 📞 *(0141) 287 2000.* 🕐 *Mon–Fri, 10:30am and 2:30pm for guided tours.* ♿ ✉ **Merchant House** 📞 *(0141) 221 8272.* ✉ *by appointment.*

GEORGE SQUARE was laid out in the late 18th century as a residential area, but re-development during Victorian times conferred its enduring status as the city's focal point. The only building not to be affected by the later 19th-century makeover is the Millennium Hotel (1807) on the north side of the Square.

The 1870s saw a building boom, with the construction of the former Post Office (1876) at the southeast corner, and the **Merchant House** (1877) to the west side. The latter is home to Glasgow's Chamber of Commerce. Founded in 1781, it is the oldest organization of its kind in the UK. The most dominant structure in George Square, however, is the **City Chambers** on the east side. Designed by William Young, in an Italian Renaissance

style, the imposing building was opened in 1888 by Queen Victoria. With the elegant proportions of the interior decorated with marble and mosaic, the opulence of this building makes it the most impressive of its kind in Scotland.

Provand's Lordship ❸

3 Castle St. 📞 *(0141) 552 8819.* 🕐 *10am–5pm, 11am–5pm Mon–Sat.*

PROVAND'S LORDSHIP was originally built as a canon's house in 1471, and is now Glasgow's oldest surviving house, as well as a museum. Its low ceilings and austere wooden furnishings create a vivid impression of life in a wealthy 15th-century household. Mary, Queen of Scots *(see p44)* may have stayed here when she visited Glasgow in 1566 to see her cousin, and husband, Lord Darnley.

Provand's Lordship, Glasgow's only medieval hou

St Mungo Museum of Religious Life and Art ❹

2 Castle St. 📞 (0141) 553 2557.
🕐 10am–5pm daily. ♿ 📷 by appt.

GLASGOW HAS strong religious roots, and the settlement that grew to become today's city started with a monastery founded in the 6th century AD by a priest called Mungo. He died in the early years of the 7th century, and his body lies buried underneath Glasgow Cathedral. The building itself dates from the 12th century, and stands on ground blessed by St Ninian as long ago as AD 397.

In recent years, the ever-growing numbers of visitors to the cathedral prompted plans for an interpretive centre. Despite the efforts of the Society of Friends of Glasgow Cathedral, however, sufficient funds could not be raised. The local authority decided to step in with money, and with the idea for a more extensive project – a museum of religious life and art. The site chosen was adjacent to the cathedral, where the 13th-century Castle of the Bishops of Glasgow once stood. The museum has the appearance of a centuries-old fortified house, despite the fact that it was completed as recently as 1993.

The top floor tells the story of the country's religion from a nondenominational perspective. Both Protestant and Catholic versions of Christianity are represented, as well as the other faiths of modern Scotland. The many, varied displays touch on the lives of communities as extensive as Glasgow's Muslims, who have had their own Mosque in the city since 1984, as well as local converts to the Baha'i faith.

Detail from the St Mungo Museum

The other floors are given over to works of art. The star of the show is Salvador Dalí's *Christ of St John of the Cross* (1951), which was brought to Glasgow in 1952 despite controversy over its subject matter. The painting was vandalized in 1961 but was subsequently restored. It now sits alongside religious artifacts and artworks, such as burial discs from Neolithic China (2000 BC), contemporary paintings by Aboriginal Australians, and some excellent Scottish stained glass from the early part of the 20th century.

Further displays in the museum examine issues of fundamental concern to people of all religions – war, persecution, death and the afterlife – and from cultures as far afield as West Africa and Mexico. In the grounds surrounding the building, there is a permanent Zen Garden, created by Yasutaro Tanaka. Such gardens have been a traditional aid to contemplation in Japanese Buddhist temples since the beginning of the 16th century.

Dalí's *Christ of St John of the Cross* at the St Mungo Museum of Religious Life and Art

Glasgow's medieval cathedral viewed from the southwest

Glasgow Cathedral and Necropolis ❺

Cathedral Square. **Cathedral** 📞 (0141) 552 6891. 🕐 Apr–Sep: 9:30am–6pm Mon–Sat, 1–5pm Sun; Oct–Mar: 9:30am–4pm Mon–Sat, 1–4pm Sun. ♿ **Necropolis** 🕐 24hrs daily.

AS ONE OF THE FEW cathedrals to escape destruction during the Scottish Reformation (*see p44*) by adapting itself to Protestant worship, Glasgow Cathedral is a rare example of an almost complete original 13th-century church.

It was built on the site of a chapel founded by the city's patron saint, St Mungo, a 6th-century bishop of Strathclyde. According to legend, Mungo placed the body of a holy man, named Fergus, on a cart yoked to two wild bulls, telling them to take it to the place ordained by God. In the "dear green place" at which the bulls stopped, he built his church.

Because of its sloping site, the cathedral is built on two levels. The crypt contains the tomb of St Mungo, surrounded by an intricate forest of columns springing up to end in delicately carved rib-vaulting. The Blacader Aisle is reputed to have been built over a cemetery blessed by St Ninian.

Behind the cathedral, a likeness of Protestant reformer John Knox (*see p44*) surveys the city from his Doric pillar, overlooking a Victorian cemetery. The necropolis is filled with crumbling monuments to the dead of Glasgow's wealthy merchant families.

Piping Centre **6**

30–34 McPhater St. 📞 (0141) 353
0220. 🕐 10am–4:30pm daily. 🏷 ♿

T HE PIPING CENTRE, which
opened its doors in a refurbished church in 1996, aims
to promote the study and
history of piping in Scotland. It offers tuition at
all levels, and houses the
**National Museum of
Piping**, which traces the
development of
the instrument.
Displays show
that bagpipes
were first
introduced to
Scotland as
early as the
14th century,
although the
golden age of
piping in the
Highlands and
islands was the
17th and 18th

**Traditional
bagpipes with
brass drones**

centuries. This was the era of
the MacCrimmons of Skye
(hereditary pipers to the chiefs
of Clan MacLeod), when complex, extended tunes (*ceol mor*,
or "the big music") were written for clan gatherings, battles
and in the form of laments.

Willow Tea Room **7**

217 Sauchiehall St. 📞 (0141) 332
0521. 🕐 9am–4.15pm Mon–Sat,
11am–4pm Sun.

T HIS IS THE SOLE survivor
of a series of delightfully
frivolous tea rooms created
by the designer Charles Rennie
Mackintosh (*see opposite page*)

**The Mackintosh-designed interior
of the Willow Tea Room**

at the turn of the century for
the celebrated restaurateur
Miss Kate Cranston. Everything in the tearoom, from
the high-backed chairs to
the tables and cutlery, was of
Mackintosh's own design. In
particular, the 1904 **Room de
Luxe** sparkles with eccen-
tricity: striking mauve and
silver furniture, coloured glass
and a flamboyant leaded door
create a remarkable venue in
which to enjoy afternoon tea.

**The exterior of the Glasgow School
of Art, Mackintosh's masterpiece**

Glasgow School
of Art **8**

167 Renfrew St. 📞 (0141) 353 4500.
🕐 Mon–Sat (by appointment).
🏷 🚗 ♿ limited.
🌐 www.gsa.ac.uk

W IDELY CONSIDERED to be
the greatest architectural
work in the illustrious career
of Charles Rennie Mackintosh,
the Glasgow School of Art was
built between 1897 and 1909
to a design he submitted in a
competition. Due to financial
constraints, it was built in two
stages. The earlier eastern half
displays a severity of style,
likened by a contemporary
critic to a prison. The later
western half is characterized
by a softer architectural style.

An art student will guide you
through the building to the
Furniture Gallery, Board Room
and the Library, the latter being a masterpiece of spatial
composition. Each room is an
exercise in contrasts between

height, light and shade, with
innovative details echoing the
architectural themes of the
structure. How much of the
school can be viewed depends
on curricular requirements at
the time of visiting, as it still
functions as an active and
highly successful art college.

Tenement House **9**

(NTS) 145 Buccleuch St. 📞 (0141)
333 0183. 🕐 Mar–Oct: 1–5pm daily.
🏷 🚗 by appointment.

M ORE A TIME CAPSULE than a
museum, the Tenement
House is an almost undisturbed
record of life as it was in a
modest Glasgow flat on a
tenement estate in the early
20th century. Glasgow owed
much of its vitality and neigh-
bourliness to tenement life,
though in later years many of
these Victorian and Edwardian apartments were to earn
a bad name for poverty and
overcrowding, and many of
them have been pulled down.

The Tenement House was
the home of Miss Agnes
Toward, who lived here from
1911 until 1965. It remained
largely unaltered during that
time and, since Agnes threw
very little away, the house has
become a treasure-trove of
social history. In the parlour,
which would have been used
only on formal occasions,
afternoon tea is laid out on a
white lace cloth. The kitchen,
with its coal-fired range and
box bed, is filled with the
tools of a vanished era, such
as a goffering-iron for ironing
lace, a washboard and a stone
hot-water bottle.

Agnes's lavender water and
medicines are still arranged in
the bathroom, and it feels
almost as though she stepped
out of the house 70 years ago
and simply forgot to return.

**The preserved Edwardian kitchen
of the Tenement House**

Glasgow Artists

THE LATE 19TH CENTURY was a time of great artistic activity in Glasgow, with influential painters such as Sir James Guthrie, Robert McGregor and others rising to prominence. But due to snobbery on the part of the Edinburgh-based arts establishment, these men often had to seek recognition outside Scotland. Only after a London exhibition in 1890 was the term "Glasgow School" coined, although the artists generally called themselves the "Glasgow Boys". Art Nouveau designer Charles Rennie Mackintosh was a contemporary, contributing his genius to the creative life of the city as well as to a new Glasgow School of Art, completed in two stages – 1899 and 1909.

More recently, the term Glasgow Boys has been used to describe the generation of artists who attended the School of Art in the 1970s and '80s.

Detail from House for an Art Lover

In **The Wayfarer**, *by Edward Arthur Walton (1860–1922), the winding path leads the viewer into the distance, in the direction of the wayfarer's gaze.*

Stirling Station, by William Kennedy *(1859–1918), depicts the crowded platform with people waiting for a train. The rich colours, and steam from the trains, contribute to the atmosphere of this bustling station.*

A Star (1891) by Sir John Lavery *is indicative of the artist's dashing, fluid, style as a portraitist. Born in Belfast, Lavery studied at Glasgow and was part of the Whistler- and Impressionist-influenced Glasgow School.*

Designed by Mackintosh in 1901, *the House for an Art Lover* (see p103) *was finally built in 1996. The design of the building and all of the furniture remains true to the original plans.*

Mackintosh's stylized tulips *on a checkered background provide a striking example of Art Nouveau decoration, juxtaposing the organic with the geometric.*

Mackintosh's unique fluidity of form *is seen in this detail from a stained-glass door in the House for an Art Lover.*

CHARLES RENNIE MACKINTOSH
Glasgow's most celebrated designer (1868–1928) entered Glasgow School of Art at the age of 16. After his success with the Willow Tea Room, he became a leading figure in the Art Nouveau movement. His characteristic straight lines and flowing detail are the hallmark of early 20th-century style.

Glasgow Science Centre ⑩

50 Pacific Quay. 【 (0141) 420 5000. ◯ daily. 📷 ♿
🆆 www.glasgowsciencecentre.org

THE IMPRESSIVE gleaming tower of this new science park is an unmistakable landmark on the city's skyline. Opened in 2001, this £75 million titanium-clad complex on the south bank of the River Clyde houses three unique but complementary venues.

A three storey science mall introduces the world of popular, everyday science through a range of dynamic interactive exhibits, laboratories and multimedia. Scotland's only IMAX Theatre stands next door, projecting breathtaking film images from the natural and scientific world onto its 24 m (80 ft) by 18 m (60 ft) screen. The 127 m (416 ft) rotating tower is the tallest freestanding structure in Scotland. Pedestrians can access the site from the north bank of the Clyde via Bell's Bridge, built in 1988.

Kelvingrove Art Gallery and Museum ⑪

Argyle St, Kelvingrove. 【 (0141) 287 2699. ◯ until mid-2006. McLellan Galleries Sauchiehall St. 【 (0141) 565 4137. ◯ 10am–5pm Mon–Thu & Sat, 11am–5pm Fri & Sun.

AN IMPOSING red sandstone building, Kelvingrove is

George Henry's *Japanese Lady with a Fan* **(1894), at Kelvingrove**

Scotland's most popular gallery, housing a magnificent art collection. The gallery is currently closed for a £27.9 million programme of restoration and refurbishment, but more than 200 exhibits from Kelvingrove can be viewed at the McLellan Galleries near the city centre. Exhibits have been chosen and grouped to reflect different aspects of the main collection. Among these are 19th-century British artists including Turner and Constable. Scottish art and design is well represented with rooms dedicated to the Scottish Colourists and the Glasgow Style (see p101). Included here are two recently acquired works by Charles Rennie Macintosh; a fine Gesso panel and a 1904 writing cabinet.

Museum of Transport ⑫

1 Bunhouse Rd. 【 (0141) 287 2720. ◯ 10am–5pm Mon–Thu & Sat, 11am–5pm Fri & Sun.

HOUSED IN Kelvin Hall, this imaginative museum conveys much of the city's industrial heyday. Model ships and ranks of steam engines, cars and motorcycles recall the 19th and early 20th centuries, when Glasgow's supremacy in shipbuilding, trade and manufacturing made her the "second city" of the British Empire. Old Glasgow can be seen through fascinating footage of the town in the cinema and through a reconstruction of a 1938 street, with Art Deco shop fronts, cinema and Underground station.

The Museum of Transport's 1938 street, with a reconstructed Underground station

Hunterian Art Gallery ⑬

82 Hillhead St. 【 (0141) 330 5431. ◯ 9:30am–5pm Mon–Sat. ◯ 24 Dec–4 Jan. 🆆 www.huntarian.gla.ac.uk

BUILT TO HOUSE a number of paintings bequeathed to Glasgow University by an ex-student and physician, Dr William Hunter (1718–83), the Hunterian Art Gallery contains Scotland's largest print collection. There are also works by many major European artists, dating from the 16th century. A collection of work by the designer Charles Rennie Mackintosh (see p101) is supplemented by a complete reconstruction of No. 6 Florentine Terrace, where he lived from

Kelvingrove Art Gallery and the Glasgow University buildings, seen from the south

1906 to 1914. There is a major collection of 19th- and 20th-century Scottish art, but by far the most famous collection is of work by the Paris-trained American painter, James McNeill Whistler (1834–1903), who influenced so many of the Glasgow School painters.

Whistler's *Sketch for Annabel Lee* (c.1869), Hunterian Art Gallery

Botanic Gardens ⓮

Great Western Rd. 📞 *(0141) 334 2422.* 🕐 *7am–dusk.* ♿ 📷 *by appt.*

THESE GARDENS form a peaceful space in the heart of the city's West End, by the River Kelvin. Originally founded at another site in 1817, they were moved to the current location in 1839 and opened to the public three years later. Aside from the main range of greenhouses, with assorted displays including palm trees and an area given over to tropical crops,

one of the most interesting features is the **Kibble Palace**. Built at Loch Long in the Highlands by John Kibble, a Victorian engineer, the glass palace was moved to its present site in the early 1870s but its splendour is now much reduced.

People's Palace ⓯

Glasgow Green. 📞 *(0141) 271 2951.* 🕐 *10am–5pm Mon–Thu & Sat, 11am–5pm Fri & Sun.* ♿

THIS VICTORIAN, sandstone structure was purpose-built in 1898 as a cultural museum for the people of Glasgow's East End. It houses everything from temperance tracts to trade-union banners, suffragette posters to the comedian Billy Connolly's banana-shaped boots, and thus provides a social history of the city from the 12th to the 20th century. A superb conservatory contains an exotic winter garden, with tropical plants and birds.

House for an Art Lover ⓰

Bellahouston Park, Dumbreck Rd. 📞 *(0141) 353 4770.* 🕐 *10am–4pm daily.* 🔴 *Fri and during functions.* 📷 ♿

PLANS FOR THE House for an Art Lover were submitted by Charles Rennie Mackintosh and his partner Margaret Macdonald in response to a competition in a German magazine in the summer of 1900.

Distinctive Mackintosh piano in the Music Room, House for an Art Lover

The competition brief was to create a country retreat for someone of elegance and taste who loved the arts. As it was a theoretical exercise, the couple were unrestrained by logistics or budget and won a special prize for their efforts.

The plans lay unused for over 80 years until consulting engineer Graham Roxburgh, who had worked on the refurbishment of other Mackintosh interiors in Glasgow (including Craigie Hall), decided to try to build the House for an Art Lover. Work began in 1989 and was successfully completed in 1996. The House is host to a digital design studio and postgraduate study centre for students at the Glasgow School of Art, as well as a café.

It is the rooms on the main floor, however, that give a real insight into the vision of Mackintosh and the artistic talent of Macdonald. The Oval Room is a beautifully proportioned space in a single light colour, meant as a tranquil retreat for ladies, while the Music Room and its centrepiece piano that is played to add to the atmosphere is also bright and inspiring.

The Main Hall is darker than the other rooms and it leads into the Dining Room, with its long table, sideboard and relief stone fireplace. The great attention to detail shown throughout the House, in the panelling, light fixtures and other elements, is enormously impressive. The exterior of the building is no exception, as that too is an extraordinary achievement in art and design.

One of the greenhouses in Glasgow's peaceful Botanic Gardens

The Georgian Pollok House, viewed from the south

Pollok House ⓱

(NTS) 2060 Pollokshaws Rd. █ (0141) 616 6410. ◯ Apr–Oct: 10am–5pm daily, Nov–Mar: 11am–4pm daily. ▨ Apr–Oct only.

Pollok house is Glasgow's finest 18th-century domestic building and contains one of Britain's best collections of Spanish paintings. The Neo-Classical central block was finished in 1750, the sobriety of its exterior contrasting with the exuberant plasterwork within. The Maxwells have lived at Pollok since the mid-13th century, but the male line ended with Sir John Maxwell, who added the grand entrance hall in the 1890s and designed most of the terraced gardens and parkland beyond.

Hanging above the family silver, porcelain, hand-painted Chinese wallpaper and Jacobean glass, the Stirling Pollok paintings are strong on British and Dutch schools, including William Blake's *Sir Geoffrey Chaucer and the Nine and Twenty Pilgrims* (1745) as well as William Hogarth's portrait of James Thomson, who wrote the words to *Rule Britannia*. Spanish 16th- to 19th-century art predominates: El Greco's *Lady in a Fur Wrap* (1541) hangs in the library, while the drawing room contains works by Francisco de Goya and Esteban Murillo. In 1966 Anne Maxwell Macdonald gave the house and 146 ha (361 acres) of parkland to the City of Glasgow. The park provides the site for the city's fascinating Burrell Collection.

Burrell Collection ⓲

Given to the city in 1944 by Sir William Burrell (1861–1958), a wealthy shipping owner, this internationally acclaimed collection is the star of Glasgow's renaissance, with objects of major importance in numerous fields of interest. The building housing these pieces was purpose-built in 1983. When the sun shines in, the stained glass blazes with colour, while the shaded tapestries seem a part of the surrounding woodland.

Figure of a Lohan
This sculpture of Buddha's disciple dates from the Ming Dynasty (1484).

Hutton Castle Drawing Room
This is a reconstruction of the Drawing Room at Burrell's own home – the 16th-century Hutton Castle, near Berwick-upon-Tweed. The Hall and Dining Room can also be seen nearby.

Bull's Head
Dating from the 7th century BC, this bronze head from Turkey was once part of a cauldron handle.

Hornby Portal
This detail shows the arch's heraldic display. The 14th-century portal comes from Hornby Castle in Yorkshire.

Main entrance

Star Exhibits
★ Stained Glass
★ Tapestries

Rembrandt van Rijn
This self-portrait, signed and dated 1632, has pride of place among the Dutch paintings hanging in the 17th- and 18th-century room.

Mezzanine floor

VISITORS' CHECKLIST

2060 Pollokshaws Rd, Glasgow.
📞 (0141) 287 2550. 🚆 Pollokshaws West. 🚌 45, 47, 48, 57 from Glasgow. ⏰ 10am–5pm Mon–Thu, Sat, 11am–5pm Fri, Sun. 🚻 ♿ 🚫 ⭕ 📷 🛗 🎧 ☎ 🛍

GALLERY GUIDE
Except for a mezzanine-floor display of paintings, the exhibitions are on the ground floor. Right of the entrance hall, rooms are devoted to tapestries, stained glass and sculpture, while ancient civilizations, Oriental art and the period galleries are ahead.

KEY TO FLOORPLAN

- ☐ Ancient civilizations
- ☐ Oriental art
- ☐ Medieval and post-medieval European art, stained glass and tapestries
- ☐ Period galleries
- ☐ Hutton Castle Rooms
- ☐ Paintings and drawings
- ☐ Temporary exhibition area

Matthijs Maris
This popular Dutch painter's ethereal style appealed to late 19th-century tastes. The Sisters (1875) is one of over 50 Maris works acquired by Burrell.

Ground floor

Lecture theatre

★ Stained Glass
A man warming himself before a fire is one of many secular themes illustrated in the stained-glass display. This 15th-century piece once decorated a church in Suffolk.

★ Tapestries
Scenes from the Life of Christ and of the Virgin *(c.1450), a Swiss work in wool, is one of many tapestries on show.*

SHOPPING IN GLASGOW

Ortak brooch

WHILE GLASGOW itself is home to some 570,000 people, as the focal point of a great conurbation in west central Scotland it provides the main shopping centre for almost half of the country's population. The large number of potential customers is allied to Glasgow's reputation as Scotland's most fashion-conscious city. This, plus the revival of the city's fortunes throughout the 1990s, has seen the arrival of some very smart stores and malls. In contrast, a trip to the colourful Barras street market, which is held every weekend, offers a more traditional, if somewhat anarchic, Glaswegian shopping experience.

St Enoch Centre, one of the city's malls

DEPARTMENT STORES AND MALLS

THE IMPRESSIVE Buchanan Galleries has many well-known shops including a **John Lewis** department store. The **Italian Centre**, in the Merchant City area and **Princes Square**, house designer boutiques. The St Enoch Centre houses a **Debenhams** department store. **House of Fraser** is one of the longest established department stores.

MARKETS

NO VISIT TO GLASGOW is complete without a trip to **The Barras**, a weekend market in the east end of the city centre. The name is a dialect version of "The Barrows", and dates from a time when goods were sold from barrows.

The current site, between the Gallowgate and London Road, has been an official market since the 1920s. Every Saturday and Sunday, thousands of bargain hunters descend on stalls that sell virtually everything from old junk to cheap clothes and CDs.

FASHION

MANY OF Glasgow's designer fashion stores are housed in the malls in the city centre. Outside the malls, **Cruise** sells all the well-known designer names for men and women while **Diesel**, one of the more streetwise fashion labels, has an outlet on Buchanan Street. Further along Buchanan Street, **Karen Millen** is the store for the chic professional woman. **Schuh** is a chain of stores selling a wide range of fashionable footwear for both men and women; **Pied à Terre** sells smart shoes for women. For special occasions **Ella Bulloch** is the best place to buy or hire a lady's hat. For a luxurious range of underwear, try **Pampas Lingerie**. Second-hand clothes stores are common. **Mr Ben** offers items with 1950s American chic, whereas **Starry Starry Night** is more classic and traditional in its style. **Graham Tiso** is the city's best shop for clothing and equipment for the outdoors. Serious tartan souvenir-hunters should seek out **Hector Russell** a Highland outfitter that produces made-to-measure kilts.

FOOD AND DRINK

GLASGOW'S finest independent delicatessen is **Fratelli Sarti**, a traditional Italian food store also offering a good selection of wines. **Peckham's**, a chain of delis, has an excellent branch on Glassford Street, and its scope goes far beyond Italy. A man once described as the UK's top cheesemonger, **Iain Mellis** opened an outlet in

Glenlivet whisky

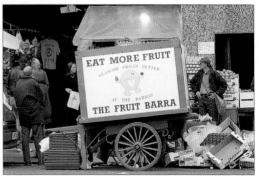

Traditional, "barrow-style" fruit stall in Glasgow's Barras Market

Glasgow in 1995. It is the best place in the entire west of Scotland for artisan cheeses made from unpasteurized milk. **Roots and Fruits** is Glasgow's leading fruit and vegetable store, and **Grass Roots** does superb breads. Aside from national chains selling beer, wine and spirits, such as **Oddbins**, there is **The Whisky Shop** in the city centre and the **Ubiquitous Chip Wine Shop** in the west end.

Shopping on Argyle Street, with its profusion of high-street stores

BOOK STORES

Glasgow is well served by bookshops. **Borders Books** on Buchanan Street, and **Waterstone's** on Sauchiehall Street are both multi-floor stores complete with coffee shops. **Ottakar's** in Buchanan Galleries is also well worth a visit.

ART AND DESIGN

THERE ARE A NUMBER of small galleries where art on display can be purchased. Many are concentrated in the streets behind the Tron Theatre, such as the **Glasgow Print Studio** and **Art Exposure**. The **Glasgow Art Fair**, held at the end of April in galleries across the city, also provides an opportunity to buy contemporary art. Fans of antiques should try the extensive **Heritage House** at Yorkhill Quay beside the River Clyde. For furniture and interior design ideas, visit **Designworks** or **Inhouse**.

DIRECTORY

DEPARTMENT STORES AND MALLS

Debenhams
97 Argyll St, G2 8AR.
(0141) 221 0088.

House of Fraser
45 Buchanan St, G1 3HR.
(0141) 221 3880.

Italian Centre
7 John St, G1 1HP.
(0141) 552 6368.

John Lewis
Buchanan Galleries, G1 2GF.
(0141) 353 6677.

Princes Square
48 Buchanan St, G1 3JX.
(0141) 221 0324.

FASHION

Cruise
180 Ingram St, G1 1DN.
(0141) 572 3232.

Diesel
116–120 Buchanan St, G1 2JW.
(0141) 221 5255.

Ella Bulloch
461 Clarkston Rd, G44 2LW.
(0141) 633 0078.

Graham Tiso
129 Buchanan St, G1 2JA.
(0141) 248 4877.

Hector Russell
110 Buchanan St, G1 2JN.
(0141) 221 0217.

Karen Millen
36 Buchanan St, G1 3JX.
(0141) 243 2136.

Mr Ben
Studio 6, 99 King St, G1 5RB.
(0141) 553 1936.

Pampas Lingerie
74 Hyndland Rd, G12 9UT.
(0141) 357 2383.

Pied à Terre
45 Buchanan St, G1 3JN.
(0141) 221 3880.

Schuh
112-114 Argyle St, G2 8BH.
(0141) 248 7331.

Starry Starry Night
19–21 Dowanside Lane, G12 9BZ.
(0141) 337 1837.

FOOD AND DRINK

Fratelli Sarti
133 Wellington St, G2 2XD.
(0141) 248 2228.

Grass Roots
20 Woodlands Road, G3 6UR.
(0141) 353 3278.

Iain Mellis
492 Great Western Rd, G12 8EW.
(0141) 339 8998.

Oddbins
26 Hope St, G2 6AA.
(0141) 248 3082.

Peckham's
61-65 Glassford St, G1 1UG.
(0141) 553 0666.

Roots & Fruits
351 Byres Rd, G12 8AU.
(0141) 339 5164.

Ubiquitous Chip Wine Shop
12 Ashton Lane, G12 8SJ.
(0141) 334 5007.

The Whisky Shop
220 Buchanan St, G1 2GF.
(0141) 331 0022.

BOOK STORES

Borders Books
98 Buchanan St, G1 3BA.
(0141) 222 7700.

Ottakar's
Buchanan Galleries, G1 2GF.
(0141) 353 1500.

Waterstone's
153–157 Sauchiehall St, G2 3EW.
(0141) 332 9105.

ART AND DESIGN

Art Exposure
19 Parnie St, G1 5RJ.
(0141) 552 7779.

Designworks
38 Gibson St, G12 8NX.
(0141) 339 9520.

Glasgow Art Fair
(0141) 204 4400.

Glasgow Print Studio
22 King St, G1 5QP.
(0141) 552 0704.

Heritage House
3b Yorkhill Quay Estate, G3 8QE.
(0141) 334 4924.

Inhouse
24–26 Wilson St, G1 1SS.
(0141) 552 3322.

ENTERTAINMENT IN GLASGOW

THE DANCE MUSIC that emerged during the 1990s found a natural home in Glasgow, which has possibly the most exuberant nightlife in Scotland. With the Scottish Exhibition and Conference Centre housing two major rock venues, and Barrowlands still a fixture on the concert circuit, popular music is very prominent. There are a number of mainstream cinemas in the city,

A flag celebrating Glasgow as "the friendly city"

as well as the Glasgow Film Theatre, a centre for arthouse releases. The annual Celtic Connections Festival in January is an international folk music event and there is plenty of culture in the city as a whole. Some major orchestras, the Scottish Ballet and Scottish Opera are based here. The Citizens' is a highly-acclaimed theatre and the Tramway and the Arches both stage large, innovative productions.

Scottish Opera performing *Eugene Onegin* on stage at the Theatre Royal

SOURCES OF INFORMATION

THE TWICE MONTHLY arts and entertainment magazine *The List* covers all events in Glasgow and Edinburgh.

CLASSICAL MUSIC AND OPERA

SCOTLAND'S NATIONAL opera company, Scottish Opera, is based at the **Theatre Royal** and stages some eight productions each season.

Glasgow Royal Concert Hall opened during the city's term as European City of Culture. The principle venue for the Royal Scottish National Orchestra, it also hosts visits from major international orchestras. The RSNO's annual concert series runs from October to April. Family classical concerts are performed all year.

For more intimate shows, the **Royal Scottish Academy of Music and Drama** has two smaller halls, while many venues across the city host recitals and concerts.

ROCK, JAZZ AND WORLD MUSIC

ROCK BANDS HAVE a choice of venues. There is the main auditorium at the **Scottish Exhibition and Conference Centre**, and the **Armadillo** in the same centre. It is **Barrowlands**, however, that remains the city's principal rock venue. Jazz sessions take place at **Cottier's**. The Royal Concert

Musicians outside City Chambers during a Festival of Jazz

Hall holds a Celtic Connections Festival. It also hosts international music, as does the **Old Fruitmarket**.

CINEMA

EIGHTEEN SCREENS are available at the **UGC Multiplex**, while the **Odeon at the Quay** on the south bank of the River Clyde has 12. The **Glasgow Film Theatre**, known by its initials GFT, shows arthouse and foreign-language movies. Glasgow's new **IMAX Theatre** is also well worth a visit.

The stylish café-bar at the Tron Theatre in the city centre

THEATRE AND DANCE

THE SCOTTISH BALLET stages its Glasgow performances at the Theatre Royal *(see Classical Music and Opera)*. Visiting dance companies, from classical to contemporary, also perform here and it is a noted stop on the touring circuit for major theatre companies from the rest of the UK and overseas.

The **Citizens' Theatre** is the main venue for serious drama, from Greek tragedies to modern pieces, and it rightly claims to be Scotland's best.

Both the **Tramway** and the **Arches** have staged extraordinary avant-garde shows, and are acclaimed for their experimental works. Smaller-scale productions can be seen at the **Tron** and Cottier's Theatre *(see Rock, Jazz and World Music)*. Commercial productions, such as musicals and pantomimes, are a staple at the popular **King's**.

Original road sign for the West End

venues are harder to find, however, **Bargo** in the Merchant City, and the first floor bar at the **Cul de Sac** in the West End continue to thrive. The city's club culture is one of the best in the UK. Each venue has different styles of music on different nights, including house, hip-hop, techno or drum-and-bash. The Arches *(see Theatre and Dance)*, **The Sub Club**, **The Tunnel**, **Archaos**, **Artá** and **Mas** are among the best.

stadium. The football season runs from August to May, and there is usually a game at least once a week during that time. Scotland's refurbished **Hampden National Stadium** hosts the finals of domestic cup competitions in November and May each year, and major international games.

Celtic fans cheering on their football (soccer) team from the stands

BARS AND CLUBS

VISITORS CAN CHOOSE from traditional pubs, which give a flavour of the old city, or fashionable bars with a contemporary atmosphere. Old-fashioned pubs such as the **Horseshoe**, the **Griffin** and the **Halt**, have long been popular in Glasgow. Modern

SPORTS

GLASGOW IS HOME to the country's most successful football (soccer) clubs, **Celtic** and **Glasgow Rangers**, and each has a large, impressive

---

DIRECTORY

CLASSICAL MUSIC AND OPERA

Glasgow Royal Concert Hall
2 Sauchiehall St, G2 3NY.
(0141) 353 8000.
www.grch.com

Royal Scottish Academy of Music and Drama
100 Renfrew St, G2 3DB.
(0141) 332 5057.

Theatre Royal
282 Hope St, G2 3QA.
(0141) 332 9000.
www.theatreroyalglasgow.com

ROCK, JAZZ AND WORLD MUSIC

Barrowlands
244 Gallowgate,
G4 0TT.
(0141) 552 4601.

Cottier's
93 Hyndland St,
G11 5PX.
(0141) 357 5825.

Old Fruitmarket
Albion St, G1 1NQ.
(0141) 353 8080.

Scottish Exhibition and Conference Centre/Armadillo
Finnieston, G3 8YW.
(0141) 248 3000.
www.secc.co.uk

CINEMA

Glasgow Film Theatre
12 Rose St, G3 6RB.
(0141) 332 8128.

IMAX Theatre
50 Pacific Quay,
G51 1EA.
(0141) 420 5000.

Odeon at the Quay
Paisley Road West, G5 8NP.
(0871) 224 4007.

UGC Multiplex
7 Renfrew St, G1 2LR.
(0141) 353 6699.

THEATRE AND DANCE

Arches
253 Argyll St, G2 8DL.
(0870) 240 7528.

Citizens' Theatre
119 Gorbals St, G5 9DS.
(0141) 429 0022.

King's
297 Bath St, G2 4JN.
(0141) 240 1111.

Tramway
25 Albert Drive, G41 2PE.
(0845) 330 3501.

Tron
63 Trongate, G1 5HB.
(0141) 552 4267.

BARS AND CLUBS

Archaos
25–27 Queen St, G1 3EF.
(0141) 204 3189.

Artá
13 Walls St, G1 1DA.
(0141) 552 2101.

Bargo
80 Albion St, G1 1NY.
(0141) 553 4771.

Cul de Sac
44–46 Ashton Lane,
G12 8SJ.
(0141) 334 4749.

Griffin
266 Bath St, G2 4JP.
(0141) 331 5171.

Halt
160 Woodlands Rd,
G3 6LF.
(0141) 352 9996.

Horseshoe
17 Drury St, G2 5AE.
(0141) 229 5711.

Mas
Royal Exchange Sq, G1.
(0141) 248 4420.

The Sub Club
22 Jamaica St, G1 4QD.
(0141) 248 4600.

The Tunnel
84 Mitchell St, G1 3NA.
(0141) 204 1000.

SPORTS

Celtic
Celtic Park,
95 Kerrydale St, G40 3RE.
(0870) 161 1888.

Glasgow Rangers
Ibrox Stadium,
G51 2YX.
(0870) 600 1993.

Hampden National Stadium
Hampden Park,
Letherby Drive, G42 9BA.
(0141) 620 4000.

CENTRAL SCOTLAND

C ENTRAL SCOTLAND *is a contrast of picturesque countryside and major urban centres, where a modern industrialized country meets an older and wilder landscape. Historically, it was here that the English-speaking Lowlands bordered the Gaelic Highlands, and there is still a strong sense of transition for anyone travelling north.*

The Highland Boundary Fault is a geological feature running through Central Scotland from Arran in the southwest to Stonehaven on the northeast coast. The Fault divides the Highlands from the Lowlands, making Central Scotland an area of contrasts, with both mountainous areas and green farmland. For hundreds of years, this line was also a meeting place, or border, between two very different cultures. To the north and west was a Gaelic-speaking people, who felt loyalty to their local clan chiefs. This way of life began to be marginalized in the late 18th century, as the more Anglicized Lowlands established their dominance.

In the Lowlands, Scotland's industry developed, drawing on coal reserves in districts such as Lanarkshire and the Lothians, while the Highlands were depopulated and eventually set aside for sporting estates and sheep farming.

Because Central Scotland is so compact, the opposing characteristics of Highland and Lowland, industrial and pre-industrial, exist side by side. Stirling Castle, parts of which date from the 16th century, is sited close to the petro-chemical plants and power plants on the upper reaches of the Forth. The tranquillity of the Trossachs and the hills of Arran are easily accessible from Glasgow, Scotland's largest, and largely industrial, city. The country's first coal-run ironworks was built at Carron in 1759, very close to Falkirk where Bonnie Prince Charlie had enjoyed one of his last military successes as claimant to the British throne 13 years earlier. Perth and Dundee are important centres of commerce positioned a short distance from the relative wildness of the Southern Highlands. There is no other area of Scotland that displays so many profound contrasts.

The view from Goatfell Ridge, near Brodick, across to the spectacular mountains of Arran

◁ A golfer in the grounds of a stately home, one of a number in Central Scotland providing golfing facilities

Exploring Central Scotland

Central Scotland presents some remarkable contrasts. The Goat-fell ridge on the Isle of Arran, off the west coast, has one of the most inspiring island hill walks in the entire country while, just to the north, the Isle of Bute is a more placid tourist destination. On the mainland, the Trossachs, near Callander, is an area of outstanding mountain beauty, very different from the lowlands of the Forth Valley further east. Stirling Castle stands at the head of the Forth under the shadow of the Ochil Hills, while Perth occupies a similar position on the Tay. The Firth of Tay, with its open views, is home to Dundee, Scotland's fourth city.

Loch Katrine in the Trossachs

GETTING AROUND

Major mainland centres such as Stirling, Perth and Dundee are easily accessible by train or motorway from Edinburgh or Glasgow but, for the mountain areas in Central Scotland (the Trossachs or minor ranges), a car is recommended. Reaching Arran or Bute is best done by car or train from Glasgow, then car ferry from ports on the Ayrshire coast (Ardrossan, Wemyss Bay). The islands are small enough to make bicycle touring possible.

SEE ALSO

• **Where to Stay** pp169–70

• **Where to Eat** pp180–81

Aberdeen

A90 A92

GLAMIS CASTLE 9

A94

Tay

A85

PERTH 8

DUNDEE 10

A914

ST ANDREWS 11

A91

A915

FALKLAND PALACE 13

EAST NEUK 12

AUCHTERARDER

GLENROTHES

GLENEAGLES

FIRTH OF FORTH

LROSS 14

DUNFERMLINE

EDINBURGH

A1 **DUNBAR**

A1

LIVINGSTON

A70 A702

B6438

Berwick-upon-Tweed

↓ Biggar   ↓ Galashiels

↓ Melrose

↓ Kelso

A68

Panoramic view of Dundee, Tayside

SIGHTS AT A GLANCE

KEY

▨ Motorway (highway)

▨ Major road

▨ Scenic route

– – Scenic path

〜 River

☸ Viewpoint

Antonine Wall 16
Arran 2
Bute 3
Culross 15
Doune Castle 7
Dundee 10
Dunfermline 14
East Neuk 12
Falkirk Wheel 17
Falkland Palace 13

Firth of Clyde 1
Glamis Castle 9
Loch Lomond 4
Perth 8
St Andrews 11
Stirling pp120–21 6
The Trossachs pp116–17 5

Firth of Clyde ❶

Numerous counties west of Glasgow.
🚍 *Helensburgh and Dumbarton in
the north; Troon and Ayr in the south.*
⛴ *from Largs to Great Cumbrae; from
Gourock to Dunoon.* 🛈 *Largs (01292)
678100; Dumbarton (01389) 742306.*
ⓦ *www.scottishheartlands.org*

As might be expected of a
waterway that leads from
Glasgow, a former economic
powerhouse of the British Empire *(see p46)*, to the Irish Sea
and the Atlantic, the Firth of
Clyde has many reminders of
its industrial past. **Greenock**,
some 40 km (25 miles) west
of Glasgow, was once a shipbuilding centre. Few go there
for the town's beauty, but the
**McLean Museum and Art
Gallery**, with its exhibits and
information on the engineer
James Watt *(see p22)*, a native
of Greenock, is worth a visit.
Princes Pier is a departure
point for cruises along the
Clyde. **Dumbarton**, 24 km
(15 miles) from Glasgow on
the northern bank, dates from
the 5th century AD. Its ancient
castle perches on a rock overlooking the rest of the town.

The Firth itself is L-shaped,
heading northwest as it opens
up beyond the Erskine Bridge.
On reaching Gourock, just
west of Greenock, the Firth
branches south to open
water. Kip Marina at nearby
Inverkip is a major yachting
centre, while many towns on
the Ayrshire coast have served
as holiday resorts for Glasgow
since Victorian times. **Largs**,
site of the clash between Scots
and Vikings in 1263, has a
multimedia centre about the
Vikings in Scotland, as well

**The old harbour at Brodick, with
Goatfell ridge in the distance**

as a modern monument to
the 1263 battle. A ferry
service is offered to **Great
Cumbrae Island**, which lies
just off the coast. The main
town on the island is
Millport, which is built
around a picturesque bay.
The western side of the
Firth of Clyde is much
less developed, bor-
dered by the Cowal
Peninsula with its
hills and lochs. The
only town of note in this
wild country is **Dunoon**.
Again once a Victorian
holiday resort, it still relies
on tourism for its income.
For many years there
was a strong American
influence in Dunoon
due to the US nuclear
submarine base at Holy
Loch that is now closed.

🏛 **McLean Museum and Art
Gallery**
15 Kelly St, Greenock. 📞 *(01475)
715624.* ⭕ *Mon–Sat.*

Arran ❷

North Ayrshire. 👥 *4,500.* ⛴ *from
Ardrossan to Brodick; from Claonaig
(Isle of Mull) to Lochranza (Apr–Oct
only).* 🛈 *Brodick (01770) 302140.*

Arran is thought to have
been populated as long
ago as the end of the last Ice
Age. The island's neolithic
chambered burial tombs, such
as the one at **Torrylinn** near
Lagg in the south, indicate
this. Bronze Age stone circles
can also be seen around
Machrie on the west coast.
Vikings arrived from about
AD 800 and exerted an
influence for more than four
centuries. After the Battle of
Largs in 1263, when Alexander
III defeated the Norsemen,
Scotland bought Arran from
the Vikings in 1266.

Today, visitors tend to
come to Arran for
outdoor pursuits. Golf
is especially popular,
with 18-hole courses at
Brodick, Whiting Bay
and Lamlash *(see
p189)*. Fishing is
also popular.
Brodick is the
island's only real
town. The more
mountainous parts
offer some of the
most spectacular
hillwalking in Cen-
tral Scotland. **The
Goatfell ridge** to
the east of Glen
Rosa and **Beinn
Tarsuinn** to the west have a
particular rugged beauty.

Robert the Bruce stayed on
Arran on his return to Scotland
in 1307. His followers had already been harassing the garrison at **Brodick Castle**, then
occupied by supporters of the
King of England. Legend states
that it was from Arran that
Bruce saw a signal fire on the
Ayrshire coast that told him it
was safe to return to the mainland and launch the campaign
against the English *(see p43)*.
Parts of the Castle still date
from the 13th century, though
it has had many later additions.

**Golfer on the
island of Arran**

♣ **Brodick Castle**
(NTS) Brodick. 📞 *(01770) 302202.*
Castle ⭕ *Apr–Oct: daily.*
Gardens ⭕ *daily.* 🖼 🚻

Largs seafront, the departure point for ferries to Great Cumbrae Island

The snowy peak of Ben Lomond rising majestically over Loch Lomond, part of the West Highland Way

Bute ❸

Argyll & Bute. 🏃 7,000. ⛴ from Wemyss Bay to Rothesay; from Colintraive to Rhubodach. ⛴ from Dunoon. 🅸 Rothesay (01700) 502151.

BUTE IS ALMOST an extension of the Cowal Peninsula, and the small ferry from Colintraive takes only five minutes to cross the Kyles of Bute to Rhubodach on the island. This route is a long drive from Glasgow, however, and most people choose to travel via Wemyss Bay on the Firth of Clyde across to the island's main town, Rothesay.

Just 25 km (16 miles) long by 8 km (5 miles) at its widest point, Bute has been occupied since at least the Bronze Age. The remains of the chapel at St Ninian's Point on the west coast date from around the 6th century, while **Rothesay Castle**, now ruined, is mostly

a 12th-century structure and was the site of struggles between islanders and Vikings in the 13th century. Over the last 120 years or so, Bute has played a more placid role as a popular holiday resort.

One of Bute's main attractions is **Mount Stuart House**, 5 km (3 miles) south of Rothesay. This great aristocratic house, built in 1877 by the third Marquess of Bute, is set in 18th-century gardens. The features of this wonderful Gothic edifice reflect the Marquess's interests in mythology, religion and astronomy.

♣ Rothesay Castle
Castle Hill St, Rothesay. 🅒 (01700) 502691. ◻ Apr–Sep: daily; Oct–Mar: Sat–Thu am (Sun: pm only). ⬤

♣ Mount Stuart House
Mount St. 🅒 (01700) 503877. ◻ daily. ⬤ May–Sep: Tue & Thu. 📷 🎥 ♿

Loch Lomond ❹

West Dunbartonshire, Argyll & Bute, Trossachs. 🚂 Balloch, Tarbet. ⛴ Balloch, Balmaha. 🅸 Balloch (08707) 200 607

OF SCOTLAND'S many lochs, Lomond is perhaps the most popular and best loved. Lying just 30 km (19 miles) northwest of Glasgow, its accessibility has helped its rise to prominence. The loch is the largest body of fresh water in the British Isles, 35 km (22 miles) long and 8 km (5 miles) at its widest point in the south, where there are a scattering of over 30 islands, some with ancient ruins. Duncryne, a small hill some 5 km (3 miles) northeast of **Balloch** on the southern shore, gives an excellent view of the Loch. Much of the area became Scotland's first national park in 2002, fronted by the new **Loch Lomond Shores** visitor centre complex in Balloch.

In general, the western shore is the more developed, with villages such as **Luss** and **Tarbet** attracting large numbers of visitors. The contrast between the Loch and **Ben Lomond**, 974 m (3,196 ft), high above its eastern shore adds to the spectacle. Many walkers pass this way since Scotland's most popular long-distance footpath, the West Highland Way *(see p191)* from Glasgow to Fort William, skirts the eastern shore. Boat trips around the loch operate regularly from Balloch Pier. The area is also good for water sports enthusiasts – speed boats, kayaks and jet skis can all be rented.

View of Bute with the 14th-century Kames Castle, at the head of Kames Bay

The Trossachs ❺

COMBINING THE RUGGEDNESS of the Grampians with the pastoral tranquillity of the Borders, this beautiful region of craggy hills and sparkling lochs is the colourful meeting place of the Lowlands and Highlands. Home to a wide variety of wildlife, including the golden eagle, peregrine falcon, red deer and the wildcat, the Trossachs and

Golden eagle

their inhabitants have inspired numerous writers, including Sir Walter Scott *(see p86)* who made the area the setting for several of his novels. In 2002, a large part of the area was designated as Loch Lomond and The Trossachs National Park, the first national park in Scotland.

Loch Katrine
The setting of Sir Walter Scott's Lady of the Lake *(1810), this freshwater loch can be explored on the Victorian steamer* Sir Walter Scott, *which cruises from the Trossachs Pier.*

Loch Lomond
Britain's largest freshwater lake was immortalized in a ballad composed by a local Jacobite soldier, dying far from home. He laments that though he will return home before his companions who travel on "the high road", he will be doing so on "the low road" (of death).

The West Highland Way provides a good footpath through the area.

Luss
With its exceptionally picturesque cottages, Luss is one of the prettiest villages in Central Scotland. Surrounded by grassy hills, it occupies one of the most scenic parts of Loch Lomond's western shore.

FORT WILLIAM

Inveruglas

LOCH ARKLET

Tarbet

BEN LOMOND
▲
974 m
(3,195 ft)

Kinlocharc

BEN UIRD
▲
596 m
(1,955 ft)

Luss

LOCH
LOMOND

Balmaha

Balloch

GLASGOW

KEY

ℹ️	Tourist information
▬	Major road
▭	Minor road
꞊	Narrow lane
= =	Footpath
☀	Viewpoint

0 kilometres   5

0 miles   5

Inchmahome Priory

Mary, Queen of Scots was hidden in this island priory to escape the armies of King Henry VIII, before fleeing for France.

VISITORS' CHECKLIST

Central. 🚆 Stirling. 🚌 Callander.
🛈 Ancaster Sq, Callander
(08707) 200628. ⏱ daily.
Inchmahome Priory, off A81,
near Aberfoyle. 📞 (0131) 668
8800. ⏱ Apr–Sep: daily. ♿
limited. **Sir Walter Scott
Steamer,** Katrine Pier 📞
(01877) 376 316.

Callander

With its Rob Roy and Trossachs Visitor Centre, Callander is the most popular town from which to explore the Trossachs.

The Duke's Pass, between Callander and Aberfoyle, affords some of the finest views in the area.

Queen Elizabeth Forest Park

There are woodland walks through this vast tract of countryside, home to black grouse and red deer, between Loch Lomond and Aberfoyle.

ROB ROY (1671–1734)

Robert MacGregor, known as Rob Roy (Red Robert) from the colour of his hair, grew up as a herdsman near Loch Arklet. After a series of harsh winters, he took to raiding richer Lowland properties to feed his clan, and was declared an outlaw by the Duke of Montrose who burned his house to the ground. After this, Rob Roy's Jacobite sympathies became inflamed by his desire to avenge the crime. Plundering the duke's lands and repeatedly escaping from prison earned him a reputation similar to that of England's Robin Hood. He was pardoned in 1725 and spent his last years freely in Balquhidder, where he is buried.

The 17th-century town house of the Dukes of Argyll

Stirling ❻

Central. 👥 28,000. 🚆 🚌
ℹ️ 41 Dunbarton Rd (01786) 475019.
🌐 www.scottishheartlands.org

SITUATED BETWEEN the Ochil Hills and the Campsie Fells, the town of Stirling grew up around its castle, historically one of Scotland's most important fortresses. Below the castle the Old Town is still protected by the original walls, built in the 16th century to keep Mary, Queen of Scots safe from Henry VIII. The medieval **Church of the Holy Rude**, on Castle Wynd, where the infant James VI was crowned in 1567, has one of Scotland's few surviving hammerbeam oak roofs. In front of the church, the ornate façade of **Mar's Wark** is all that remains of a grand palace which, though never completed, was commissioned in 1570 by the first Earl of Mar. It was destroyed by the Jacobites in 1746.

ENVIRONS: Three kilometres (2 miles) south of Stirling, the **Bannockburn Heritage Centre** stands by the field where Robert the Bruce defeated the English in 1314 *(see p43).* After the battle, he dismantled the castle so it would not fall back into English hands. A bronze equestrian statue commemorates the man who became an icon of Scottish independence.

ℹ️ **Bannockburn Heritage Centre**
(NTS) Glasgow Rd. 📞 *(01786) 812664.* ⭕ *daily* ⬤ *24 Dec–Feb.* 📷 ♿

Stirling Castle

RISING HIGH on a rocky crag, this magnificent castle, which dominated Scottish history for centuries, now remains one of the finest examples of Renaissance architecture in Scotland. Legend says that King Arthur wrested the original castle from the Saxons, but there is no evidence of a castle before 1124. The present building dates from the 15th and 16th centuries and was last defended, against the Jacobites, in 1746. From 1881 to 1964 the castle was used as a depot for recruits into the Argyll and Sutherland Highlanders, though it now serves no military function.

Gargoyle on castle wall

Robert the Bruce
In the esplanade, this modern statue shows Robert the Bruce sheathing his sword after the Battle of Bannockburn in 1314.

Prince's Tower

Forework

Entrance

***Stirling Castle in the Time of the Stuarts**, painted by Johannes Vorsterman (1643–99)*

◁ **Loch Ard, near Stirling, in the Trossachs**

★ **Palace**
The otherwise sparse interiors of the royal apartments contain the Stirling Heads. These Renaissance roundels depict 38 figures, thought to be members of the royal court at that time.

VISITORS' CHECKLIST

Castle Wynd, Stirling. ☎ (01786) 450000. ⬜ Apr–Sep: 9:30am–6pm daily; Oct–Mar: 9:30am–5pm daily. 📷 🚫 museum. ♿ limited. 🎫 🚻 🛍 ▣
Ⓦ www.historic-scotland.gov.uk

The King's Old Building houses the Regimental Museum of the Argyll and Sutherland Highlanders.

★ **Chapel Royal**
Seventeenth-century frescoes by Valentine Jenkins adorn the chapel, reconstructed in 1594.

Nether Bailey

STAR FEATURES

★ **Palace**

★ **Chapel Royal**

The Great Hall, built in 1500, has a roof similar to that of Edinburgh Castle *(see pp60–61)*.

The Elphinstone Tower was levelled into a gun platform in 1714.

STIRLING BATTLES

At the highest navigable point of the Forth and holding the pass to the Highlands, Stirling occupied a key position in Scotland's struggles for independence. Seven battlefields can be seen from the castle; the 67-m (220-ft) Wallace Monument at Abbey Craig recalls William Wallace's defeat of the English at Stirling Bridge in 1297, foreshadowing Bruce's victory in 1314.

The Victorian Wallace Monument

Grand Battery
Following the unrest after the deposition of the Stuarts (see p45), this parapet was built in 1708, to strengthen the castle's defences.

Perth seen from the east across the Tay

Doune Castle ❼

Doune, Central. **📞** *(01786) 841742.*
🚊 **🚌** *Stirling then bus.* **🕐** *daily.*
⬤ *Oct–Mar: Thu & Fri.* 🎫 **♿**
limited. **w** *www.historic-scotland.gov.uk*

BUILT AS THE residence of
Robert, Duke of Albany,
in the late 14th century,
Doune Castle was a Stuart
stronghold until it fell into
ruin in the 18th century. Now
fully restored, it offers a
unique view into the life of
the medieval royal household.
The Gatehouse leads
through to the central courtyard from which the Great
Hall can be entered. Com-
plete with its reconstructed
open-timber roof, minstrels'
gallery and central fireplace,
the Hall adjoins the Lord's
Hall and Private Room with
its original privy and well-
hatch. A number of private
stairs and narrow passages
illustrate the ingenious means
by which the royal family
tried to protect itself during
times of danger.

Perth ❽

Perthshire. **🏛** *45,000.* **🚊** **🚌**
ℹ *Lower City Mills, West Mills St.*
📞 *(01738) 450600.*
w *www.perthshire.co.uk*

ONCE THE CAPITAL of medi-
eval Scotland, Perth's rich
heritage is reflected in many
of its buildings. It was in the
Church of St John, founded
in 1126, that the preacher
John Knox delivered the fiery
sermons which led to the destruction of many local mon-
asteries. The Victorianized
Fair Maid's House (c.1600),
on North Port, is one of the
oldest houses in town and
was the fictional home of the
heroine of Sir Walter Scott's
The Fair Maid of Perth (1828).
In **Balhousie Castle**, the
Museum of the Black Watch

commemorates the first ever
Highland regiment, while the
Museum and Art Gallery has
displays on local industry and
exhibitions of Scottish painting.

ENVIRONS: Three km (2 miles)
north of Perth, the Gothic
Scone Palace stands on the
site of an abbey destroyed by
John Knox's followers in 1559.
Between the 9th and 13th
centuries, Scone guarded the
sacred Stone of Destiny, now
housed in Edinburgh Castle
(see pp60–61), on which the
Scottish kings were crowned.
The embroideries of Mary,
Queen of Scots are on display
within the palace.

♣ Balhousie Castle
RHQ Black Watch, Hay St. **📞** *(0131)*
310 8530. **🕐** *19 Mar–Oct:*
10am–6pm daily; Nov–22 Dec: daily.
⬤ *23 Dec–18 Mar.*
🏛 Museum and Art Gallery
78 George St. **📞** *(01738) 632488.*
🕐 *Mon–Sat.* **♿**
♣ Scone Palace
A93 to Braemar. **📞** *(01738) 552300.*
🕐 *Easter–Oct: daily.* 🎫 **♿**

Glamis Castle ❾

Glamis, outside Forfar, Tayside.
📞 *(01307) 840242.* **🚊** **🚌** *Dundee*
then bus. **🕐** *Apr–Oct: daily.* 🎫 🎫
♿ *grounds.*

WITH THE pinnacled out-
line of a Loire chateau,
the imposing medieval tower-
house of **Glamis Castle**

Glamis Castle with statues of James VI (left) and Charles I (right)

began as a royal hunting lodge in the 11th century but underwent reconstruction in the 17th century. It was the childhood home of Queen Elizabeth the Queen Mother, and her former bedroom can be seen with a youthful portrait by Henri de Laszlo (1878–1956).

Behind the castle's grey-pink walls, many rooms are open to the public, including Duncan's Hall, the oldest in the castle and Shakespeare's setting for the king's murder in *Macbeth*. Together, the rooms present an array of china, paintings, tapestries and furniture spanning 500 years. In the grounds stand a pair of wrought-iron gates made for the Queen Mother on her 80th birthday in 1980.

Dundee ❿

Tayside. 🏛 *150,000.* ✈ 🚲 🚉
🚹 *7–21 Castle St (01382) 527527.*
🅿 *Tue, Fri–Sun.*
🆆 *www.angusanddundee.co.uk*

FAMOUS FOR ITS cake and marmalade, **Dundee** was also a major ship-building centre in the 18th and 19th centuries, a period which is recreated at the Victoria Docks.

HMS Unicorn, built in 1824, is the oldest British-built warship still afloat and is fitted as it was on its last voyage. Berthed at Riverside is the royal re-search ship **Discovery**. Built here in 1901 for the first of Captain Scott's voyages to the Antarctic, the *Discovery* was one of the last sailing ships to be made in Britain. Housed in a Victorian Gothic building, the

View of St Andrews over the ruins of the cathedral

McManus Galleries provide a glimpse of Dundee's industrial heritage, with exhibitions of archaeology and Victorian art.

ENVIRONS: Along the coast, **Arbroath** is famed for its red stonework, ancient Abbey and "Arbroath Smokies" (smoked haddock). Arbroath Abbey displays a copy of *The Declaration of Arbroath*, attesting Scotland's independence.

🏛 **HMS Unicorn**
Victoria Docks,
📞 *(01382) 200900.*
🅾 *Easter–Oct: 10am–5pm* ● *late Dec–early Jan.* 🖼 🦽 *limited.* 🆆
www.frigateunicorn.org
🏛 **Discovery**
Discovery Point.
📞 *(01382) 201245.*
🅾 *daily.* 🖼 🦽 🏛 *by appt.*
🏛 **McManus Galleries**
Albert Institute, Albert Square.
📞 *(01382) 432350.* 🅾 *daily.*

Insignia of St Mary's College, St Andrews University

St Andrews ⓫

Fife. 🏛 *14,000.* 🚲 *Leuchars.* 🅿
🚹 *70 Market St (01334) 472021.*
🆆 *www.standrews.co.uk*

SCOTLAND'S OLDEST UNIVERSITY town and one-time ecclesiastical capital, **St Andrews** is now a shrine to golfers from all over the world. Its main streets and cobbled alleys, full of crooked house-fronts, dignified university buildings and medieval churches, converge on the venerable ruins of the 12th-century **cathedral**. Once the largest cathedral in Scotland, it was later pillaged for its stones, which were used to build the town. **St Andrew's Castle** was built for the town's bishops in the year 1200 and the dungeon can still be seen. St Andrews' golf courses occupy the land to the west of the city, and each is open for a modest fee.

The **British Golf Museum**, which tells how the city's Royal and Ancient Golf Club became the ruling arbiter of the game, will delight golf enthusiasts.

⛳ **St Andrew's Castle**
The Scores. 📞 *(01334) 477196.*
🅾 *daily.* 🖼 🦽 🏛
🏛 **British Golf Museum**
Bruce Embankment.
📞 *(01334) 4600046.*
🅾 *daily.* 🖼 🦽

THE BIRTHPLACE OF GOLF

Scotland's national game *(see pp188–9)* was pioneered on the sandy links around St Andrews. The earliest record of the game being played dates from 1457, when golf was banned by James II because it was interfering with his subjects' archery practice. Mary, Queen of Scots was berated in 1568 for playing immediately after her husband, Darnley, had been murdered.

Mary, Queen of Scots at St Andrews in 1563

The central courtyard of Falkland Palace, bordered by rose bushes

East Neuk ⓬

Fife. ⚏ *Leuchars.* ⬛ *Glenrothes & Leuchars.* ⓘ *St Andrews (01334) 472021.*

A STRING of pretty fishing villages peppers the shoreline of the **East Neuk** (the eastern "corner") of Fife, stretching from Earlsferry to Fife Ness. Much of Scotland's medieval trade with Europe passed through these ports, a connection reflected in the Flemish-inspired crow-stepped gables of many of the cottages. Although the herring industry has declined and the area is now a peaceful holiday centre, the sea still dominates village life. The harbour is the heart of St Monans, a charming town of narrow twisting streets, while Pittenweem is the base for the East Neuk fishing fleet.

The town is also known for **St Fillan's Cave**, the retreat of a 9th-century hermit whose relic was used to bless the army of Robert the Bruce before the Battle of Bannockburn. A church stands among the cobbled lanes and colourful cottages of Crail; legend goes that the stone by the church gate was hurled across to the mainland from the Isle of May by the Devil.

A number of 16th- to 19th-century buildings in the village of Anstruther contain the **Scottish Fisheries Museum**, which tells the area's history with the aid of cottage interiors, boats and displays on whaling. From the village you can also embark for the nature reserve on the **Isle of May**, which teems with seabirds and a colony of grey seals. The statue of Alexander Selkirk in Lower Largo recalls the local boy whose seafaring adventures inspired Daniel Defoe's novel *Robinson Crusoe* (1719). After disagreeing with his captain, he was put ashore on an uninhabited island where he survived for four years.

🏛 Scottish Fisheries Museum
St Ayles, Harbour Head, Anstruther. 【 *(01333) 310628.* ◯ *daily.* ⚏ 🖬 ♿

THE PALACE KEEPER

Due to the size of the royal household and the necessity for the king to be itinerant, the office of Keeper was created by the medieval kings who required custodians to maintain and replenish the resources of their many palaces while they were away. Now redundant, it was a hereditary title and gave the custodian permanent and often luxurious lodgings.

James VI's bed in the Keeper's Bedroom at Falkland Palace

Falkland Palace ⓭

(NTS) Falkland, Fife. 【 *(01337) 857397.* ⚏ 🚌 *Ladybank, Kirkcaldy, then bus.* ◯ *Mar–Oct: 10am–6pm daily (Sun: pm).* 🖼

T HIS STUNNING Renaissance palace was designed as a hunting lodge for the Stuart kings. Although its construction was begun by James IV in 1500, most of the work was carried out by his son, James V, in the 1530s. Under the influence of his two French wives, he employed French workmen to redecorate the façade of the East Range with dormers, buttresses and medallions, and to build the beautifully proportioned South Range. The palace fell into ruin during the years of the Commonwealth and was occupied briefly by Rob Roy *(see p117)* in 1715.

After buying the estates in 1887, the third Marquess of Bute became the Palace Keeper and subsequently restored the building. The richly panelled interiors are filled with superb furniture and contemporary portraits of the Stuart monarchs. The royal tennis court, built in 1539 for King James V, is the oldest in Britain.

Dunfermline ⓮

Fife. 🏠 *45,000.* ⚏ 🚌 ⓘ *1 High St, (01383) 720999.*

S COTLAND'S CAPITAL until 1603, Dunfermline is dominated by the ruins of the 12th-century abbey and palace, which recall its royal past. The town first came to prominence in the 11th century as the seat of King Malcolm III, who founded a priory on the present site of the **Abbey Church**. With its Norman nave and 19th-century choir, the abbey church contains the tombs of 22 Scottish kings and queens, including that of the renowned Robert the Bruce.

The ruins of the **palace** soar over the beautiful gardens of Pittencrieff Park. Dunfermline's most famous son, the philanthropist Andrew Carnegie (1835–1919), had been forbidden entrance to the park as a boy. After making his fortune, he bought the entire Pittencrieff estate and gave it to the people of Dunfermline. Carnegie emigrated to Pennsylvania in his teens and through iron and steel, became one of the wealthiest men in the world. He donated some $350 million for the benefit of mankind. The town's **Carnegie Birthplace Museum** tells his story.

🏛 Carnegie Birthplace Museum
Moodie St. 📞 *(01383) 723638.* ⏰
Apr–Oct: daily (Sun pm). ♿ &

The 12th-century Norman nave of Dunfermline Abbey Church

Culross ⓯

Fife. 👥 *450.* 🚉 *Dunfermline.* 🚌 *Dunfermline.* 🛈 *National Trust, The Palace (01383) 880359.* ⏰ *Easter–Sep: daily.* ♿ & *limited.*

AN IMPORTANT religious centre in the 6th century, the town of Culross is reputed to have been the birthplace of St Mungo in 514. Now a beauti-

fully preserved 16th- and 17th-century village, Culross prospered in the 16th century due to the growth of its coal and salt industries, most notably under the genius of Sir George Bruce. Descended from the family of Robert the Bruce, Sir George took charge of the Culross colliery in 1575 and created a drainage system called the "Egyptian Wheel" which cleared a mine 1.5 km (1 mile) long, running underneath the River Forth.

The National Trust for Scotland began restoring the town in 1932 and now provides a guided tour. This starts at the **Visitors' Centre**, housed in the one-time village prison.

Built in 1577, Bruce's **palace** has the crow-stepped gables, decorated windows and red pantiles typical of the period. The interior retains its original early 17th-century painted ceilings, which are among the finest in Scotland. Crossing the square past the **Oldest House**, dating from 1577, head for the **Town House** to the west. Behind it, a cobbled street known as the Back Causeway leads to the turreted **Study**, built in 1610 as a house for the Bishop of Dunblane. The main room is open to visitors and should be seen for its original Norwegian ceiling. Continuing northwards to the ruined abbey, fine church and Abbey House, don't miss the Dutch-gabled **House with the Evil Eyes**.

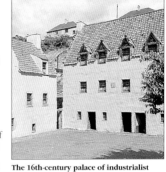

The 16th-century palace of industrialist George Bruce, at Culross

Antonine Wall ⓰

Falkirk. 🛈 *2–4 Glebe St (01324) 620244.* 🚉 *Falkirk.* ⏰ *Mon–Sat.*

THE ROMANS invaded Scotland for a second time around AD 140, in the reign of Emperor Antonius and built a 60 km (37 mile) earth rampart across Central Scotland from the Firth of Clyde to the Firth of Forth. The rampart was further defended by ditches and forts at strategic points. One of the best preserved sections of the fortifications can be seen at Rough Castle, west of Falkirk.

Falkirk Wheel ⓱

Lime Rd, Tamfourhill, Falkirk. 📞 *(01324) 619888; booking line: (08700) 500208.* 🚉 *Falkirk.* ⏰ *daily.* ♿ *for boat trip.* 🚗 🚻 🌐 *www.thefalkirkwheel.co.uk*

THIS IMPRESSIVE, elegant boat lift is the first ever to revolve and the centrepiece of Scotland's ambitious canal regeneration scheme. Once important for commercial transport, the Union and the Forth and Clyde canals were blocked by numerous roads during the 1960s. Now the Falkirk Wheel gently swings boats between the two waterways creating an uninterrupted link between Glasgow and Edinburgh. This huge, moving sculpture rotates continuously, lifting boats 35m, a height equivalent to 11 traditional locks, in just 15 minutes. Visitors can ride the wheel on one of the boats that leave the visitor's centre every half hour.

The rotating Falkirk Wheel boat lift

THE HIGHLANDS AND ISLANDS

OST OF THE *stock images of Scottishness – clans and tartans, whisky and porridge, bagpipes and heather – originate in the Highlands, and enrich the popular picture of Scotland as a whole. But for many centuries the Gaelic-speaking, cattle-raising Highlanders had little in common with their southern neighbours.*

Clues to the non-Celtic ancestors of the Highlanders lie scattered across the Highlands and islands in the form of stone circles, brochs and cairns spanning over 5,000 years. By the end of the 6th century, the Gaelic-speaking Celts had arrived from Ireland, as had St Columba who taught Christianity to the monastic community he established on the island of Iona. It was the fusion of Christianity with Viking culture in the 8th and 9th centuries that produced the beautiful St Magnus Cathedral in the Orkney Islands.

For over 1,000 years, Celtic Highland society was founded on a clan system, built on family ties to create loyal groups dependent on a feudal chief. However, the clans were systematically broken up by England after 1746, following the defeat of the Jacobite attempt on the British crown, led by Bonnie Prince Charlie *(see p153).* A more romantic vision of the Highlands began to emerge in the early 19th century. Its creation was largely due to Sir Walter Scott, whose novels and poetry depicted the majesty and grandeur of a country previously considered merely poverty-stricken and barbaric. Another great popularizer was Queen Victoria, whose passion for Balmoral Castle helped to establish the trend for acquiring Highland sporting estates. But behind the sentimentality lay harsh economic realities that drove generations of Highland farmers to seek a new life overseas.

Today, over half the inhabitants of the Highlands and islands still live in communities of less than 1,000 people. But thriving oil and tourist industries have supplemented fishing and whisky, and population figures are rising.

A group of puffins congregating on the rocks, a common sight on Scottish islands

◁ **The castle of Eilean Donan, Loch Duich in Glen Shiel**

Exploring the Highlands and Islands

To the north and west of Stirling, the historic gateway to the Highlands, lie the magnificent mountains and glens, fretted coastlines and lonely isles that are the epitome of Scottish scenery. Inverness, the Highland capital, makes a good starting point for exploring Loch Ness and the Cairngorms, while Fort William holds the key to Ben Nevis. Inland from Aberdeen lie Royal Deeside and the Spey Valley whisky heartland. The romantic Hebridean Islands are a ferry-ride from Oban, Mallaig or Ullapool.

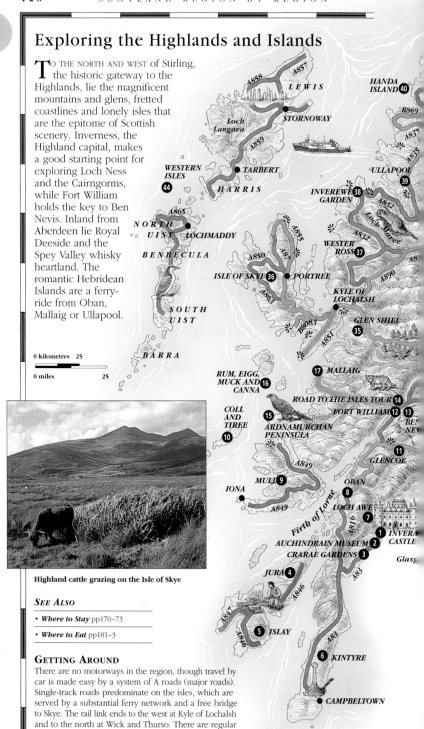

0 kilometres 25

0 miles 25

Highland cattle grazing on the Isle of Skye

See Also

• *Where to Stay* pp170–73

• *Where to Eat* pp181–3

Getting Around

There are no motorways in the region, though travel by car is made easy by a system of A roads (major roads). Single-track roads predominate on the isles, which are served by a substantial ferry network and a free bridge to Skye. The rail link ends to the west at Kyle of Lochalsh and to the north at Wick and Thurso. There are regular flights from London to Inverness, Aberdeen and Wick.

KEY

Major road	
Scenic route	
Scenic path	
River	
Viewpoint	

SIGHTS AT A GLANCE

Aberdeen pp142–3 ㉓
Ardnamurchan Peninsula ⑮
Auchindrain Museum ②
Ben Nevis ⑬
Black Isle ㉜
Blair Castle ⑲
The Cairngorms pp140–41 ㉒
Cape Wrath and the North Coast ㊶
Cawdor Castle ㉙
Coll and Tiree ⑩
Crarae Gardens ③
Culloden ㉘
Dornoch ㉞
Dunkeld ㉑
Elgin ㉖
Fort George ㉗
Fort William ⑫

Glencoe ⑪
Glen Shiel ㉟
The Great Glen
   pp148–9 ㉛
Handa Island ㊵
Inveraray Castle ①
Inverewe Garden ㊳
Inverness ㉚
Islay ⑤
Isle of Skye pp152–3 ㊱
Jura ④
Kintyre ⑥
Loch Awe ⑦
Mallaig ⑰
Mull ⑨
Oban ⑧
Orkney Islands ㊷

Pitlochry ⑳
Rum, Eigg, Muck
   and Canna ⑯
Shetland Islands ㊸
Speyside Malt Whisky
   Trail ㉕
Strathpeffer ㉝
Ullapool ㊴
Western Isles ㊹
Wester Ross ㊲

Walks and Tours
Killiecrankie Walk ⑱
Road to the Isles Tour ⑭
Royal Deeside Tour ㉔

Inveraray Castle ❶

Inveraray, Argyll & Bute. 🚆 *Arrochar, then bus.* 📞 *(01499) 302203.* ☐ *Apr–Oct: Mon–Sat 10am–5:45pm, Sun1pm–5:45pm.* ⬤ *Apr, May, Oct: Fri.* 📷 ✔
♿ w *www.inveraray-castle.com*

The pinnacled Gothic exterior of Inveraray Castle

T HIS MULTI-TURRETED mock Gothic palace is the family home of the powerful Clan Campbell, who have been the Dukes of Argyll since 1701. It was built in 1745 by architects Roger Morris and William Adam on the site and ruins of a 15th-century castle. The conical towers were added later, after a fire in 1877.

The magnificent interiors, designed by Robert Mylne in the 1770s, form a backdrop to such treasures as Regency furniture, a huge collection of Oriental and European porcelain and portraits by Ramsay, Gainsborough and Raeburn. The Armoury Hall contains early weaponry collected by the Campbells to fight the Jacobite rebels. The Combined Operations Museum commemorates the 250,000 allied troops who trained at Inveraray during World War II.

Auchindrain Museum ❷

Inveraray, Argyll & Bute. 📞 *(01499) 500235.* 🚆 *Inveraray, then bus.* ☐ *Apr–Sep: 10am–5pm daily.* 📷 ♿ *limited.*

T HE FIRST OPEN-AIR museum in Scotland, Auchindrain illuminates the working lives of the kind of farming community typical of the Highlands until the late 19th century. Constituting a township of some 20 thatched cottages, the site was communally farmed by its tenants until the last one retired in 1962. Visitors can wander through the houses, most of which combine living space, kitchen and a cattle shed all under one roof. They are furnished with box beds and rush lamps, and edged by herb gardens. Auchindrain is a fascinating memorial to a time before the Highland farmers made the transition from subsistence to commercial farming.

A traditional crofter's plough at the Auchindrain Museum

Crarae Gardens ❸

Crarae, Argyll & Bute. 📞 *(01546) 886614, (01852) 200366.* 🚆 *Inveraray, then bus.* ☐ *9:30 am–sunset, daily.* 📷 ✔ *by appointment.* ♿ *limited.*

W IDELY CONSIDERED the most beguiling of the many gardens of the West Highlands, the Crarae Gardens *(see also pp20–21)* were created in the 1920s by Lady Grace Campbell. She was the aunt of explorer Reginald Farrer, whose specimens from Tibet were the beginnings of a collection of exotic plants. The gardens now resemble a Himalayan ravine, nourished by the warmth of the Gulf Stream and the high rainfall of the region. Although many unusual Himalayan rhododendrons flourish here, the gardens are also home to exotic plants from Tasmania, New Zealand and the United States. Great plant collectors still contribute to the gardens, which are at their best in late spring.

Jura ❹

Argyll & Bute. 🧍 *250.* ⛴ *from Kennacraig to Islay, Islay to Jura.* ℹ️ *Bowmore (01496) 810254.*

B ARREN, MOUNTAINOUS and overrun by red deer, the Isle of Jura has only one road, which connects the single village of Craighouse to the Islay ferry. Though walking is restricted from August to October during the stalking (deer-hunting) season, Jura offers superb hill-walking, especially on the slopes of the three main peaks known as the Paps of Jura. The tallest of these is Beinn An Oir at 784 m (2,572 ft). Beyond the northern tip of the isle are the notorious whirlpools of Corryvreckan. The author George Orwell, who came to the island to write his final novel, *1984*, nearly lost his life here in 1946 when he fell into the water. A legend tells of Prince Breackan who was

Lagavulin distillery, producer of one of Scotland's finest malts, on Islay

Mist crowning the Paps of Jura, seen at sunset across the Sound of Islay

drowned in his attempt to win the hand of a princess. He tried to keep his boat anchored in the whirlpool for three days, held by ropes made of hemp, wool and maidens' hair, until one rope, containing the hair of an unfaithful girl, finally broke.

Islay ❺

Argyll & Bute. 🎿 3,500. 🚢 from Kennacraig. 🚹 Bowmore (08707) 200617. W www.isle-of-islay.com

THE MOST SOUTHERLY of the Western Isles, Islay (pronounced 'Eyeluh') is the home of such respected Highland single malt whiskies *(see p30)* as Lagavulin and Laphroaig. Most of the island's distilleries produce heavily-peated malts with a distinctive tang of the sea. The Georgian village of Bowmore has the island's oldest distillery and a circular church designed to minimize the Devil's possible lurking-places. The **Museum of Islay Life** in Port Charlotte contains a wealth of fascinating information concerning the island's social and natural history. Eleven kilometres (7 miles) east of Port Ellen stands the Kildalton Cross. A block of local green stone adorned with Old Testament scenes, it is one of the most impressive 8th-century

Celtic crosses in Britain. Worth a visit for its archaeological and historical interest is the medieval stronghold of the Lords of the Isles, **Finlaggan**, which is under excavation. Islay's superb beaches support a variety of bird life, some of which can be seen at the Royal Society for the Protection of Birds (RSPB) reserve at Gruinart.

🏛 **Museum of Islay Life**
Port Charlotte. 📞 (01496) 850358. ⏰ Easter– Oct: daily (Sun pm). 🅿 ♿

Kintyre ❻

Argyll & Bute. 🎿 8,000. 🚢 Oban. 🚌 Campbeltown. 🚹 Campbeltown (01586) 552056.
W www.visitscottishheartlands.com

A LONG, NARROW PENINSULA stretching far south of Glasgow, Kintyre has superb views across to the islands of Gigha, Islay and Jura. The 14 km (9 mile) Crinan Canal,

which opened in 1801 and has a total of 15 locks, bustles with pleasure craft in the summer. The town of Tarbert (meaning "isthmus" in Gaelic) takes its name from the neck on which it stands, which is narrow enough to drag a boat across, between the waters of Loch Fyne and West Loch Tarbert. This feat was first achieved by the Viking King Magnus Barfud who, in 1198, was granted by treaty as much land as he could sail around.

Travelling further south past Campbeltown, the B842 road ends at the headland known as the Mull of Kintyre, which was made famous when former Beatle Paul McCartney commercialized a traditional pipe tune of the same name. Westward from Kintyre lies the isle of Rathlin. It is here that Robert the Bruce learned patience in his constant struggles against the English by observing a spider weaving an elaborate web in a cave.

Sailing boats moored at Tarbert harbour, Kintyre

Loch Awe **7**

Argyll. � 🚉 *Dallamally.* ℹ️ *Inveraray*
(01499) 302063.

O NE OF THE longest freshwater lochs in Scotland,
Loch Awe stretches 40 km (25
miles) across a glen in the
southwestern Highlands. A
short drive east from the town
of Lochawe are the remains of
Kilchurn Castle, abandoned
after being struck by lightning
in the 18th century. Dwarfing
the castle is Ben Cruachan.
The huge summit of 1,125 m
(3,695 ft) can be reached by
the narrow Pass of Brander,
where Robert the Bruce fought
the Clan MacDougal in 1308.
Near the village of Taynuilt, the
preserved Lorn Furnace at
Bonawe is a reminder of the
iron-smelting industry that
destroyed much of the area's
woodland in the last centuries.
On the A816, to the south of
the loch, is **Kilmartin House**.
The museum here displays
artifacts from local prehistoric
sites, as well as reconstructions
of boats, utensils and jewellery,
providing a vivid glimpse of
life in prehistoric Scotland.

🏛 **Kilmartin House**
Kilmartin. 📞 *(01546) 510278.* ⭕
daily. 🏷🔗 🌐 www.kilmartin.org

**McCaig's Tower looming over the
houses and fishing boats of Oban**

Oban **8**

Argyll. 🏔 *8,500.* 🚂 🚉 🚢
ℹ️ *Argyll Square (01631) 563122.*
🌐 www.visitscotland.com

K NOWN AS THE "Gateway to
the Isles", this bustling
port on the Firth of Lorne
commands fine views of the
Argyll coast. Shops crowd the
seafront around the "little bay"
which gives Oban its name,
and fresh fish is always for
sale on the busy pier. Regular
ferries leave for Mull, Coll,
Tiree, Barra, South Uist, Islay,
Colonsay and Lismore, making
Oban one of the most visited

places on the west coast.
Built on a steep hill, the town
is dominated by the immense
McCaig's Tower, an eccentric
Colosseum-like structure built
in the 1800s. Other major landmarks are the pink granite
cathedral and the 600-year-old
ruined keep, **Dunollie Castle**,
once the northern outpost of
the Dalriadic Scots. Among
Oban's other attractions are
working centres for glass and
pottery, and Oban Distillery,
producers of fine malt whisky.
Early in August yachts converge on the town for West
Highland Week, while at the
end of the month, Oban's
Highland Games take place.
Nearby Kilmore, Taynuilt and
Tobermory, on Mull, also host
summer Highland Games.

ENVIRONS: A few miles north
of Oban, off the A85, is the
13th-century **Dunstaffnage
Castle** where Flora MacDonald
was briefly imprisoned for
helping Bonnie Prince Charlie
escape in 1746. Further north
at Barcaldine is the **Scottish
Sealife Sanctuary**. This
centre combines looking after
injured and orphaned seals,
with displays of underwater
life. The **Rare Breeds Park**,
situated 3 km (2 miles) south
of Oban, has unusual breeds
of farm animals such as Soay
and Jacobs sheep. The Isle of
Seil is reached via the 18th
century "Bridge over the
Atlantic." The **Island Folk
Museum** on the small island
off Easdale describes the
history of slate mining in the
area. To the south is **Arduaine
Garden**, noted for its varieties
of spring blooming rhododendrons and azaleas.

⚓ **Dunstaffnage Castle**
Connel. 📞 *(01631) 562465.* ⭕ *daily.*
🔴 *Oct–Mar: Thu pm & Fri.* 🏷 ✔
🐟 **Scottish Sealife
Sanctuary**
Barcaldine, near Connel. 📞 *(01631)*
720386. ⭕ *daily.* 🏷🔗
🐟 **Rare Breeds Park**
New Barren. 📞 *(01631) 770608.*
⭕ *Easter–Oct: daily.* 🏷🔗
🏛 **Island Folk Museum**
Easdale. 📞 *(01852) 300370.*
⭕ *Apr–Oct: daily.*
🌿 **Arduaine Garden**
(NTS) Kilmelford. 📞 *(01852) 200366.*
⭕ *daily.* 🏷🔗 ✔ *by appointment.*

The ruins of Kilchurn Castle on the shore of Loch Awe

The picturesque kaleidoscope of houses in Tobermory, one of Mull's most favoured tourist stops

Mull ❾

Argyll. 🏠 *2,800.* ⛴ *from Oban,
Lochaline and Kilchoan; from
Fionnphort, on Mull, to Iona.*
🛈 *Tobermory (01688) 302182;
Craignure (01680) 812377.*

THE LARGEST of the Inner
Hebridean islands, Mull
features rough moorlands, the
rocky peak of Ben More and
a splendid beach at Calgary.
Most roads follow the coastline, affording wonderful sea-
views. From Craignure, the
Mull and West Highland Railway offers a short trip to the
baronial **Torosay Castle**. The
gardens are lined with statues,
and inside is a wealth of 19th-
century paintings and furniture.
On a promontory to the east
lies the 13th-century **Duart
Castle**, home of the chief of
Clan Maclean. You can visit the
Banqueting Hall, State Rooms
and the dungeons that once
held prisoners from a Spanish
Armada galleon, sunk in 1588
by one Donald Maclean. At the
northern end of Mull is the
town of **Tobermory**, with its
brightly coloured buildings
along the seafront. Built as a
fishing village in 1788, it is now
a popular harbour for yachts.

ENVIRONS: The small and very
beautiful island of **Iona** is
one of the biggest attractions
on Scotland's west coast. A
restored abbey stands on the
site where Irish missionary
St Columba began his crusade
in 563 and made Iona the
home of Christianity in
Europe. In the abbey graveyard, 48 Scottish kings are

said to be buried. During the
summer months the abbey
has a large influx of visitors.
If the weather is fine, make
a trip to **Fingal's Cave** on the
Isle of Staffa *(see p15).* One of
Scotland's natural wonders, the
cave is surrounded by "organ
pipes" of basalt, the inspiration
for Mendelssohn's *Hebrides
Overture.* Boat trips run there
from Fionnphort and Ulva, and
to the seven **Treshnish Isles**.
These uninhabited isles are a
sanctuary for thousands of seabirds, including puffins, razorbills, kittiwakes and skuas.
Dutchman's Cap is the most
distinctive in shape, but Lunga
is the main stop for tour boats.

♣ **Torosay Castle**
Near Craignure. (*(01680) 812421.*
Castle ◯ *Easter–end-Oct: daily.* ✔
Gardens ◯ *daily.* ◙ ♿ *gardens.*
♣ **Duart Castle**
Off A849, near Craignure. (*(01680)
812309.* ◯ *May–mid-Oct: daily.* ◙
🚢 **Fingal's Cave and
Treshnish Isles**
⛴ *Easter–Oct.* (*(01688) 400242.
Timetable varies, call for details.* ◙

Coll and Tiree ❿

Argyll. 🏠 *950.* ⛴ *from Oban.*
✗ *from Glasgow to Tiree only.*
🛈 *Oban (01631) 563122.*

THESE LOW, FERTILE islands are
the most westerly in the
Inner Hebrides and, despite
frequent notices of winter gale
warnings, record higher hours
of sunshine than the rest of
Britain. Predominantly crofting
communities, they offer beautiful beaches and impressive
surf. Tiree's soil is 60 per cent
shell sand, so no trees can
grow. In spring, both islands
are ablaze with wild flowers.
Breacachadh Castle, the restored 15th-century home of
Clan Maclean until 1750, overlooks a bay in south Coll but
is not open to the public. Tiree
has two free museums, the
**Sandaig Thatched House
Museum**, with items from life
in the late 19th and early 20th
centuries, and the **Skerryvore
Lighthouse Museum** in
Hynish – the lighthouse stands
20 km (12 miles) offshore.

A traditional croft building on the island of Coll

The Three Sisters, Glencoe, rising majestically in the late autumn sunshine

Glencoe ⓫

Lochaber. 🚆 *Fort William.*
🚌 *Glencoe.* ℹ️ *NTS Visitor Centre,*
Ballachulish (01855) 811307. ⏱ *Apr–*
Oct: 9:30am–5:30pm daily. 🖼 ♿

R ENOWNED for its awesome
scenery and savage history,
Glencoe was compared by
Dickens to "a burial ground of
a race of giants". The precipitous cliffs of Buachaille Etive
Mor and the knife-edged ridge
of Aonach Eagach present a
formidable challenge even to
experienced mountaineers.

Against a backdrop of craggy
peaks and the tumbling River
Coe, the Glen offers superb
hill-walking. Stout footwear,
waterproofs and attention to
safety warnings are essential.
Details of routes, ranging from
an easy walk in the vicinity of
Signal Rock (from which the
signal was given to com-
mence the massacre) to a stiff
10-km (6-mile) haul up the
Devil's Staircase can be had
from the Visitor Centre.
Guided walks are offered in
summer by the NTS Ranger
Service. East of Glencoe lies

Rannoch Moor, one of the
emptiest areas in Britain. A
dramatic way to view it is
from the chairlift at the
Glencoe Ski Centre.
    To the southwest, a minor
road leads down beautiful
Glen Etive to the head of
Loch Etive. This impressive
sea loch eventually emerges
on the coast at the Connel
Bridge north of Oban.
    At the Ballachulish Bridge a
side road branches to Kinloch-
leven. This village, at the head
of a long attractive loch, combines two contrasting images
of dramatic mountains and an
austere aluminium works.

⛷ **Glencoe Ski Centre**
Kingshouse, Glencoe. ☎ *(01855)*
851226. ⏱ *daily.* 🖼 ♿ *limited.*

Fort William ⓬

Lochaber. 🏘 *11,000.* 🚆 🚌
ℹ️ *(01397) 703781.*
🌐 *www.visitscotland.com*

F ORT WILLIAM, one of the
major towns on the west
coast, is noted not for its looks
but for its location at the foot
of Ben Nevis. The **Jacobite**
Steam Train runs the magical
route from here to Mallaig *(see*
p137), as do ordinary trains.

🚂 **Jacobite Steam Train**
🚆 *Fort William.* ☎ *(01463) 239026.*
Departs late-May–mid-Oct: 10:20am
Mon–Fri.

THE MASSACRE OF GLENCOE

In 1692, the chief of the Glencoe MacDonalds was five
days late in registering an oath of submission to William III,
giving the government an excuse to root out a nest of
Jacobite supporters. For ten days 130 soldiers, captained
by Robert Campbell, were hospitably entertained by the
unsuspecting MacDonalds. At dawn on 13 February, in a
terrible breach of trust, the soldiers fell on their hosts, kill-
ing some 38 MacDonalds. Many more died in their wintry
mountain hideouts. The mas-
sacre, unsurprisingly, became
a political scandal, though
there were to be no
official reprimands
for three years.

Detail of *The*
Massacre of Glencoe
by James Hamilton

Ben Nevis

Lochaber. 🚆 *Fort William.* 🚌 *Glen Nevis.* ℹ️ *Ionad Nibheis Visitor Centre, Glen Nevis (01397) 705922.* 🕐 *Easter–Oct: daily.* ♿

WITH ITS SUMMIT in cloud for about nine days out of ten, and capable of developing blizzard conditions at any time of the year, Britain's highest mountain is a mishmash of metamorphic and volcanic rocks. The sheer northeastern face poses a technical challenge to experienced rock climbers. By contrast, thousands of visitors each year make their way to the peak via a relatively gentle, but long and stony, western path. Motorbikes, even cars, have ascended via this path, and runners pound up and down it during the annual Ben Nevis

Ben Nevis as seen from the northwest

Race. On one of the rare fine days, visitors who make their way to the summit will be rewarded with breathtaking views. On a cloudy day, a walk through the lush landscape of

Glen Nevis may be more rewarding than making an ascent, which will reveal little more at the summit than a ruined observatory and memorials testifying to the tragic deaths of walkers and climbers.

To the north of Ben Nevis, the **Nevis Range Gondola** provides access to a ski centre, restaurant and other tourist facilities, all situated at 650 m (2,130 ft).

🚠 **Nevis Range Gondola**
Off A82, Torlundy. 🕐 *(01397) 705825.* 🕐 *10am–5pm daily, (weather permitting).*

CLIMBING BEN NEVIS

The main path up Ben Nevis, called the Old Bridle Path, starts in Glen Nevis. Numerous visitors each year are lulled into a false sense of security by mild weather conditions in the Glen, occasionally with fatal results. You must wear stout footwear (not trainers) and take hat and gloves and enough layers of clothing to allow for sub-zero temperatures at the top, even on a summer day. Also take plenty of food and drink, and an Ordnance Survey map and compass even if you think you won't need them. It is amazingly easy to lose the path in cloudy or snowy conditions, especially when starting the descent.

TIPS FOR WALKERS

Starting Point ①: *Visitor Centre.*
Starting Point ②: *Achintee.*
Starting Point ③: *400 m (440 yds) beyond campsite (very limited parking).*
Length: *16 km (10 miles); 6–8 hours average for round trip.*
Weather Information: *Western Highlands (09068) 500442.*
Level: *moderate difficulty on a dry day with broken cloud, but prone to rapid weather change; extremely difficult in snow.*

KEY

■ ■ Old Bridle Path
═══ Minor road
🔺 Camping
☀ Viewpoint
🅿 Parking
ℹ️ Visitor centre

0 metres   1,000
0 yards   1,000

Road to the Isles Tour ⑭

THIS SCENIC ROUTE goes past vast mountain corridors, breathtaking beaches of white sand and tiny villages to the town of Mallaig, one of the ferry ports for the isles of Skye, Rum, Eigg, Muck and Canna. In addition to stunning scenery, the area is steeped in Jacobite history *(see p147).*

SKYE

LOCH MORAR

TIPS FOR DRIVERS

Tour length: *72 km (45 miles).*
Stopping-off points: *Glenfinnan NTS Visitors' Centre (01397 722-250) explains the Jacobite risings and serves refreshments; the Old Library Lodge in Arisaig serves excellent Scottish food.*

Mallaig ⑦
The Road to the Isles ends at Mallaig, an active little fishing port with a very good harbour and one of the ferry links to the Isle of Skye *(see pp152–3).*

Morar ⑥
The road continues through Morar, renowned for its white sands, and Loch Morar, rumoured to be the home of a 12-m (40-ft) monster known as Morag.

Prince's Cairn ⑤
The road crosses the Ardnish Peninsula to Loch Nan Uamh, where a cairn marks the spot from which Bonnie Prince Charlie left for France in 1746.

Ardnamurchan Peninsula ⑮

Argyll. 🚗 *Corran Ferry on A82 from Glencoe to Fort William, or Fishnish (Mull) to Kilchoan.* ℹ️ *Fort William (01397) 703781.*

THIS PENINSULA and the adjacent areas of Moidart and Morvern are some of the west coast's best-kept secrets. They are characterized by a sinuous coastline, rocky mountains and beaches. Some of the best beaches are found at the tip of the peninsula, the most westerly point of mainland Britain.
    The **Ardnamurchan Point Visitor Centre** at Kilchoan explores the history of lighthouses and light-keeping. The 1846 lighthouse was designed by Alan Stevenson, father of author Robert Louis Stevenson. It is one of many built by the Stevenson family throughout Britain.
    The award-winning **Ardnamurchan Natural History Centre** at Glenmore has encouraged wildlife to

A view from Roshven, near Arisaig, across to the islands of Eigg and Rum

inhabit its "living building", and wild red deer can even graze on its turf roof. An enchanting wooded road runs from Salen to Strontian, or you can go north to Acharacle.

ℹ️ **Ardnamurchan Point Visitor Centre**
Kilchoan. ☎️ *(01972) 510210.* ⏰ *Apr–Oct: daily.* 📷 ♿
🏛 **Ardnamurchan Natural History Centre**
Glenmore. ☎️ *(01972) 500209.* ⏰ *Easter–Oct: daily.* 📷 *exhibition only.* ♿

Rum, Eigg, Muck and Canna ⑯

Small Isles. 🚶 *150.* 🚢 *from Mallaig or Arisaig.* ♿ *Canna only.* ℹ️ *Mallaig (01687) 462170.*

EACH OF THE four "small isles" has an individual character and atmosphere, but shares a sense of tranquillity. Canna is a narrow island surrounded by cliffs and has a scattering of unworked archaeological sites.

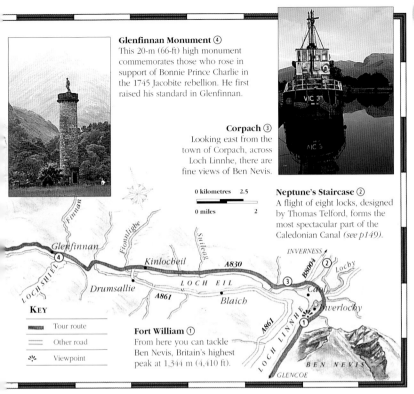

Glenfinnan Monument ④
This 20-m (66-ft) high monument commemorates those who rose in support of Bonnie Prince Charlie in the 1745 Jacobite rebellion. He first raised his standard in Glenfinnan.

Corpach ③
Looking east from the town of Corpach, across Loch Linnhe, there are fine views of Ben Nevis.

0 kilometres 2.5
0 miles 2

Neptune's Staircase ②
A flight of eight locks, designed by Thomas Telford, forms the most spectacular part of the Caledonian Canal (see p149).

Fort William ①
From here you can tackle Ben Nevis, Britain's highest peak at 1,344 m (4,410 ft).

KEY
Tour route
Other road
Viewpoint

Once owned by Gaelic scholar John Lorne Campbell, it now belongs to the National Trust for Scotland. It has few inhabitants and little accommodation.

Eigg is the most varied of the four islands. Dominated by the distinctive sugarloaf hill, the Sgurr of Eigg, it has a glorious beach with "singing sands" that make odd noises when moved by feet or by the wind. Here the islanders symbolize the spirit of community land ownership, having successfully led a high-profile campaign to buy their island from their landlord.

Muck takes its name from the Gaelic for "pig", which it is said to resemble in shape. The smallest of the islands, but no less charming, it is owned by a family who live and farm on the island. Rum

is the largest and most magnificent island, with scabrous peaks that bear Norse names and are home to an unusual colony of Manx shearwater birds. The island's rough tracks make it best suited to the active visitor. Now owned by Scottish Natural Heritage and a centre for red deer research, it previously belonged to the wealthy Bullough family who built

Colourful fishing boats in Mallaig harbour

Kinloch Castle. Its design and furnishings were revolutionary at the time and it remains a fascinating piece of design history.

⚓ **Kinloch Castle, Rum**
📞 (01687) 462037. ⬜ Apr–Oct: daily; Nov–Mar: call for details.

Mallaig ⑰

Lochaber. 🏃 980. 🚂 🚌 ⛴ from Ardvasar (Skye). 🛈 (01687) 462170.

THE HEART OF Mallaig is its harbour, which has an active fishing fleet and ferries that serve the "small isles" and Skye. The atmosphere is rather more commercial than leisurely, but it is set in an area of outstanding beauty. In the village itself is **Mallaig Marine World**, which incorporates aquariums and a permanent fishery exhibition.

🐟 **Mallaig Marine World**
📞 (01687) 462292. ⬜ Mar–Oct: daily; Nov–Feb: Mon–Sat. by appointment.

Killiecrankie Walk ⑱

In an area famous for its scenery and historical connections, this circular walk offers views that are typical to the Highlands. The route is fairly flat, though ringed by mountains, and meanders through a wooded gorge, passing the Soldier's Leap and a Victorian viaduct.

There are ideal picnic spots along the way, and the shores of man-made Loch Faskally are lined with beautiful trees. Returning along the River Tummel, the route crosses one of Queen Victoria's favourite Highland areas before it doubles back to complete the circuit.

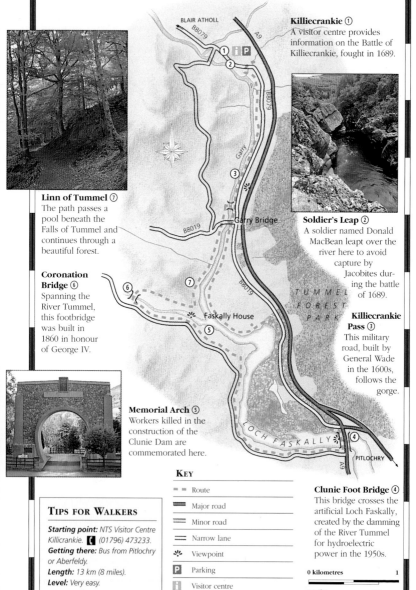

Killiecrankie ①
A visitor centre provides information on the Battle of Killiecrankie, fought in 1689.

Linn of Tummel ⑦
The path passes a pool beneath the Falls of Tummel and continues through a beautiful forest.

Coronation Bridge ⑥
Spanning the River Tummel, this footbridge was built in 1860 in honour of George IV.

Soldier's Leap ②
A soldier named Donald MacBean leapt over the river here to avoid capture by Jacobites during the battle of 1689.

Killiecrankie Pass ③
This military road, built by General Wade in the 1600s, follows the gorge.

Memorial Arch ⑤
Workers killed in the construction of the Clunie Dam are commemorated here.

Clunie Foot Bridge ④
This bridge crosses the artificial Loch Faskally, created by the damming of the River Tummel for hydroelectric power in the 1950s.

Map labels: BLAIR ATHOLL, B8079, A9, B8079, Garry, Garry Bridge, B8019, B8019, Faskally House, TUMMEL FOREST PARK, LOCH FASKALLY, PITLOCHRY, A9

KEY

▪ ▪	Route
	Major road
	Minor road
	Narrow lane
☀	Viewpoint
P	Parking
i	Visitor centre

0 kilometres   1
0 miles   0.5

TIPS FOR WALKERS

Starting point: NTS Visitor Centre Killicrankie. **C** (01796) 473233.
Getting there: Bus from Pitlochry or Aberfeldy.
Length: 13 km (8 miles).
Level: Very easy.

The distinctive white turrets and façade of the ducal Blair Castle

One of Scotland's most famous stages, the **Festival Theatre**, is located in Port-na-Craig. It operates a year-round programme with performances changing daily.

Blair Athol Distillery
Perth Rd. (01796) 482003.
Easter–Sep: daily (Sun: pm); Oct–Easter: Mon–Fri. limited.
Festival Theatre
Port-na-Craig. (01796) 472680.
mid-May–Oct: daily. for plays.
Power Station Visitor Centre
Port-na-Craig. (01796) 473152.
Apr–Oct: daily.

Blair Castle 19

Blair Atholl, Perthshire. (01796) 481207. Blair Atholl. Apr–Oct: 9:30am–4:30pm daily. limited. www.blair-castle.co.uk

THIS RAMBLING, turreted castle has been altered and extended so often in its 700-year history that it now provides a unique insight into the history and changing tastes of aristocratic life in the Highlands.

The elegant 18th-century wing, with its draughty passages hung with antlers, has a display that includes the gloves and pipe of Bonnie Prince Charlie (see p153), who spent two days here gathering support for a Jacobite uprising (see p147). Family portraits span 300 years, and include paintings by such masters as Johann Zoffany and Sir Peter Lely. Sir Edwin Landseer's *Death of a Hart in Glen Tilt* (1850) was painted nearby and hangs in the ballroom.

Queen Victoria visited the castle in 1844 and conferred on its owners, the Dukes of Atholl, the distinction of being allowed to maintain a private army. The Atholl Highlanders, are still in existence today.

Pitlochry 20

Perthshire. 2,500. 22 Atholl Rd (01796) 472215. www.perthshire.co.uk

SURROUNDED BY the pine-forested hills of the central Highlands, Pitlochry became a famous town after Queen Victoria described it as one of the finest resorts in Europe.

In early summer, wild salmon leap up the ladder built into the Power Station Dam on their way to spawning grounds further up the river. The **Power Station Visitor Centre** outlines the hydro-electric scheme, which harnesses the waters of the River Tummel.

Blair Athol Distillery, the home of Bell's whisky, offers guided tours in the art of whisky making (see pp30–31).

The ruins of Dunkeld Cathedral

Dunkeld 21

Tayside. 2,200. Birnam. The Cross (01350) 727688.

SITUATED BY the River Tay, this ancient and charming village was all but destroyed in the Battle of Dunkeld, a Jacobite defeat, in 1689. The **Little Houses** lining Cathedral Street were the first to be rebuilt, and remain fine examples of an imaginative restoration.

The sad ruins of the 14th-century **cathedral** enjoy an idyllic setting on shady lawns beside the Tay, against a backdrop of steep and wooded hills. The choir is used as the parish church, and its north wall contains a Leper's Squint (a little hole through which lepers could see the altar during mass). It was while on holiday in the countryside around Dunkeld that the children's author, Beatrix Potter, found the inspiration for her Peter Rabbit stories.

Salmon ladder at the Power Station Dam in Pitlochry

The Cairngorms ㉒

Wild goat

Rising to a height of 1,309 m (4,296 ft), the Cairngorm mountains form the highest landmass in Britain. Cairn Gorm itself is the site of one of Britain's first ski centres. A weather station at the summit provides regular reports, essential in an area known for sudden changes of weather. Walkers should be sure to follow the mountain code without fail. During the summer a funicular railway climbs Cairn Gorm affording superb views over the Spey Valley. Many estates in the valley have centres which introduce the visitor to Highland land use.

Strathspey Steam Railway
This track between Aviemore and Broomhill dates from1863.

Aviemore, the commercial centre of the Cairngorms, provides buses to the ski area 13 km (8 miles) away.

Kincraig Highland Wildlife Park
Driving through this park, the visitor can see bison alongside bears, wolves and wild boar. All of these animals were once common in the Highlands.

The Cairngorms by Aviemore

Rothiemurchus Estate
Highland cattle can be seen among many other creatures at Rothiemurchus. A visitor centre provides guided walks and illustrates life on a Highland estate.

Loch Garten Nature Reserve
Ospreys now thrive in this reserve, which was established in 1959 to protect the first pair seen in Britain for 50 years.

GRANTOWN-ON-SPEY

Broomhill

A 95

B970

Nethy Bridge

CH
RTEN

CH
LICH

Nethy

P

CAIRN GORM
1,245 m
(4,084 ft)

BEN MACDHUI
1,309 m
(4,296 ft)

CAIRNGORM
MOUNTAINS

Ben MacDhui is Britain's second highest peak, after Ben Nevis.

VISITORS' CHECKLIST

The Highlands. 🚂 🚌 *Aviemore.*
ℹ️ *Grampian Rd, Aviemore (01479) 810363.* **Cairngorm Reindeer Centre**, *Loch Morlich.*
📞 *(01479) 861228.* ⭘ *daily.*
🎿 **Kincraig Highland Wildlife Park** 📞 *(01540) 651270.* ⭘ *daily (weather permitting).* **Rothiemurchus Visitor Centre**, *near Aviemore.* 📞 *(01479) 810858.*
⭘ *daily.* **Loch Garten Nature Reserve** 📞 *(01479) 821409.*
⭘ *daily.* **Skiing & Funicular Railway** 📞 *(01479) 861261.*

The Cairngorm Reindeer Centre provides walks in the hills among Britain's only herd of reindeer.

Skiing
During the winter, chairlifts and tows provide access to more than 28 ski runs on Cairn Gorm's northern flanks.

FLORA OF THE CAIRNGORMS

With mixed woodland at their base and the summits forming a sub-polar plateau, the Cairngorms present a huge variety of flora. Ancient Caledonian pines (once common in the area) survive in Abernethy Forest, while arctic flowers flourish in the heights.

The Cairngorm plateau holds little life except lichen (Britain's oldest plant), wood rush and cushions of moss campion, which is often completely covered with pink flowers.

Shady corries are important areas for alpine plants such as arctic mouse-ear, hare's foot sedge, mountain rock-cress and alpine speedwell.

Pinewoods occupy the higher slopes, revealing purple heather as they become sparser.

Mixed woodland covers the lower ground which is carpeted with heather and deergrass.

1,200 m (3,950 ft)
1,000 m (3,300 ft)
800 m (2,650 ft)
600 m (2,000 ft)
400 m (1,300 ft)
200 m (650 ft)
0 m (0 ft)

An idealized section of the Cairngorm plateau

KEY

ℹ️	Tourist information
▬▬▬	Major road
⋯⋯	Minor road
═══	Narrow lane
– –	Footpath
🎿	Viewpoint

Aberdeen ㉓

Scotland's third largest city and Europe's offshore oil capital, Aberdeen has prospered since the discovery of oil in the North Sea in the early 1970s. The sea bed has now yielded 50 oilfields. Widely known as the Granite City, its forbidding and rugged outlines are softened by year-round floral displays in the public parks and gardens, the Duthie Park Winter Gardens being the largest indoor gardens in Europe. Aberdeen's busy harbour can be observed from the picturesque village of Footdee at the southern end of the city's 2 mile (3 km) sandy beach.

The spires of Aberdeen, rising behind the city harbour

Exploring Aberdeen

The city centre flanks the 1.5-km (1-mile) long Union Street, ending to the east at the Mercat Cross. The cross stands by Castlegate, the one-time site of the city castle, and now only a marketplace. From here, the cobbled Shiprow meanders southwest and passes Provost Ross's House on its way to the harbour. A bus can be taken 1.5 km (1 mile) north of the centre to Old Aberdeen, which, with its medieval streets and wynds (narrow, winding lanes), has the peaceful character of a separate village. Driving is restricted in some streets.

♛ King's College

College Bounds, Old Aberdeen. ((01224) 273702. ◯ daily. ᴧ
Founded in 1495 as the city's first university, the college now has a visitor centre that provides details of its history. The interdenominational chapel, consecutively Catholic and Protestant in the past, has a distinctive lantern tower, rebuilt after a storm in 1633. Douglas Strachan's stained-glass windows add a modern touch to the interior, which contains a 1540 pulpit, later carved with heads of Stuart monarchs.

♜ St Andrew's Cathedral

King St. ((01224) 640119. ◯ May–Sep: Tues–Fri. ᴧ ☑ by arrangement.
The Mother Church of the Episcopal Church in the United States, St Andrew's has a memorial to Samuel Seabury, the first Episcopalian bishop in the US, who was consecrated in Aberdeen in 1784. A series of coats of arms adorns the ceiling above the north and south aisles, contrasting colourfully with the white walls and pillars. They represent the American states and the Jacobite families of Aberdeenshire.

The elegant lantern tower of the chapel at King's College

♜ Art Gallery

Schoolhill. ((01224) 523700. ◯ daily. ᴧ ☑ www.aberdeencity.gov.uk
Housed in a Neo-Classical building, the Art Gallery has a wide range of exhibitions, with an emphasis on modern works. A collection of Aberdonian silver is included among the decorative arts on the ground floor. A permanent collection of 18th- to 20th-century art features such names as Toulouse-Lautrec, Raeburn and Reynolds. Local granite merchant Alex Macdonald bequeathed a number of the works on display.

♞ St Nicholas Kirk

Union St. ((01224) 643494. ◯ May–Sep: daily; Oct–Apr: Mon–Fri (am). ᴧ
Founded in the 12th century, St Nicholas is Scotland's largest parish church. Though the present structure dates from 1752, many earlier relics can be seen inside. After damage during the Reformation, the interior was divided into two. A chapel in the East Church holds iron rings used to secure witches in the 17th century, while in the West Church there are embroidered panels attributed to Mary Jameson (1597–1644).

♜ Maritime Museum

Shiprow. ((01224) 337700. ◯ daily. ᴧ ☑ www.aagm.co.uk
Overlooking the harbour is the Provost Ross's House, which dates back to 1593. The Maritime Museum housed here traces the history of Aberdeen's long seafaring tradition. The exhibitions cover numerous topics from shipwrecks, rescues and ship-building to models that illustrate the workings of the many oil installations situated off the east coast of Scotland.

♞ St Machar's Cathedral

The Chanonry. ((01224) 485988. ◯ daily. ᴧ ☑ www.stmachar.com
Dominating Old Aberdeen, the 15th-century St Machar's Cathedral is the oldest granite building in the city. The stonework of one arch dates back to the 14th century. The nave now serves as a parish church and its magnificent oak ceiling is adorned with the coats of arms of 48 popes, emperors and princes of Christendom.

PROVOST SKENE'S HOUSE

Guestrow. **(** *(01224) 641086.* **(** *daily.* **▨** **W** www.aagm.co.uk
Once the home of Sir George Skene, a 17th-century provost
(mayor) of Aberdeen, the house was built in 1545 and remains
one of the oldest houses in the city. Inside, period rooms span
200 years of design. The Duke of Cumberland stayed here
during the weeks preceding the Battle of Culloden *(see p146).*

VISITORS' CHECKLIST

Grampian. **▥** *212,000.*
✕ *13 km (8 miles) NW Aberdeen.*
≥ **🚌** *Guild St.* **ℹ** *Union St*
(01224) 288828. **▦** *Fri, Sat.*

The 18th-century Parlour,
with its walnut harpsichord and
covered fire-side chairs, was the
informal room in which the
family would have tea.

The Regency Room typifies
early 19th-century elegance. A
harp dating from 1820 stands
by a Grecian-style sofa and a
French writing table.

The Painted Gallery has
one of Scotland's most important cycles of religious art. The
panels are early 17th century,
though the artist is unknown.

The 17th-century Great Hall
contains heavy oak dining
furniture. Provost Skene's
wood-carved coat of arms
hangs above the fireplace.

The Georgian Dining Room,
with its Classical design, was
the main formal room in the
16th century and still has its
original flagstone floor.

Entrance

ABERDEEN CITY CENTRE

Art Gallery ①
St Andrew's Cathedral ⑤
St Nicholas Kirk ②
Marischal College ④
Maritime Museum ⑦
Mercat Cross ⑥
Provost Skene's
  House ③

KEY

🚌 Bus station

≥ Train station

⛴ Ferry service

P Parking

ℹ Tourist information

✝ Church

0 metres   200

0 yards   200

Royal Deeside Tour ㉔

SINCE QUEEN VICTORIA'S purchase of the Balmoral Estate in 1852, Deeside has been best known as the summer home of the British Royal Family, though it has been associated with royalty since the time of Robert the Bruce in the 1300s. This route follows the Dee, one of the world's most prolific salmon rivers, through some magnificent Grampian scenery.

Muir of Dinnet Nature Reserve ④
An information centre on the A97 provides an excellent place from which to explore this beautiful mixed woodland area, formed by the retreating glaciers of the last Ice Age.

Balmoral ⑥
Bought by Queen Victoria for 30,000 guineas in 1852, after its owner choked to death on a fishbone, the castle was rebuilt in the Scottish Baronial style at Prince Albert's request.

Ballater ⑤
The old railway town of Ballater has royal warrants on many of its shop fronts. It grew as a 19th-century spa town, its waters reputedly providing a cure for tuberculosis.

Speyside Malt Whisky Trail ㉕

Moray. 🛈 *Elgin (01343) 542666.*
Ⓦ *www.maltwhiskytrail.com*

SUCH ARE THE climate and geology of the Grampian mountains and glens bordering the River Spey that half of Scotland's whisky distilleries are found on Speyside. They span a large area so a car is required. The signposted "Malt Whisky Trail" takes you to seven distilleries and one cooperage (a place where barrels are made), all with excellent visitor centres and tours of their premises.

There is no secret to whisky distilling (*see pp 30 –31*): essentially barley is steeped in water and allowed to grow, a process called "malting"; the grains are then dried with peat smoke, milled, mixed with water and allowed to ferment; the frothy liquid goes through a double process of distillation.

Oak casks, in which the maturing whisky is stored at the distilleries

The final result is a raw, rough whisky that is then stored in old oak sherry casks for 3 to 16 years, during which time it mellows. Worldwide, an average of 30 bottles of Scotch whisky are sold every second.

The visitor centres at each Whisky Trail distillery provide similar, and equally good, guided tours of the workings and audio-visual displays of their individual histories. Their entry charges are usually redeemable against the purchase of a bottle of whisky. A different slant on the process is given at the **Speyside Cooperage**. Here the visitor can learn about the making of the wooden casks that are eventually used to store the whisky.

TIPS FOR DRIVERS

Length: *111 km (69 miles).*
Stopping-off points: *Crathes
Castle café.* ☐ *May–Sep: daily;
Station Restaurant, Ballater serves
traditional meals all day.*

Drum Castle ①
This impressive 13th-century keep
was granted by Robert the Bruce to
his standard bearer in 1323,
in gratitude for his services.

PETERHEAD
A96
A956
ABERDEEN
A93
A956

Banchory ③
Just south of the town is the
18th-century Brig o' Feugh,
where salmon leap.

• Peterculter

A980
A93
Dee
B9077
A90
STONEHAVEN

③

B974

Crathes Castle
and Gardens ②
This is the family home of
the Burnetts, who were
made Royal Foresters of
Drum by Robert the Bruce.
Along with the title, he
gave Alexander Burnett
the ivory Horn of Leys,
which is still on display.

0 kilometres   5

0 miles   4

KEY

▬▬ Tour route

▬▬ Other road

☆ Viewpoint

⚑ Benromach Distillery
Forres. 🄲 *(01309) 675968.* ☐
*Oct–Mar: Mon–Fri; Apr–Sep: Mon–
Sat; Jun, Jul, Aug: Sun.* 🏷 ⅙ ☑
⚑ Cardhu Distillery
Knockando. 🄲 *(01340) 872555.*
☐ *Jan–Jun: Mon–Fri; Jul–Sep:
Mon–Sun; Oct–Dec: Mon–Fri.* 🏷 ⅙
⊞ Dallas Dhu Distillery
Forres. 🄲 *(01309) 676548.* ☐ *Jan–
Mar: Mon–Thu, Sat, Sun; Apr–Sep: daily;
Oct–Mar: Mon–Wed, Sat, Sun.* 🏷 ⅙
⚑ Glenfiddich Distillery
Dufftown. 🄲 *(01340) 820373.*
☐ *Easter–mid-Oct: daily; mid-
Oct–Easter: Mon–Fri.* ⅙ ☑
⚑ Glen Grant Distillery
Rothes. 🄲 *(01340) 832118.* ☐
Apr–Oct: daily. 🏷 ☑ ⅙ *limited.*
⚑ The Glenlivet Distillery
Glenlivet. 🄲 *(01340) 821720.*
☐ *mid-Mar–Oct: daily.*
🏷 ☑ ⅙ *limited.*
⚑ Speyside Cooperage
Craigellachie. 🄲 *(01340) 871108.*
☐ *9:30am–4pm daily.*
🏷 ☑ ⅙ *limited.*
⚑ Strathisla Distillery
Keith. 🄲 *(01542) 783044.*
☐ *Apr–Oct: daily.* 🏷 ⅙ *limited.*

Elgin 26

Moray. 🏠 *25,000.* 🚊 🚌 🛈 *17
High St (01343) 542666.* 🏪 *Sat.*

WITH ITS COBBLED market-
place and crooked lanes,
the popular town of Elgin still
retains much of its medieval
layout. The 13th-century
cathedral ruins are all that
remain of one of Scotland's
architectural triumphs. Once
known as the Lantern of the
North, the cathedral was
severely damaged in 1390 by
the Wolf of Badenoch (the
son of Robert II) in revenge
for his excommunication by
the Bishop of Moray. Further
damage came in 1576 when
the Regent Moray ordered the
lead roofing to be stripped.
Among the remains is a Pictish
cross-slab in the nave and a
basin where one of the town's
benefactors, Andrew Anderson,
was kept as a baby by his
homeless mother. The **Elgin
Museum** has anthropological

and geological displays, while
the **Moray Motor Museum**
has over 40 cars and motorbikes, dating back to 1904.

⊞ Elgin Museum
1 High St. 🄲 *(01343) 543675.* ☐
Apr–Oct: Mon–Sat. 🏷 ⅙ ☑
⊞ Moray Motor Museum
Bridge St, Bishopmill. 🄲 *(01343)
544933.* ☐ *Easter–Oct: daily.* 🏷 ⅙

**Details of the central tower of
the 13th-century Elgin Cathedral**

An aerial picture of Fort George, illustrating its imposing position

Fort George ㉗

Inverness. ((01667) 460232. ≊ ⊟
Inverness, Nairn. ○ 9:30am–6:30pm
daily (Sun pm). ⬜ ✔ ⅃
w www.historic-scotland.gov.uk

ONE OF THE FINEST examples of European military architecture, Fort George holds a commanding position on the Moray Firth, ideally located to suppress the Highlands. Completed in 1769, the fort was built after the Jacobite risings to discourage further rebellion in the Highlanders, and has remained a military garrison ever since.

The **Regimental Museum** of the Highlanders Regiment is housed in the Fort. Some of the barrack rooms have been reconstructed to show the conditions of the common soldiers stationed here more than 200 years ago. The **Grand Magazine** contains an outstanding collection of arms and military equipment. Fort George's battlements also make an excellent place from which to watch dolphins playing in the waters of the Moray Firth.

Culloden ㉘

(NTS) Inverness. ≊ ⊟ Inverness.

THE DESOLATE battlefield of Culloden looks much as it did on 16 April 1746, the date of the last battle to be fought on British soil (see p45). Here the Jacobite cause, with the help of Bonnie Prince Charlie's

leadership (see p153), perished under the onslaught of nearly 9,000 troops, led by the Duke of Cumberland. Visitors can roam the battlefield, visit the clan graves and experience the audio-visual displays at the **NTS Visitor Centre**.

ENVIRONS: Roughly 1.5 km (1 mile) east of Culloden are the outstanding Neolithic burial sites at **Clava Cairns**.

🛈 **NTS Visitor Centre**
On the B9006 east of Inverness.
((01463) 790607. ○ daily.
● Jan. ⬜ ⅃

Cawdor Castle ㉙

On B9090 (off A96). ((01667) 404
401. ≊ Nairn, then bus or taxi. ▭
from Inverness. ○ Easter– Sep:
9:30am– 6:30pm; Oct–Easter: 9:30am–
4:30pm. ⬜ ⅃ gardens and ground
floor only. w www.cawdorcastle.com

WITH ITS TURRETED central tower, moat and drawbridge, Cawdor Castle is one of the most romantic stately homes in the Highlands. Though the castle is famed for being the 11th-century home of Shakespeare's tragic character Macbeth, and the scene of his murder of King Duncan, it is historically unproven that either figure came here.

An ancient holly tree preserved in the vaults is said to be the one under which, in 1372, Thane William's donkey stopped for a rest during its master's search for a place to build a fortress. According to legend, this was how the site for the castle was chosen. Now, after 600 years of con-

tinuous occupation (it is still the home of the Thanes of Cawdor) the house contains a number of rare tapestries and portraits by the 18th-century painters Joshua Reynolds (1723–92) and George Romney (1734–1802). Furniture in the Pink Bedroom and Woodcock Room includes work by the 18th-century designers Chippendale and Sheraton. In the Old Kitchen, the huge Victorian cooking range stands as a shrine to below-stairs drudgery. The castle's grounds provide beautiful nature trails, as well as a nine-hole golf course.

The drawbridge on the eastern side of Cawdor Castle

Inverness ㉚

Highland. ⛰ 60,000. ≊ ⊟
🛈 Castle Wynd (01463) 234353.
w www.visithighlands.com

IN THE HIGHLANDS, all roads lead to the region's "capital", Inverness, the centre of communication, commerce and administration for six million outlying acres and their scattered populations. Despite

A contemporary picture, *The Battle of Culloden* (1746), by D Campbell

The red sandstone exterior of Inverness Castle high above the city centre, aglow in the light of the setting sun

being the largest city in the north, it is more like a town in its atmosphere, with a compact and easily accessible centre. Although sadly defaced by modern architecture, Inverness earns a worthy reputation for its floral displays in summer, and for the River Ness, which flows through the centre and adds considerable charm. The river is frequented by salmon fishermen during the summer, even where it runs through the city centre. Holding the high ground above the city is **Inverness Castle**, a Victorian building of red sandstone, now used as the court house. Just below the castle, next to the tourist information office, is **Inverness Museum and Art Gallery,** which houses permanent and touring exhibitions and runs workshops for children. The main shopping area fans out in three directions from here and includes a lively pedestrian precinct where pipers and other musicians can be found busking.

Just across the river is the **Scottish Kiltmaker Visitor Centre**, part of the Highland House of Fraser Group. Here visitors will get an insight into the history, culture and tradition of the kilt, with audiovisual and workshop presentations of kiltmaking. On the banks of the Ness, stands **Eden Court Theatre**, which

Kilt maker with Royal Stuart tartan

has a varied programme of local and international performers. Following the tree-lined banks of the river further upstream leads to the **Island Walks**, accessed by a pedestrian suspension bridge. Beyond this, further upstream still, is **Inverness Sports Centre and Aquadome**, which offers swimming pools, spas and a variety of wild, spiralling flumes. Thomas Telford's Caledonian Canal *(see pp148–9)*, constructed between 1804 and 1822, is still in constant use and can be viewed at Tomnahurich Bridge. From here, **Jacobite Cruises** runs summer cruises along the length of Loch Ness – an excellent way to spend a sunny afternoon. Inverness is

an ideal base for touring the rest of the Highlands as it lies within easy reach of most of the region's best-known attractions, including the emotive battlesite of Culloden, 8 km (5 miles) to the east.

🏛 **Inverness Museum and Art Gallery**
Castle Wynd. 📞 *(01463) 237114.*
🕙 *9am–5pm Mon–Sat.* ♿
🏛 **Scottish Kiltmaker Visitor Centre**
4–9 Huntly St. 📞 *(01463) 222781.*
🕙 *May–Sept: daily; Oct–May: Mon–Sat.* 📷
🎭 **Eden Court Theatre**
Bishop's Rd. 📞 *(01463) 234234.* 📷
📷 ♿ W www.eden-court.co.uk
🏊 **Inverness Sports Centre and Aquadome**
Bught Park. 📞 *(01463) 667500.*
🕙 *daily.* 📷 ♿
⛴ **Jacobite Cruises**
Tomnahurich Bridge, Glenurquhart.
📞 *(01463) 233999.* 📷 ♿

THE JACOBITE MOVEMENT

The first Jacobites (mainly Catholic Highlanders) were the supporters of James VII of Scotland (James II of England) who was deposed by his Parliament in the "Glorious Revolution" of 1688. With the Protestant William of Orange on the throne, the Jacobites' desire to restore the Stuart monarchy led to the uprisings of 1715 and 1745. The first, in support of James VIII, the "Old Pretender", ended

James II, by Samuel Cooper (1609–72)

at the Battle of Sheriffmuir (1715). The failure of the second uprising, with the defeat at Culloden, saw the end of Jacobite hopes and led to the demise of the clan system and the suppression of Highland culture for more than a century.

The Great Glen ③

Following the path of a geological fault, the Great Glen forms a scenic route from Inverness on the east coast to Fort William on the west. The glacial rift valley was created when the landmass split and moved 400 million years ago. A series of four lochs includes the famous Loch Ness, home of the elusive monster. The Caledonian Canal, built by Thomas Telford, provides a link between the lochs, and has been a shipping channel as well as a popular tourist route since 1822. Hiring a boat or taking a leisurely drive are ideal ways to view the Glen.

Common redpoll

THE GREAT GLEN

Spean Bridge is home to a Woollen Mill selling traditional knitwear and tweeds. Close to the village is the impressive Memorial to all the Commandos who lost their lives in World War II. The surrounding rugged terrain was their training ground.

Loch Lochy

Lochy is one of the four beautiful lochs of the Great Glen, formed by a fissure in the earth and erosion by glaciers. There are caves nearby where Bonnie Prince Charlie is said to have hidden after the Battle of Culloden.

STAR SIGHTS

★ **Loch Ness**

★ **Caledonian Canal**

Steall Waterfall

Located at the foot of the magnificent Ben Nevis, this impressive waterfall tumbles down into a valley of wild flowers. Found at the end of a walk through a dramatic gorge, this is the perfect place to picnic.

Ben Nevis (*see p135*) is Britain's highest mountain at 1,343 m (4,406 ft), but its broad, indefinable shape belies its immense size.

0 kilometres   10

0 miles   10

Fort Augustus is a pretty village situated at the southwestern end of Loch Ness. The base for boat cruises around the loch, it is also the site of a Benedictine Abbey.

VISITORS' CHECKLIST

Highland. ■ *Castle Wynd, Inverness (01463) 234353; (01397) 703781.* Ⓦ *www.visitscotland.com.*
The Official Loch Ness Exhibition Ⓒ *(01456) 450573.* ◯ *daily.* ♿ Ⓚ **Urquhart Castle** Ⓒ *(01456) 450551.* ◯ *daily.* ♿

★ **Loch Ness**

Scotland's most famous loch, the 37 km (23 miles) of Loch Ness provide a beautiful route through the Glen. Urquhart Castle rises imposingly over the water.

Falls of Foyers nestle among the trees above Loch Ness; a winding path yields spectacular views.

KEY

▦	Main route through the Glen
▦	Major road
▭	Minor road
♦	Good walking area
☼	Viewpoint
■	Tourist information
⛴	Car ferry
⚑	Boating and watersports centre

THE LOCH NESS MONSTER

First sighted by St Columba in the 6th century, "Nessie" has attracted increasing attention since ambiguous photographs were taken in the 1930s. Though serious investigation is often undermined by hoaxers, sonar techniques continue to yield enigmatic results: plesiosaurs, giant eels and too much whisky are the most popular explanations. The Official Loch Ness Exhibition, at Drumnadrochit, presents the photographic evidence and wide variety of scientific explanations proffered over the years.

★ **Caledonian Canal**

This splendid canal provides a base from which to view the Glen's beautiful surroundings. From Inverness, the canal travels via Fort Augustus to the eight locks at Neptune's Staircase – a feat of engineering.

The shores of the Black Isle in the Moray Firth

Black Isle ❷

Ross & Cromarty. 🏛 10,600. ⬌ ⬛
Inverness. 🛈 W www.visitscotland.com
(01463) 731505.

THOUGH THE DRILLING plat-
forms in the Cromarty Firth
recall how oil has changed
the local economy, the broad
peninsula of the Black Isle is
still largely composed of farmland and fishing villages.
The town of **Cromarty** was
an important 18th-century port
with thriving rope and lace
industries. Many of its merchant houses still stand. The
award-winning museum in
the **Cromarty Courthouse**
provides heritage tours of
the town. The thatched **Hugh
Miller Museum** celebrates
the life of theologian and geologist Hugh Miller (1802–56),
who was born in Cromarty.

Fortrose boasts a ruined
14th-century cathedral, while
a stone on Chanonry Point
commemorates the Brahan
Seer, a 17th-century prophet.
He was burnt alive in a barrel
of tar by the Countess of
Seaforth after he foresaw her
husband's infidelity. For local
archaeology, the **Groam
House Museum** in the town
of Rosemarkie is worth a visit.

🏛 **Cromarty Courthouse**
Church St, Cromarty. 🅲 (01381)
600418. ◯ Apr–Oct: daily; Nov–Mar:
daily (pm). ● 23 Dec–Feb. 🈂
🏛 **Hugh Miller Museum**
(NTS) Church St, Cromarty.
🅲 (01381) 600245. ◯ Mar–Sep:
noon–5pm daily. 🈂 🅱 limited.
🏛 **Groam House Museum**
High St, Rosemarkie. 🅲 (01381)
620961. ◯ Easter week: pm only;
May–Sep: daily (Sun: pm); Oct–Apr: Sat
& Sun (pm). 🈂 🅱 ground floor only.

Strathpeffer ❸

Ross & Cromarty. 🏛 1,400. ⬌
Dingwall. ⬛ Inverness. 🛈 W www.
visitscotland.com (01463) 731505.

STANDING 8 km (5 miles) east
of the Falls of Rogie, the
holiday centre of Strathpeffer
still retains the refined charm
that made it well-known as a
Victorian spa and health resort.
The town's huge hotels and
gracious layout recall the days
when European royalty and
lesser mortals flocked to the
chalybeate- and sulphur-laden
springs, believed to alleviate
tuberculosis. It is still possible
to sample the water at the
unmanned **Water Tasting
Pavilion** in the town centre.

🏛 **Water Tasting Pavilion**
The Square. ◯ Easter–Oct: daily.

Dornoch ❹

Sutherland. 🏛 2,200. ⬌ Golspie,
Tain. ⬛ Inverness, Tain. 🛈 The
Square (01862) 810400.
W www.visithighlands.com

WITH ITS FIRST-CLASS golf
course and extensive
sandy beaches, Dornoch is a
popular holiday resort, but it
has retained a peaceful atmosphere. The medieval cathedral
(now the parish church) was
all but destroyed in a clan
dispute in 1570; it was finally
restored in the 1920s for its
700th anniversary. More
recently, the pop star Madonna
chose the cathedral for the
christening of her child.
A stone at the beach end of
River Street marks the place
where Janet Horne, the last
woman to be tried for witch-
craft in Scotland, was
executed in 1722.

ENVIRONS: Nineteen kilometres
(12 miles) northeast of the
resort is the stately, Victorianized pile of **Dunrobin Castle**,
magnificently situated in a
great park with formal gardens
overlooking the sea. Since
the 13th century this has been
the seat of the Earls of
Sutherland. Many of its rooms
are open to visitors.
The peaceful town of **Tain**
to the south became an

THE HIGHLAND CLEARANCES

During the heyday of the clan system (see pp26–7), tenants
paid their land-holding chieftains rent in the form of military
service. However, with the destruction of the clan system
after the Battle of Culloden (see p146), landowners began
to demand a financial rent, which their tenants were unable
to afford, and the land was gradually bought up by Lowland
and English farmers. In what became known as "the year
of the sheep" (1792), thousands of tenants were evicted,
sometimes forcibly,
to make way for live-
stock. Many emigrated
to Australia, America
and Canada. The ruins
of their crofts can still
be seen, especially in
Sutherland and the
Wester Ross.

The Last of the Clan
(1865) by Thomas Faed

administrative centre for the Highland Clearances, when the tolbooth was used as a jail. All is explained in the heritage centre, **Tain Through Time**.

♠ **Dunrobin Castle**
Near Golspie. ☎ (01408) 633177. ◐ Mar–Oct: daily (Sun:pm). 🎥 📷
🏛 **Tain Through Time**
Tower St. ☎ (01862) 894089. ◐ Apr–Oct: daily (Sun:pm); Nov–Mar: by appt. 🎥 ♿

The serene cathedral precinct in the town of Dornoch

Glen Shiel 🕦

Skye & Lochalsh. ⊇ Kyle of Lochalsh.
🚌 Glen Shiel. 🚹 Bayfield House, Bayfield Road (01478) 612137.

DOMINATING one of Scotland's most haunting regions, the awesome summits of the Five Sisters of Kintail rear into view at the northern end of Loch Cluanie as the A87 enters Glen Shiel. The **visitor centre**

at Morvich offers ranger-led excursions in the summer. Further west, the road passes the romantic **Eilean Donan Castle**, connected to the land by a causeway. After becoming a Jacobite (see p147) stronghold, it was destroyed in 1719 by English warships. In the 19th century it was restored, and it now contains a number of relics of the Jacobite cause.

♠ **Eilean Donan Castle**
Off A87, near Dornie. ☎ (01599) 555202. ◐ Apr–Oct: daily. 🎥

Isle of Skye 🕦

See pp152–3.

Wester Ross 🕥

Ross & Cromarty. ⊇ Achnasheen, Strathcarron. 🚌 Gairloch. 🚹 ⓦ www.visitscotland.com (01445) 712130.

LEAVING LOCH CARRON to the south, the A890 suddenly enters the northern Highlands and the great wilderness of Wester Ross. The Torridon Estate, sprawling on either side of Glen Torridon, includes some of the oldest mountains on earth (Torridonian rock is over 600 million years old), and is home to red deer, wild cats and wild goats. Peregrine falcons and golden eagles nest in the towering sandstone mass of Beinn Eighe, above the village of Torridon, with its breathtaking views over Applecross towards Skye. The **Torridon**

Typical Torridonian mountain scenery in the Wester Ross

Countryside Centre offers guided walks in season, and essential information on the natural history of the region.
Further north, the A832 cuts through the **Beinn Eighe National Nature Reserve**, Britain's oldest wildlife sanctuary. Remnants of the ancient Caledonian pine forest still stand on the banks and isles of Loch Maree, providing shelter for pine martens and wildcats. Buzzards and golden eagles nest on the alpine slopes. **Beinn Eighe Visitor Centre** has information on the reserve.
Along the coast, a series of exotic gardens thrive in the warming influence of the Gulf Stream. The most impressive is Inverewe Gardens (see p156).

🏛 **Torridon Countryside Centre**
(NTS) Torridon. ☎ (01445) 791221. ◐ Easter–Sep: daily. 🎥 📷 ♿
❅ **Beinn Eighe Visitor Centre**
Near Kinlochewe, on A832. ☎ (01445) 760258. ◐ Easter–Oct: daily. ♿

The western side of the Five Sisters of Kintail, seen from a viewpoint above Ratagan

Isle of Skye 36

Otter by the coast at Kylerhea

THE LARGEST of the Inner Hebrides, Skye can be reached by the bridge linking Kyle of Lochalsh and Kyleakin. A turbulent geological history has given the island some of Britain's most varied and dramatic scenery. From the rugged volcanic plateau of northern Skye to the ice-sculpted peaks of the Cuillins, the island is divided by numerous sea lochs, leaving the traveller never more than 8 km (5 miles) from the sea. Limestone grasslands predominate in the south, where the hillsides, home of sheep and cattle, are scattered with the ruins of crofts abandoned during the Clearances *(see p150)*. Historically, Skye is best known for its association with Bonnie Prince Charlie.

Skeabost has the ruins of a chapel which is associated with St Columba. Medieval tombstones can be found in the graveyard.

Grave of Flora MacDonald

Kilmuir

WESTERN ISLES

Uig

L O C H S N I Z O R T

• Lusta

B886

• Milovaig

Dunvegan

Skeabo

B884

B885

A850

A863

0 kilometres   10

0 miles   5

A863

Portnalong

B8009

Talisker   Carbost

The Talisker distillery
at Carbost, is famous for its Highland malts, often described as "the lava of the Cuillins".

C U

Dunvegan Castle
For over seven centuries, Dunvegan Castle has been the seat of the chiefs of the Clan Mac-Leod. It contains the Fairy Flag, a fabled piece of magical silk treasured for its protection.

Cuillins
Britain's finest mountain range is within walking distance of Sligachan, and in summer a boat sails from Elgol to the desolate inner sanctuary of Loch Coruisk. As he fled across the surrounding moorland, Bonnie Prince Charlie is said to have claimed: "even the Devil shall not follow me here!"

S O

KEY

	Tourist information
	Major road
	Minor road
	Narrow lane
	Viewpoint

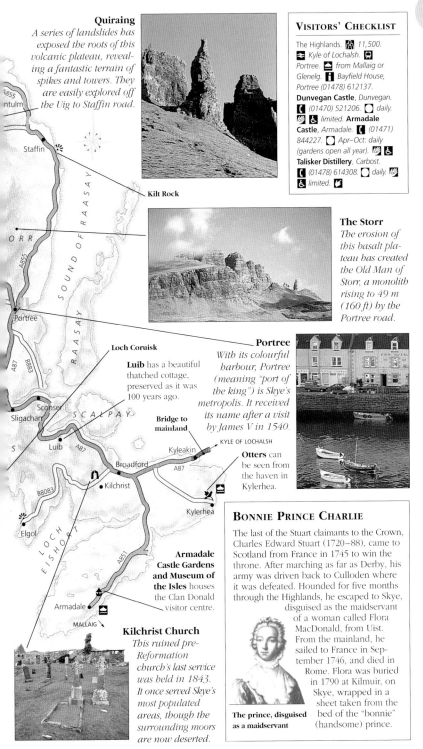

Quiraing

A series of landslides has exposed the roots of this volcanic plateau, revealing a fantastic terrain of spikes and towers. They are easily explored off the Uig to Staffin road.

Staffin

Kilt Rock

VISITORS' CHECKLIST

The Highlands. 🏠 *11,500.*
✈ *Kyle of Lochalsh.* 🚢
Portree. ⛴ *from Mallaig or
Glenelg.* ℹ *Bayfield House,
Portree (01478) 612137.*
Dunvegan Castle, *Dunvegan.*
📞 *(01470) 521206.* ○ *daily.*
🅿 ♿ *limited.* **Armadale
Castle**, *Armadale.* 📞 *(01471)
844227.* ○ *Apr–Oct: daily
(gardens open all year).* 🅿 ♿
Talisker Distillery, *Carbost.*
📞 *(01478) 614308.* ○ *daily.* 🅿
♿ *limited.* 🎟

The Storr

The erosion of this basalt plateau has created the Old Man of Storr, a monolith rising to 49 m (160 ft) by the Portree road.

Loch Coruisk

Luib has a beautiful thatched cottage, preserved as it was 100 years ago.

Portree

With its colourful harbour, Portree (meaning "port of the king") is Skye's metropolis. It received its name after a visit by James V in 1540.

Bridge to mainland

KYLE OF LOCHALSH

Otters can be seen from the haven in Kylerhea.

Armadale Castle Gardens and Museum of the Isles houses the Clan Donald visitor centre.

Kilchrist Church

This ruined pre-Reformation church's last service was held in 1843. It once served Skye's most populated areas, though the surrounding moors are now deserted.

BONNIE PRINCE CHARLIE

The last of the Stuart claimants to the Crown, Charles Edward Stuart (1720–88), came to Scotland from France in 1745 to win the throne. After marching as far as Derby, his army was driven back to Culloden where it was defeated. Hounded for five months through the Highlands, he escaped to Skye, disguised as the maidservant of a woman called Flora MacDonald, from Uist. From the mainland, he sailed to France in September 1746, and died in Rome. Flora was buried in 1790 at Kilmuir, on Skye, wrapped in a sheet taken from the bed of the "bonnie" (handsome) prince.

The prince, disguised as a maidservant

Dawn over the desolate tablelands of northern Skye, viewed from the Quiraing ▷

Inverewe Garden ❸

On A832, near Poolewe, Highland.
📞 (01445) 781200. 🕐 daily. 🖼 ✔
♿ 🅆 www.nts.org.uk

INVEREWE GARDEN attracts over 130,000 visitors a year for the simple reason that they are considered a national treasure. The gardens contain an extraordinary variety of trees, shrubs and flowers from around the world, despite being at a latitude of 57.8° north.

Inverewe was started in 1862 by the 20-year-old Osgood Mackenzie after being given an estate of 4,860 ha (12,000 acres) of exposed, barren land next to his family's holding. At that time there was just one dwarf willow growing there. Mackenzie began by planting shelter trees and then went on to create a walled garden using imported soil. He found that the west coast's climate, warmed by the North Atlantic Drift from the Gulf Stream *(see p21)*, encouraged the growth of exotic species. By 1922, the garden had achieved international recognition as one of the great plant collections. In 1952 it was donated to the National Trust for Scotland. At Inverewe today you can find Blue Nile lilies,

Some of the many unusual plants cultivated at Inverewe Garden

the tallest Australian gum trees growing in Britain and fragrant rhododendrons from China. Planting is designed to provide colour all year, but the gardens are at their best between spring and autumn.

Ullapool ❸

Highland. 🚶 1,800. ✈ Inverness.
🚌 ⛴ 🛈 Argyle St (01854) 612135.

WITH ITS WIDE streets, white-washed houses, palm trees and street signs in Gaelic, Ullapool is one of the prettiest villages on the west coast. Planned and built as a fishing station in 1788, it occupies a peninsula jutting into Loch Broom. Fishing is no longer important, except when East European "klondyker" factory ships moor in the loch in the winter. The major activity is now the ferry to Stornoway on Lewis *(see table, p213)*. The **Ullapool Museum** offers an insight into local history.

🏛 **Ullapool Museum**
7–8 West Argyle St. 📞 (01854) 612987. 🕐 Mon–Sat. 🖼 ♿

ENVIRONS: The natural wonders of this area include the rugged Assynt Mountains, a short drive north, and, to the south, the deep and precipitous Corrieshalloch Gorge.

At **Achiltibuie**, it is worth visiting the **Hydroponicum**, a "Garden of the Future", where flowers grow without soil. The town also has a **Smokehouse** where the process of curing salmon can be viewed. Tour boats run from here, and from Ullapool, to the **Summer Isles** – a small, sparsely populated group, once the home of noted environmentalist, Fraser Darling. Achiltibuie is worth a visit for the scenic drive alone.

🌿 **Hydroponicum**
Achiltibuie. 📞 (01854) 622202. 🕐 Mar–Sep: daily. 🖼 ♿ limited.
🐟 **Smokehouse**
Achiltibuie. 📞 (01854) 622353. 🕐 Easter–end Sep: Mon–Sat.

A tranquil, late-evening view of Ullapool and Loch Broom on the northwestern coast of Scotland

Majestic cliffs on Handa Island, a welcome refuge for seabirds

Handa Island ⑩

Highland. 🚢 *from Tarbet, near Scourie, Apr–Aug.* 🛈 *Scottish Wildlife Trust, Edinburgh (0131) 312 7765.*

LOCATED JUST offshore from Scourie on the west coast, this small island is an important breeding sanctuary for many species of seabirds.

In past centuries it was inhabited by a hardy people, who had their own queen and parliament. The last 60 inhabitants were evacuated in 1847 when their potato crop failed. The island was also used as a burial ground as it was safe from the wolves that inhabited the mainland.

The island is now managed by the Scottish Wildlife Trust. A walk takes visitors to the 100-m (328-ft) high northern cliffs. On the way you are liable to experience the intimidating antics of great and Arctic skuas (large migratory birds) swooping low over your head. Early in the year 11,000 pairs of razorbills can be found on Handa, and 66,000 pairs of guillemots, the largest breeding colony of this species in Britain.

ENVIRONS: The highest waterfall in Britain is **Eas Coul Aulin**, at 180 m (590 ft). It is best seen after rainfall, from a tour boat based at Kylesku, 24 km (15 miles) to the south of Handa.

Cape Wrath and the North Coast ⑪

Highland. 🚌 🚢 *May–Sep (01971) 511376.* 🛈 *John O'Groats (01955) 611373.*

THE NORTHERN edge of mainland Scotland spans the full variety of Highland geography, from mountainous moorlands and dazzlingly white beaches to flat, green farmland.

Cape Wrath is alluring not only for its name but for its cliffs, constantly pounded by the Atlantic. There are many stacks rising out of the sea that swarm with seabirds. The lighthouse was among the last in Scotland to be automated in 1998. In summer, a minibus serves the 13-km (8-mile) road leading to Cape Wrath. In order to reach the bus, you must take the connecting **Cape Wrath Ferry** from the pier by the Cape Wrath Hotel, as the cape is cut off by the Kyle of Durness. At Durness is **Smoo Cave**, an awesome cavern hollowed out of limestone. **Smoo Innercave Tours** run trips there. Just outside Durness, a community of artists has established the **Balnakeil Craft Village**, displaying pottery, enamelwork, wood carving, printmaking and paintings. Astonishingly white beaches follow one after the other along the coast, and the road then loops round Loch Eriboll – the

A nesting kittiwake

deepest of the sea lochs and a base for Atlantic and Russian convoys during World War II.

The **Strathnaver Museum** in Bettyhill explains the notorious Sutherland "Clearances", the forced evictions of 15,000 people to make way for sheep. At Rossal, 16 km (10 miles) south of Bettyhill, is an archaeological walk around an excavated village, which provides important information on life in pre-Clearance days.

A gigantic white dome at **Dounreay** marks the nuclear reprocessing plant, where you can tour the works and visit the free exhibition centre in summer. The main town on the coast here is Thurso, a village of solid stone buildings. Once famous for its locally quarried stone slabs, Thurso's industry died with the advent of cement. Each September, Thurso hosts "Northlands", the Scottish Nordic Music Festival.

John O'Groats is probably the most famous name on the map here, said to be the very northerly tip of the mainland, although this is in fact nearby **Dunnet Head**. Apart from a quaint harbour where day trips leave for Orkney, John O'Groats is a tourist trap. More rewarding are the cliffs at **Duncansby Head**, where you can enjoy the natural ferocity of the Pentland Firth.

🚢 **Smoo Innercave Tours**
38 Sango Mor, Durness. 📞 *(01971) 511704.* 🕐 *Apr–Sep: daily.* 📷
🏛 **Strathnaver Museum**
Clachan, Bettyhill. 📞 *(01641) 521418.* 🕐 *Apr–Oct: Mon–Sat.* 📷 ♿ *limited.*

Duncansby Head, Caithness, at the far northeast corner of Scotland

Orkney Islands ❷

IT IS SAID THAT THE DIFFERENCE between Orkney and Shetland is that Shetlanders are fishermen with farms while Orcadians are farmers with boats. Orkney's geology is radically different from its neighbour and so is its character – flat and gently undulating islands with rich soil that makes the grass lush green and nurtures summer crops of grain. The 70 islands contain the densest concentration of archaeological sites in Britain, testifying to their long history of settlement. Orcadians are warm and easy-going, except during the fierce Christmas and New Year football matches, known as the *Ba'*, in Kirkwall.

VISITORS' CHECKLIST

Orkney. 🚶 19,800. ✕ ⛴ from
Scrabster or Gill's Bay (Caithness),
Aberdeen, Lerwick (Shetland), and
John O' Groats (May–Sep only).
ℹ Kirkwall (01856) 872856.
🌐 www.visitorkney.com

The Old Man of Hoy, a majestic stone column off the coast of Hoy

Kirkwall

A charming town with flag-stoned streets and a small, busy harbour, Kirkwall is mainland Orkney's administrative centre. **St Magnus Cathedral** is an 860-year-old architectural masterpiece made of yellow and red stone. Each June it is host to a week-long festival of classical music. Opposite the cathedral is the ruin of **Earl's Palace**, a once splendid example of Renaissance architecture. Boats run to the island of Shapinsay where the stylish **Balfour Castle**, with its original furnishings, has stood since 1840.

🏛 **Earl's Palace**
ℹ (01856) 871918. ○ Apr–Sep. 🏚
⛴ **Balfour Castle**
🏰 (01856) 711282. ○ May–Sep: Sun. 🏚 🚻 ♿ ground floor only.

Mainland Orkney

Five miles from the town of Stromness is **Maes Howe**, the finest chambered tomb in Western Europe, built before 2,700 BC to align with the winter solstice. Vikings plundered the tomb around 1150, and their graffiti is itself a treasure of ancient linguistic inscriptions. Nearby are the huge Standing Stones of Stenness and the famous Ring of Brodgar, consisting of 36 standing stones.

Even better known, however, is the astonishing prehistoric village of **Skara Brae**, inhabited from about 3,100 BC for 500 years until buried by shifting sands. A storm uncovered the remains in 1850. On display are Stone Age beds, dressers and kitchens. To the south of Kirkwall, the road runs over the Churchill Barriers, great causeways built by Italian prisoners of war to protect the British fleet stationed in the bay of Scapa Flow. They also built the Italian Chapel, which lies close to the road and is worth visiting.

The colourful stone exterior of St Magnus Cathedral

♜ **Maes Howe and Skara Brae**
ℹ (0131) 668 8800. ○ daily. 🏚 ♿

Other Islands

The **Scapa Flow Centre** on the island of **Hoy** has an exceptional exhibition, graphically reviving the events of Scapa Flow on 16 June 1919, when the surrendered German Fleet was scuttled by its crews, and 74 ships were sunk.

The Old Man of Hoy, a stack at the west end of the island measuring 137 m (450 ft), is well worth the 6 km (4 mile) walk to reach it. **Rousay** has so many archaeological sites it is known as the "Egypt of the North", while **Sanday**, as its name suggests, consists largely of sandy beaches.

ℹ **Scapa Flow Centre**
🏰 (01856) 791300. ○ May–Sep: Sat, Sun; Oct–Apr: Mon–Fri. 🏚 ♿

SEABIRDS OF THE ORKNEY AND SHETLAND ISLANDS

As seabirds spend most of their time away from land, nesting is a vulnerable period in their lives. Inaccessible cliffs such as those at Herma Ness on Unst in the Shetland Islands and St John's Head on the Orkney island of Hoy provide security for thousands of migrant and local birds.

Herring gull

Fulmar

Shetland Islands ❸

THIS GROUP OF OVER A HUNDRED cliff-edged islands forms the most northerly domain of Scotland. Shetlanders are a friendly people, with a distinctive dialect derived from their long connection with Norway. Nowhere in Shetland is further than 5 km (3 miles) from the sea, and fishing and salmon farming still provide a major contribution to the economy. In recent times, North Sea oil has brought important revenue and employment. In winter Shetland suffers severe storms, but in summer the sun can shine for 19 hours. The islands are famous for their profusion of fiddle music and annual Viking festivals.

VISITORS' CHECKLIST

Shetland. 🏠 23,000. ✈
🚢 from Aberdeen and from
Stromness on mainland Orkney.
🛈 Lerwick (01595) 693434.
w www.visitshetland.com

The prehistoric settlement of Jarlshof, with its Norse and Viking remains

Lerwick
Mainland Shetland's chief town is attractive, with flag-stoned wynds (narrow lanes), grey stone buildings and old "lodberries" (houses with a private pier). The **Shetland Museum** contains artifacts from shipwrecks and the whaling era, and replicas of the St Ninian's Isle Treasure. The Clickimin *broch* (prehistoric fort) is easy to get to, but the one at Mousa is its superior. Tour boats run from the harbour to the gannet colony at **Noss**. Lerwick's *Up Helly Aa* Viking fire festival takes place in late January, and there are folk music festivals in April and October.

🏛 **Shetland Museum**
((01595) 695057. ● until summer 2006. ♿

Mainland Shetland
Fine beaches and pretty inlets provide the visitor with lengths of striking coastline. **Jarlshof Prehistoric and Norse Settlement**, in the extreme south, is the archaeological site of a settlement that spanned 3,000 years from Neolithic to Viking times. The nearby cliffs of Sumburgh Head are worth a visit, and on the west coast, the sand isthmus at St Ninian's Isle offers an interesting walk. The ornate **Mousa Broch**, on the island of Mousa, is the best-preserved of its kind in Britain.

🏠 **Jarlshof Prehistoric and Norse Settlement**
((01950) 460112. ● Mar–Sep: daily. 🏠 ♿ limited. 📷 by request.
🏠 **Mousa Broch**
((01950) 431367. ● Mar–Sep.

Other Islands
All islands in Shetland have regular ferry connections, though the outlying ones are weather-dependent. It is worth visiting **Hermaness National Nature Reserve** on Unst, not only to see the startling numbers of birds, but also to look out over the most northerly tip of Scotland, to the lighthouse islets of Muckle Flugga. **Unst Heritage Centre and Boat Haven** has a museum. **Fair Isle** is famed for its seabirds and brightly patterned sweaters, and **Foula** (where Christmas is celebrated on 6 January) has the most dramatic 365-m (1,200-ft) cliffs. Every island has its own character, and many, such as the islands of Out Skerries, hold community dances where traditional Shetland dances are still performed with enthusiasm.

☒ **Hermaness National Nature Reserve**
((01957) 711278. ● Apr–Sep: daily.
🛈 **Unst Heritage Centre and Boat Haven**
((01957) 711528. ● May–Sep: daily (pm only). 🏠 donation. ♿

The dramatic Viking fire festival of *Up Helly Aa*, a major Shetland event

Puffin   **Great skua**   **Razorbills**   **Black guillemot**

Western Isles 🌀

WESTERN SCOTLAND ENDS with this remote chain of islands, made of some of the oldest rock on earth. Almost treeless landscapes are divided by countless waterways, while the western, windward coasts are edged by miles of white sandy beaches. For centuries, the eastern shores, composed largely of peat bogs, have provided islanders with fuel. Man has been here for 6,000 years, living off the sea and the thin turf, though abandoned monuments including a Norwegian whaling station on Harris attest to the difficulties faced in commercializing the islanders' traditional skills. Gaelic, part of an enduring culture, is widely spoken.

The interior of a croft house at the Black House Museum

The monumental Standing Stones of Callanish in nothern Lewis

Lewis and Harris

Forming the largest landmass of the Western Isles, Lewis and Harris are a single island, though Gaelic dialects differ between the two areas. From the administrative centre of **Stornoway**, with its bustling harbour and colourful house fronts, the ancient **Standing Stones of Callanish** are only 26 km (16 miles) to the west. Just off the road on the way to Callanish are the ruins of **Carloway Broch**, a Pictish (see p41) tower over 2,000 years old. The more recent past can be explored at Arnol's **Black House Museum** – a showcase of crofting life as it was until 50 years ago.

South of the rolling peat moors of Lewis, a range of mountains marks the border with Harris, which is entered by passing Aline Lodge at the head of Loch Seaforth. The mountains of Harris are a paradise for the hillwalker. From their summits on a clear day, the distant isle of St Kilda can be seen 80 km (50 miles) to the west.

The ferry port of Tarbert stands on a slim isthmus separating North and South Harris. The tourist office provides addresses for local weavers of the tough Harris Tweed. Some weavers still use indigenous plants to create the various dyes. From Leverburgh, on Harris' southern tip, a ferry sails to North Uist, linked by a causeway to Berneray.

🏛 Black House Museum & Visitor Centre

📞 *(01851) 710395.* ⭕ *all year: Mon–Sat.* 🖼 🗲

The Uists and Benbecula

After the dramatic scenery of Harris, the lower-lying, largely waterlogged southern isles may seem an anticlimax, though they nurture secrets well worth discovering. Long, white, sandy beaches fringe the Atlantic coast, edged with one of Scotland's natural treasures: the lime-rich soil known as *machair*. During the summer months, the soil is covered with wild flowers, the unique fragrance of which can be detected far out to sea.

From **Lochmaddy**, North Uist's main village, the A867 crosses 5 km (3 miles) of causeway to **Benbecula**, the isle from which the brave Flora MacDonald smuggled Bonnie Prince Charlie to Skye (see p153). Benbecula is a flat island covered by a mosaic of small lochs. Like its neighbours, it is known for good trout fishing. Here, and to the north, the Protestant religion holds sway, while Catholicism prevails in the southern islands. Benbecula's chief source of employment is the Army Rocket Range, which

The harbour at Stornoway, the principal town on Lewis and Harris

has its headquarters in the main village of Bailivanich. Another causeway leads to South Uist, with its golden beaches, which are renowned as a National Scenic Area.

Eriskay
One of the smallest and most enchanting of the Western Isles, Eriskay epitomizes their peace and beauty. The island is best known for the wrecking of the *SS Politician* in 1941, which inspired the book and film *Whisky Galore*. A bottle from its cargo and other relics can be seen in Eriskay's only bar. It was at the beautiful beach of Coilleag A'Phrionnsa (Prince's beach) that Bonnie Prince Charlie first set foot on Scotland at the start of his 1745 campaign. As a result, a rare convolvulus flower that grows here has become associated with him.

Blue waters off the coast of Barra, looking east to the Isle of Rum

Barra
The dramatic way to arrive on Barra is by plane – the airstrip is a beach and the timetable depends on the tide. Barra is a pretty island, with its central core of hills and circular road. The western side is almost all beaches. Over 1,000 species of flowers have been recorded.

The view over Castlebay from the Madonna and Child statue, on the top of Heaval hill, is particularly fine. The romantic **Kisimul Castle**, set on an island, is the 15th seat of the Clan MacNeil. It is currently being restored. Other attractions are the **Barra Heritage Centre** and also a golf course.

🏰 **Kisimul Castle**
(*(01871) 810313.* ⏰ *Apr–Sep:* 🚢 *includes boat trip.*
ℹ️ **Barra Heritage Centre**
(*(01871) 810336.* ⏰ *May–Sep: Mon–Sat.* ♿

A group of St Kildan men with their catch of fulmar seabirds

St Kilda
These "Islands on the Edge of the World" were the most isolated habitation in Scotland until the ageing population requested to be evacuated in 1930. The St Kildans developed a unique lifestyle based on harvesting seabirds. The largest gannetry in the world (40,000 pairs) is now to be found here. There are three islands and three stacks of awesome beauty, each with soaring cliffs

VISITORS' CHECKLIST

Western Isles. 🏘 *29,600.*
✈ *Stornoway, Benbecula, Barra.*
🚢 *from Uig (Skye), Oban, Mallaig, Kyle of Lochalsh and Ullapool.* ℹ️ *26 Cromwell St, Stornoway (01851) 703088.*
🌐 *www.visithebrides.com*

rising sheer to 425 m (1,400 ft) at their highest. Such is their isolation that separate sub-species of mouse and wren have evolved. Tours are run by **Westernedge Charters** and **Murdo Macdonald**. Volunteers can also pay to join summer work parties on the island, run by the **National Trust for Scotland**, which owns St Kilda.

ℹ️ **Westernedge Charters**
Linlithgow. **(** *(01506) 204053.*
ℹ️ **Murdo Macdonald**
1 Erista, Uig, Isle of Lewis.
(*(01851) 672381.*
ℹ️ **National Trust for Scotland**
Balnain House, Inverness.
(*(01463) 232034.*

CROFTING

Crofts are small parcels of agricultural land, worked in conjunction with another source of income as they are too small to provide total subsistence. They originated in the early 1800s when landlords made available units of poor land on the coast, clearing the people from the more fertile areas, and making them dependent on wages from either fishing or collecting kelp (seaweed used to make commercial alkali). When these sources of income diminished, crofters endured over 50 years of extreme hardship through famine, high rents, eviction and lack of security. Not until 1886 was an Act passed which gave crofters security and allowed families the right of inheritance (but not ownership). Today there are 17,000 registered crofts, almost all in the Highlands and islands. Governed by special regulations prohibiting the creation of new crofts, the crofters are eligible for special grants. Most crofters raise sheep, but recent trends are tree planting and providing habitats for rare birds. Crofting remains a vital part of Highland communities.

A traditional, thatched crofter's house on the island of North Uist

TRAVELLERS'
NEEDS

WHERE TO STAY 164–173

WHERE TO EAT 174–183

SPECIAL INTERESTS AND
OUTDOOR ACTIVITIES 184–195

WHERE TO STAY

THE RANGE OF HOTELS and other accommodation available in Scotland is extensive, and whatever your budget, you should be able to find something to suit your needs. Different types of accommodation are described below, and the hotel listings section on pages 166–173 includes over 90 of the best places to stay, from luxurious country-house hotels and castles, to cosy bed-and-breakfasts, to basic campsites. Many offer non-smoking rooms. This selection represents both excellence and good value. Self-catering holidays are also growing in popularity. This type of accommodation is particularly well suited to those on a tight budget or families with young children, who may find hotels to be a little formal and inflexible. We have also added some useful introductory information on the campsites and caravan parks in Scotland, which provide an adventurous, reasonably priced alternative to hotels and guest houses.

Malmaison Hotel's distinctive sign

Stately interior of Kildrummy Castle Hotel (see p172) in the Grampians

HOTEL CLASSIFICATIONS

THE QUALITY Assurance Scheme run by VisitScotland is a useful guide when choosing holiday accommodation. Hotels, bed-and-breakfasts and self-catering are all covered in the scheme. A grade from "acceptable" to "exceptional" is awarded along with a classification of stars from one to five, indicating the facilities available.

PRICES, HIDDEN EXTRAS AND BOOKING

HOTEL RATES ARE normally quoted per room and include VAT (value-added tax) and service charge. Top-of-the-range hotels can cost over £200 and an average hotel in Edinburgh or Glasgow about £70–£150 for two people, including breakfast. Outside the city, expect to pay £50–£90 for a similar standard, or £12.50–

£30 for bed-and-breakfast. Tipping is not expected other than in very exclusive hotels. High rates are charged for telephone calls made from your room, so it may be worth buying a phonecard and using the lobby telephone instead.

Some hotels require a non-refundable deposit. If you cancel a room early on, you should not have to pay the full price. Tourist Information Centres offer a Book-a-Bed-Ahead scheme and, for a small fee, they will reserve a room.

COUNTRY HOUSE HOTELS AND CASTLES

THE TERM "country house hotel" has been applied liberally by some hoteliers who think gas log-fires and reproduction furniture are sufficient to warrant the name on their brochures. The genuine article is not hard to spot, however, as the buildings are invariably of architectural value, filled with antiques and fine furnishings, and situated in extensive grounds. Converted castles offer visitors the chance to live and dine like a lord. The atmosphere is intimate yet refined, with cordon bleu cooking and a well-stocked wine cellar. Room tariffs are high, but the height of comfort and luxury is guaranteed.

COACHING INNS AND SHOOTING LODGES

COACHING INNS can be found throughout Scotland. In former times they were staging points for people journeying by horse and carriage, where horses could rest and travellers could find food and lodging.

Generally attractive, historic buildings, inns are often the town's focal point. Some are cottage style with a thatched roof, others are Georgian or Victorian with sash windows and doorways framed with pillars and porticoes. They nearly always have traditional decor, and usually a reliable restaurant serving regional, home-cooked food in a friendly and informal atmosphere.

The authentic dining area at Dalhousie Castle

◁ **A colourful display of flowers outside Deacon Brodie's Tavern on the Royal Mile in Edinburgh**

In the more rural areas of Scotland, there are shooting lodges which also provide accommodation. These are often part of a large estate, and the property of a local landowner. They are comfortably furnished without being overly luxurious, which helps to keep down the price of a room. It is not obligatory to go shooting while staying at these lodges, but that may be a facility on offer, and fresh game will be served in the restaurant.

The majestic Malmaison Hotel *(see p167)* on the quayside in Leith

BED-AND-BREAKFASTS AND GUESTHOUSES

FOR INEXPENSIVE accommodation and a chance to meet local Scottish people, bed-and-breakfast is the ideal choice. Often family-owned, they are basic, no-frills establishments with a choice of a full, cooked breakfast or cereal and toast included in the price.

B & Bs, as they are commonly known, dominate the lower price range, and in the remote areas of Scotland can be the only form of accommodation available. The buildings are often cosy farmhouses with homely decor, and you are likely to receive a more personal, friendly welcome than at the larger, busier hotels.

Guesthouses also offer reasonably priced, basic accommodation. They usually contain a number of bedrooms, as well as a communal sitting or dining area. VisitScotland publishes the "Scotland: Bed-and-Breakfast" guide, which lists over 1,500 B & Bs and guesthouses.

A traditional croft cottage, one of many self-catering properties in Scotland

SELF-CATERING

THE FREEDOM OF self-catering accommodation (efficiency units) will appeal to those who prefer to stay in one place and be independent, or those with young children and a limited budget. There are many places all over Scotland, ranging from luxury apartments in the cities to converted barns or cottages in the country. Local tourist offices have the most comprehensive and up-to-date lists, and provide a booking service.

CAMPING AND CARAVANNING

A CHOICE OF campsites and caravan (recreational vehicle) parks, normally open from Easter to October, can be found all over Scotland. During the summer months parks fill up quickly, so book ahead. Road signs indicate where to find the campsites and caravan parks off the main roads. Two clubs, the **Caravan Club**

www.caravanclub.co.uk (01342 326944) and the **Camping and Caravanning Club** www. campingandcaravaningclub.co. uk (02476 694995), publish guides listing their parks, and it may be worthwhile becoming a member. A typical camping or caravan pitch (site) costs from £6–£10 per night, making it an economical way to see Scotland.

YOUTH HOSTELS

THERE ARE AROUND 80 hostels in Scotland, owned by the **Scottish Youth Hostels Association** or SYHA, e-mail syha@syha.org.uk (01786 891400). Most offer central heating, hot showers and cheap evening meals. Accommodation is usually single-sex dormitories, but occasionally there are separate family rooms. You must be a member of the SYHA to stay, but anyone over the age of five can join upon arrival.

Invercoe campsite in the Highlands – basic facilities but wonderful views

Choosing a Hotel

HOTELS in this guide have been selected across a wide price range for their excellent facilities and locations. Many also have a recommended restaurant. The chart lists hotels by region; colour-coded thumb tabs indicate the regions covered on each page. Map references pertain to the inside back cover. For restaurant listings, see pages 176–83.

	Credit Cards	Restaurant	Children Welcome	Garden/Terrace	Number of Rooms
EDINBURGH					
OLD TOWN: *Ibis Hotel* w www.ibishotels.com (£) 6 Hunter Square. ((0131) 240 7000. FAX (0131) 240 7007. An attractive hotel that blends into the fabric of the Old Town, ideally situated close to the Royal Mile and Princes Street.	AE DC MC V		●		99
OLD TOWN: *Jury's Edinburgh Inn* w www.jurysdoyle.com (£)(£) 43 Jeffrey Street. ((0131) 200 3300. FAX (0131) 200 0400. With great views to Calton Hill, this hotel is conveniently situated close to the Royal Mile, Princes Street and Waverley Station.	AE DC MC V	■	●		186
OLD TOWN: *Apex International Hotel* w www.apexhotels.co.uk (£)(£)(£) 31-35 Grassmarket. ((0131) 300 3456. FAX (0131) 220 5345. A comfortable modern building in the historic Grassmarket, amid shops and eating places. Some bedrooms overlook the castle.	AE MC V	■		■	169
OLD TOWN: *Bank Hotel* @ bank-hotel@festival-inns.co.uk (£)(£)(£) 1 South Bridge. (FAX (0131) 622 6800. An imaginative new conversion of a former bank, situated at the heart of the Old Town, close to the Royal Mile. Each of the bedrooms is individually designed to commemorate a famous Scot.	AE MC V		●		9
OLD TOWN: *Point Hotel* w www.pointhotel.co.uk (£)(£)(£) 34 Bread Street. ((0131) 221 5555. FAX (0131) 221 9929. This striking, stylish conversion, with colour-themed floors, is only a few minutes' walk from Edinburgh Castle and the Grassmarket.	AE DC MC V	■	●		140
NEW TOWN: *Duthus Lodge* @ duthus.lodge@ukgateway.net (£)(£) 5 West Coates. ((0131) 337 6876. FAX (0131) 313 2264. Detached, family-run Victorian sandstone villa with conservatory and gardens, about 10 minutes' walk from city centre.	MC V		●	■	7
NEW TOWN: *Melvin House* w www.melvinhouse.co.uk (£)(£) 3 Rothesay Terrace. ((0131) 225 5084. FAX (0131) 226 5085. Within easy walking distance of Princes Street, this hotel is in a Victorian house of exceptional character with a galleried library.	AE DC MC V		●	■	24
NEW TOWN: *Stuart House* w www.stuartguesthouse.com (£) 12 East Claremont Street. ((0131) 557 9030. FAX (0131) 557 0563. This attractive, family-run hotel, in the northeastern part of the New Town, is set in a residential area just 15 minutes' walk from Princes Street.	AE DC MC V		●		8
NEW TOWN: *Parliament House* w www.parliamenthouse-hotel.co.uk (£)(£)(£) 15 Calton Hill. ((0131) 478 4000. FAX (0131) 478 4001. An original Georgian town house, with an impressive, convenient location next to Calton Hill.	DC MC V	■	●		53
NEW TOWN: *Albany Town House Hotel* w www.albanyhoteledinburgh.co.uk (£)(£)(£) 39 Albany Street. ((0131) 556 0397. FAX (0131) 557 6633. An elegant and luxurious hotel incorporating three historically listed Georgian terraced houses, situated in the eastern part of the New Town. The Haldanes restaurant in the basement is very good.	AE MC V	■	●		21
NEW TOWN: *Channings* w www.channings.co.uk (£)(£)(£) South Learmonth Gardens. ((0131) 315 2226. FAX (0131) 332 9631. Close to the city centre, this hotel consists of five converted Edwardian houses. Smart and very well kept, but still homely.	AE DC MC V	■	●	■	42
NEW TOWN: *Caledonian Hilton* w www.hilton.co.uk (£)(£)(£)(£) Princes Street. ((0131) 222 8888. FAX (0131) 222 8889. This hotel is an institution in Edinburgh. Centrally located, it is a popular place to meet. Excellent restaurant – La Pompadour.	AE DC MC V	■	●	■	251

Price categories for a standard double room per night, inclusive of breakfast, service charges and any additional taxes such as VAT:
£ under £80
££ £80–£130
£££ £130–£180
££££ £180–£230
£££££ over £230.

RESTAURANT
Hotel restaurant or dining room usually open to non-residents unless otherwise stated.

CHILDREN WELCOME
Child cots and a baby-sitting service available. Some hotel restaurants have children's portions and high chairs.

GARDEN/TERRACE
Hotels with a garden, courtyard or terrace.

CREDIT CARDS
Indicates which credit cards are accepted: *AE* American Express; *DC* Diners Club; *MC* MasterCard/Access; *V* VISA.

	CREDIT CARDS	RESTAURANT	CHILDREN WELCOME	GARDEN/TERRACE	NUMBER OF ROOMS
NEW TOWN: *Howard Hotel* w www.thehoward.com £££££ 32–36 Great King Street. (0131) 557 3500. FAX (0131) 557 6515. A stylish and urbane small hotel, converted from three adjoining Georgian houses. Superb facilities and exemplary service.	AE DC MC V	■	●	■	18
FURTHER AFIELD: *Old Aberlady Inn* £ Main Street, Aberlady, East Lothian. (01875) 870503. FAX (01875) 870209. Situated close to Aberlady Bay nature reserve and beaches, the inn has attractive rooms and a bistro with good traditional cooking.	MC V	■	●	■	6
FURTHER AFIELD: *The Malmaison Hotel* w www.malmaison.com £££ Tower Place, Leith. (0131) 468 5000. FAX (0131) 468 5002. A converted sailor's home situated on the historic Leith quayside. Individual and stylishly designed rooms overlook the harbour.	AE DC MC V	■	●	■	100
FURTHER AFIELD: *Greywalls Hotel* w www.greywalls.co.uk £££££ Gullane, East Lothian. (01620) 842144. FAX (01620) 842241. An outstanding Lutyens country house set in walled gardens designed by Gertrude Jekyll. Adjacent to the Muirfield golf course.	AE DC MC V	■	●	■	23

SOUTHERN SCOTLAND

	CREDIT CARDS	RESTAURANT	CHILDREN WELCOME	GARDEN/TERRACE	NUMBER OF ROOMS
AUCHENCAIRN: *Balcary Bay* w www.balcary-bay-hotel.co.uk £££ Auchencairn, Castle Douglas, D & G. **Map** D5. (01556) 640217. FAX (01556) 640272. A family-run hotel in an excellent position on the shores of Balcary Bay. Quality of service is evident as many visitors return year after year to this friendly, traditional establishment. ● mid-Nov–Feb.	AE MC V	■	●	■	20
DRYBURGH: *Dryburgh Abbey Hotel* w www.dryburgh.co.uk ££ Dryburgh, Roxburghshire. **Map** E5. (01835) 822261. FAX (01835) 823945. This country house hotel, set in secluded grounds next to the ruins of Dryburgh Abbey and the River Tweed, is ideal for fishing.	AE MC V	■	●	■	38
JEDBURGH: *Hundalee House* w www.accommodation-scotland.org £ Jedburgh, Roxburgh, Borders. **Map** E5. & FAX (01835) 863011. A well-presented bed-and-breakfast, in an attractive 18th-century house set in large gardens. ● Nov–Mar				■	5
KELSO: *Roxburghe Hotel* w www.roxburghe.net ££££ Kelso, Roxburghshire. **Map** E5. (01573) 450331. FAX (01573) 450611. A delightful country house hotel, owned by the Duke of Roxburgh. Elegant and relaxed, it is set in large grounds running down to the River Teviot. Golf, tennis, fishing and shooting are available to residents.	AE DC MC V	■	●	■	22
KIRKCUDBRIGHT: *Gladstone House* w www.kirkcudbrightgladstone.co.uk £ 48 High Street, Kirkcudbright, D & G. **Map** D6. & FAX (01557) 331734. Exceptional bed-and-breakfast hotel in this appealing town. Decorated with taste, it is an attractive and civilized place to stay.	MC V				3
LAUDER: *The Lodge at Carfraemill* w www.carfraemill.co.uk ££ Berwickshire. Map E5. (01578) 750750. FAX (01578) 750751. Traditional stone coaching inn in the heart of the Scottish Borders, 21 miles south of Edinburgh.	DC AE MC V	■	●	■	10
PEEBLES: *Cringletie House* w www.cringletie.com £££ Peebles, Borders, **Map** D5. (01721) 725750. FAX (01721) 725751. Comfortable and peaceful country house hotel set in beautiful grounds. It has an excellent restaurant and a relaxed atmosphere.	AE MC V	■	●	■	14
PEEBLES: *Traquair* w www.traquair.co.uk £££ Innerleithen, Peebles, Borders. **Map** D5. (01896) 830323. FAX (01896) 830639. The oldest inhabited house in Scotland (see pp87) provides unique accommodation, with a cottage restaurant and brewery on site.	MC V		●	■	3

Price categories for a standard double room per night, inclusive of breakfast, service charges and any additional taxes such as VAT:
£ under £80
££ £80–£130
£££ £130–£180
££££ £180–£230
£££££ over £230.

RESTAURANT
Hotel restaurant or dining room usually open to non-residents unless otherwise stated.

CHILDREN WELCOME
Child cots and a baby-sitting service available. Some hotel restaurants have children's portions and high chairs.

GARDEN/TERRACE
Hotels with a garden, courtyard or terrace.

CREDIT CARDS
Indicates which credit cards are accepted: *AE* American Express; *DC* Diners Club; *MC* MasterCard/Access; *V* VISA.

	CREDIT CARDS	RESTAURANT	CHILDREN WELCOME	GARDEN/TERRACE	NUMBER OF ROOMS
PORTPATRICK: *Crown* @ crownportpatrickhotel@aol.com £ North Crescent, Portpatrick, Stranraer. **Map C6.** ((01776) 810261. **FAX** (01776) 810551. A popular pub-hotel overlooking the harbour. Food is served in the traditional-style bar and the smarter conservatory restaurant. ☎ TV P	AE DC MC V	■	●	■	12

GLASGOW

	CREDIT CARDS	RESTAURANT	CHILDREN WELCOME	GARDEN/TERRACE	NUMBER OF ROOMS
CITY CENTRE: *Babbity Bowster* £ 16–18 Blackfriars Street. ((0141) 552 5055. **FAX** (0141) 552 7774. An unusual hotel with immense character. Behind the finely restored Adam façade are a few simple, neat bedrooms. ☎ P	AE MC V	■	●	■	6
CITY CENTRE: *The Brunswick* W www.brunswickhotel.co.uk £ 106-108 Brunswick Street. ((0141) 552 0001. **FAX** (0141) 552 1551. Situated in the restored "Merchant City" area, this hotel has an individual, contemporary style. It is compact but comfortable. ☎ TV ↥ ✍ ✦	AE DC MC V	■	●		18
CITY CENTRE: *Carlton George* W www.carltonhotels.co.uk £££ 44 West George Street. ((0141) 353 6373. **FAX** (0141) 353 6263. This luxury hotel in the heart of the city, caters for leisure visitor and business traveller alike and is very well placed for Glasgow's main shopping areas. ☎ TV ↥ 24 ✦	AE DC MC V	■	●		64
CITY CENTRE: *Hilton Glasgow* W www.hilton.com ££££ 1 William Street. ((0141) 204 5555. **FAX** (0141) 204 5004. Large city-centre hotel that is both smart and stylish. Predominantly catering for the business market. ☎ TV ↥ 24 P ≋ ✦	AE DC MC V	■	●		319
CITY CENTRE: *Langs* W www.langshotels.co.uk ££ 2 Port Dundas Place. ((0141) 333 1500. **FAX** (0141) 333 5700. A style-conscious, glamorous boutique hotel with two trendy restaurants. Bedrooms are comfortably minimalist. Gym. ☎ TV ↥ ✍ P ✦	AE DC MC V	■	●		100
CITY CENTRE: *Malmaison* W www.malmaison.com £££ 278 West George Street. ((0141) 572 1000. **FAX** (0141) 572 1002. Beautifully decorated rooms, with satellite TV and CD player, provide a stylish stay. The brasserie serves French cuisine. ☎ TV ↥ 24 ✍ ✦	AE DC MC V	■	●		72
CITY CENTRE: *Millennium Hotel* W www.millenniumhotels.com ££££ 40 George Square. ((0141) 332 6711. **FAX** (0141) 332 4264. The Millennium is a large hotel facing George Square, with traditional comforts and an attractive conservatory for breakfast, drinks or simply to watch the world go by. ☎ TV ↥ 24 ✍	AE DC MC V	■	●		117
WEST END: *Hillhead Hotel* W www.hillheadhotel.co.uk £ 32 Cecil Street. ((0141) 339 7733. **FAX** (0141) 339 1770. Set in a quiet residential location, this hotel is close to Glasgow University, the Botanic Gardens and a number of restaurants and bars. ☎ TV ✍	AE MC V		●		11
WEST END: *Kirklee Hotel* W www.kirkleehotel.co.uk £ 11 Kensington Gate. ((0141) 334 5555. **FAX** (0141) 339 3828. This Edwardian town house is in a quiet location, but close to the Botanic Gardens, Glasgow University, bars and restaurants. ☎ TV ✍	MC V		●	■	9
WEST END: *Town House* W www.thetownhouseglasgow.com £ 4 Hughenden Terrace. ((0141) 357 0862. **FAX** (0141) 339 9605. An expertly restored Victorian house, where you are assured a friendly welcome. The bedrooms have grand proportions. ☎ TV P	MC V		●	■	10
WEST END: *Wickets Hotel* W www.wicketshotel.co.uk £ 52 Fortrose Street. (& **FAX** (0141) 334 9334. This family-run hotel is close to the Scottish Exhibition Centre and Glasgow University. ● 24–26 Dec, 31 Dec–2 Jan. ☎ TV P	AE MC V	■	●	■	11

WEST END: *One Devonshire Gardens* [W] www.onedevonshiregardens.com £££ AE DC MC V 35
1 Devonshire Gardens. [C] *(0141) 339 2001.* FAX *(0141) 337 1663.*
The ultimate smart town-hotel. Lavish furnishings and stylish decor.
First class service and an excellent restaurant. 🚗 TV 24 ⚡ P

CENTRAL SCOTLAND

ABERDOUR: *Hawkcraig House* £   2
Hawkcraig Point, Aberdour, Fife. **Map** D4. [C] *(01383) 860335.*
Staying in this small, whitewashed, old ferryman's house is a pleasant
experience. Lovely setting and friendly owners. ● *Nov–Apr.* 🚗 TV P

ARRAN: *Kilmichael House Hotel* [W] www.kilmichael.com ££ MC V 7
Glen Cloy, Brodick, Isle of Arran. **Map** C5. [C] *(01770) 302219.* FAX *(01770) 302068.*
This small hotel provides a warm welcome and every comfort in elegant
surroundings. It also affords some of the best food in Arran. 🚗 TV P 🐕 ⚡

AUCHTERARDER: *Gleneagles* [W] www.gleneagles.com £££££ AE DC MC V 273
Auchterarder. **Map** D4. [C] *(01764) 662231.* FAX *(01764) 662134.*
Originally built by the Caledonian Railway Company in 1924, this
magnificent hotel is internationally renowned. 🚗 TV 🏊 24 ⚡ P 🌊 ♿

BALQUHIDDER: *Monachyle Mhor Farmhouse* £££ MC V 10
[W] www.monachylemhor.com
Balquhidder, Perthshire. **Map** C4. [C] *(01877) 384622.* FAX *(01877) 384305.*
This hotel overlooks Loch Voil and has a fine restaurant. 🚗 TV ⚡ P ♿

BLAIRGOWRIE: *Kinloch House* [@] info@kinlochhouse.com £££££ MC V 18
Near Blairgowrie, Perthshire. **Map** D3. [C] *(01250) 884237.* FAX *(01250) 884333.*
A handsome baronial house, with wonderful, relaxed surroundings and a
superb restaurant. ● *last two weeks in Dec.* 🚗 TV ⚡ P ♿

CALLANDER: *Roman Camp Country House* [W] www.roman-camp-hotel.co.uk ££ AE DC MC V 14
Callander. **Map** D4. [C] *(01877) 330003.* FAX *(01877) 331533.*
Set in extensive gardens, this peaceful, charming retreat has a unique atmos-
phere. The menu offers innovative and modern cuisine. 🚗 TV ⚡ P ♿

DUNBLANE: *Cromlix House* [W] www.cromlixhouse.com £££££ AE DC MC V 14
Kinbuck, nr Dunblane, Stirlingshire. **Map** D4. [C] *(01786) 822125.* FAX *(01786) 825450.*
A fine Edwardian mansion set in a large estate. The rooms are furnished
with antiques and original furniture. 🚗 TV P

GLAMIS: *Castleton House* [W] www.castletonglamis.co.uk £££ AE MC V 6
Eassie, nr Glamis, Forfar. **Map** D3. [C] *(01307) 840340.* FAX *(01307) 840506.*
Reasonably close to Dundee and Glamis Castle, this family-run, country
house hotel is set in peaceful, attractive countryside. Good food. 🚗 TV ⚡ P

IRVINE: *Annfield House* [W] www.annfieldhousehotel.co.uk £ AE DC MC V 9
6 Castle St, Irvine. **Map** C4. [C] *(01294) 278903.* FAX *(01294) 278904.*
A comfortable hotel with a country house atmosphere overlooking the River
Irvine. The restaurant has a reputation for high quality cuisine. 🚗 TV ⚡ P

LARGS: *Brisbane House* [W] www.brisbanehousehotel.co.uk ££ AE DC MC V 23
14 Greenock Rd, Esplanade, Largs. **Map** C5. [C] *(01475) 687200.* FAX *(01475) 676295.*
Attractive 18th-century house which has been modernized to make it smart
and stylish. Some bedrooms overlook the Firth of Clyde. 🚗 TV 24 P ♿

MARKINCH: *Balbirnie House* [W] www.balbirnie.co.uk ££££ AE DC MC V 30
Balbirnie Park, Markinch, Fife. **Map** D4. [C] *(01592) 610066.* FAX *(01592) 610529.*
Surrounded by extensive parkland, the setting for this Georgian mansion
is outstanding. It is unashamedly luxurious, but the atmosphere remains
informal and unstuffy. 🚗 TV 24 ⚡ P ♿

ST ANDREWS: *Old Course Hotel* [W] www.oldcoursehotel.co.uk £££££ AE DC MC V 134
St Andrews. **Map** E4. [C] *(01334) 474371.* FAX *(01334) 477668.*
Not a very beautiful hotel outside but no expense has been spared
inside – the result is tasteful luxury.
🚗 TV 🏊 24 ⚡ P 🌊 ♿

SCONE: *Murrayshall Country House Hotel* [W] www.murrayshall.co.uk £££ AE DC MC V 41
Scone, Perthshire. **Map** D4. [C] *(01738) 551171.* FAX *(01738) 552595.*
A turreted, baronial hall with two golf courses. The rooms are rather
formal and starchy, but still luxuriously comfortable. Excellent food is
served in the restaurant. 🚗 TV P ♿

		Price categories / legend			CREDIT CARDS	RESTAURANT	CHILDREN WELCOME	GARDEN/TERRACE	NUMBER OF ROOMS

Price categories for a standard double room per night, inclusive of breakfast, service charges and any additional taxes such as VAT:
£ under £80
££ £80–£130
£££ £130–£180
££££ £180–£230
£££££ over £230.

RESTAURANT
Hotel restaurant or dining room usually open to non-residents unless otherwise stated.

CHILDREN WELCOME
Child cots and a baby-sitting service available. Some hotel restaurants have children's portions and high chairs.

GARDEN/TERRACE
Hotels with a garden, courtyard or terrace.

CREDIT CARDS
Indicates which credit cards are accepted: *AE* American Express; *DC* Diners Club; *MC* MasterCard/Access; *V* VISA.

Entry	Credit Cards	Restaurant	Children Welcome	Garden/Terrace	No. of Rooms
STRACHUR: *Creggans Inn* w www.creggans-inn.co.uk **££** Strachur, Argyll, Strathclyde. **Map** C4. ☎ (01369) 860279. FAX (01369) 860637. Convivial inn with pretty bedrooms, in a superb spot overlooking Loch Fyne. The food is excellent, both in the formal restaurant and at the bar, and the service is superb throughout the whole establishment. 🔲 TV P	AE MC V	▩	●		14
TROON: *Piersland House* w www.piersland.co.uk **££** Craigend Rd, Troon, Ayrshire. **Map** C5. ☎ (01292) 314747. FAX (01292) 315613. An appealing mock-Tudor house close to the championship golf course. A cottage annexe has been added in which each suite has its own sitting room. Good food is available. 🔲 TV 24 P &	AE DC MC V	▩	●	▩	30
TURNBERRY: *Turnberry* w www.westin.com-turnberry **£££££** Turnberry, Ayrshire. **Map** C5. ☎ (01655) 331000. FAX (01655) 331706. Huge Edwardian hotel and health spa refurbished to luxurious standards. What the Turnberry perhaps lacks in atmosphere it more than makes up for in comfort. 🔲 TV 🔼 24 P 🏊	AE DC MC V	▩	●	▩	221

THE HIGHLANDS AND ISLANDS

Entry	Credit Cards	Restaurant	Children Welcome	Garden/Terrace	No. of Rooms
ABERDEEN: *Maryculter House Hotel* w www.maryculterhousehotel.co.uk **££** South Deeside Road, Maryculter, Aberdeen. **Map** E3. ☎ (01224) 732124. FAX (01224) 733510. A historic hotel set in quiet, rural surroundings on the banks of the River Dee, with riverside walks close by. 🔲 TV 24 🔁 P & limited.	AE DC MC V	▩	●	▩	22
ABERDEEN: *Udny Arms* w www.udny.demon.co.uk **£** Main Street, Newburgh, Aberdeen. **Map** E3. ☎ (01358) 789444. FAX (01358) 789012. A village pub with character and comfortable rooms. Close to a golf course and the Ythan estuary nature reserve and known for its good food. ● 26 Dec. 🔲 TV 🔁 P & limited.	DC MC V	▩	●	▩	26
ACHILTIBUIE: *Summer Isles* w www.summerisleshotel.co.uk **££** Achiltibuie, near Ullapool, Ross & Cromarty, Highlands. **Map** C2. ☎ (01854) 622282. FAX (01854) 622251. A special hotel that meets all expectations. Well-appointed rooms, a superb restaurant and fabulous views to the Summer Isles. ● mid-Oct–Easter 🔲 P	MC V	▩	●		13
ARDUAINE: *Loch Melfort Hotel* w www.lochmelfort.co.uk **£** Arduaine, by Oban, Argyll. **Map** C4. ☎ (01852) 200233. FAX (01852) 200214. Comfortable accommodation here, with the best views on the west coast. The panoramic restaurant, looking to Scarba and Jura, serves local seafood. Arduaine Garden (*see p132*) lies adjacent to the grounds. ● Jan. 🔲 TV P &	AE MC V	▩	●	▩	26
ARISAIG: *Old Library Lodge* w www.oldlibrary.co.uk **£** Arisaig, Highlands. **Map** B3. ☎ (01687) 450651. FAX (01687) 450219. A modest restaurant-with-rooms offering a minimum five choices at each course, and much fresh, locally sourced produce. Peaceful, spacious bedrooms, mostly in a modern rear extension. ● Dec–Feb 🔲 TV 🔁	AE MC V	▩		▩	6
AULDEARN: *Boath House* w www.boath-house.com **££££** Auldearn, Nairn, Highlands. **Map** D2. ☎ (01667) 454896. FAX (01667) 455469. Close to the Moray Firth, this imposing Georgian mansion stands in secluded 20-acre grounds. The strikingly decorated contemporary interior is cool and spacious. Outstanding food (organic and seasonal). ● Christmas week 🔲 TV 🔁 &	AE MC V	▩	●	▩	6
BALLATER: *Balgonie Country House* w www.balgonie-hotel.co.uk **£** Braemar Place, Ballater, Aberdeenshire. **Map** D3. ☎ & FAX (013397) 55482. Family-run country house hotel on the outskirts of Ballater. The excellent fare features Scottish cuisine, and the wonderful hospitality favours any guest who likes home-from-home comforts. ● Jan–mid Feb 🔲 TV P	AE MC V	▩	●	▩	9

BALLINDALLOCH: *Delnashaugh Hotel* (£) MC V 9
Ballindalloch, Banffshire, Grampian. **Map** D2.
(01807) 500255. FAX (01807) 500389.
Overlooking the River Avon in the Spey Valley, this hotel makes a perfect base for exploring the area, and is lovely to return to after a day's sightseeing. The food is especially good.

BARRA: *Castlebay Hotel* W www.castlebay-hotel.co.uk (£) MC V 12
Castlebay, Isle of Barra, Western Isles. **Map** A3.
(01871) 810223. FAX (01871) 810455.
A friendly, family-owned hotel overlooking the bay, where you can take a boat to Mingulay and Eriskay. The food is highly recommended.

CRINAN: *Crinan Hotel* W www.crinanhotel.com (£)(£)(£)(£)(£) MC V 20
Crinan, Lochgilphead, Argyll. **Map** C4. (01546) 830261. FAX (01546) 830292.
This hotel is in a superb position by the harbour, where Loch Crinan meets the Sound of Jura. The service is excellent, but a visit is worthwhile for the stunning views alone.

CROMARTY: *Royal* W www.royalcromartyhotel.co.uk (£) MC V 10
Marine Terrace, Cromarty, Highlands. **Map** D2. (01381) 600217. FAX (01381) 600813.
With beautiful views overlooking the Firth of Cromarty, this friendly, unpretentious hotel has a traditional feel. The well-decorated bedrooms are comfortable and spotless.

DORNOCH: *Dornoch Castle Hotel* W www.dornochcastlehotel.com (£)(£) AE MC V 24
Castle Street, Dornoch, Sutherland. **Map** D2. (01862) 810216. FAX (01862) 810981.
An interesting, historic building dating from the late 15th, early 16th centuries, and formerly part of the Bishop's Palace. There is a secluded garden and the food is very good.

DULNAIN BRIDGE: *Auchendean Lodge* W www.auchendean.com (£)(£) AE DC MC V 5
Dulnain Bridge, by Grantown on Spey, Inverness-shire. **Map** D2. & FAX (01479) 851347.
Set in spectacular scenery near Aviemore and Cairngorm, this welcoming hotel is an Edwardian shooting lodge. Conveniently situated for exploring the Speyside distilleries and the alluring countryside. Nov.

DUNKELD: *Kinnaird* W www.kinnairdestate.com (£)(£)(£)(£)(£) AE MC V 9
Kinnaird Estate, near Dunkeld, Tayside. **Map** D3. (01796) 482440. FAX (01796) 482289.
Surrounded by a vast, beautiful country estate, this 18th-century house has been converted into a sumptuous, luxurious hotel where no expense has been spared.

FORRES: *Milton of Grange Farm* W www.forres-accommodation.co.uk (£)(£) MC V 3
Forres, Moray. **Map** D2. (01309) 676360. FAX (01309) 676360.
Comfortable family farm overlooking Findhorn Nature Reserve and the Moray Firth. An excellent base for beaches, watersports, golf and the Speyside whisky and castle trail.

FORT WILLIAM: *Old Pines Hotel* W www.oldpines.co.uk (£)(£) MC V 8
Spean Bridge, near Fort William, Argyll. **Map** C3. (01397) 712324.
Situated nine miles from Fort William this timber framed ski lodge offers warm and friendly accommodation. A good base from which to tour the surrounding countryside.

GAIRLOCH: *Rua Reidh Lighthouse Hostel* W www.ruareidh.co.uk (£) MC V 8
Melvaig, Gairloch, Ross-shire. **Map** C2. (01445) 771263.
The former lighthouse keeper's house offers a friendly and relaxed atmosphere with home cooking.

IONA (NEAR MULL): *Argyll Hotel* W www.argyllhoteliona.co.uk (£)(£)(£) MC V 16
Isle of Iona, Argyll. **Map** B4. (01681) 700334. FAX (01681) 700510.
An unpretentious, friendly hotel on this very special island. Ask for a bedroom facing the sea for the most wonderful views. Dec–Jan.

INVERNESS: *Glenmoriston Town House* W www.glenmoriston.com (£)(£) AE DC MC V 30
Inverness, Inverness-shire. **Map** D2. (01463) 223777. FAX (01463) 712378.
Riverside hotel with tasteful, contemporary décor. Bedrooms attain high standards, with marble bathrooms and lavish furnishings.

INVERNESS: *Dunain Park* W www.dunainparkhotel.co.uk (£)(£)(£) DC MC V 13
Inverness, Inverness-shire. **Map** D2. (01463) 230512. FAX (01463) 224532.
Surrounded by a large garden, this comfortable hotel provides a peaceful base for touring the area.

Price categories for a standard double room per night, inclusive of breakfast, service charges and any additional taxes such as VAT: £ under £80 ££ £80–£130 £££ £130–£180 ££££ £180–£230 £££££ over £230.	**RESTAURANT** Hotel restaurant or dining room usually open to non-residents unless otherwise stated. **CHILDREN WELCOME** Child cots and a baby-sitting service available. Some hotel restaurants have children's portions and high chairs. **GARDEN/TERRACE** Hotels with a garden, courtyard or terrace. **CREDIT CARDS** Indicates which credit cards are accepted: *AE* American Express; *DC* Diners Club; *MC* MasterCard/Access; *V* VISA.	CREDIT CARDS	RESTAURANT	CHILDREN WELCOME	GARDEN/TERRACE	NUMBER OF ROOMS
ISLE ORNSAY (SKYE): *Eilean Iarmain* w www.eileaniarmain.co.uk ££ Sleat, Isle of Skye, Highlands. **Map** B3. [(01471) 833332. FAX (01471) 833275. Traditional 19th-century seaside inn with a Gaelic feel. Wonderful views from the comfy bedrooms and public rooms. 🛏 TV 🍴 P	AE MC V	▪	●	▪	16
KILDRUMMY: *Kildrummy Castle* w www.kildrummycastlehotel.co.uk £££ Kildrummy, near Alford, Gordon, Grampian. [(01975) 571288. **Map** E3. FAX (01975) 571345. Large, rather stately, Victorian castellated building, set in lovely gardens overlooking a 13th-century castle ruin. The superb interior decoration is every bit as beautiful as the surroundings. ● *Jan.* 🛏 TV P	MC V	▪	●	▪	16
KILLIECRANKIE: *Killiecrankie Hotel* w www.killiecrankiehotel.co.uk ££££ Killiecrankie, by Pitlochry, Perthshire. **Map** D3. [(01796) 473220. FAX (01796) 472451. Smart country house hotel in a scenic setting. The excellent meals, which are chosen from a menu of hearty fare, may be taken in the enjoyable surroundings of the conservatory. 🛏 TV 🍴 P	MC V	▪	●	▪	10
KYLESKU, BY LAIRG: *Kylesku Hotel* w www.kyleskuhotel.co.uk £ Kylesku, by Lairg, Sutherland. **Map** D2. [(01971) 502231. FAX (01971) 502313. A family-run hotel with a welcoming atmosphere, situated on the shore of Loch Glencoul. The restaurant specializes in local seafood. ● *Nov–Mar.* 🛏 TV 🍴 P	MC V	▪	●	▪	8
LEDAIG: *Isle of Eriska* w www.eriska-hotel.co.uk £££££ Ledaig, near Oban, Argyll. **Map** C3. [(01631) 720 371. FAX (01631) 720 531. Situated on its very own island, this grand, 19th-century baronial hall has charming rooms. Service in the dining room is formal in the evenings, and guests are expected to change for dinner; an air of comforting tradition pervades. ● *Jan–mid-Feb.* 🛏 TV 24 P 🏊 🚫	AE MC V	▪	●	▪	22
LEWIS, TIMSGARRY: *Baile Na Cille* ££ Timsgarry, Isle of Lewis, Highlands. **Map** B1. [(01851) 672242. FAX (01851) 672241. A very friendly hotel in an amazing location at the end of a long beach. A perfect place to get away from it all. ● *mid-Oct–mid-Mar.* 🛏 🍴 P	MC V	▪	●	▪	12
MUIR OF ORD: *The Dower House* w www.thedowerhouse.co.uk ££ Highfield, Muir of Ord, Ross-shire, Highlands. **Map** C2. [& FAX (01463) 870090. An extremely agreeable small hotel that is attractively decorated. Pleasing bedrooms and a first-rate restaurant. 🛏 TV 24 🍴 P 🚫 limited.	MC V	▪	●	▪	5
MULL, DERVAIG: *Druimard Country House* w www.druimard.co.uk ££ Dervaig, by Tobermory, Isle of Mull, Strathclyde. **Map** B4. [& FAX (01688) 400345. This restored Victorian house offers every comfort including an excellent restaurant, overlooking the River Bellart. ● *Jan.* 🛏 P	MC V	▪	●	▪	7
MULL, TOBERMORY: *Western Isles Hotel* w www.mullhotel.com ££ Tobermory, Isle of Mull, Strathclyde. **Map** B3. [(01688) 302012. FAX (01688) 302297. A grand, traditional establishment, with views over Tobermory Bay and the Sound of Mull. Very welcoming and comfortable, with log fires in winter. There is a choice of restaurants, including a conservatory which is particularly delightful. ● *Christmas.* 🛏 TV P	MC V	▪	●	▪	28
OLD MELDRUM: *The Redgarth* @ redgarth1@aol.com £ Old Meldrum, Aberdeenshire. **Map** E3. [(01651) 872353. Enjoying magnificent views over Bennachie and the surrounding countryside, this small, comfortable hotel is well placed for exploring the local castle and whisky trails. The restaurant offers a varied choice of home cooked meals. 🛏 TV 🍴 P	AE MC V	▪		▪	3

ONICH: *Cuilcheanna House* W www.smoothhound.co.uk/hotels/cuilcheanna.htm £££
Onich, by Fort William, Inverness-shire. **Map** C3. (01855) 821226.
Expect exceptional home cooking by chef Linda Scott at this country house hotel overlooking the beautiful Loch Linnhe. The four-course dinners change daily and are outstanding value, although they are available only to residents of the hotel. ● *Nov–Easter.*
MC V — 7

ORKNEY: *Foveran* W www.foveranhotel.co.uk ££
St Ola, Kirkwall, Orkney. (01856) 872389. FAX (01856) 876430.
A modern hotel with great views over Scapa Flow and the South Isles. Comfortable rooms and a good restaurant.
MC V — 8

PORT APPIN: *Airds* W www.airds-hotel.com £££££
Port Appin, Appin, Argyll. **Map** C3. (01631) 730236. FAX (01631) 730535.
A former ferry inn with a modest whitewashed exterior, inside it is smart and comfortable with a very good restaurant.
MC V — 12

SHETLAND, BUSTA: *Busta House* W www.bustahouse.com ££
Busta, Brae, Shetland. (01806) 522506. FAX (01806) 522588.
A civilized family-run hotel beside its own little harbour. This early 18th-century house is relaxed and comfortable. limited.
AE DC MC V — 22

SHETLAND, WALLS: *Burrastow House* W www.userszetnet.co.uk/burrastow-house £
Walls, Shetland. (01595) 809307. FAX (01595) 809213.
In a very remote part of western Shetland, this is a wonderful place to escape to for absolute calm and tranquillity. Comfort is not sacrificed here, and the food is delicious. ● *Jan–Mar.*
AE DC MC V — 5

SHIELDAIG: *Tigh-an-Eilean* W www.theaa.com/hotels/3194.html £££
Shieldaig, near Strathcarron, Ross & Cromarty, Highlands. **Map** C2.
(01520) 755251. FAX (01520) 755321.
On the bank of Loch Shieldaig, this small hotel is comfortable and homely. The rooms are on the small side but the view is spectacular.
● *mid-Nov–Mar.*
MC V — 11

SKYE, HEREBOST: *Dunorin House* @ stay@dunorin.freeserve.co.uk ££
Herebost, Dunvegan, Isle of Skye, Highlands. **Map** B2. & FAX (01470) 521488.
Enjoying outstanding views of the Cuillin mountains, this family-run hotel offers a comfortable, relaxing atmosphere. All bedrooms are on the ground floor and the restaurant has an excellent menu. ● *Oct–Mar.*
MC V — 10

SKYE, PORTREE: *Viewfield House* W www.viewfieldhouse.com ££
Portree, Isle of Skye, Highlands. (01478) 612217. FAX (01478) 613517
A rambling building that has been a family house for 200 years. Guests are made welcome and everyone dines together. ● *mid-Oct–mid-Apr.*
MC V — 12

SKYE, SLIGACHAN: *Sligachan Hotel* W www.sligachan.co.uk ££
Sligachan, Isle of Skye, Highlands. (01478) 650204. FAX (01478) 650207.
This famous hotel sits beside Loch Sligachan below the northern end of the Black Cuillin hills. An excellent base for walkers, climbers and lovers of Highland scenery. ● *mid-Oct–mid-Apr.*
MC V — 22

SKYE, STAFFIN: *Flodigarry Hotel* W www.flodigarry.co.uk £
Flodigarry, Staffin, Isle of Skye. **Map** B2. (01470) 552203. FAX (01470) 552301.
Set on the spectacular Trotternish Peninsula with magnificent views, the building was originally associated with Flora Macdonald. The hotel has a conservatory and offers friendly, traditional hospitality.
AE MC V — 18

TALLADALE: *The Old Mill Highland Lodge* £££
W www.theoldmillhighlandlodge.co.uk
Loch Maree, Highlands. **Map** C2. (01445) 760271.
Located in a rennovated mill dating from 1840 on the shores of Loch Maree with fine views of the surrounding mountains.
— 6

THURSO: *Forss House* W www.forsshousehotel.co.uk ££
Thurso, Caithness, Highlands. **Map** D1. (01847) 861201. FAX (01847) 861301.
A welcoming hotel on the wilds of the northern coast. Imposing on the outside, but inside it is comfortable and cheerful.
AE DC MC V — 13

ULLAPOOL: *Ceilidh Place* W www.theceilidhplace.com ££
14 West Argyle St, Ullapool, Wester-Ross, Highlands. **Map** C2.
(01854) 612103. FAX (01854) 612886.
Lots going on here – musical evenings and exhibitions, a café and bookshop. Residents have their own peaceful sitting room.
MC V — 13

WHERE TO EAT

SCOTTISH FOOD NEED strike no terror in the visiting gourmet's heart; Scotland's restaurant scene has moved far from its once dismal reputation. This is partly due to an influx of foreign chefs and cooking styles. You can now sample a wide range of international cuisine throughout Scotland, with the greatest choice in Edinburgh and Glasgow. Home-grown restaurateurs have also risen to the challenge of redeeming Scottish food, and the indigenous cooking has improved beyond all

Ryan's Bar in Edinburgh

recognition in the last decade. You can now eat extremely well in Scotland regardless of your budget, and at most times of the day in the major towns and cities, although the more rural establishments are less flexible. Affordable, well-prepared but less elaborate food is making a mark in all types of brasseries, restaurants and cafés throughout the country. The restaurant listings on pages 176–83 feature some of the best places to eat, as well as those with a consistently good track record.

The vast selection of beer and whisky available in a typical Scottish pub

PRICES AND BOOKING

ALL RESTAURANTS are required by law to display their current prices outside the door. These amounts include VAT (value-added tax) at 17.5 per cent, and any service or cover charge should also be specified. This should give a rough idea of what the meal will cost before you enter the restaurant.

Wine can be pricey when dining out in Scotland, and extras like coffee and bottled water may be disproportionately expensive compared to the cost of the food. Service charges (usually between 10 and 15 per cent) are sometimes added automatically to the bill. If service has not been included, you are expected to leave a tip – the amount will depend on the level of service that you have received. The majority of restaurants accept cheques with a cheque guarantee card, or credit cards. Pubs

usually prefer cash to cards. It is advisable to book a table before making a special journey to a restaurant. City restaurants are very busy, and some of the more renowned establishments can be fully booked up to a month in advance. If you cannot keep a reservation, cancel it by telephone.

BREAKFAST, LUNCH AND DINNER

TRADITIONALLY, breakfast in Scotland begins with cereal and milk, followed by bacon, eggs and tomato, and usually black pudding (blood sausage) too. It finishes with toast and marmalade, and a pot of tea. The alternative is a continental breakfast of black coffee, fruit juice and a croissant or two.

The most popular lunchtime foods are sandwiches, salads, baked potatoes and ploughman's lunches (a roll, hunk of cheese or ham and relishes),

found mainly in pubs. A traditional Sunday lunch of roast meat and vegetables is served in some pubs and restaurants.

Grand hotels can offer five or six courses for dinner, but usually there are only three. Dessert is often followed by a range of specialist cheeses and oatcakes. Outside the larger towns and cities, dinner is usually eaten between 6pm and 9pm, and no later. In Scotland lunch is sometimes called "dinner" and the evening meal may be called "tea".

AFTERNOON TEA

NO VISITOR SHOULD miss the experience of a proper Scottish afternoon tea, which can rival breakfast as the most enjoyable meal of the day. There are hundreds of tearooms all over Scotland, offering a choice of delicious sandwiches and cakes. Dundee Cake, fruit scones and shortbread are particular favourites and are wonderful eaten with a cup of tea. Scotch pancakes swimming in butter are another appetizing speciality.

One of Glasgow's many new and fashionable Italian restaurants

Fast food in Edinburgh: a fish and chip shop on the Portobello promenade

CHILDREN

MANY PLACES now welcome junior diners *(see the listings for details)* and some actively encourage families, at least during the day or early evening. They may offer a separate children's menu, or simply adapt the portions to suit a child's appetite. Some also provide highchairs. Italian, Spanish, Indian and fast-food restaurants nearly always welcome children, and even pubs are relaxing their rules and may provide special play areas.

VEGETARIAN FOOD

BRITAIN IS AHEAD of many of its European counterparts in providing vegetarian alternatives to meat dishes, and Scotland is no exception. A few of the establishments listed in this guide serve only vegetarian meals, and most cater for non-meat-eaters *(see the listings for an indication of restaurants serving vegetarian dishes)*. Edinburgh and Glasgow have the widest choice, but smaller towns and villages are also beginning to experiment with meat-free dishes. Vegetarians wishing to find a wider choice than is offered by Scottish and English food should try South Indian, Chinese and other ethnic restaurants as they have a tradition of good vegetarian cuisine.

SEAFOOD

WITH MORE THAN 16,000 km (10,000 miles) of coastline, fish and shellfish play an important part in the Scottish diet and economy. North Sea cod, haddock (often smoked as kippers or Arbroath Smokies), herring and mackerel, can all be found in shops and restaurants, while farms on the west coast rear much of Scotland's Atlantic salmon and rainbow trout. Lobsters, crabs and prawns are all common in Scottish waters and in recent years more emphasis has been placed on the cultivation and conservation of natural shellfish stocks including mussels, oysters and scallops.

The Mitre pub on Edinburgh's Royal Mile

FAST FOOD

SCOTLAND IS RIGHTLY famed for its "fish suppers" (fish and chips) and there are many seaside fish bars selling wonderfully fresh fish and chips (French fries). Most also offer chicken suppers. Away from the coast the fish may not be as amazingly fresh, but there are plenty of good places from which to choose.

Visitors will find the usual fast food chains, such as Pizza Hut, McDonald's, Burger King and KFC, as well as sandwich bars and "greasy spoon" cafés that serve mainly fried food.

Taking afternoon tea in Scotland – an elegant and enjoyable pastime

PUBS AND STYLE BARS

SCOTTISH ALCOHOL licensing laws are different from the rest of Britain, most apparent in the later closing times of pubs and bars. Whereas in England and Wales most places close at 11pm, many in Scotland, particularly in the towns and cities, stay open until midnight or even 1 or 2am. During the Festival in August *(see pp78–9)*, Edinburgh's drinking holes often do not close until 3am.

While the old-fashioned, dark and occasionally slightly shabby pubs still exist, a new breed of bar has become popular in Scotland in recent years. In the towns and cities, 'style' bars have become two-a-penny. Unlike the traditional pubs, the choice of drink is not limited to a few beers. They tend to be noisy, with a predominantly young clientele. Here, the emphasis is on variety, with lively happy hours and interesting cocktails.

Choosing a Restaurant

THE RESTAURANTS in this guide have been selected across a wide price range for their good value, exceptional food and interesting location. Many are in recommended hotels. The chart lists the restaurants by region starting with Edinburgh; colour-coded thumb tabs indicate the regions covered on each page. For hotel listings, see pp166–73.

	CREDIT CARDS	CHILDREN WELCOME	FIXED-PRICE MENU	VEGETARIAN	TRADITIONAL SCOTTISH
EDINBURGH					
OLD TOWN: *Café Florentin* ⓕ 8 St Giles Street. 【 *(0131) 225 6267.* A cosmopolitan, informal café serving a full range of coffees, teas and light meals. French breads and pastries are the speciality here. ● *25 Dec.* ⚡		●	▨	●	
OLD TOWN: *Black Bo's* ⓕⓕ 57-61 Blackfriars St. 【 *(0131) 557 6136.* Small vegetarian restaurant in the Old Town which really cares about food. Imaginative and well flavoured dishes form the menu. ● *1-2 Jan, 25–6 Dec.* ¶	MC V	●	▨	●	
OLD TOWN: *Petit Paris* ⓕⓕⓕ 38-40 Grassmarket. 【 *(0131) 226 2442.* Checked tablecloths and wall posters set the scene for this relaxed and friendly restaurant using local and imported French produce. The slowly baked rabbit and roast seabass are recommended. ● *Mon, Oct-Apr.* ¶				▨	●
OLD TOWN: *The Atrium and the Blue Bar Café* ⓕⓕⓕ 10 Cambridge Street. 【 *(0131) 228 8882.* Stylish interior reflects the light, simple dishes in The Atrium – the cutting edge of modern Scottish food. For light lunches or dinners, try the Blue Bar upstairs. ● *Sat lunch, Sun, 25-6 Dec, 1-2 Jan.* 🔁 ¶	AE DC MC V	●		●	
OLD TOWN: *The Grain Store* ⓕⓕⓕ 30 Victoria Street. 【 *(0131) 225 7635.* On the upper floor of an unusual building, in a cobbled street with interesting shops, this restaurant is close to the Castle, Grassmarket and St Giles. Good food in an informal atmosphere. ● *first week of Jan, 25–6 Dec.* ¶	AE MC V		▨	●	▨
OLD TOWN: *The Witchery and the Secret Garden Restaurant* ⓕⓕⓕⓕ @ mail@thewitchery.com Castlehill, Royal Mile. 【 *(0131) 225 5613.* Sample contemporary Scottish cuisine in style. Located beside the entrance to Edinburgh Castle at the top of the Royal Mile. ● *25–26 Dec.* ¶	AE DC MC V	●	▨	●	▨
SOUTH SIDE: *Sweet Melinda's* ⓕⓕⓕ 11 Roseneath Street, Marchmont. 【 *(0131) 229 7953.* With ingredients from nearby Eddie's Chinese fish market, this is seriously good seafood with a Pacific Rim accent. ● *Sun, Mon, 1–2 Jan, 25–6 Dec.* 🔁 ¶	MC V	●		●	
NEW TOWN: *Queen Street Café* ⓕ Scottish National Portrait Gallery, 1 Queen Street. 【 *(0131) 557 2844.* A delightful coffee shop providing delicious and imaginative home cooking in interesting surroundings. (There is also a good café in the Scottish National Gallery of Modern Art.) ● *25–6 Dec.* 🔁 ⚡ *entire premises.*	AE DC MC V			●	
NEW TOWN: *Howie's* �W www.howies.uk.com ⓕⓕ 29 Waterloo Place. 【 *(0131) 556 5766.* This eclectic bistro serving contemporary Scottish food, has a monthly changing menu that ensures its lasting appeal. ● *1 Jan, 25–6 Dec.* ¶	AE MC V	●	▨	●	
NEW TOWN: *Indigo Yard* ⓕⓕⓕ 7 Charlotte Lane. 【 *(0131) 220 5603.* An informal café/bistro, with outdoor tables, combining restaurant and bar services. Popular in the evenings. Great atmosphere. 🔁 ⚡ ¶	AE MC V	●		●	
NEW TOWN: *The Dome* �W www.thedomeedinburgh.com ⓕⓕⓕ 14 George Street. 【 *(0131) 624 8624.* In a magnificent building, constructed for the Royal College of Physicians in 1775, the restaurant has a sophisticated menu. Coffee, light lunches and afternoon tea are served al fresco in the courtyard. ● *1–2 Jan, 25–6 Dec.* ¶	AE MC V	●		●	

Price categories include a three-course meal for one, half a bottle of house wine, and all unavoidable extra costs such as cover charge and VAT:
£ under £15
££ £15–£25
£££ £25–£35
££££ £35–£50
£££££ over £50.

CHILDREN WELCOME
Restaurants offering smaller portions and high chairs for children. Special menus sometimes available.
FIXED-PRICE MENU
A good value fixed-price meal, at lunch, dinner or both, usually consisting of three courses.
VEGETARIAN
Vegetarian specialities are included on the menu.
TRADITIONAL SCOTTISH
Several, if not all, of the items on the menu are traditional Scottish recipes, using fresh local produce.

	Credit Cards	Children Welcome	Fixed-Price Menu	Vegetarian	Traditional Scottish
NEW TOWN: *Martin's* — £££ 70 Rose Street, North Lane. (0131) 225 3106. Excellent city-centre restaurant offering a range of imaginative, contemporary Scottish cuisine. The superb Celtic cheeseboard is highly recommended. ● Sat lunch, Sun, Mon, 24 Dec–20 Jan.	AE DC MC V		■	●	
NEW TOWN: *Ochre Vita (Channings Hotel)* www.channings.co.uk — £££ 12-15 South Learmouth Gardens. (0131) 315 2226. Channings' conservatory restaurant is a Mediterranean style bistro offering classic dishes with an exotic twist in an informal setting.	AE DC MC V	●	■	●	
NEW TOWN: *Haldane's* www.haldinesrestaurant.co.uk — £££££ 39A Albany Street. (0131) 556 8407. Elegant, tranquil restaurant with charming staff and stylish, flavourful contemporary food. ● 24-6 Dec.	AE DC MC V	●	■	●	■
NEW TOWN: *Vincaffé* — £££ 11 Multrees Walk. (0131) 557 0088. This restaurant and wine bar is situated in the heart of the city close to St Andrew's Square and Princes Street. The pizzas made from organic Canadian flour are particularly recommended. ● 25 Dec. 1–Jan.	AE MC V			●	
NEW TOWN: *Number One Princes Street* www.thebalmoralhotel.com — £££££ 1 Princes Street. (0131) 556 2414. The restaurant of Edinburgh's finest hotel enjoys a well-deserved reputation for excellence. Also a brasserie offering light meals.	AE DC MC V	●	■	●	■
FURTHER AFIELD: *Daniel's* — ££ 88 Commercial Street, Leith. (0131) 553 5933. One of the best of the new conservatory restaurants opposite the Scottish Office and piazza. The restaurant serves hearty Alsace food with French charm, and lighter snacks in the café at the back. ● 1 Jan, 24-5 Dec.	AE MC V	●	■	●	■
FURTHER AFIELD: *The Waterfront* www.skippers.co.uk — £££ 1C Dock Place, Leith. (0131) 554 7427. The restaurant combines small, cosy rooms and a conservatory facing the dock, with outside terraces and a pontoon. The menu reflects the best of Scottish ingredients available, especially fish. ● 25-6 Dec.	AE MC V	●	■	●	●
FURTHER AFIELD: *Whitekirk Golf Club and Restaurant* — £££ Whitekirk, near North Berwick, East Lothian. (01620) 870300. This restaurant has a rural setting, with lovely views. It offers good value and a friendly atmosphere. ● 24-6 Dec, 1–Jan, dinner.	MC V	●		●	■
FURTHER AFIELD: *Open Arms Hotel* openarms@clara.co.uk — £££ Dirlton, East Lothian. (01620) 850241. On the village green, overlooking Dirlton Castle. Diners can chose between the formal restaurant, or the brasserie.	MC V	●	■	●	●
FURTHER AFIELD: *Skippers Bistro* www.skippers.co.uk — £££ 1A Dock Place, Leith. (0131) 554 1018. Offers intimate and relaxing dining. The menu, specializing in fish, changes daily. ● 25 Dec, 1 Jan.	AE MC V	●		●	■
FURTHER AFIELD: *Suruchi Too* www.suruchirestaurant.co.uk — £££ 121 Constitution Street, Leith. (0131) 554 3268. Indian cuisine with a distinct Scottish flavour; vegetable haggis fritters and menus written in the Scots vernacular.	AE MC V	●	■	●	
FURTHER AFIELD: *Valvona & Crolla* — £££ 19 Elm Row, Leith. (0131) 556 6066. Fresh southern Mediterreanean cuisine, using Italian and local produce. The chocolate cake and lemon tart are recommended.		●		●	

Price categories include a three-course meal for one, half a bottle of house wine, and all unavoidable extra costs such as cover charge and VAT:
£ under £15
££ £15–£25
£££ £25–£35
££££ £35–£50
£££££ over £50.

CHILDREN WELCOME
Restaurants offering smaller portions and high chairs for children. Special menus sometimes available.
FIXED-PRICE MENU
A good value fixed-price meal, at lunch, dinner or both, usually consisting of three courses.
VEGETARIAN
Vegetarian specialities are included on the menu.
TRADITIONAL SCOTTISH
Several, if not all, of the items on the menu are traditional Scottish recipes, using fresh local produce.

	CREDIT CARDS	CHILDREN WELCOME	FIXED-PRICE MENU	VEGETARIAN	TRADITIONAL SCOTTISH

FURTHER AFIELD: *Vintners Rooms* w www.thevintnersrooms.demon.co.uk £££
87 Giles Street, Leith. ((0131) 554 6767.
This unusual and unpretentious candlelit restaurant is housed in a wine warehouse. ● Mon, Sun dinner, last week Dec, first week Jan. ♦ ♦
AE MC V — Children Welcome ●, Fixed-Price ■, Vegetarian ●

SOUTHERN SCOTLAND

ABBEY ST BATHANS: *The Riverside Restaurant* w www.abbeyartifacts.co.uk ££
Abbey St Bathans, near Duns, Berwickshire. Map E4. ((01361) 840312.
This small, friendly restaurant in a delightful setting near the river serves freshly prepared food all day. ● Mon. ♦
MC V — Children ●, Vegetarian ●

JEDBURGH: *Simply Scottish* ££
High Street, Jedburgh, the Borders. Map E5. ((01835) 864696.
This combined restaurant and coffee shop, located in the centre of Jedburgh, offers simple, contemporary Scottish cooking with style.
● Sun–Thu dinner, Nov–mid-Mar. ♦ ♦
MC V — Children ●, Fixed-Price ■, Vegetarian ●, Traditional ■

KELSO: *Floors Garden Centre Coffee Shop* ££
Floors Castle Garden Centre, Kelso, Roxburghshire. Map E5. ((01573) 225714.
Friendly coffee shop attached to attractive garden centre, serving home-made lunches and afternoon teas. ● 24 Dec–4 Jan. ♦ ♦ entire premises.
AE MC V — Children ●, Vegetarian ●, Traditional ■

KIPPFORD: *The Anchor Hotel* ££
Kippford, Dalbeattie, Kirkcudbrightshire. Map D6. ((01556) 620205.
Situated on the waterfront, with views of the boating activity, this friendly pub offers good bar food. ● 25 Dec. ♦ limited. ♦ ♦
AE MC V — Children ●, Vegetarian ●, Traditional ■

MELROSE: *Burts Hotel* ££££
Market Square, Melrose. Map E5. ((01896) 822285.
The restaurant of this townhouse hotel presents the best Scottish game and fish with imagination and flair. ● 25 Dec dinner, 26 Dec. ♦ limited. ♦ ♦
AE MC V — Fixed-Price ■, Vegetarian ●, Traditional ■

PEEBLES: *Kailzie Gardens Restaurant* ££
Kailzie Gardens, near Peebles, Peeblesshire. Map D5. ((01721) 722807.
A delightful courtyard setting on the Peebles to Traquair road, for excellent home-cooked lunches and afternoon teas. ● Fri–Sun dinner. ♦ ♦ entire premises. ♦
MC V — Children ●, Fixed-Price ■, Vegetarian ●, Traditional ■

PORTPATRICK: *Knockinaam Lodge* w www.knockinaamlodge.com ££££
Off A77 near Portpatrick, Dumfries & Galloway. Map C6. ((01776) 810471.
This converted 19th-century hunting lodge is set in an idyllic location overlooking the sea. The cuisine on offer is smart, modern and French. ♦ limited. ♦ ♦
AE DC MC V — Children ●, Fixed-Price ■, Vegetarian ●

TWEEDSMUIR: *The Crook Inn* w www.crookin.co.uk ££
Tweedsmuir, Peeblesshire. Map D5. ((01899) 880272.
Set a short way north of Tweedsmuir, this historic inn's 1930s interior has a cosy atmosphere and log fires. ● 25 Dec. ♦
MC V — Children ●, Vegetarian ●, Traditional ■

GLASGOW

CITY CENTRE: *Willow Tea Room* w www.willowtearooms.co.uk £
217 Sauchiehall Street. ((0141) 332 0521.
Tucked away above a jeweller's shop, this reconstruction of a Mackintosh tearoom (see p100) has an impressive range of light lunches and afternoon teas in an Art Nouveau setting. ● 1–2 Jan, 25–6 Dec.
— Children ●, Vegetarian ●, Traditional ■

CITY CENTRE: *Café Gandolfi* w www.cafegandolfi.co.uk £££
64 Albion Street. ((0141) 552 6813.
A stunning interior, with stained glass windows and individual pieces of Tim Stead furniture, creates a stylish and stimulating atmosphere for a drink, snack or meal. ● 1–2 Jan, 25–6 Dec. ♦ ♦
AE MC V — Children ●, Vegetarian ●, Traditional ■

CITY CENTRE: *Le Chardon d'Or* ££££ AE DC MC V
176 West Regent Street. ((0141) 248 3801.
Traditional French technicques and textures using Scottish produce. Fine formal dining in a relaxed atmosphere and one of the finest restaurants in the city. ● *two weeks at Christmas, two weeks Jul or Aug.*

CITY CENTRE: *Crème de la Crème* ££ AE DC MC V
1071 Argyle Street. ((0141) 221 3222.
Extravagantly decorated, bustling Indian restaurant on Glasgow's famous shopping street. ● *Sun lunch.*

CITY CENTRE: *Fratelli Sarti* ££ AE DC MC V
121 Bath Street. ((0141) 204 0440.
This excellent Italian restaurant offers mouth-watering *dolci, gelati* and probably the best pizza in Glasgow. There are other branches at 133 Wellington Street and 42 Renfield Street. ● *1 Jan, 25 Dec.*

CITY CENTRE: *Gumbo* £££ MC V
33 Ingram Street. ((0141) 552 2929.
1900s fire station converted into a restaurant with a lively atmosphere. Louisianan and Creole dishes and varied music including jazz and soul.
● *1 Jan, 25–6 Dec, Mon.*

CITY CENTRE: *Bouzy Rouge* w www.bouzy-rouge.com £££ AE DC MC V
111 West Regent Street. ((0141) 221 8804.
This fashionable, busy restaurant concentrates on contemporary Scottish cuisine with an international influence. Bookings are essential. There are two other branches in the city. ● *1 Jan.*

CITY CENTRE:: *78 St Vincent Street* £££ AE DC MC V
78 St Vincent Street. ((0141) 248 7878.
Decorated with a mural by Glaswegian artist Donald McLeod, this restaurant offers French cuisine with a Scottish touch.

CITY CENTRE: *Thai Fountain* £££ AE MC V
2 Woodside Crescent. ((0141) 332 2599.
The Charing Cross area is the location of the finest of Glasgow's few Thai restaurants. Prawn and fish dishes abound, and a great vegetarian menu is also available.

CITY CENTRE: *The Buttery* ££££ AE MC V
652 Argyle Street. ((0141) 221 8188.
A converted tenement is the unusual location for one of Glasgow's finest restaurants, where traditional Scottish food is dished up with creative flair.
● *Sat lunch, Sun, Mon.*

CITY CENTRE: *The Corinthian* w www.corinthian.uk.com £££ AE MC V
191 Ingram Street. ((0141) 552 1101.
Traditional Scottish cuisine using the best produce prepared with flair and imagination and served in the architecturally stunning interior of a renovated Victorian bank.

CITY CENTRE: *Rogano* w www.rogano.co.uk ££££ AE DC MC V
11 Royal Exchange Place. ((0141) 248 4055.
This spacious restaurant has been fashionable in Glasgow since the 1930s. Seafood is a speciality. A lighter menu is available downstairs.
● *1 Jan, 25 Dec.* limited

WEST END: *Antipasti* ££ MC V
337 Byres Road. ((0141) 337 2737.
A good value restaurant with a great atmosphere. Cheerful staff serve hearty portions of pasta and all the trimmings with great efficiency. Worth the wait at busy times; there are some outside tables. ● *1 Jan, 25 Dec.*

WEST END: *Two Fat Ladies* w www.twofatladies.5pm.co.uk £££ AE DC MC V
88 Dumbarton Road. ((0141) 339 1944.
This informal restaurant features quality fresh fish and thoughtful and creative cooking, to provide Glasgow with one of its best fish restaurants.
● *Sun lunch, 25 Dec, 1 Jan.*

WEST END: *Stravaigin* w www.stravaigin.com ££££ AE DC MC V
28 Gibson Street, West End. ((0141) 334 2665.
This award-winning restaurant and café bar, offers a Scottish menu with Eastern influences. ● *Mon, 1–2 Jan, 25–6 Dec.* café bar only.

For key to symbols see back flap

<table>
<tr><td colspan="2">

Price categories include a three-course meal for one, half a bottle of house wine, and all unavoidable extra costs such as cover charge and VAT:
£ under £15
££ £15–£25
£££ £25–£35
££££ £35–£50
£££££ over £50.

</td><td>

CHILDREN WELCOME
Restaurants offering smaller portions and high chairs for children. Special menus sometimes available.
FIXED-PRICE MENU
A good value fixed-price meal, at lunch, dinner or both, usually consisting of three courses.
VEGETARIAN
Vegetarian specialities are included on the menu.
TRADITIONAL SCOTTISH
Several, if not all, of the items on the menu are traditional Scottish recipes, using fresh local produce.

</td></tr>
</table>

	CREDIT CARDS	CHILDREN WELCOME	FIXED-PRICE MENU	VEGETARIAN	TRADITIONAL SCOTTISH
WEST END: *The Ubiquitous Chip* W www.ubiquitouschip.co.uk ££££ 12 Ashton Lane, West End. (0141) 334 5007. Famous for its innovative Scottish recipes and an outstanding wine list. A less expensive, less formal restaurant is upstairs. ● *1 Jan, 25 Dec, 31 Dec.*	AE DC MC V	●	▦	●	▦
FURTHER AFIELD: *La Fiorentina* ££ 2 Paisley Road West, South Side. (0141) 420 1585. A traditional Italian restaurant, situated close to Kingston Bridge. Great atmosphere with characterful waiters. ● *Sun, 1 Jan.*	AE DC MC V	●	▦	●	
FURTHER AFIELD: *Gingerhill* ££ Hillhead Street, Milngavie. (0141) 956 6515. Situated in the town centre, at the start of the West Highland Way, this cheerful restaurant specializes in modern Scottish fare with a leaning towards seafood. ● *Mon–Tue dinner, 1 Jan.*	MC V		▦	●	

CENTRAL SCOTLAND

	CREDIT CARDS	CHILDREN WELCOME	FIXED-PRICE MENU	VEGETARIAN	TRADITIONAL SCOTTISH
ANSTRUTHER: *The Cellar* ££££ 24 East Green, Anstruther, Fife. **Map E4.** (01333) 310378. One of the finest fish restaurants in Scotland is situated behind the fisheries museum (see pp124) at the east end of the harbour. ● *Sun–Mon (Nov–Easter), 24 Dec–28 Dec.*	AE DC MC V		▦	●	
ARRAN, BRODICK: *Creelers Restaurant* £££ The Home Farm, Brodick, Isle of Arran. **Map C5.** (01770) 302810. Located outside Brodick, near the castle. A friendly and relaxed restaurant offering a menu of great fish and shellfish, fresh from the boats. ● *Mon (except bank holidays), Nov–early March.*	MC V	●		●	▦
BALLOCH: *Georgian Room, Cameron House Hotel* £££££ Loch Lomond, Dumbarton & Clydebank. **Map C4.** (01389) 755565. Fine contemporary cooking is offered by the restaurant of this luxurious hotel on the very pretty southern bank of Loch Lomond. *entire premises.*	AE DC MC V		▦	●	
CUPAR: *The Peat Inn* W www.thepeatinn.co.uk ££££ Peat Inn, near Cupar, Fife. **Map D4.** (01334) 840206. Located in the middle of rural Fife, David Wilson has led the revival of great Scottish restaurants. Dining here is a real gastronomic experience. The inn also has eight bedrooms. ● *Sun–Mon, 25 Dec. entire premises.*	AE MC V	●	▦	●	
DALRY: *Braidwoods* ££££ Drumastle Mill Cottage, by Dalry, Ayrshire. **Map C5.** (01294) 833544. Michelin star restaurant in a 200 year old converted miller's cottage offering modern Scottish cuisine. Among the specialities is fillet of roasted turbet with pea purée. ● *three weeks in Jan, two weeks in Sep.*	AE MC V	●	▦	●	
DRYMEN: *The Pottery* £ The Square, Drymen, Stirlingshire. **Map C4.** (01360) 660458. Friendly restaurant and coffee shop alongside a pottery, serving good home-cooked food all day and delicious afternoon teas. Roaring fires in winter and a delightful terrace in summer. ● *1 Jan, 25 Dec.*	AE DC MC V	●		●	▦
FAIRLIE: *Fins Restaurant* W www.fencebay.co.uk £££ Fencefoot Farm, Fairlie, near Largs. **Map C4.** (01475) 568989. Delightful, small seafood restaurant in a converted stone barn, using produce from own fishery and smokehouse, as well as other local supplies. ● *Sun dinner, Mon, 1–2 Jan, 25–26 Dec. entire premises.*	MC V	●	▦	●	▦
GIRVAN: *Wildings* £££ Harbour Road, Maidens, Ayrshire. **Map C5.** (01655) 331401. This comfortable family-run restaurant offers a varied menu with seafood specialities among the best on the west coast. Superb flavours at good prices. ● *25–6 Dec, 1–2 Jan.*	MC V	●	▦	●	

INVERARAY: *Loch Fyne Oyster Bar* [W] www.lochfyne.com £££
Cairndow, near Inveraray, Argyll. **Map** C4. (*(01499) 600264.*
The Oyster Bar on the banks of this famous fishing loch enjoys an excellent
reputation for its fresh seafood. Booking is advised. ● *1–2 Jan, 25 Dec.*

AE DC MC V

KINCARDINE ON FORTH: *The Unicorn Inn* [W] www.theunicorn.co.uk £££
15 Excise Street, Kincardine, Clackmannanshire. **Map** D4. (*(01259) 739129.*
Surprisingly unassuming location in the heart of this historic village on
the River Forth. The restaurant offers excellent seafood and a welcoming
and informal atmosphere. ● *Sun lunch, Mon.*

AE DC MC V

KINCLAVEN: *Ballathie House Hotel* [W] www.ballathiehousehotel.com ££££
Kinclaven, near Perth, Perth & Kinross. **Map** D4. (*(01250) 883268.*
Scottish dishes of the highest quality are on offer in the restaurant of this
Victorian country house hotel overlooking the River Tay.
entire premises

AE DC MC V

PERTH: *Let's Eat* [W] www.letseatperth.co.uk £££
77–79 Kinnoull Street, Perth. **Map** D4. (*(01738) 643377.*
A high-quality restaurant in the former Theatre Royal. Good value, imaginative dishes. ● *Sun–Mon, two weeks mid-Jul, 25–6 Dec, 1–2 Jan, last two weeks
Jan.*

AE MC V

ST ANDREWS: *Dolls House Restaurant* [W] www.dolls-house.co.uk ££
3 Church Sq, St Andrews, Fife. **Map** E4. (*(01334) 477422.*
Fresh Scottish seafood and game cooked with a Mediterranean influence in
a restaurant with a Dolls House theme.

AE DC MC V

STIRLING: *The River House Restaurant* [W] www.leonardoco.com ££
Castle Business Park, Craigforth, Stirling. **Map** D4. (*(01786) 465577.*
Situated close to the M9 (junction 10), this restaurant extends out over a
lake to offer an interesting venue. Modern ambience with food to match.
● *25 Dec, 1 Jan.*

AE DC MC V

STIRLING: *Scholars Stirling Highland Hotel* [W] www.paramount-hotels.co.uk £££
Spittal Street, Stirling. **Map** D4. (*(01786) 475444.*
Set in the old town of Stirling, at the foot of the entrance to the castle, this
hotel's restaurant serves fine Scottish fare. ● *Sat lunch.*

AE DC MC .V

THE HIGHLANDS AND ISLANDS

ABERDEEN: *Restaurant on the Terrace* £££
10-14 Union Terrace, Aberdeen. **Map** E3. (*(01224) 640233.*
This traditional hotel, located in the heart of the city, offers European
cuisine and also more traditional Scottish cuisine.
limited.

AE DC MC V

ABERDEEN: *The Silver Darling* ££££
Pocra Quay, Footdee, North Pier, Aberdeen. **Map** E3. (*(01224) 576229.*
Well worth finding on the north side of Aberdeen Harbour, this restaurant
provides superb seafood which varies according to the daily catch. Great
puddings. ● *Sat lunch, Sun, two weeks from 24 Dec.*

AE DC MC V

ACHILTIBUIE: *Summer Isles Hotel* [W] www.summerisleshotel.co.uk ££££
Achiltibuie, near Ullapool, Ross and Cromarty. **Map** C2. (*(01854) 622282.*
An idyllic setting overlooking the Summer Isles. The Michelin starred
restaurant offers exceptionally fine dinners, and superb seafood lunches
and suppers in the adjacent bar. ● *mid-Oct–Easter.*

MC V

ARCHIESTOWN: *Archiestown Hotel* [W] www.archiestownhotel.co.uk £££
Archiestown, near Aberlour, Aberdeenshire. **Map** D2. (*(01340) 810218.*
West of Craigellachie, in the heart of Speyside whisky country, this
informal bistro is noted for its warm and inviting atmosphere and
good Scottish fare.

MC V

AUCHMITHIE: *The But'n'Ben* ££
Auchmithie, near Arbroath. **Map** E3. (*(01241) 877223.*
Converted cottages create a cosy setting for this village restaurant. Fresh
seafood with a Scottish emphasis. Reasonably priced lunches, high teas
and evening meals. ● *Sun eve, Tue.*

AE MC V

AVIEMORE: *Corrour House Hotel* [W] www.corrourhousehotel.co.uk £££
Rothiemurchus, near Aviemore, Inverness-shire. **Map** D3. (*(01479) 810220.*
Family-run Victorian house with superb views of the Cairngorm Mountains.
Traditional Scottish fare in a pretty setting. ● *mid-Nov–Dec.*

MC V

<table>
<tr><td colspan="2">

Price categories include a three-course meal for one, half a bottle of house wine, and all unavoidable extra costs such as cover charge and VAT:
£ under £15
££ £15–£25
£££ £25–£35
££££ £35–£50
£££££ over £50.

</td><td>

CHILDREN WELCOME
Restaurants offering smaller portions and high chairs for children. Special menus sometimes available.
FIXED-PRICE MENU
A good value fixed-price meal, at lunch, dinner or both, usually consisting of three courses.
VEGETARIAN
Vegetarian specialities are included on the menu.
TRADITIONAL SCOTTISH
Several, if not all, of the items on the menu are traditional Scottish recipes, using fresh local produce.

</td></tr>
</table>

	CREDIT CARDS	CHILDREN WELCOME	FIXED-PRICE MENU	VEGETARIAN	TRADITIONAL SCOTTISH
BALLATER: *Darroch Learg* W www.darroch.co.uk **££££** Braemar Road, Ballater, Aberdeenshire. **Map D3.** ((013397) 55443. Victorian lodge with views of the Cairngorms. Modern Scottish cooking with delicate flavours. ● *Christmas, last three weeks in Jan.* & ⇥ *restaurant only.* ▯	AE DC MC V	●	■	●	■
BEAULY: *The Glass Restaurant* W www.glassrestaurant.supanet.com **££** Struy, by Beauly, Inverness-shire. **Map D2.** ((01463) 761219. Modern and classical cuisine using local ingredients. Among the specialities are venison collops (panfried anise dusted venison with a spiced roast pimento and red onion chutney). ● *mid-Oct–early Mar.*	DC MC V	●		●	■
CRINAN: *Lock 16, Crinan Hotel* W www.crinanhotel.com **££££** Crinan Hotel, Crinan, by Lochgilphead, Argyll. **Map C4.** ((01546) 830261. The third floor restaurant has great views of Jura and Scarba, to complement fabulously fresh seafood. Excellent ground floor restaurant and good lunches in the bar. Coffee shop on the quayside. & ⇥ ▯	MC V	●	■		■
HARRIS (WESTERN ISLES): *Scarista House* W www.scaristahouse.com **££££** Scarista, Isle of Harris, Western Isles. **Map B2.** ((01859) 550238. In an idyllic, west-facing position above the white sand beaches and adjacent to the golf course, this restaurant has superb views and excellent food. Rooms are also available. ⇥ ▯	MC V			●	■
INVERKIRKAIG: *Achin's Bookshop Tea Room* **£** Inverkirkaig, near Lochinver, Sutherland. **Map C1.** ((01571) 844262. Near the start of a footpath up the Kirkaig River (Suilven), open for lunches and teas only. ● *Oct–Easter.* & ⇥ *entire premises.*	MC V	●		●	■
INVERNESS: *Café One* **££** 75 Castle Street, Inverness. **Map D2.** ((01463) 226200. Attractive restaurant in the town centre, using good ingredients cooked in a modern Scottish style. ● *Sun, 1 Jan, 25–6 Dec.* ⇥ ▯	AE MC V	●		●	■
INVERNESS: *Adam's Dining Room (Culloden House)* **££££** W www.cullodenhouse.co.uk Off A96 at Culloden, Inverness. **Map D2.** ((01463) 790461. The food is country house style at this historic hotel, with sauces, jellies, sorbets, mousses, and fresh meat, game and fish dishes. ⇥ ▯	AE DC MC V	●	■	●	■
INVERNESS: *La Riviera* **££££** Glenmoriston Town House, Inverness. **Map D2.** ((01463) 223777. Modern gastronomic French cooking on the riverside, just five minutes from the town centre. ● *Mon.* & ⇥ ▯		●	■	●	
KIRKTON OF GLENISLA: *Glenisla Hotel* @ glenislahotel@btinternet.com **££** Kirkton of Glenisla, near Alyth, Perthshire. **Map D3.** ((01575) 582223. Tranquil setting and an ideal base for skiing, walking and fishing. Traditional inn with log fires, hearty food and a range of malts. ● *25 Dec.* & ⇥ ▯	MC V	●		●	■
KISHORN: *Kishorn Seafood Bar* **££** Kishorn, Strathcarron, Ross-Shire. **Map C2.** ((01520) 733240. Fresh local shellfish and lobster selected from counter and water tank. Superb views to Skye and the Allpecross hills.	AE MC V	●		●	■
LAGGAN BRIDGE: *Caoldair Kiln Room Coffee Shop* **£** Laggan Bridge, near Newtonmore, Inverness-shire. **Map D3.** ((01528) 544231. Delicious home-made light lunches and baking, as well as quality crafts, are available here. Some outside tables. ● *Oct–Easter.* & ⇥ *entire premises.*	MC V	●		●	■
LOCHINVER: *Lochinver Larder* @ lochlarder@btinternet.com **££** Main Street, Lochinver, Sutherland. **Map C1.** ((01571) 844356. Family run bistro, offering good value home-cooked local produce with an emphasis on seafood. ● *Dec–Mar (Nov dinner).* & ⇥ *entire premises.* ▯	MC V	●		●	■

MULL: *Dovecote Restaurant* W www.calgary.co.uk   ££   MC V
Calgary, Isle of Mull, Argyll. **Map** B3. (*01688) 400256.*
West of Dervaig, close to a fabulous shell beach, is this restaurant in a converted dovecote. Interesting menu based on fresh local produce. Rooms available at the Calgary Hotel. ● *Nov–Easter.*

ORKNEY: *The Creel Restaurant* W www.thecreel.co.uk   £££   MC V
Front Rd, St Margaret's Hope, South Ronaldsay, Orkney. (*01856) 831311.*
Cosy gastronomic haven in a remote part of the island. Fresh local ingredients, especially seafood. ● *Jan, Feb, two weeks mid-Oct.* & *entire premises.*

PITLOCHRY: *Moulin Hotel* W www.moulinhotel.co.uk   ££   MC V
11 Kirkmichael Road, Moulin, Pitlochry, Perthshire. **Map** D3. (*01796) 472196.*
Historic inn situated at the foot of Ben Vrackie, on the Pitlochry to Braemar road. The roaring fires and warm welcome make the Moulin a great venue for lunches, afternoon teas or evening meals. &

PORT APPIN: *The Pier House* W www.pierhousehotel.co.uk   £££   MC V
Port Appin, Argyll. **Map** C3. (*01631) 730302.*
A stunning position on the quayside, facing west over Lismore, provides one of the best locations on the west coast. Conservatory dining room with glorious views serves superb seafood. ● *25 Dec.* &

SHETLAND: *Burrastow House*   £££   AE MC V
Walls, Shetland. (*01595) 809307.*
Georgian house in remote, peaceful location on the west coast of the island. Excellent home cooking complements the use of local ingredients. & *entire premises.*

SKYE, COLBOST: *The Three Chimneys*   £££££   AE MC V
Colbost, near Dunvegan, Isle of Skye. **Map** B2. (*01470) 511258.*
This award-winning restaurant offers lovingly prepared local ingredients for an epicurean treat in delightful surroundings. Accommodation is also available. & *entire premises.*

SKYE, SLEAT: *Kinloch Lodge* W www.kinloch-lodge.co.uk   ££££   AE MC V
Sleat, Isle of Skye. **Map** B3. (*01471) 833214.*
This is the home of the High Chief of the Clan Donald and his wife Lady Claire, a renowned cook who is responsible for the wonderful traditional Scottish cuisine. ● *23–28 Dec.* & *entire premises.*

STONEHAVEN: *The Tolbooth Restaurant*   £££   MC V
The Old Pier, The Harbour, Stonehaven, Aberdeen. **Map** E3. (*01569) 762287.*
Set in an imaginatively converted historic building on the quay. Charming, staff present an interesting contemporary dinner menu, specializing in local fresh seafood. ● *Sun, Mon, 1–15 Jan, 25 Dec.*

TARBET: *Seafood Café* W www.seafoodrestaurant-tarbet.co.uk   ££   MC
Tarbet, near Scourie, Sutherland. **Map** C1. (*01971) 502251.*
Situated in a remote crofting settlement, where boats cross to the nearby bird reserve on Handa Island. The proprietors catch and cook your dinner. Self-catering accommodation is also available. ● *Sep–Easter.*

THURSO: *Forss Country House Hotel* W www.forsshousehotel.co.uk   £££   AE DC MC V
Near Thurso, Caithness, Highlands. **Map** D1. (*01847) 861201.*
Peaceful Highland hotel set in 20 acres of woodland. Fresh local produce used in traditional Scottish dishes. ● *24 Dec–4 Jan.* *entire premises.*

TONGUE: *Ben Loyal Hotel* W www.benloyal.co.uk   ££££   MC V
Tongue, Sutherland, Highlands. **Map** D1. (*01847) 611216.*
A comfortable, family-run restaurant on the north coast, with views of the sea and spectacular Ben Loyal. The well-balanced menu uses quality local ingredients. Restaurant only from Apr–Oct. ● *24 Dec–1 Mar.*

ULLAPOOL: *Morefield Mariners Restaurant* W www.morefieldmotel.co.uk   ££   MC V
Cruachan Place, off North Road, Ullapool, Highlands. **Map** C2. (*01854) 612161.*
Popular, inexpensive restaurant specializing in seafood, with excellent meat and vegetarian dishes. Bar meals served in winter.

ULLAPOOL: *The Ceilidh Place* W www.theceilidhplace.co.uk   £££   AE DC MC V
14 West Argyle Street, Ullapool, Highlands. **Map** C2. (*01854) 612103.*
An interesting building with great atmosphere, incorporating a formal restaurant, table service coffee shop, bars and bookshop, as well as rooms above. Imaginative menus at various prices. &

SPECIAL INTERESTS AND OUTDOOR ACTIVITIES

SCOTLAND MAY NOT be able to guarantee sunshine or offer beach culture, but its popularity as a holiday destination is due in no small part to its opportunities for outdoor activities, as well as cultural pursuits. Over the years, the tourist industry has matured to occupy an important role in the Scottish economy, and local businesses have become adept at providing visitors with what they are looking for. That could be playing golf by the sea, fishing on the Tweed, cruising to see whales off the west coast during the summer, skiing in the Cairngorms in winter, eating fresh oysters at a lochside restaurant or searching for information on ancestors who left the country 200 years ago. Facilities for all kinds of activities have never been better, and this section outlines some of the best.

A lone piper of the Highlands

Searching for records of ancestors, Edinburgh

TRACING GENEALOGY

FROM THE TIME of the infamous Clearances of the 18th century onwards (*see p150*), Scots have emigrated to Australia, Canada, New Zealand, South Africa, the US and elsewhere in search of an easier life. There are now millions of foreign nationals who can trace their heritage back to Scotland, and uncovering family history is a popular reason for visiting the country.

Professional genealogists can be commissioned, but those interested in conducting investigations themselves should try the **General Register Office for Scotland** (which has records of births, deaths and marriages dating from the 1500s), the **Scottish Genealogy Society** or the **Scottish Record Office**, all found in Edinburgh.

GAELIC STUDIES

THE NORTHWEST of Scotland is the heartland for the Gaelic language. Historically, this was a Celtic language that spread from mainland Europe to Ireland in the 4th century BC, and later into Scotland where it became the national language. By the 18th century, however, under English rule, Gaelic had become identified with a rebellious clan system that was persecuted after the Jacobite rising of 1745 (*see p45*). It was marginalized and suffered a decline.

A recent renaissance aims to revive this once-dominant culture with Gaelic broadcasts and by teaching it to children. **An Comunn Gaidhealach**, Scotland's official Gaelic society, organizes the annual Royal National Mod (*see p38*), a performing arts competition. Other Gaelic societies are **Comunn An Luchd Ionnsachaidh** and **Comunn na Gàidhlig**. **Sabhal Mor Ostaig**, a college on the Isle of Skye, runs short Gaelic courses for visitors.

FOOD AND DRINK TOURS

SCOTLAND HAS a justified reputation for fine produce, and recent years have seen an upsurge in the number of noteworthy restaurants in Edinburgh and Glasgow. Indeed, Edinburgh has established itself as the number two city for eating out in the British Isles, after London.

One way of sampling Scottish cuisine is to book a holiday through **Connoisseurs Scotland**, which arranges stays at country house hotels with a reputation for top-class cooking, such as the Crinan Hotel in Argyll, or Gleneagles.

The **Scotch Malt Whisky Society** has information for lovers of this spirit. Distilleries are a popular attraction (*see pp30–31 and p144*), with

Learning about whisky, the "water of life", at a Speyside distillery

names such as **Glenfiddich Distillery** operating tours.

The production of cask-conditioned beers is explained at Edinburgh's **Caledonian Brewery**. An exhibition at **Inverawe Smokehouses**, near Taynuilt in the Highlands, shows the techniques used in smoking fish such as salmon.

VIEWING WILDLIFE

IN COMPARISON with much of the rest of the British Isles, Scotland still has large areas of moor and mountain wilderness and a long, relatively undeveloped coastline that supports a range of animals

Sighting a porpoise as it breaks the calm surface of a sea loch

Walkers on the lookout for red deer and birds of prey at Glen Coe

(see pp16–17). In the mountains near Aviemore, rangers from the **Cairngorm Reindeer Centre** take parties of people on to the mountain to walk among a herd of reindeer.

A convenient way to see the abundant sealife is on a boat trip run by **Maid of the Forth Cruises**, which operates from South Queensferry on the Forth near Edinburgh – dolphins and common seals are resident in these waters. More adventurous are the trips in search of whales offered by **Sea Life Cruises** from the Isle of Mull, but even a casual tourist in the Highlands can spot birds of

prey, otters in the lochs and herds of red deer on the mountainsides. With a large share of Britain's resident and visiting birds, Scotland is also home to a number of important bird sanctuaries, the most celebrated being Handa Island off Scourie on the far northwest coast *(see p157)*. St Abb's Head *(see p84)* east of Edinburgh and Baron's Haugh near Motherwell (on the outskirts of Glasgow) are nearer the cities.

Many wildlife tours are small-scale private businesses that operate according to seasonal and daily demand, so always check the details with the local tourist information offices.

(see pp16–17), (see p157), (see p84)

DIRECTORY

TRACING GENEALOGY

General Register Office for Scotland
New Register House,
3 West Register St,
Edinburgh, EH1 3YT.
((0131) 334 0380.
W www.scotlands
people.gov.uk

Scottish Genealogy Society
15 Victoria Terrace,
Edinburgh, EH1 2JL.
((0131) 220 3677. W
www.scotsgenealogy.com

Scottish Record Office
General Register House,
2 Princes St,
Edinburgh, EH1 3YY.
((0131) 535 1314.

GAELIC STUDIES

An Comunn Gaidhealach
109 Church St,
Inverness, IV1 1EY.
((01463) 231226.
W www.ancomunn.co.uk

Comunn An Luchd Ionnsachaidh
Inverness.
((01463) 226 710.
W www.cli.org.uk

Comunn na Gàidhlig
5 Mitchell's Lane,
Inverness, IV3 2AQ.
((01463) 234138.
W www.cnag.org.uk

Sabhal Mor Ostaig
Teangue, Sleat,
Isle of Skye, IV44 8RQ.
((01471) 844373.

FOOD AND DRINK TOURS

Caledonian Brewery
42 Slateford Rd,
Edinburgh, EH11 1PH.
((0131) 337 1286.

Connoisseurs Scotland
PO Box 26164,
Dunfermline, KY11 9WQ.
((01383) 825 800.

Glenfiddich Distillery
Dufftown,
Keith, Banffshire,
AB55 4DH.
((01340) 820373.

Inverawe Smokehouses
Taynuilt,
Argyll, PA35 1HU.
((01866) 822446.

Scotch Malt Whisky Society

The Vaults,
87 Giles St,
Edinburgh, EH6 6BZ.
((0131) 554 3451.
W www.smws.com

VIEWING WILDLIFE

Cairngorm Reindeer Centre
Glenmore, Aviemore,
PH22 1QU.
((01479) 861228.

Maid of the Forth Cruises
Hawes Pier,
South Queensferry, EH30.
((0131) 331 4857.

Sea Life Surveys
Ledaig, Tobermory,
Isle of Mull, PA75 6NU.
((01688) 302916.

Outdoor Activities at a Glance

O NLY A HANDFUL OF INLAND LOCHS and coastal waters have been exploited by commercial boating and watersports companies, though it is possible to use private vessels on many minor lochs in wilderness areas. Likewise, organized skiing is confined to just five centres. Of the country's several hundred golf courses, most are concentrated in Central and Southern Scotland. This map plots the main centres for various popular activities. For further information about particular sports across Scotland, see pages 188–95.

Handa Island, off the far northwest coast, is one of a number of seabird reserves.

Rock climbers and mountaineers (see p192) *usually head for Glencoe, the Cairngorms and the Cuillin Hills on Skye. The Torridon range and other formations further north are also popular choices.*

The five skiing centres (see p193) *are White Corries (Glencoe), the Nevis Range, Cairngorm, Glenshee and the Lecht. The skiing season usually gets under way in December and lasts until April.*

The West Highland Way is the most famous long-distance walk in Scotland, encompassing a wonderful variety of terrain.

Culzean Castle

KEY

🏄	Watersports
⛵	Sailing
⛳	Major golf course
🦅	Birdwatching
🧗	Mountaineering
⛷	Skiing
🎣	Fishing
🐴	Pony trekking
🚶	Major walking area
▪ ▪	Long-distance walk route

Sailing (see p195) *is popular off the west coast and the islands. The calm waters of sheltered bays are suitable for beginners, while the open sea can be both exhilarating and treacherous. Inland, Loch Ness offers sailing opportunities.*

SHETLAND

ORKNEY

John o'Groats

HIGHLANDS

SPEYSIDE

Cairngorms

GRAMPIAN MOUNTAINS

GLASGOW   EDINBURGH

PENTLAND HILLS

CHEVIOT HILLS

0 kilometres   50

0 miles   50

Bird-watching (see p185) *is in itself a reason to visit Scotland. The best sanctuaries are in remote coastal areas where such delightful species as puffins make their home on the sheer, wave-lashed cliffs.*

Watersports (see p195) *include canoeing, surfing, windsurfing and diving. Visitors can book equipment and courses through activities centres scattered around the country.*

Golf *(see pp188–9)* attracts thousands of visitors every year, especially to the most famous courses in Central Scotland, such as St Andrews and Carnoustie.

Walking (see pp190–91) *is tremendously popular in Scotland, and vast swathes of the countryside are open to the public.*

Fishing *(see p194)* is well catered for on the River Tweed in Southern Scotland, and on Loch Ness in the Highlands.

Pony trekking *opportunities* (see p194) *are within easy reach of the cities, in the gentle countryside of southern and central Scotland, and in the great moor and mountain wilderness of the Highlands.*

Golf in Scotland

British-made golf tees

THE ANCIENT GAME OF GOLF is synonymous with Scotland and has been played here for hundreds of years. One of the most popular sports in the country, it is enjoyed by people of all ages and capabilities. Wherever you choose to stay, there will always be a golf course within easy reach, from the legendary championship courses to the smaller, intimate locations set amid dramatic countryside or along the coast. Few other countries can rival Scotland in the number, quality and variety of courses. Golf, it is believed by the Scots, is a game for everyone to enjoy.

A scenic view of Gleneagles, one of Scotland's championship courses

EARLY HISTORY

VARIATIONS ON the game of golf as we know it today were being played across Europe as long ago as the 14th century, and possibly even in Roman times. Yet it is the Scottish who must be credited with establishing the official game, and encouraging its development across the world. It was in Scotland that the passion for golf was born. By the middle of the 16th century, the game had become a popular pastime at the highest levels of society – James VI himself was a keen player, as was his mother, Mary, Queen of Scots.

In the late 1800s, wealthy middle-class Englishmen began to follow the example of the Royal Family by taking their holidays in Scotland.

Duncan Forbes

The expansion of the railway system at this time allowed people to get to the seaside links, and the English were so infatuated with the game of golf that they took it home with them. In 1744 the Gentlemen Golfers of Leith, led by Duncan Forbes, drew up the first *Articles & Laws in Playing at Golf.* Although later revised and updated, these original rules, set down by the Scottish professionals of the time, formed the framework for the modern game of golf.

TOOLS OF THE TRADE

THE SCOTTISH influence on golf was not to end there. Many of the professionals playing at the time were also skilled carpenters, instrumental in developing the clubs and balls used in the game. Willie Park Senior was a master club-maker, and winner of the first Scottish Open in 1860, and Old Tom Morris became a legend in the game for both his playing and craftsmanship. In the days before machinery, the wooden clubs were made entirely by hand.

The earliest irons were also fashioned by hand, followed by aluminium-headed clubs that differ very little from clubs today. The "guttie" ball was invented in 1848, replacing the expensive and easily damaged "feathery", thus making the game more affordable. The modern, rubber-core ball in use today appeared at the beginning of the 20th century.

THE COURSES

MANY OF Scotland's courses are steeped in history and tradition, such as the championship courses of St Andrews and Carnoustie. But an increasing number of newer courses now offer the same standard of play and variety of landscape. There is something for everyone, and if your purse does not stretch to a round at a top professional course like Gleneagles, there are plenty of smaller, more affordable options, each with their own character, often with stunning views of the coastline.

Some clubs offer accommodation but, if not, there are always hotels and bed-and-breakfasts nearby. Caddy cars (golf cars) and catering facilities are common in all clubs. Nearly all the courses are 18-hole, and are open to visitors, but be aware of occasional restrictions (some clubs do not allow players to wear jeans or joggers, for example). The chart shows some of the many courses available. Map references pertain to the map on the inside back cover.

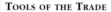

An old railway poster illustrating the lure of St Andrews as a paradise for golfing enthusiasts

Price categories	Description		Pay Per Round	Pay Per Day	Entry Restrictions	Coastal View
Price categories based on the cost of a round of golf on a weekday (weekends may be more expensive): £ £10–£25 ££ £25–£40 £££ £40–£60 ££££ over £60.	**PAY PER ROUND** It is possible to pay for a single round. **PAY PER DAY** It is possible to pay for a whole day's golf. Prices shown represent day rates only if no round rate is available. **ENTRY RESTRICTIONS** There are either restrictions on playing at certain times or special entry requirements – telephone ahead for details. **COASTAL VIEW** The course is situated on the coast with views of the sea.					

Entry	Price	Pay Per Round	Pay Per Day	Entry Restrictions	Coastal View
ABERDOUR: *Aberdour Golf Club* Seaside Place, Aberdour, Fife. **Map** D4. *(01383) 860256.*	£	●	▨	●	▨
ARBROATH: *Arbroath Artisan Golf Club* Elliot, Near Arbroath, Angus. **Map** E3. *(01241) 875837.*	££	●	▨	●	▨
AUCHTERARDER: *Gleneagles Hotel Golf Courses* w www.gleneagles.com The Gleneagles Hotel, Auchterarder, Perthshire. **Map** D4. *(01764) 694469.*	££££	●			
CARNOUSTIE: *Carnoustie Golf Club* w www.carnoustiegolflinks.co.uk 3 Links Parade, Carnoustie, Angus. **Map** E4. *(01241) 853789.*	££££	●		●	▨
CRAIGSTON: *Cochrane Castle Golf Club* Craigston, Johnstone, Renfrewshire. **Map** C4. *(01505) 320146.*	£	●	▨	●	
CRUDEN BAY: *Cruden Bay Golf Club* Aulton Road, Cruden Bay, Aberdeenshire. **Map** E2. *(01779) 812285.*	£££	●	▨		▨
DORNOCH: *Royal Dornoch Golf Club* w www.royaldornoch.com Golf Road, Dornoch, Sutherland. **Map** D2. *(01862) 810219.*	££££	●		●	▨
DUNFERMLINE: *Pitreavie Golf Club* Queensferry Road, Dunfermline, Fife. **Map** D4. *(01383) 723151.*	£	●	▨		
EDINBURGH: *Merchants of Edinburgh Golf Club* 10 Craighill Gardens, Edinburgh. **Map** D4. *(0131) 447 1219.*	££	●	▨		
GLASGOW: *Haggs Castle Golf Club* 70 Dumbreck Road, Glasgow. **Map** D4. *(0141) 427 1157.*	££	●	▨	●	
KINROSS: *Green Hotel Golf Courses* Green Hotel, Kinross, Kinross-shire. **Map** D4. *(01577) 863407.*	£	●	▨		
KIRKCALDY: *Kirkcaldy Golf Club* Balwearie Road, Kirkcaldy, Fife. **Map** D4. *(01592) 203258.*	£	●	▨		▨
LAMLASH: *Lamlash Golf Club* Lamlash, Isle of Arran. **Map** C5. *(01770) 600296.*	£		▨		▨
LARGS: *Largs Golf Club* w www.largsgolfclub.co.uk Irvine Road, Largs, Ayrshire. **Map** C4. *(01475) 673594.*	£££	●	▨		▨
MILLPORT: *Millport Golf Club* Golf Road, Millport, Isle of Cumbrae. **Map** C4. *(01475) 530306.*	£	●	▨		▨
NAIRN: *Nairn Golf Club* Seabank Road, Nairn, Nairnshire. **Map** D2. *(01667) 453208.*	££££	●	▨	●	▨
NEWMACHAR: *Newmachar Golf Club* Swailend, Newmachar, Aberdeenshire. **Map** E2. *(01651) 863002.*	££	●	▨	●	
ST ANDREWS: *St Andrews Links* w www.standrews.org.uk Pilmour House, St Andrews, Fife. **Map** E4. *(01334) 466666.*	££££	●	▨	●	▨
SCONE: *Murrayshall Golf Course and Lyndoch Course* Murrayshall Hotel & Golf Course, Scone, Perthshire. **Map** D4. *(01738) 551171.*	££	●	▨		
SKEABOST: *Skeabost Golf Club* Skeabost Country House Hotel, Skeabost Bridge, Isle of Skye. **Map** B2. *(01470) 532202.*	£		▨		▨
STONEHAVEN: *Stonehaven Golf Club* Cowie, Stonehaven, Kincardineshire. **Map** E3. *(01569) 762124.*	£	●	▨		▨
TROON: *Royal Troon Golf Club Old Course* w www.royaltroon.com Craigend Road, Troon, Ayrshire. **Map** C5. *(01292) 311555. Quoted cost includes lunch.*	££££		▨	●	▨

Walking in Scotland

Thermos flask

I︎T CAN TRULY BE SAID that Scotland is a paradise for walkers. The scenery is superb without being overwhelming, and the variety of terrain encompasses everything from craggy mountains to gentle river valleys, not to mention a magnificent coastline. In recent years there has been an increase in the number of walks available to the public. The local tourist information centre is always a good first port of call if you are looking for advice or suggested routes. Whether you wish to walk for an hour or spend a day on the trail, you will find that Scotland can satisfy all of your walking needs.

Walking boots

not on rough ground where you may need ankle support. Lightweight walking boots are suitable for most seasons.

WALKING OPPORTUNITIES

T︎HIS SECTION deals with low-level walking; mountain activities are covered on pages 192–3, and you can also obtain information from the **Mountaineering Council of Scotland**. In recent years, greatly improved path networks have been developed, some through the national **Paths for All Partnership**. The networks provide excellent, safe walking opportunities for visitors. Some of the best networks are in the Borders and around Galloway, in Perthshire (around Dunkeld and Pitlochry), in Aberdeenshire (around Huntly), at Braemar and on the island of Bute.

Local authorities and other agencies have created paths and published walking guides for remote areas, such as Wester Ross, the Western Isles, Orkney and Shetland. Some of these walks tie in with ferry services. Most have a cultural or natural history theme, or incorporate a castle, waterfall or other place of interest. The walks are generally from 6 to 12 km (4 to 7 miles) in length.

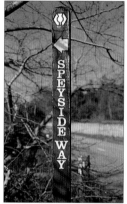

Long-distance trail signpost for walkers in the Spey river valley

RIGHT OF ACCESS

I︎N SCOTLAND there is a statutory right of access to most land for recreational purposes. New access laws implemented in 2005 are balanced by a Scottish Outdoor Access Code giving guidance on responsible conduct for users and managers of such land.

Scotland's long tradition of open access has resulted in few routes being shown on Ordnance Survey or other maps, although historic rights of way are usually marked. **Scotways** hold the definitive maps showing these routes.

Guidebooks available at large bookshops such as **Ottakar's** in Edinburgh or **Borders** in Glasgow, describe easily walkable routes, many of which are signposted. Access restrictions may be requested

in mountain areas during the stag stalking season (August to October), but on any areas owned by the **National Trust for Scotland** there is open access all year *(see p193)*.

CLOTHING AND EQUIPMENT

T︎HE WEATHER in Scotland is fickle. It can snow in June or be balmy in February, and conditions are liable to change rapidly. This makes selecting the right clothing and equipment tricky. Even in summer, you should take a waterproof jacket if venturing far from shelter. When going on a day walk, take waterproof trousers and a fleece or warm sweater.

The art of being comfortable is to make your clothing adaptable; several thin layers are better than one thick one. Head covering is worth considering – a cap for sunny days or a warmer hat for cold days.

For any walk of more than a couple of hours' duration, take a drink and snack. If you are going to be out all day, take energy foods and liquids.

Good footwear is essential. Countryside walks generally demand strong shoes or boots. Sturdy trainers can be worn on roads or firm tracks, but

Summer walking in Glen Etive

Above the clouds in Knoydart, looking to the Cuillin Hills on Skye

Tourist information centres are good starting places for more details, or you can contact **VisitScotland** to obtain their *New Walking Scotland* brochure, which describes walks in all parts of Scotland. Their brochure also lists walking festivals. These events, that last up to a week, offer a wide range of guided walks along with a programme of evening entertainment. The first such festival, held in the Borders, started in 1995. Others are now held in the Highlands, Deeside and Perthshire, with more starting up each year.

Compass of the type commonly used by walkers

For information on organized walks, contact the **Ramblers' Association Scotland**. There are also hundreds of miles of forest trails and walks across the country. The **Forestry Commission** can provide you with general information.

Longer low-level routes being developed include the Fife Coastal Path, the Clyde Walkway and the Speyside Way extension to Aviemore. All of these can easily be sampled as day walks.

Spring and autumn are especially lovely times of the year for walking in Scotland. The colouring is superb, and there is often a wider choice of accommodation available.

LONG-DISTANCE WALKS

SCOTLAND HAS relatively few formal long-distance routes, though the potential for making up your own is limitless. The three "official" routes are the 152-km (95-mile) West Highland Way from Glasgow to Fort William, the 340-km (211-mile) Southern Upland Way from Portpatrick to Cockburnspath, and the 84-km (52-mile) Speyside Way from Spey Bay to Tomintoul.

Other routes developed by local authorities include the 100-km (62-mile) St Cuthbert's Way from Melrose to Lindisfarne, and the Fife Coastal Path from North Queensferry to Tayport near the bridge over the Tay to Dundee.

The three principal routes are shown on the activities map *(see pp186–7)*. For information about them, and others being developed, contact **Scottish Natural Heritage** and local tourist information centres.

Surveying the scenery on a wintry day in the Cairngorms

DIRECTORY

Borders Books
98 Buchanan St,
Glasgow G1 3BA.
(*(0141) 222 7700.*

Forestry Commission
231 Corstorphine Rd,
Edinburgh EH12 7AT.
(*(0131) 314 6322.*
w www.forestry.gov.uk

Mountaineering Council of Scotland
The Old Granary, West Mill St,
Perth PH1 5QP.
(*(01738) 638227.*
w www.mountaineering-scotland.org.uk

National Trust for Scotland
28 Charlotte Square,
Edinburgh EH2 4ET.
(*(0131) 243 9300.*
w www.nts.org.uk

Ottakar's
57 George St,
Edinburgh EH2 2JQ.
(*(0131) 225 4495.*

The Paths for All Partnership
Inglewood House,
Tullibody Rd,
Alloa FK10 2HU
(*(01259) 218888.*
w www.pathsforall.org.uk

Ramblers' Association Scotland
Kingfisher House,
Auld Mart Business Park,
Milnathort KY13 9DA.
(*(01577) 861222.*
w www.ramblers.org.uk

Scottish Natural Heritage
12 Hope Terrace,
Edinburgh EH9 2AS.
(*(0131) 447 4784.*
w www.snh.org.uk

Scotways
24 Annandale St,
Edinburgh EH7 4AN.
(*(0131) 558 1222.*
w www.scotways.com

VisitScotland
23 Ravelston Terrace,
Edinburgh EH4 3TP.
(*(0845) 2255 121.*
w www.visitscotland.com

Activities in the Mountains

Detailed area maps

ALTHOUGH SCOTLAND'S highest mountains rise to little over 1,200 m (4,000 ft), they offer a true challenge to the hill walker and rock climber alike. Noted worldwide for their beauty of form and variety of character, the mountains of Scotland command respect among all mountaineers, not least because the climate is so variable. During the winter, conditions can be arctic. Long days in the hills offer a sense of satisfaction and refreshment that is highly valued as a contrast to the hectic pace of modern life.

A rucksack for carrying provisions

Scotland may be small, but the maritime climate and frequently wild winter weather produce ice climbs that are among the most serious and demanding in the world. The only "closed season" on Scotland's mountains is the short period between mid-August and late October, when restrictions apply in certain areas during the stag shooting season. *Heading for the Scottish Hills*, published jointly by the **Mountaineering Council of Scotland** and the Scottish Landowners' Federation gives estate maps and telephone numbers to call for local advice. See the Directory opposite for details of the **Hillphones** message system.

Hard hats and safety ropes – vital equipment for rock climbing

SAFETY IN THE MOUNTAINS

THE MOUNTAINS of Scotland demand respect at any time of the year, and this means being properly prepared. You should always take with you full waterproofs, warm clothes (including hat and gloves), and food and drink. Take a map and compass and know how to use them. Good boots are essential. Winter mountaineering demands knowledge of ice-axe and crampon techniques. **Glenmore Lodge** in Aviemore is a good centre offering courses in skiing, hill craft and mountaineering.

MOUNTAINEERING IN SCOTLAND

RECREATION IN the mountains takes several forms. Many people aim for the higher hills, known as "Munros" and "Corbetts". These vary in character from the rounded heathery domes of the Monadhliath or the Southern Uplands to the steep, craggy eminences of the

west, many of which command superb sea views. Narrow ridges such as the Aonach Eagach above Glencoe, and the peerless Cuillins of Skye, offer exhilarating sport and a special challenge. Given the right conditions, most hills can be climbed in a day, but more remote peaks may demand an overnight camp, or a stay in one of the simple huts known as a "bothy". Winter mountaineering needs extra skills but it also reaps the fantastic reward of the most breathtaking scenery.

Rock and ice climbing in Scotland has a long and distinguished history stretching back over a century. The main climbing areas, including Glencoe, the Cairngorms and Skye, have provided tough training grounds for many climbers who later gained world renown. All year the huge northern faces of Ben Nevis (*see p135*) offer a multitude of climbs at all levels. New areas, including the far northwest and the islands, have been developed more recently, as have particular disciplines such as sea-stack climbing. Techniques are being continually extended and skills refined, so that ever tougher routes can be completed. The mountains of

MUNROS AND CORBETTS

SCOTTISH MOUNTAINS rising just above 914 m (3,000 ft) are often called "Munros" after Sir Hugh Munro, first president of the Scottish Mountaineering Club (SMC). In 1891 Munro published the first comprehensive list of mountains fulfilling

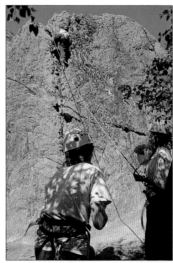

Rock climbers ascending Polldubh, Glen Nevis

Enjoying a superb mountain panorama in the northern Highlands

this criterion. The list has been maintained by the SMC ever since, and the hills are now officially classed as Munros. Normally, the principal summits on a hill are Munros; the lesser summits are called "Tops". Revised several times, the list now totals 284 Munros.

The first known Munroist was the Rev AE Robertson in 1901. He finished his tour of the Munros on Meall Dearg, above Glencoe, and it is recorded that he kissed the cairn before kissing his wife, such was his enthusiasm as the first of many dedicated Munroists.

In the 1920s, J Rooke Corbett published a list of the summits that measured 760–915 m (2,500–3,000 ft). These 221 "Corbetts", as they became known, have a clearer definition than the Munros – they must be single summits.

A third list is available, of summits of 610–760 m (2,000–2,500 ft) called "Grahams". All summits in Scotland over 610 m have now been categorized and published. The hills are described, with ascent routes, in the SMC guides *The Munros* and *The Corbetts, and other Scottish Hills*, and in *The Munros Almanac* and *The Corbetts Almanac*. The third set is listed in a publication called *The Grahams*.

SKIING IN SCOTLAND

THERE ARE FIVE ski centres in Scotland: **White Corries** at Glencoe, **Nevis Range** *(see pp135)*, **The Lecht**, **Cairngorm** *(see pp140–41)* and **Glenshee**. The Lecht tends to have the gentlest runs, while White Corries has the steepest.

These two centres are more informal than the others. Nevis Range, Glenshee and Cairngorm offer good facilities and runs for skiers of all abilities, including nursery slopes.

Ski centres are usually open from December to April, depending on the amount of snow cover. Unfortunately, snow is not wholly reliable in Scotland but when it does snow, the skiing is exhilarating. Hotels and guesthouses in the ski areas offer weekend and midweek packages, and there are ski schools in all the areas. The best advice is to keep an eye on the weather and take your chance as it arises.

Cross-country or Nordic skiing is a popular, informal sport in Scotland. Given good snow cover, there are many suitable areas, ranging from the Southern Uplands to the hills of the north and west, as well as hundreds of miles of forest trails all over Scotland.

Downhill skiing on the Scottish slopes

DIRECTORY			

SAFETY IN THE MOUNTAINS

Scotland has a well organized network of voluntary mountain rescue teams. Calls for rescue should be made to the police on **999**.

Weather Forecasts
(the Highlands)
((09068) 500442.

Mountaineering Council of Scotland
The Old Granary, West Mill St, Perth PH1 5QP.
((01738) 638227.
FAX (01738) 442095.

Hillphones
W www.hillphones.info
This service offers hill-walkers a recorded telephone message detailing daily stag stalking in various parts of the Highlands from Aug 1st until Oct 31st. It is organized by the Mountaineering Council of Scotland, Scottish Natural Heritage and participating estates.

Athol and Lunde
((01796) 481740.
Balmoral–Lochnagar
((013397) 55532.
Callater and Clunie
((013397) 41997.
Drumochter
((01528) 522200.

Glen Clova
((01575) 550335.
Glen Dochart/Glen Lochay
((01567) 820886.
Glen Shee
((01250) 885288.
Grey Corries/Mamores
((01397) 732362.
Invercauld
((013397) 41911.
North Arran
((01770) 302363.
Paps pf Jura
((01496) 820151.
South Glen Shiel
((01599) 511425.

Glenmore Lodge
Aviemore,
Inverness-shire PH22 1QU.
((01479) 861256.

SKI CENTRES

W www.visitscotland.com

Cairngorm
Aviemore, Inverness-shire.
((01479) 861261.

Glenshee
Cairnwell, Aberdeenshire.
((013397) 41320.

The Lecht
Strathden, Aberdeenshire.
((01975) 651440.

Nevis Range
Torlundy, Inverness-shire.
((01397) 705825.

White Corries
King's House,
Glencoe, Argyll.
((01855) 851226.

Other Outdoor Activities

Dunkeld fishing fly

SCOTLAND HAS A FEW surprises up its sleeve for people who still associate the country with old-fashioned tourist images. While traditional pursuits such as deerstalking or salmon fishing still thrive, they are now complemented by a wide range of more contemporary sports including mountain biking and even surfing. Flanked by the North Sea and the Atlantic, Scotland has ample water for sailing, windsurfing and fishing, while horse riding and cycling present excellent ways to explore the country's varied and dramatic landscapes.

Splendid catch of the day from the River Tweed, southern Scotland

Mountain biking on low-level tracks

CYCLING AND MOUNTAIN BIKING

CYCLING AROUND Scotland is one of the best ways to view the country. The trails of the Highlands are near perfect mountain bike territory and **Forest Enterprise** has opened a lot of the forest road network to mountain bikers. There is also an expanding national cycle path network to explore.

Edinburgh has a system of cycle paths on old train tracks. **Edinburgh Central Cycle Hire** is just one of many hire shops in the city. The **Scottish Cyclists Union** has information on cycling events and races in and around the capital.

A *Cycling in Scotland* booklet is available from tourist offices. For details of cycling trips in Scotland, contact the **C.T.C. National Cyclists Organisation** and **Scottish Cycling Holidays**.

FISHING

ALTHOUGH SCOTLAND is most associated with salmon fishing, there are opportunities for sea angling, coarse fishing, and game fishing for trout too.

The **Salmon and Trout Association** has information on game fishing – the season runs from mid-February to the end of October. For coarse fishing and sea angling a landowner's permission is required before casting off. The **Scottish Federation for Coarse Angling** and **Scottish Federation of Sea Anglers** provide all the necessary information. Contact the **Scottish Anglers National Association** for general advice.

HUNTING

THE TRADITION of recreational hunting can be traced back to the mid-1800s, when Queen Victoria and Prince Albert set up residence in Balmoral on Deeside. It became fashionable for British aristocrats to spend the autumn shooting in Scotland. Large parts of the Highlands became sporting estates.

Scotland is recognized as providing Europe's best game-shooting and deerstalking. Red deer and grouse are plentiful, while many estuaries and firths are wintering grounds for birds.

Over the last 30 years or so, hunting in Scotland has also attracted overseas visitors. For information on gun licensing and where to shoot, contact the **British Association for Shooting and Conservation.**

PONY TREKKING AND HORSE RIDING

THERE ARE MORE than 60 trekking and riding centres across Scotland, catering to a wide range of abilities, including trips deep into the Highlands for experienced riders. Some offer accommodation, tuition and trail riding, others provide trekking by the hour. The **Trekking and Riding Society of Scotland** has a complete list of all the centres.

Pentland Hills Icelandics, south of Edinburgh, offers rides on rare Icelandic ponies. On Deeside is the **Glen Tanar Equestrian Centre**, and visitors to Skye should try **Portree Riding Stables**.

Visitors taking in the Scottish scenery on horseback

SAILING

SCOTLAND IS A country of firths, islands and sea lochs, and the best way to explore them is by boat. You do not necessarily have to be a skilled sailor to do this, as some companies now offer supervised

Wooden sailboat in the Sound of Sleat, just off the Isle of Skye

yachting holidays for novices. Visitors also have the option of chartering a yacht. Centres such as **Port Edgar Marina** near Edinburgh or the **Scottish National Watersports Centre** on Cumbrae in the Firth of Clyde offer tuition for beginners, while experienced sailors will find serviced moorings for their own craft in beauty spots up and down the west coast and among the islands.

WATERSPORTS

SURFING IS NOT an activity normally associated with Scotland, but a good wetsuit and a sense of determination are all that is needed. Pease Bay in East Lothian is a popular spot, as are some north coast locations such as Dunnet Bay by Thurso and the northwest tip of Lewis. September to October is the best time for the waves. Windsurfing is also a

Kayaking on Loch Eil in the shadow of magnificent Ben Nevis

favourite activity. The **Scottish Windsurfing Association** has information on sites across the country. The top venue is the remote island of Tiree, which hosts a major windsurfing event in October every year.

Canoes and kayaks can be rented on lochs and in sheltered bays. The **Scottish Water Ski Centre** has details on the best places to water ski.

DIRECTORY

CYCLING AND MOUNTAIN BIKING

C.T.C. National Cyclists Organisation
69 Meadrow, Godalming, Surrey GU7 3HS, England.
((08708) 730060.
w www.ctc.org.uk

Edinburgh Central Cycle Hire
13 Lochrin Place, Edinburgh EH3 9QX.
((0131) 228 6633.

Forest Enterprise
1 Highlander Way, Inverness IV2 7GB.
((01463) 232811.

Scottish Cycling Holidays
87 Perth St, Blairgowrie, Perthshire PH10 6DT.
((01250) 876100.

Scottish Cyclists Union
The Velodrome, Meadowbank Sports Centre, London Road, Edinburgh EH7 6AD.
((0131) 652 0187.

FISHING

Salmon & Trout Association
National Game Angling Centre, The Pier, Loch Leven, Kinross KY13 8UF
((01577) 861116

Scottish Anglers National Association
National Game Angling Centre, The Pier, Loch Leven, Kinross KY13 8UF
((01577) 861116
w www.sana.org.uk

Scottish Federation for Coarse Angling
8 Longbraes Gardens, Kirkcaldy, Fife KY2 5YJ.
((01592) 642242.
w www.sfca.co.uk

Scottish Federation of Sea Anglers
Unit 28, Evans Business Centre, Mitchelston Industrial Estate, Kirkcaldy KY1 3NB.
((01592) 657520.

HUNTING

British Association for Shooting and Conservation (Scotland)
Trochry, Dunkeld, Perthshire PH8 0DY.
((01350) 723226.
w www.basc.org.uk

PONY TREKKING AND HORSE RIDING

Glen Tanar Equestrian Centre
Glen Tanar, Aboyne, Royal Deeside AB36 8XJ.
((01339) 886448.

Pentland Hills Icelandics
Windy Gow Farm, Carlops, Midlothian EH26 9NL.
((01968) 661095.
w www.phicelandics.co.uk

Portree Riding Stables
Garalatin, Portree, Isle of Skye, IV51 9LN.
((01478) 613124.
w www. portreeriding.co.uk

Trekking and Riding Society of Scotland (TRSS)
Druaich Na-H Abhainne, Killin, Perthshire SK21 8TN.
((01567) 820909.

SAILING

Port Edgar Marina
South Queensferry, Edinburgh EH30 9SQ.
((0131) 331 3330.

Scottish National Watersports Centre
Cumbrae KA28 0HQ.
((01475) 530757.

WATERSPORTS

Royal Yacht Association
Caledonia House, South Gyle, Edinburgh EH12 9DQ.
((0131) 317 7388.
w www. ryascotland.org.uk

Scottish Water Ski Centre
Town Hill Loch, Townhill, Dunfermline KY12 0HT.
((01383) 620123.

SURVIVAL
GUIDE

PRACTICAL INFORMATION 198-207
TRAVEL INFORMATION 208-215

PRACTICAL INFORMATION

TO ENJOY SCOTLAND FULLY, it is best to know something about the workings of everyday life. The range of facilities for tourists in Scotland has never been better – indeed tourism has become a major part of the country's economy – and VisitScotland is continually promoting better services around the country. This chapter gives advice about when best to visit Scotland; customs and immigration requirements; where to find tourist information; what to do or whom to turn to if things go wrong; banking and communications; and how to get around the country by public and private transport, including ferries to the islands.

Logo of VisitScotland

Whether or not you find Scotland an expensive country will depend on the exchange rate between the pound and your own currency.

Visitors travelling to Edinburgh from London will find that costs are generally lower in Scotland's capital.

Visitors' Centre in Callander, at the heart of the Trossachs

WHEN TO VISIT

SCOTLAND'S CLIMATE is very changeable (see pp36–9). May and June are usually drier than July and August, although the latter are usually the warmest months. The west coast tends to be mild and wet, while the east coast is cool and drier.

Scotland's towns and cities are all-year destinations, but many attractions open only between Easter and October. The main family holiday months, July and August, and public holidays (see p38) are always busy. Hotels are crammed at Christmas and New Year, particularly in Edinburgh for the Hogma-nay street party (see p39). Spring and autumn offer a moderate climate and a lack of crowds. Whatever the time of year, it is wise to get an up-to-date weather forecast before you set off on foot to remote hills or mountainous locations. Walkers and climbers can be surprised by the weather, and the Mountain Rescue services are frequently called out due to unexpectedly severe conditions. Weather reports are given on television and radio, in newspapers and by a weather phone service (see p193).

INSURANCE

IT IS SENSIBLE to take out travel insurance before travelling, to cover cancellation or curtailment of your holiday, theft or loss of money and possessions, and the cost of any medical treatment (see p202). If your country has a reciprocal medical arrangement with the UK you can obtain free treatment under the National Health Service. Australia, New Zealand and everywhere in the European Union (EU) has this arrangement. North American health plans, and student identity cards may give some protection against incurred costs, but always check the small print.

Sign for the Mountain Rescue

If you want to drive a car in Scotland, it is advisable to take out fully comprehensive insurance. You must carry a valid driver's licence. If you are not an EU citizen, you must have an international driver's licence, available through the AAA for those in the US.

ADVANCE BOOKING

OUT OF SEASON, you should have few problems booking accommodation or transport at short notice, but in high season always try to book ahead if possible. Before travelling, contact **VisitBritain**, www.visitbritain.com, or a travel agent, for advice and information.

CUSTOMS AND IMMIGRATION

A VALID PASSPORT is needed to enter the United Kingdom. Visitors from the European Union (EU), the United States, Canada, Australia and New Zealand do not require visas to enter the UK, nor any inoculations or vaccinations. Once within the UK, visitors are free to travel to and from Scotland, England, Wales and Northern Ireland without passing any other frontier formalities.

When you arrive at any international air or sea port in the UK, you will find separate queues at immigration control: one for EU nationals and several others for everyone else. Scotland is a member of the EU, which means that anyone arriving from an EU member country can pass through a blue channel. Random checks are still made, however, for illegal goods, especially drugs.

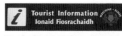

Standard tourist information sign

◁ **The busy Royal Mile in Edinburgh, with the Firth of Forth in the distance**

Travellers entering from outside the EU have to pass through the usual customs channels. Go through the green channel if you have nothing to declare over the customs allowances for overseas visitors, and the red channel if you have goods to declare. If you are unsure of importation restrictions, go through the red channel. Full details of these restrictions are available from HM Customs and Excise in London. Beware – never carry luggage or parcels through customs for someone else.

Tourist brochure

TOURIST INFORMATION

Tourist bookings in Scotland are handled by **VisitScotland** via its call centre and website. The organization also has a base in central London. In addition to these, every region of Scotland has its own tourist board, providing information about local accommodation, entertainment and places of interest. Smaller, subsidiary tourist information offices can be found in many towns and public places, and at some of the principal locations of historical interest. Look out for the tourist information symbol, indicating an office. The British Tourist Authority operates offices overseas.

DISABLED TRAVELLERS

The facilities on offer in Scotland for disabled visitors are steadily improving. An increasing number of hotels and guesthouses now offer easy wheelchair access. This information is given in the headings for each entry throughout the guide. Given advance notice, FirstScotRail *(see p211)*, ferry or coach (long-distance bus) staff will help any disabled passengers. Ask a travel agent about the Disabled Persons Railcard, which entitles the holder to discounted rail fares on services across the country.

Specialist tour operators, such as **Holiday Care**, cater for the physically handicapped visitor. You can contact them on (0845) 1249971, www.holidaycare.org.uk. **Hertz Rent A Car** offers hand-controlled vehicles without any extra cost *(see p215)*. For permission to use any disabled parking space, you need to display a special sign in your car.

Visitors from the US can telephone the **Society for the Advancement of Travel for the Handicapped (SATH)** on (212) 447 7284 before leaving. They publish *ACCESS to Travel*, a magazine full of information.

DIRECTORY

VISITSCOTLAND

For brochures to any area in Scotland, or to book accommodation contact:
[C] (0845) 2255121.
[W] www.visitscotland.com

VisitScotland Centre
19 Cockspur St, London SW1Y 5BL

REGIONAL TOURIST BOARDS

Aberdeen & Grampian
[C] (0845) 2255121.
[W] wwwcastlesandwhisky.com

Angus & Dundee
[C] (01382) 527527.
[W] www.angusanddundee.co.uk

Argyll, The Isles, Loch Lomond, Stirling & The Trossachs
[C] (0845) 2255121.
[W] www.visitscotland.com

Ayrshire & Arran
[C] (01292) 678100.
[W] www.ayrshire-arran.com

Dumfries & Galloway
[C] (01387) 253862.
[W] www.visit-dumfries-and-galloway.co.uk

Edinburgh & Lothians
[C] (0845) 2255121.
[W] www.edinburgh.org

Greater Glasgow & Clyde Valley
[C] (0141) 204 4480.
[W] www.seeglasgow.com

Highlands of Scotland
[C] (0845) 2255121.
[W] www.visithighlands.com

Kingdom of Fife
[C] (0845) 2255121.
[W] www.standrews.co.uk

Orkney Islands
[C] (01856) 872856.
[W] www.visitorkney.com

Perthshire
[C] (0845) 2255121.
[W] www.perthshire.co.uk

Scottish Borders
[C] (0870) 608404.
[W] www.scot-borders.co.uk

Shetland Islands
[C] (08701) 999440.
[W] www.visitshetland.com

Western Isles
[C] (0845) 2255121.
[W] www.visithebrides.com

Tobermory harbour on the Isle of Mull, popular with tourists

Glamis Castle, one of the castles charging admission to visitors

TRAVELLING WITH CHILDREN

PUBLIC HOLIDAYS and school holidays (July–mid-August) have most to offer in the way of children's entertainment. Many places have activities suitable for children over the Christmas period, particularly pantomimes. Discounts for children and family tickets are available for travel, theatre and other entertainments.

Choose accommodation that welcomes children (see pp164–73), or opt for self-catering (efficiency apartments). Many hotels provide baby-sitting or baby-listening services, and offer reductions or free accommodation for the very young.

Nowadays restaurants are better equipped for children; many provide highchairs and special menus (see pp174–83). Pubs often admit children, if accompanied by an adult. The legal drinking age is 18.

Playing with interactive exhibits at Edinburgh's Museum of Childhood

ADMISSION CHARGES

THESE VARY WIDELY, from a nominal fee to a more substantial charge for popular attractions. Reductions are often available for groups, senior citizens, children or students. The majority of local churches, museums and art galleries are free, unless a special exhibition is showing, but donations are often expected. Some attractions in Scotland are run privately, either as a commercial venture or on a charitable basis.

OPENING HOURS

MANY SHOPS in Scotland open on Sundays, particularly in the city centres. Monday to Friday hours are around 9:30am to 5:30pm, but shop hours do vary, opening late one evening a week – usually on a Thursday. Museums and art galleries generally open for fewer hours on Sundays, and many attractions continue to open on public and bank holidays, especially on Christmas Day and New Year's Day.

VAT AND REFUNDS

VALUE ADDED TAX (VAT) is charged at 17.5 per cent on most goods and services. When leaving the UK, non-residents can redeem VAT on goods purchased from shops in the Retail Export Scheme. Refunds will be given if goods are faulty and are returned with the receipt as proof of purchase.

STUDENT TRAVELLERS

FULL-TIME STUDENTS who have an International Student Identity Card (ISIC) are often entitled to discounts on travel, sports facilities and entrance fees. North American students can also get medical cover but it may be very basic (see p202). ISIC cards are available from **STA Travel**, or the **National Union of Students**. Inexpensive accommodation is also available (out of term) at the

Student ISIC card

university halls of residence in the main cities. This is a good way of staying in central locations when on a tight budget.

An **International Youth Hostel Federation** card enables you to stay in one of Scotland's many youth hostels. Contact the **Scottish Youth Hostels Association** direct.

Charlotte Square, Edinburgh, home of the National Trust for Scotland

NATIONAL TRUST FOR SCOTLAND

MANY OF SCOTLAND's historic buildings, parks, gardens, and vast tracts of countryside and coastline are cared for by the **National Trust for Scotland** (NTS). Entrance fees are often relatively high compared to fees at other sights, so if you wish to visit several NTS properties it may be worth taking out annual membership, which allows free access thereafter to all NTS properties. Beware, however, that many NTS properties close in the winter.

Typical newspaper stand, Glasgow

MEDIA

NATIONAL newspapers in Scotland fall into two categories: serious publications, such as Edinburgh's *The Scotsman* or Glasgow's *The Herald*; and those that are heavy on gossip, such as *The Sun* or *The Daily Record*. Weekend newspapers, such as *Scotland on Sunday* and the *Sunday Herald*, are more expensive than dailies, with many supplements including sections on arts, restaurants, entertainment, travel and reviews.

Newsagents sell a huge range of specialist periodicals. In major towns, main train stations and some of the larger book stores stock foreign magazines and newspapers.

The BBC (British Broadcasting Corporation) operates nine TV channels and produces some of the best television programmes in the world, without commercial breaks. The BBC's three main rivals are ITV, Channel 4 and Channel 5.

The BBC owns a number of radio stations from the popular Radio One to the middle-brow Radio Four, as well as the national station, BBC Radio Scotland. There are many local

ELECTRICITY

THE VOLTAGE IN Scotland is 220/240 AC, 50 Hz. The electrical plugs have three square pins and take fuses of 3, 5 and 13 amps. In order to use your foreign appliances, such as hair dryers, you will need an adaptor. Most hotel bathrooms have two-pronged sockets for electric shavers.

SMOKING AND ALCOHOL

SCOTLAND'S PARLIAMENT intends making smoking in all public places illegal from 2006. This ban will include public transport systems, taxis, train stations, theatres and cinemas, bars, restaurants and shops.

There is a general ban on drinking in public in Greater Glasgow and the Clyde Valley area, although public drinking is discouraged throughout Scotland. This ban is usually lifted for the New Year street party at Hogmanay (31 December).

CONVERSION CHART

Britain is officially metricated in line with the rest of Europe, but imperial measures are still in common usage, including road distances (measured in miles). Imperial pints and gallons are 20 per cent larger than US measures.

Imperial to metric
1 inch = 2.5 centimetres
1 foot = 30 centimetres
1 mile = 1.6 kilometres
1 ounce = 28 grams
1 pint = 0.6 litres
1 gallon = 4.5 litres

Metric to imperial
1 millimetre = 0.04 inch
1 centimetre = 0.4 inch
1 metre = 3 feet 3 inches
1 kilometre = 0.6 mile
1 gram = 0.04 ounce
1 kilogram = 2.2 pounds

TIME

SCOTLAND IS ON Greenwich Mean Time (GMT) during the winter months – that is, five hours ahead of Eastern Standard Time and ten hours behind Sydney. From the middle of March to the end of October, the clocks go forward one hour to British Summer Time (which is one hour ahead of GMT). To check the correct time, you can dial 123 to contact the Speaking Clock service.

DIRECTORY

National Trust for Scotland (NTS)
📞 *(0131) 243 9300.*
🖥 www.nts.org.uk

STUDENT TRAVELLERS

International Youth Hostel Federation
📞 *(01707) 324170.*
🖥 www.hihostels.com

National Union of Students
📞 *(0131) 556 6598.*

Scottish Youth Hostels Association
📞 *(01786) 891400.*
🖥 www.syha.org.uk

STA Travel
📞 *(08701) 600599.*
🖥 www.statravel.co.uk

EMBASSIES AND CONSULATES

United States Consulate
3 Regent Terrace,
Edinburgh EH7 5BW.
📞 *(0131) 556 8315.*

Australian High Commission
Australia House, Strand,
London WC2B 4LA.
📞 *(08700) 056701.*

Canadian Consulate
30 Lothian Rd,
Edinburgh EH1 2DH.
📞 *(0131) 220 4333.*

New Zealand High Commission
New Zealand House,
1 Haymarket,
London SW1Y 4TQ.
📞 *(08700) 056962.*

A selection of Scottish newspapers

Personal Security and Health

Pharmacy sign

LIKE ANY OTHER country, Scotland has its share of social problems, but it is very unlikely that you will come across any violence. If you do encounter difficulties, do not hesitate to contact the police for help. The UK's National Health Service (NHS) can be relied upon for an emergency or routine treatment. However, you may have to pay for treatment if your country has no reciprocal arrangement with the UK. Below is some guidance for enjoying a trouble-free visit.

HOSPITALS AND MEDICAL TREATMENT

ALL VISITORS to Scotland, especially those from outside the European Union (EU), are strongly advised to take out medical insurance against the cost of emergency hospital care, repatriation and specialists' fees. Emergency medical treatment in an NHS Accident and Emergency department is free, but additional medical care could prove very expensive. Visitors from the US should check with their insurance companies before leaving home to be sure they are covered if medical care is needed.

EU residents and nationals of some other Commonwealth and European countries are entitled to free medical treatment under the NHS, though the process is bureaucratic. Before travelling, obtain an E111 form that confirms that your country of origin has adequate reciprocal health arrangements with the UK. Some treatments are not covered, however, and repatriation is not included, so medical insurance is preferable.

If you need to see a dentist while staying in Scotland, you will have to pay. The cost will vary depending on your entitlement to NHS treatment. Emergency dental treatment is available in some hospitals.

PHARMACISTS

YOU CAN BUY a wide range of medicines without prescription from pharmacies in Scotland. Boots is the best-known and largest supplier, with branches in most towns.

A traditional, privately owned pharmacy in Leith, Edinburgh

Many medicines are available only with a doctor's prescription, which you must take to a dispensing chemist (pharmacist). Either bring your own supply or ask your doctor to write out the generic name of the drug (as opposed to the brand name). If you are entitled to an NHS prescription, you will be charged a standard rate; without this, you will be charged the full cost. Ask for

a receipt for any insurance claim. Some pharmacies stay open until midnight. Doctors' surgeries (offices) are usually open mornings and early evenings. Hospital Accident and Emergency departments are always open.

THE MIDGE

BEING BITTEN BY midges is one of the most common hazards for visitors to Scotland. The chance of encountering these tiny biting flies is particularly heightened around lochs and on the coast, as they love damp conditions. They breed between April and October, and are at their worst at the start and end of the day. There is no way of escaping them altogether, but to ensure that you suffer only the minimum of bites, apply insect repellent (such as Autan) and avoid sitting near bright lights after dark. If they really are a nuisance you may want to invest in a midge net.

CRIME AND SUITABLE PRECAUTIONS

SCOTLAND IS NOT a dangerous place for visitors, and it is most unlikely that your stay will be blighted by crime. There are, however, practical steps that can be taken to help you avoid loss of property or personal injury. Take good care of your belongings

Woman police constable   **Police constable**   **Traffic police officer**

Police patrol car with the familiar yellow stripe and blue light

at all times. Make sure your possessions are adequately insured before you arrive. Never leave them unattended in public places. Keep your valuables well concealed, especially in crowds. In cinemas or theatres, keep handbags on your lap, not on the floor. It is advisable not to carry too much cash or jewellery with you; leave it in the safe in the hotel instead. Pickpockets tend to frequent crowded places like bustling markets, busy shops and rush-hour public transport.

By far the safest way of carrying large amounts of cash around is in traveller's cheques *(see p205)*. Or you can withdraw small amounts of cash from cashpoints (ATMs). If you are travelling alone at night try to avoid deserted and poorly lit buildings and places such as back streets and car parks.

WOMEN TRAVELLING ALONE

IT IS NOT UNUSUAL in Scotland for women to travel unaccompanied, or to visit a bar or restaurant with a group of female friends. Nor is it especially dangerous. But caution is advisable in deserted places, especially after dark. Try to avoid using public transport when there is just one other passenger or a group of young men. It is best to summon a licensed taxi *(see p215)* rather than walk through a lonely area of a city at night, especially if you do not know the area well. It is illegal to carry any offensive weapons, including knives, guns, mace or tear-gas, even for self-defence. Personal alarms are permitted however.

Ambulance

Fire engine

POLICE

THE SIGHT of a traditional British bobby patrolling the streets in a tall hat is now less common than the police patrol car, usually with wailing sirens and flashing lights. But the old-fashioned police constable does still exist in Scotland, particularly in rural areas and crowded city centres, and continues to be courteous, approachable and helpful. Unlike in many other countries, the police in Scotland do not carry guns. If you are lost, the traditional advice to ask a policeman or woman still applies. Traffic wardens may also be able to help with directions.

In a crisis, dial 999 to reach police, fire and ambulance services who are on call 24 hours a day. Calls are free from any public or private phone, but they should only be made in real emergencies. In Scotland's coastal areas this number will also put you in touch with Britain's voluntary coastguard rescue service, the RNLI (Royal National Lifeboat Institution).

Logo of the Royal National Lifeboat Institution

LOST PROPERTY

IF YOU ARE unlucky enough to lose anything or have anything stolen, go straight to the nearest police station to report your loss. If you want to claim on insurance for any theft, you will need a written report from the local police. All of the main bus and train stations have lost property centres. Most hotels disclaim all responsibility for valuables not kept in their safe.

It is advisable to make photocopies of your vital documents such as passports and travel papers. If you lose your passport, contact your embassy or consulate in either Edinburgh or London *(see p201)*.

(see p201)

DIRECTORY

POLICE, FIRE AND AMBULANCE SERVICES

999. Calls are free (24-hour phoneline).

HOSPITAL ACCIDENT AND EMERGENCY DEPARTMENTS

Aberdeen Royal Infirmary
(01224) 840506.

Edinburgh Royal Infirmary
(0131) 536 1000.

Glasgow Royal Infirmary
(0141) 211 4484.

Inverness Raigmore
(01463) 704000.

Perth Royal Infirmary
(01738) 473838.

EMERGENCY DENTAL CARE

Edinburgh Dental Hospital
(0131) 536 4900.

DISABLED HELPLINE

The Disability Helpline
(08457) 123456.

Banking and Local Currency

Visitors to most Scottish cities and large towns will find a number of options for exchanging currency and cashing travellers' cheques. High-street banks, travel agencies and bureaux de change all offer this service at different exchange and commission rates. Cashpoints (ATM)s can be found at many locations and can be used to dispense cash via your debit card. Credit cards and traveller's cheques are the safest methods of bringing currency with you to Scotland.

One of many banks to offer bureau de change facilities

Bureaux de Change

Although bureaux de change are often more conveniently located than banks and have longer opening hours, the exchange rates can vary considerably and commission charges can be high.

The reputable firms such as **International Currency Exchange**, **Thomas Cook** and **American Express** offer good exchange facilities. International Currency Exchange has just one branch at Edinburgh Airport; both Thomas Cook and American Express have branches throughout Scotland.

Banks

Every large town and city in Scotland should have a branch of at least one of the following banks – Bank of Scotland, Royal Bank of Scotland, TSB Scotland, Girobank and Clydesdale.

Most banks have a cashpoint (ATM), as do many building societies, shops and garages, from which you can obtain money with a bank or credit card and your personal identification number (PIN). Some of the most modern machines have easy-to-read computerized instructions in several languages. Cardholders from principal English banks, such as NatWest, HSBC, Lloyds and Barclays, can withdraw money from certain banks in Scotland. Check that your bank card is compatible with the cashpoint you are using or you may be charged a fee or have your card rejected.

You can also obtain money by contacting your own bank and asking them to wire cash to the nearest Scottish bank. Branches of Thomas Cook or American Express will do this for you. Visitors from the US can have cash dispatched through **Western Union** to a bank or post office. Take your passport as proof of identity. Banking hours vary from bank to bank, but the minimum opening times are 9:30am to 3:30pm Monday to Friday.

Credit Cards

Credit and store cards are widely accepted throughout Scotland, but some smaller shops, guesthouses and cafés may not take them. VISA is the most widely used card, but MasterCard, Access, Diners Club and American Express are also accepted. For a small fee you can get cash advances with a credit card at any bank displaying the card sign.

Traveller's Cheques

Traveller's cheques can be purchased at American Express, Travelex or your bank. All are accepted in Scotland. If you exchange American Express cheques at an American Express office, commission is not charged.

Scottish Banks

Branches of the three main Scottish banks (Royal Bank of Scotland, Bank of Scotland and Clydesdale), will be found in all cities and many towns. English banks such as NatWest and Barclays are rare outside the main cities. Most banks offer exchange facilities, but proof of identity may be required and the commission charges will vary.

Bank of Scotland logo

Royal Bank of Scotland logo

NatWest logo

Clydesdale Bank logo

DIRECTORY

Exchange Facilities

International Currency Exchange
(0131) 333 3146.

Thomas Cook
(0141) 201 7200.

American Express
(0131) 7182505.

Western Union
(0800) 833833.

CURRENCY AND TRAVELLER'S CHEQUES

Bᴿɪᴛᴀɪɴ'ꜱ ᴄᴜʀʀᴇɴᴄʏ is the pound sterling (£), which is divided into 100 pence (p). There are no exchange controls in Britain, so you may bring in and take out as much cash as you like. Scotland has its own notes that are legal tender throughout Britain (with the exception of the £1 note), although they are not generally accepted abroad. Bank of England and Northern Ireland notes can be used throughout Scotland. Ask for some small notes when changing money, as they are easier to use. Traveller's cheques are a safer alternative to carrying large amounts of cash. Be sure to keep the receipts separate from the cheques so you can easily obtain a refund if your cheques are lost or stolen. Some high-street banks issue traveller's cheques free of commission to their account holders, but the normal charge is around 1 per cent.

Bank Notes

Scottish notes are produced in denominations of £1, £5, £10, £20, £50 and £100. Always get small denominations, as some shops may refuse the larger notes. Although Scotland has a £1 note, the English £1 coin, and all Bank of England currency, is legal tender.

£100 note

£10 note

£1 note

£20 note

£5 note

Coinage

Coins currently in use are £2, £1, 50p, 20p, 10p, 5p, 2p and 1p. The same coins are produced and accepted throughout the UK.

2 pounds (£2)

1 pound (£1)

50 pence (50p)

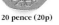

20 pence (20p)

10 pence (10p)

5 pence (5p)

2 pence (2p)

1 penny (1p)

Communications

Modern BT phone box

Wᴵᴛʜ ᴄᴏɴᴛɪɴᴜᴏᴜꜱʟʏ ɪᴍᴘʀᴏᴠɪɴɢ telecommunication systems and the spread of e-mail, staying in contact and making plans while travelling has never been easier. The telephone system in Scotland is efficient and inexpensive. Charges depend on when, where and for how long you talk. The cheapest time to call is between 6pm and 8am Monday to Friday, and throughout the weekend. Local calls made on public payphones, however, are charged at a fixed rate per minute.

Payphones

Yᴏᴜ ᴄᴀɴ ᴘᴀʏ for a payphone using coins or a card. Payphones accept 10p, 20p, 50p and £1 pieces, while newer phones also accept £2 coins. The minimum cost of a call is 30p. If you expect a call to be short, use 10p or 20p pieces, as payphones only return unused coins. Some payphones accept credit and debit cards. The minimum fee for local and national calls is 95p and £1.20 for international calls, calls to premium rate numbers, mobile phones and calls made through the operator.

Telephone Directories

Dɪʀᴇᴄᴛᴏʀɪᴇꜱ, ꜱᴜᴄʜ ᴀꜱ *Yellow Pages* and *Thomson Local*, list local businesses and services. They can be found at local Post Offices, libraries and often at your hotel. A number of operators now offer telephone directory enquiry services at different levels of cost to the caller.

Using a Card and Coin Phone

1 Lift the receiver and wait for the dial tone.

2 Insert your phone card into the slot or deposit any of the following coins: 10p, 20p, 50p, £1, £2. The minimum amount is 20p.

3 Dial the number and wait to be connected.

4 The display indicates how much credit you have left. A rapid bleeping noise means your money has run out. Deposit more coins or insert another phone card.

5 If you want to make another call and you have money left in credit, do not replace the receiver, press the follow-on-call button.

6 When you have finished speaking, replace the receiver and retrieve your card or collect your change. Only wholly unused coins are refunded.

£1

50p

20p

10p

USEFUL NUMBERS

A number of telephone services exist to help you find or reach a specific phone number.

Emergency Calls
999. Police, Fire, Ambulance, Coastguard, Mountain and Cave Rescue.

Directory Enquiries
118500 (BT).

International Directory Enquiries
118505 (BT).

International Operator
155.

Operator Assistance
100.

Overseas Calls
00 followed by country code: Australia (61), Canada (1), Ireland (353), New Zealand (64), South Africa (27), United States (1).

Talking Pages
118247. Provides numbers for specific kinds of shops or services in any area.

Accessing the Internet

Mᴏꜱᴛ ᴄɪᴛɪᴇꜱ ᴀɴᴅ towns now have some form of public access to computers and the Internet. Free Internet access is often available at main library branches, although you may have to book a time slot. Internet cafés usually charge by the minute for computer use.

EasyEverything, a chain of massive Internet cafés, has branches in Edinburgh (58 Rose Street and Princes Street) and Glasgow (57–61 St Vincent Street and Trongate Shopping Centre). Internet access is very cheap and is most reasonable during off-peak times.

24-hour Internet access at the easyInternetcafé

Sending a Letter

The distinctive Post Office logo

BESIDES MAIN POST OFFICES that offer all the mail services available, there are many sub-Post Offices in newsagents, grocery stores and general information centres, particularly in more isolated areas and smaller towns. In many villages the Post Office is also the only shop. Post Offices are usually open from 9am to 5:30pm Monday to Friday, and until 12:30pm on Saturday. Mailboxes – in all shapes and sizes but always red – are found throughout cities, towns and villages.

Postbus collection in rural Scotland

MAIL SERVICES

STAMPS CAN BE BOUGHT at many outlets, including supermarkets and petrol stations. Hotels often have mailboxes at their reception. When writing to an address anywhere in the UK always include the postcode. Letters and postcards can be sent either first or second class within the UK. First-class

1st-class aerogramme

1st-class stamp   2nd-class stamp

Greetings stamps featuring characters from children's fiction

service is more expensive but quicker, with most letters reaching their destination the following day (except Sunday); second-class mail takes a day or two longer.

POSTE RESTANTE

LARGE URBAN Post Offices have a poste restante service where letters can be sent for collection. To use the service be sure to print the surname (last name) clearly so it will be filed correctly. Send it to Poste Restante followed by the address of the Post Office. To collect your mail you will have to show your passport or other form of identification. Mail will be kept for one month. One of the most central Post Offices in Edinburgh is the one situated in the St James Centre, EH1, close to the main bus station. This Post Office also offers the poste restante service.

MAILBOXES

THESE MAY BE either freestanding "pillar boxes" or wall safes, both painted bright red. Some pillar boxes have separate slots, one for overseas and first-class mail, another for second-class mail. Initials on older mail boxes indicate who was monarch at that time.
    Mailboxes are often embedded in Post Office walls. Collections are usually made several times a day during weekdays (less often on Saturdays and rarely on Sundays and public holidays); times are marked on the box.

A rural mailbox, embedded in a stone wall

MAILING ABROAD

Pillar box

AIRMAIL PROVIDES a speedy and cost-effective method of communication. Aerogrammes go first class anywhere in the world and cost the same regardless of destination. They take about three to four days to reach European cities, and between four and seven days for destinations elsewhere. All mail sent within Europe goes via airmail, while overseas mail rates are classed by weight. Sending post overseas by surface mail may be more economical, but it can take anywhere up to 12 weeks for it to reach its final destination. The Post Office offers an express delivery service called **Parcelforce International**. Available from most main Post Offices, Parcelforce is comparable in price to many private companies such as **DHL**, **UPS**, **Crossflight**, or **Expressair**.

Crossflight
((0870) 2241122.

DHL
((08701) 100300.

Expressair
((020) 8897 3336.

Parcelforce International
((0870) 8501150.

UPS
((08457) 877877.

TRAVEL INFORMATION

A S THE UK IS an international gateway for air and sea traffic, travelling to Scotland poses few problems. There are direct flights from North America and continental Europe. Coach travel from Europe via the ferries is a cheap, albeit rather slow form of transport. Travelling by train using the Channel Tunnel is an efficient way of crossing to the UK. Travelling within Scotland itself is fairly easy. Internal flights are

A British Airways plane in mid-flight

available between the cities on the mainland, and also to the island groups. Another easy way to island-hop is to take the ferries. There is an extensive network of roads in urban areas and renting a car can be the best way of travelling around. The inter-city rail network is limited in Scotland, though a small network of trains serves the country. Travelling by coach is the cheapest option; there are services between most cities.

Check-in desks at Glasgow International Airport

INTERNATIONAL FLIGHTS TO AND FROM SCOTLAND

E DINBURGH AND Glasgow are the principal airports in Scotland. The four other international airports are Prestwick, Aberdeen, Inverness and Sumburgh on Shetland. **Air France**, **bmi** and **KLM UK** (formerly AirUK) offer direct flights from continental Europe. Glasgow and Edinburgh have the most frequent services, with direct and indirect flights to many major

European destinations including Paris, Dublin, and Brussels.

A number of transatlantic airlines offer direct services to Glasgow airport, including **British Airways, American Airlines**, **Continental Airlines** and **Air Canada**. Flights to Edinburgh and Glasgow are available from long-haul destinations such as North Africa, South Africa, Australia and the Far East. These are routed via a European capital, often Brussels or Amsterdam.

A more economical option can be to fly to London and take a cheap domestic flight north. These flights can cost as little as £29 one way.

The airports at Glasgow, Edinburgh and Aberdeen offer up-to-date facilities, including banking, shops, cafés, hotels and restaurants. Glasgow has a new international terminal, while Edinburgh has recently undergone a £55 million programme of development and renovation. This work was completed in spring 2001, with the opening of a new international arrivals hall.

TRAVELLING WITHIN THE UK FROM SCOTLAND

F LIGHTS FROM Scotland to other British destinations operate from all the mainland international airports. British Airways offers express services to London's Heathrow and Gatwick airports. bmi also flies direct to Heathrow. **easyJet**, **Ryanair** and KLM UK operate between Scotland and the English airports of Luton, Stansted and London City.

There are also direct flights to other major cities in the UK, including Manchester, Newcastle upon Tyne, Leeds, Birmingham, Belfast and Cardiff, and to some of the

Passengers from abroad passing through International Arrivals

AIRPORT	☏ INFORMATION	DISTANCE TO CITY CENTRE	TAXI FARE TO CITY CENTRE	PUBLIC TRANSPORT TO CITY CENTRE
Aberdeen	(0870) 0400006	7 miles (11 km)	£12	Bus: 30 min Taxi: 20 min
Edinburgh	(0870) 0400007	8 miles (13 km)	£16	Bus: 25 min Taxi: 20 min
Glasgow	(0870) 0400008	8 miles (13 km)	£16.50	Bus: 25 min Taxi: 20 min
Prestwick	(01292) 511115	29 miles (47 km)	£40	Train: 45 min Taxi: 40 min

The terminal at Glasgow International Airport

smaller ones such as Bristol and Southampton, but the relatively high cost of these flights can sometimes outweigh the time saved.

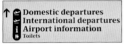

Sign directing passengers to locations within an airport

← ⊘ HM Customs enquiries

Directions to the department for information on customs

TRAVELLING WITHIN SCOTLAND BY AIR

SCOTLAND'S SIZE means that internal air travel is quick, but it can prove an expensive mode of travel compared to rail, coach or car. There are good air connections between the Highlands and central Scotland. When travelling to the islands off the coast of Scotland, flying becomes a particularly viable option. **British Airways CitiExpress** and **Loganair**, both subsidiaries of British Airways, provide regular flights from all the major cities on the mainland to the Western Isles, Orkney Islands and Shetland Islands.

TRANSPORT FROM THE AIRPORTS

SCOTLAND'S MAIN international airports lie on the outskirts of Glasgow, Edinburgh and Aberdeen, where there are efficient transportation links. Taxis are the most convenient form of door-to-door travel,

but they are also fairly expensive. Coaches or buses provide cheaper transport to the town centres, though during rush hour or heavy traffic, coaches, buses and taxis may be slow. **National Express** as well as **Scottish Citylink** (see p211) provide direct coach services from the major airports to various destinations.

Prestwick International is served by its own train station; a service runs to Glasgow city centre every half an hour.

AIR FARES

AIR FARES TO Scotland are usually at their highest from June to September. The best deals are available from November to April, excluding the Christmas period – if you want to travel then, you should book well in advance.

Apex (Advance Purchase Excursion) fares are often the best value, though they must be booked a month ahead and are subject to restrictions, such as minimum and maximum stays and no refunds. Charter flights offer even cheaper seats, but with less flexibility.

Promotional fares are often available, and it is worth checking direct with the airlines for special offers. Cheap deals are sometimes offered by package operators and are

Rental car collection point at Glasgow International Airport

advertised in newspapers and travel magazines. Students, those under 26 years old and senior citizens may be eligible for a discount. Children and babies travel for less.

If you choose a discount fare, always buy from a reputable operator, and check with the airline to ensure your seat has been confirmed. Packages may also be worth considering for cost-savings, even if you enjoy independent travel. Airlines and tour operators can put together a great range of flexible deals to suit your needs, sometimes with car rental or rail travel included. This can often be cheaper than arranging transport once you have arrived. A small airport tax is imposed on all those departing from British airports.

DIRECTORY
AIRLINE INFORMATION

Air Canada
📞 (08705) 247226.
🌐 www.aircanada.ca

Air France
📞 (08450) 845111.
🌐 www.airfrance.co.uk

American Airlines
📞 (08457) 789789.
🌐 www.aa.com

British Airways
📞 (0870) 8509850.
🌐 www.british-airways.com

bmi
📞 (08457) 554554.
🌐 www.flybmi.com

British Airways CitiExpress
📞 (01624) 826000.

Continental Airlines
📞 (0845) 607 6760.
🌐 www.continentalairlines.com

easyJet
📞 (0905) 821 0905.
🌐 www.easyjet.com

KLM UK
📞 (08705) 074074.
🌐 www.klmuk.com

Loganair
📞 (0141) 848 7594.

Ryanair
📞 (08712) 460000.
🌐 www.ryanair.ie

Travelling by Rail and Coach

SCOTLAND HAS A PRIVATIZED rail network, FirstScotRail,
that covers most of the country and is generally
efficient and reliable. A quarter-hourly service operates
between Edinburgh and Glasgow, and lines radiate from
both cities, with frequent services to many Scottish destinations and to most parts of England. Journey times to
London are just over four hours from Edinburgh and just
over five from Glasgow. Scotland also has a good coach
(long-distance bus) service that is generally cheaper than
the trains, although journeys can be slow. Weekend rail
and coach services are popular, so book ahead.

**The Flying Scotsman, one of the
many swift inter-city train services**

**The Virgin Superfast train at
Edinburgh's Waverley station**

TRAIN TICKETS

ALLOW PLENTY OF time to buy
your ticket, and always
ask about any special offers
or reduced fares. There are
four types of discounted fares
for adults. Apex (Advance
Purchase Excursion) and
SuperApex tickets are available
in limited numbers on some
inter-city routes. SuperApex
fares must be purchased 14
days in advance, and Apex at
least a week in advance. Savers
can be used at weekends and
on most weekday trains outside rush hours. Supersavers
cannot be used on Fridays, or
on any peak-hour service to,
from or through London.
First-class tickets cost about
one-third more than standard
fares, and returns are cheaper
than buying two singles.

RAIL PASSES

IF YOU PLAN to travel a lot by
train, it is a good idea to buy
a rail pass. These can be purchased from agents such as
Rail Europe, which operates
in Europe, the US and Canada.
There are different passes
available to suit every need.
The Freedom of Scotland pass
allows unlimited rail travel
around the country for a set

period. The Highland Rover
permits travel on the West
Highland lines and the Inver-
ness-to-Kyle line. The Festival
Cities Rover, available during
the Edinburgh International
Festival in August, is for use
between Glasgow's Queen
Street and Edinburgh's
Waverley station on
any three out of seven
consecutive days. The
passes are also valid
on some coach and
ferry services and on
the Glasgow Under-
ground (see p96).
    One-third price dis-
counts are available for
16- to 25-year-olds using
a Young Person's Rail
Card. The Senior Rail-
card and Disabled Railcard en-
title the holder to a one-third
discount on most fares. Those
aged 5 to 15 travel for less, and
there are also family tickets.

**A leaflet about
the steam train**

GENERAL TIPS

BRITAIN'S FASTEST and most
comfortable trains are those
on the inter-city routes. These
popular services book up
quickly. It is always advisable
to reserve your seat in advance,
especially if you want to travel
at peak times such as Friday
evenings and Sunday after-
noons. Inter-city trains
are fast, with a limited
number of stops. The
trip from Edinburgh to
Glasgow, for example,
takes around 50
minutes. A reduced
service is usually in
operation on Sundays
and public holidays.
Porters are often scarce
at British stations,
although trolleys are
usually available for
passengers to help themselves.
If you are disabled and need
assistance, contact the rele-
vant train company before
the day you travel.

RAIL MAP OF SCOTLAND

KEY

— Principal routes

— Other routes

● Rail junction

○ Train station

SCENIC TRAIN RIDES

WHEN MOTOR transportation made many rural railways redundant in the mid-20th century, picturesque sections of track, and many of the old steam engines, were rescued and restored to working order. Tourist offices or train ticket offices can provide you with information on where the lines are, and how much it will cost to take a ride on the trains.

Ride the Jacobite steam train from Fort William to Mallaig, passing over a spectacular viaduct at Glenfinnan; or take the Strathspey Steam Railway from Aviemore to Boat of Garten.

The Jacobite steam train on its picturesque journey to Mallaig

INTERNATIONAL COACH TRAVEL

ALTHOUGH TRAVELLING by coach (long-distance bus) is cheap compared with other methods of transport, it is not the most comfortable way of crossing Europe. If you have a lot of spare time, however, and want to stop off en-route at other destinations, it can be a convenient mode of transport. The ticket usually covers all parts of the journey, including the ferry or Channel Tunnel.

NATIONAL COACH NETWORK

THE LARGEST coach operators in Scotland are **Scottish Citylink**, **Stagecoach** and **National Express**, which runs services only between the main cities and to destinations in the rest of Great Britain. Buy a reserved ticket to guarantee a seat.

Discounts are available for full-time students or anyone under 25 with a coach pass. Over-50s and children aged between 5 and 15 years also qualify for reductions. Under-5s travel free on Scotland's nation-

al coaches. The Tourist Trail Pass is ideal for those planning to cover many destinations over a limited period. It allows unlimited travel on all National Express services in Scotland and the rest of Britain. You can buy the pass in the UK at major international airports, at Glasgow's Buchanan Bus Station and at Edinburgh's Tourist Information Centre. The Scottish Explorer Pass, available from Scottish Citylink agents and from Glasgow Airport, allows travel only within Scotland.

COACH AND BUS TOURS

DOZENS OF COACH tours are available in Scotland, catering for all interests, age groups and a host of different destinations. They may last anything from a couple of hours for a city tour to several days for a national tour.

OcttopusTravel.com offers scheduled sightseeing tours of Edinburgh, Glasgow and Inverness, or can arrange a tour to your own itinerary for Edinburgh and Glasgow. The Edinburgh-based **Scotline Tours** offers half- and full-day tours, while **Prestige Tours** and **Rabbie's Trail Burners** offer tours of three days or more.

Ask at your hotel or tourist office for details of local bus and coach tours. Most major towns and cities offer open-top bus tours.

Local buses are generally a cheap way to get about. In the more remote rural areas not served by public transport, **Royal Mail** operates the Post-bus. Fare-paying passengers travel in the postal delivery van – an interesting if rather slow way to travel around. Details of routes are available from the Royal Mail and via its website.

The Postbus provides transport in remote parts of the Highlands

Open-top bus tour on the Royal Mile in Edinburgh

DIRECTORY

UK AND OVERSEAS RAIL NUMBERS

Disabled Information
[(08457) 443366.

Lost Property
[(0141) 335 3276 (Glasgow).

National Rail Enquiries
[(08457) 484950.
W www.nationalrail.com

Rail Europe
[(0870) 8371371 (UK).
[(877) 257 2887 (US).
[(800) 361 7245 (Canada).
W www.raileurope.co.uk

First ScotRail Telesales
[(0845) 601 5929 (bookings).
W www.firstscotrail.com

COACH AND BUS INFORMATION

British Travel Associates
[(800) 327 6097 (US only).

OctopusTravel.com
[(800) 462 8678.
W www.octopustravel.com

National Express
[(08705) 808080.

Prestige Tours
[(0141) 886 1000.

Rabbie's Trail Burners
[(0131) 226 3133.

Royal Mail
[(0131) 228 7407.
W www.royalmail.com

Scotline Tours
[(0131) 557 0162.

Scottish Citylink
[(08705) 505050.
W www.citylink.co.uk

Travelling by Ferry

IF YOU ARE travelling to Scotland from continental Europe by foot, car, coach or train, you will need to cross the English Channel or North Sea by ferry or Channel Tunnel. Ferry services operate between several ports on the Continent and Scotland and England, while the Channel Tunnel provides a nonstop rail link from France and Belgium. Fares between ferries and the Channel Tunnel are fiercely competitive. Island-hopping by ferry is an enjoyable and economical way to visit the beautiful islands situated off the coast of Scotland.

Logo of a Scottish ferry company

A car ferry travelling from Oban to Lochboisdale on South Uist

TRAVELLING DIRECT TO SCOTLAND BY FERRY

SCOTLAND'S ONLY ferry link to Europe is provided by **Superfast Ferries**. This service links Rosyth on the opposite side of the Firth of Forth to Edinburgh, with Zeebrugge in Belgium. The overnight sailing takes about 17 hours 30 minutes. From Northern Ireland, there are two routes available. **Seacat** runs a frequent service between Belfast and Troon and **Stena Line** between Belfast and Stranraer. **P&O Irish Sea Ferries** offers daily crossings between Larne and Cairnryan, just north of Stranraer.

SERVICES TO ENGLAND FROM THE CONTINENT

A NETWORK OF ferry services regularly crosses the North Sea and the English Channel from northern Europe to ports in the UK. Of those travelling to the north of England, **P&O North Sea Ferries** runs a daily crossing from Rotterdam or Zeebrugge to Hull, and **DFDS Seaways** runs from Kristiansand, Gothenburg and Amsterdam to Newcastle.

An alternative way to travel to Scotland from the Continent via England is the Channel Tunnel, which links the UK with France.

Passengers travelling by coach or car board the **Eurotunnel** train, and remain in their vehicle throughout the 35-minute journey from Calais to Folkstone. For those travelling on foot, the **Eurostar** train runs frequent services between Paris, Brussels, and London.

Any visitors from outside the European Union should allow plenty of time for immigration control and customs clearance at British ports *(see pp198–9)*.

ISLAND-HOPPING IN SCOTLAND

SCOTLAND HAS just under 800 islands scattered off its coastline, and travelling by ferry is a wonderful way to experience their rugged beauty. The islands can be roughly divided into two main groups: the Hebrides, situated off the west coast, and Orkney and Shetland, lying to the northeast of the mainland.

Caledonian MacBrayne has 30 ships, linking 23 of the westerly isles to the mainland and to each other. Destinations include Arran, Islay, Mull, Barra, Lewis, Harris, Skye, Raasay, Coll, Tiree and Eigg. The summer timetable runs from Easter to mid-October with a reduced service for the rest of the year. Most of the routes have two or three trips a day, but some have only one, so be sure to call ahead and check. Single, return and five-day tickets are available.

In addition, there are two special travel tickets. Island Hopscotch tickets are valid on a choice of fifteen routes for one month from the date of the first journey. The Island Rover gives you the freedom to choose your own route between the islands for 8 or 15 consecutive days from the date of the first journey. Although the Island Rover ticket is valid on all of Caledonian's services, it does not ensure a place on any particular sailing, and it is advisable to make vehicle reservations.

Northlink Ferries, a venture between Caledonian MacBrayne and The Royal Bank of Scotland has ferry routes from the Scottish mainland to Orkney and Shetland. All routes have large capacity purpose built roll-on roll-off ferries with modern facilities including restaurants, cabins, shop and childrens' play area.

Passengers on the deck of a ferry leaving Tobermory on the Isle of Mull

**A Caledonian MacBrayne ferry
leaving the port of Mallaig**

NorthLink sails from Scrabster, north of Thurso, to Stromness on Orkney Mainland and direct from Aberdeen to Orkney or Shetland. Another service links Orkney and Shetland.

Pentland Ferries also offers a car service to Orkney. This runs between Gill's Bay west of John o' Groats and St Margaret's Hope on South Ronaldsay. This island is linked to Orkney Mainland via the Churchill Barrier causeways. The vehicle capacity of this older ferry is limited to 46 and booking in advance is recommended.

During the summer, **John o' Groats Ferries** runs a 40-minute passenger only crossing to Burwick on South Ronaldsay with a coach link to Kirkwall on Orkney Mainland. Small passenger and car ferries link Orkney's nine large outer islands with Orkney Mainland.

CRUISES

A CRUISE IS A leisurely way to see the many different Scottish islands. Caledonian MacBrayne offers various non-landing, evening cruises departing from a number of locations on the west coast.

John o' Groats Ferries offers day cruises to Orkney Mainland from John o' Groats and Inverness. These can be extended to include accommodation in Kirkwall and a tour of the island's historic sites by bus.

It is also possible to take a cruise on some of Scotland's lochs and rivers. **Caledonian Discovery** offers six-day cruises along the Caledonian Canal from Fort William to Inverness.

DIRECTORY

Caledonian Discovery
☏ (01397) 772167.
🅆 www.fingalcruising.co.uk

Caledonian MacBrayne
☏ (08705) 650000.
🅆 www.calmac.co.uk

DFDS Seaways
☏ (08705) 333111.
🅆 www.dfdsseaways.co.uk

Eurostar
☏ (08705) 186186.
🅆 www.eurostar.com

Eurotunnel
☏ (08705) 353535.
🅆 www.eurotunnel.com

John o' Groats Ferries
☏ (01955) 611353.
🅆 www.jogferry.co.uk

NorthLink Ferries
☏ (0845) 6000449.
🅆 www.northlinkferries.co.uk

P&O Irish Sea Ferries
☏ (0870) 2424777.
🅆 www.poirishsea.com

P&O North Sea Ferries
☏ (0870) 1296002.
🅆 www.poferries.com

Pentland Ferries
☏ (01856) 831226.
🅆 www.pentlandferries.co.uk

Seacat
☏ (0870) 5523523.
🅆 www.seacat.co.uk

Stena Line
☏ (0870) 4006798.
🅆 www.stenaline.co.uk

Superfast Ferries
☏ (0870) 4585120.
🅆 www.directferries.com

Cruising on Loch Ness with Caledonian Discovery's *Fingal of Caledonia*

CAR FERRY ROUTE	INFORMATION	DAYS	LAST CHECK-IN	JOURNEY TIME
Aberdeen–Kirkwall (Orkney)	(0845) 6000449	alternate days	30 mins	6 hrs, 30 mins
Aberdeen–Lerwick (Shetland)	(0845) 6000449	daily	30 mins	13 hrs
Ardrossan–Brodick (Arran)	(01294) 463470	daily	30 mins	55 mins
Gill's Bay–St Marg's Hope (Ork.)	(01856) 831226	daily	30 mins	1 hr
Kennacraig–Port Ellen (Islay)	(01880) 730253	daily	45 mins	2 hrs, 10 mins
Kilchoan–Tobermory (Mull)	(01688) 302017	Mon–Sun	30 mins	35 mins
Lerwick (Shet.)–Kirkwall (Ork.)	(0845) 6000449	alternate days	30 mins	5 hrs 30 mins
Mallaig–Armadale (Skye)	(01687) 462403	daily	30 mins	30 mins
Oban–Castlebay (Barra)	(01631) 566688	daily ex. Wed	45 mins	5 hrs, 15 mins
Oban–Craignure (Mull)	(01631) 566688	daily	30 mins	45 mins
Scrabster–Stromness (Orkney)	(0845) 6000449	daily	30 mins	1 hr, 30 mins
Uig (Skye)–Tarbert (Harris)	(01470) 542219	Mon–Sat	30 mins	1 hr, 35 mins
Ullapool–Stornoway (Lewis)	(01854) 612358	Mon–Sat	45 mins	2 hrs, 40 mins

Travelling by Car

IN SCOTLAND, AND THE REST of the UK, driving is on the left-hand side of the road, and distances are measured and signposted in miles. A network of toll-free motorways exists in the south and between Edinburgh and Glasgow; using these can reduce travelling time. In the larger towns traffic density can cause delays, and during public holiday weekends heading north to the Highlands is often slow work. Rural Scotland, with its striking scenery, is an enjoyable place to drive, and the roads to even the remote parts are generally good.

The A68 from Northern England to Scotland

WHAT YOU NEED

TO DRIVE IN Scotland you need a current driving licence, with an international driving permit if required. In any vehicle you drive, you must carry proof of ownership or a rental agreement, plus insurance documents.

A motorway sign

ROADS IN SCOTLAND

PEAK RUSH-HOUR traffic can last from 8–9:30am and 5–6:30pm on weekdays in the cities. Radio Scotland and local radio stations broadcast regular reports of road conditions throughout the day. You can also contact **AA Road Watch** for information on road conditions. You can save vital travel time by knowing which routes should be avoided.

Outside the cities, a good touring map is essential; the AA or RAC motoring atlases are straightforward to use. For exploration of more remote areas, the Ordnance Survey series is the best. Such areas often have only single-track roads with passing places and blind bends, that demand cautious driving.

On all road maps, motorways are indicated by an M followed by a number, such as the M8. Major roads, which are often dual (2-lane) carriageways, are labelled A roads. Secondary roads, often less congested than A roads, are called B roads. There are fewer roads in the Highlands.

Disabled drivers can contact the **AA Disability Helpline** for general motoring information.

ROAD SIGNS

SIGNS ARE NOW generally standardized in line with the rest of Europe. Directional signs are colour-coded: blue for motorways, green for major (A) roads and white for minor (B) roads. In the Highlands and islands, road signs display both English and Gaelic names. Brown signs with a blue thistle give visitor information on attractions and tourist centres. Warning signs are usually triangles in red and white, with easy to understand pictograms. Watch for electronic notices on motorways that warn of road works, accidents or dangerous driving conditions.

Level crossings at train tracks often have automatic barriers. If the lights are flashing red, it means a train is approaching; you are required to stop.

No stopping | Speed limit (mph)

No entry | No right-turn allowed

Railway level crossing | Yield to all vehicles

One-way traffic | Gradient of a road

RULES OF THE ROAD

SPEED LIMITS are 50–65 km/h (30–40 mph) in built-up areas and 110 km/h (70 mph) on motorways or dual carriageways – look out for speed signs on other roads. Wearing seatbelts is compulsory in Scotland and it is illegal to drive and use a hand-held mobile phone. Severe penalties are imposed for drinking and driving.

PARKING

IN SCOTLAND'S TOWNS and cities, on-street parking is often paid for by purchasing a ticket from a roadside machine. The ticket is then left on display inside the car. Some cities have "park and ride" schemes, where you take a bus from an out-of-city car park into the centre. Other towns have a "disc" parking scheme; ask the tourist office or a local newsagent for a disc to mark your arrival time. Many car parks operate on a pay-and-display system. Avoid double yellow lines at all times; you can park on single lines at evenings and weekends, but check roadside signs for variations to the rule. Traffic wardens will not hesitate to ticket, clamp or tow away your car if in breach of the rules. If in doubt, find a car park. Outside urban and popular visitor areas, parking is not such a problem. Look out for the letter P, which indicates legal parking spaces.

It is best to avoid driving in Edinburgh, as cars have limited access to the centre and the vast majority of sights can be reached on foot. Taxis, which you can hail on the street or find waiting at a taxi rank, are another option. Licensed cabs must display a "For Hire" sign. Mini-cabs must display a card proving the identity of the licensed driver. If there is no meter, ask the fare in advance.

The busy M8 motorway on the outskirts of Glasgow

One of Glasgow's black cabs

FUEL

Nᴏʀᴛʜ ᴀᴍᴇʀɪᴄᴀɴ visitors to Scotland may find petrol (gasoline) very expensive, particularly at motorway service stations. It is the large supermarkets that often have the lowest prices. Petrol is sold in four grades: diesel, 4-star (regular) super unleaded and premium unleaded. Most modern cars use unleaded petrol. Diesel and unleaded fuel are cheaper than 4-star. Most petrol stations are self-service but instructions at the pumps are easy to follow. Green hoses denote unleaded fuel pumps and deliveries are in litres.

BREAKDOWN SERVICES

Bʀɪᴛᴀɪɴ's ᴍᴀᴊᴏʀ motoring organizations, the **AA** (Automobile Association) and the **RAC** (Royal Automobile Club), provide a comprehensive 24-hour breakdown and recovery service. Both motoring organizations offer reciprocal assistance for

RAC logo

members of overseas motoring organizations – before arrival check with your own group to see if you are covered. You can contact the AA or RAC from roadside SOS phones on all motorways. Most car rental agencies have their own cover, which includes membership of either the AA or the RAC while you are driving. Even if you are not a member of an organization, you can still call out a rescue service, although it will be expensive.

Always take the advice given on the insurance policy or rental agreement. If you have an accident that injures you or damages a vehicle, contact the police straight away.

CAR RENTAL

Rᴇɴᴛɪɴɢ ᴀ ᴄᴀʀ can be costly, but one of the more competitive companies is **Hire for Lower**. Others include **Arnold Clark**, **Budget**, **Hertz Rent A Car**, **Europcar** and **National Car Rental**.

Many companies require a credit card number or a substantial cash deposit as well as your driving licence and passport. The normal age requirements are over 21 and under 70. Major airports, train stations and city centres have car rental outlets. Value for money car hire can also be found in some smaller towns.

DIRECTORY

BREAKDOWN SERVICES

AA
📞 *(0800) 887766.*
🖥 *www.theaa.com*

RAC
📞 *(0800) 828282.*
🖥 *www.rac.co.uk*

CAR RENTAL

Arnold Clark
📞 *(0800) 838245.*

Avis
📞 *(0870) 6060100.*
🖥 *www.avis.co.uk*

Budget
📞 *(0870) 1565656.*
🖥 *www.budgetdrive.com*

**Europcar/
British Car Rental**
📞 *(08457) 222525.*
🖥 *www.europcar.com*

Hertz Rent A Car
📞 *(0141) 248 7736 (Glasgow).*
🖥 *www.hertz.com*

Hire for Lower
📞 *(0870) 0667788.*
🖥 *www.autosabroad.com*

National Car Rental
📞 *(08705) 365365.*
🖥 *www.nationalcar.co.uk*
🖥 *www.nationalcar.com (in US).*

GENERAL INFORMATION

AA Road Watch
📞 *(09003) 401100.*

AA Disability Helpline
📞 *(0800) 262050.*

General Index

Page numbers in **bold** type refer to main entries.

A

AA 215
Abbey St Bathans, restaurants 178
Abbeys
 Dryburgh Abbey 81, 85
 Inchmahome Priory 117
 Jedburgh Abbey 84, 85
 Kelso Abbey 84, 85
 Melrose Abbey 81, 82, 85, **86**
 Tour of the Border Abbeys **85**
Abbotsford House 81, **86**
Aberdeen **142–3**
 airport 208
 ferries 213
 hotels 170
 map 143
 restaurants 181
Aberdeen Royal Infirmary 203
Aberdour, golf 189
Aberfoyle, restaurants 180
Achiltibuie 156
 hotels 170
 restaurants 181
Achray, Loch 13
Act of Union (1707) 45
Adam, John 57
Adam, Robert
 Culzean Castle 50, 92, 93
 New Town (Edinburgh) 64
 portrait 92
 West Register House (Edinburgh) 65
Adam, William
 Floors Castle 84
 Hopetoun House 70
 Inveraray Castle 130
 Tolbooth (Sanquhar) 88
Admission charges 200
Ainslie Place (Edinburgh)
 Street-by-Street map 64
Air Canada 209
Air France 209
Air travel **208–9**
Albany, Robert, Duke of 122
Albert, Prince Consort 144
Alcohol 201
 Scotch whisky **30–31**
Alexander II, King 43
Alexander III, King 43, 114
Ambulances 203
American Airlines 209
American Express 204
An Comunn Gaidhealach 185
Animals **16–17**
Anstruther, restaurants 180
Antiques shops **73**
Antonine Wall 41, **125**
Aquariums
 Mallaig Marine World 137
 Oban Seal and Marine Centre 132
Arbroath 123
 golf 189
Arbroath, Declaration of (1320) 43
Archaos (Glasgow) 109
Arches (Glasgow) 109
Archiestown, restaurants 181
Architecture, The Scottish Castle **18–19**
Ard, Loch 120
Ardnamurchan Peninsula **136**
Ardrossan, ferries 213
Arduaine, hotels 170
Arduaine Garden 132
Argyll, Dukes of 120, 130
Arisaig, hotels 170
Armadale, ferries 213
Armadale Castle Gardens and Museum
 of the Isles 153
Arnold Clark 215
Arran **114**
 ferries 213
 hotels 169
 restaurants 180
Art
 Glasgow Artists **101**
 shops **73**, **107**
 see also Museums and galleries

Art Exposure (Glasgow) 107
Art Gallery (Aberdeen) **142**
Art Gallery and Museum (Perth) 122
Arthur, King 120
Arthur's Seat **67**
Assembly (Edinburgh) 77
Assembly Rooms (Edinburgh) 77
Assynt Mountains 156
Atholl, Dukes of 139
Auchencairn, hotels 167
Auchindrain Museum **130**
Auchmithie, restaurants 182
Auchterarder
 golf 189
 hotels 169
Austin Reed (Edinburgh) 73
Austin Reed (Glasgow) 107
Australian High Commission 201
Auto Shuttle Express 215
Aviemore 140
 restaurants 182
Avis 215
Awe, Loch **132**
Ayr Gold Cup 38

B

Ba' Game 39
Bagpipes 28
 National Museum of Piping (Glasgow) 100
 Piping Centre (Glasgow) **100**
 World Pipe Band Championships 37
 World Piping Championships 38
Baird, John Logie 23
Balfour Castle 158
Balhousie Castle 122
Ballater
 hotels 170
 restaurants 182
 Royal Deeside tour 144
Ballindalloch, hotels 170
Balloch 115
 restaurants 180
Balmoral 46
 Royal Deeside tour 144
Balnakeil Craft Village 157
Balquhidder, hotels 169
Banchory, Royal Deeside tour 145
Bank notes 205
Banks 204
Banks, Iain 25, 46
Bannockburn, Battle of (1314) 43, 63, 120, 124
Bannockburn Heritage Centre (Stirling) 120
Barbour, John 24
Bargo (Glasgow) 109
Barclays Scottish Open 37
Barra **161**
 ferries 213
 hotels 171
Barrowlands (Glasgow) 109
Bars
 Edinburgh 77
 Glasgow 109
The Battle of Culloden (Campbell) 146
Bed-and-breakfast 165
Bedlam (Edinburgh) 77
Beinn Eighe National Nature Reserve 151
Beinn Tarsuinn 114
Bell, Alexander Graham 23, 46
Beltane 36
Ben Lomond 115
Ben Nevis **135**, 148
Ben Nevis Hill Race 38
Benbecula **160–61**
Bennet's (Edinburgh) 77
Benson, Gordon 62
Birds 16–17
Black Isle **150**
Blackadder, Elizabeth 98
The Blacksmith (Meunier) 105
Blair Castle 19, **139**
Blairgowrie, hotels 169
Blind Harry 24
bmi (British Midland) 209
Boats
 ferries **212–13**
 sailing **195**
 Traditional Boats Festival 37
Bongo Club (Edinburgh) 77
Book of Kells 42

Books
 Edinburgh Book Festival **79**
 shops **73**, **107**
Borders Books (Glasgow) 107
Boswell, James 24
Botanic Garden, Edinburgh *see* Royal
 Botanic Garden
Botanic Gardens (Glasgow) 20, **103**
Bow Bar (Edinburgh) 77
Braemar Castle 18
Braemar Gathering 12, 38
Brahan Seer 150
Breakdown services 215
Breakfast 174
Bridges, Forth **69**
Bridie, James 25
Britannia (Royal Yacht) 68
British Airways 209
British Airways CitiExpress 209
British Association for Shooting and
 Conservation (Scotland) 195
British Golf Museum (St Andrews) 123
Brodick
 ferries 213
 restaurants 180
Brodick Castle 114
Brown, George Douglas 25
Bruce, George 25
Bruce, Sir George 125
Bruce, Robert *see* Robert the Bruce
Bruide, King 42
Bryden, Bill 25
Buchan, John 25
Budget (car rental) 215
Bullough family 137
Bunessan, hotels 172
Bureaux de change 204
Burgundy, Duke of 60
Burnett family 145
Burns, Robert 24, 46, 47
 Burns Cottage (Alloway) 89
 Burns Heritage Trail **89**
 Burns House (Dumfries) 89
 Burns House and Museum (Mauchline) 89
 Ellisland Farm 89
 portrait of 63
 Robert Burns Centre (Dumfries) 89
 Tam O'Shanter Experience (Alloway) 89
 Writer's Museum (Edinburgh) 57
Burns Night 39
Burrell, Sir William 104
Burrell Collection (Glasgow) 51, **104–5**
Busta, hotels 173
Bute **115**
Bute, 3rd Marquess of 115, 124
Bute House (Edinburgh) 65
Byrne, John 25

C

CTC National Cyclists Organisation 195
Cadenheads (Edinburgh) 73
Caerlaverock Castle **90**
Café-bars, Edinburgh **77**
Café Royal (Edinburgh) 77
Cairngorm Reindeer Centre 141, 185
Cairngorms 51, **140–41**
 skiing 193
Caledonian Brewery 185
Caledonian Canal 137, 147, 148, 149
Caledonian Discovery 213
Caledonian MacBrayne 213
Callander 117, 198
 hotels 169
Callanish 41
Calton Hill (Edinburgh) **66**
Camera Obscura (Edinburgh) 56
Cameron, Richard 88
Campbell, D, The Battle of Culloden 146
Campbell, Lady Grace 130
Campbell, John Lorne 137
Campbell, Robert 134
Campbell clan 130
Camping 165
Canadian Consulate 201
Canna **136–7**
Canongate Tolbooth: The People's Story
 (Edinburgh) **58–9**
Cape Wrath **157**
Caravanning 165

Carloway Broch 160
Carlyle, Thomas 25
Carnegie, Andrew 124–5
Carnegie Birthplace Museum 125
Carnoustie, golf 189
Cars **214–15**
  insurance 198
  Moray Motor Museum (Elgin) 145
  rental 215
  see also Tours by car
Cassilis, Earls of 92
Castle Rock (Edinburgh) 53
Castlebay, ferries 213
Castles (general)
  accommodation in 164
  The Evolution of the Scottish Castle **18–19**
Castles (individual)
  Armadale Castle 153
  Balfour Castle 158
  Balhousie Castle 122
  Blair Castle 19, **139**
  Braemar Castle 18
  Brodick Castle 114
  Caerlaverock Castle **90**
  Cawdor Castle **146**
  Claypotts Castle 18
  Crathes Castle and Garden 145
  Culzean Castle 50, **92–3**
  Dirleton Castle 71
  Doune Castle **122**
  Drum Castle 19, 145
  Drumlanrig Castle 19, **88–9**
  Duart Castle 133
  Duffus Castle 18
  Dunollie Castle (Oban) 132
  Dunrobin Castle 19, 150
  Dunstaffnage Castle 132
  Dunvegan Castle 152
  Edinburgh Castle 11, 53, **60–61**
  Eilean Donan Castle 127, 151
  Floors Castle 84, 85
  Glamis Castle **122–3**
  Inveraray Castle **130**
  Inverness Castle 147
  Jedburgh Castle 84
  Kames Castle 115
  Kilchurn Castle 132
  Kinloch Castle 137
  Kisimul Castle (Barra) 161
  MacLellan's Castle (Kirkcudbright) 90
  Neidpath Castle 18
  Rothesay Castle 115
  St Andrews Castle 123
  Stirling Castle **120**
  Tantallon Castle 71
  Threave Castle **89**
  Torosay Castle 133
  Tower-houses 18–19
  Traquair House 19
  see also Stately homes
Cathedrals
  Dunkeld 139
  Elgin 145
  Glasgow Cathedral and Necropolis 99
  St Andrews 123
  St Andrew's Cathedral (Aberdeen) 142
  St Giles Cathedral (Edinburgh) 57
  St Machar's Cathedral (Aberdeen) 142
  St Magnus Cathedral 158
Catholic Church 44
Cawdor Castle **146**
Celtic (Glasgow) 109
Celtic Church 42
Celtic Connections 39
Celts 41, 127
Central Scotland **111–25**
  hotels 169–70
  map 112–13
  restaurants 180–81
Charles I, King of England 62, 90, 122
Charles II, King of England 57, 66
Charlie, Bonnie Prince 45, 127, **153**
  Battle of Falkirk 111
  Benbecula 160
  Blair Castle 139
  Culloden 146
  Drumlanrig Castle 89
  Eriskay 161
  Glenfinnan Monument 137
  Isle of Skye 152
  Loch Lochy 148

Charlie, Bonnie Prince (cont.)
  Mercat Cross (Edinburgh) 58
  Palace of Holyroodhouse 67
  Prince's Cairn 136
  Scottish National Portrait Gallery
    (Edinburgh) 63
  Traquair House 87
Charlotte Square (Edinburgh) 65
Children 200
  Museum of Childhood (Edinburgh) **58**, 59
  in restaurants 175
Christ of St John of the Cross (Dalí) 99
Christianity 42, 90
Churches see Cathedrals and individual
  towns and cities
Cinema see Film
Citizens' Theatre (Glasgow) 109
City Café (Edinburgh) 77
City Observatory (Edinburgh) 66
Clans **26–7**, 127
Clava Cairns 146
Claypotts Castle 18
Clearances 46, **150**, 152
Climate **36–9**, 198
Clothes
  shops 72, 73, **106**
  walking 190
Clubs
  Edinburgh **77**
  Glasgow **109**
Clunie Foot Bridge, Killiecrankie Walk 138
Clyde, River 88, 95
  Firth of Clyde **114**
Coach travel **211**
Coaching inns 164–5
Cockburn, Lord 64
Cockburns of Leith 73
Coins 205
Colbost, restaurants 183
Coll **133**
Collective Gallery (Edinburgh) 73
Colonsay, hotels 171
Columba, St 42, 63, 127, 133, 149
Comunn An Luchd Ionnsachaidh 185
Comunn na Gàidhlig 185
Connoisseurs Scotland 185
Consulates 201
Continental Airlines 209
Conversion chart 201
Cooper, Samuel, James II 147
"Corbetts", mountaineering 193
Corniche (Edinburgh) 73
Coronation Bridge, Killiecrankie Walk 138
Corpach, Road to the Isles Tour 137
Cottier's Theatre (Glasgow) 109
Country-house hotels 164
Covenanters
  Greyfriars Kirk (Edinburgh) 62
  Martyrs' Monument 91
  Sanquhar 88
Craig, James 64
Craignure, ferries 213
Craigston, golf 189
Cranston, Kate 100
Crarae Gardens 20, **130**
Crathes Castle and Gardens 21
  Royal Deeside tour 145
Credit cards 204
Crime 202–3
Crinan
  hotels 171
  restaurants 182
Crockett, SR 25
Crofting **161**
Cromarty 150
  hotels 171
Crossflight 207
Cruden Bay, golf 189
Cruise (Edinburgh) 73
Cruise (Glasgow) 107
Cuillins 152
Cul de Sac (Glasgow) 109
Culloden 146
Culloden, Battle of (1746) 45, 46, **146**
Culross **125**
Culzean Castle 50, **92–3**
Cumberland, Duke of 143, 146
Cumberland (Edinburgh) 77
Cupar, restaurants 180
Currency see Bank notes and Coins
Customs and immigration 198–9
Cycling **194**, 195

D

Dale, David 88
Dalí, Salvador, Christ of St John of the Cross 99
Dance
  Edinburgh **76**, 77
  Glasgow **108–9**
  Highland dancing 29
Darien Expedition 45
Darnley, Lord 67, 98, 123
David I, King 9, 42, 43
  Border abbeys 85
  Edinburgh Castle 61
  Holyrood Abbey 53
  Holyrood Park (Edinburgh) 67
  Kelso Abbey 85
  Melrose Abbey 86
Dawyck Botanic Garden 21
Dean Bridge (Edinburgh)
  Street-by-Street map 64
Dean Village **69**
Debenhams (Glasgow) 107
Dee, River 89, 90
Deeside, Royal Deeside tour 144–5
Defoe, Daniel 124
Dentists 202, 203
Department stores
  Edinburgh **72**, 73
  Glasgow **106**, 107
Designworks (Glasgow) 107
Dewar, Sir James 23
DFDS 213
Dirleton Castle 71
Disabled travellers 199
  Disability Helpline 203
  train information 211
Discovery 123
Distilleries see Whisky
Doctors 202
Dominion (Edinburgh) 77
Dornoch **150–51**
  golf 189
  hotels 171
Douglas, Gavin 24
Douglas, Sir James ("Black Douglas") 86, 89
Douglas family 60, 88
Doune Castle 122
Dounreay 157
Doyle, Arthur Conan 25
Drum Castle 19
  Royal Deeside tour 145
Drumlanrig Castle 18, 19, **88–9**
Drummond, George 64
Drummond, James, The Return of Mary,
  Queen of Scots 40
Drummond Castle Gardens 21
Dryburgh, hotels 167
Dryburgh Abbey 81
  Tour of the Border Abbeys 85
Drymen, restaurants 180
Duart Castle 133
Duffus Castle 18
Duich, Loch 127
Dulnain Bridge, hotels 171
Dumbarton 114
Dunbar, William 24
Duncan, King 146
Duncansby Head 157
Dundee 113, **123**
  restaurants 181
Dunfermline **124–5**
  golf 189
Dunkeld **139**
  hotels 171
Dunnet Head 157
Dunollie Castle (Oban) 132
Dunoon 114
Dunrobin Castle 19, 150
Dunstaffnage Castle 132
Dunvegan, hotels 173
Dunvegan Castle 152

E

Eas Coul Aulin 157
East Lothian Coast **70–71**
East Neuk **124**
Easyeverything 206
easyJet 209
Edinburgh 51, **53–79**
  airport 208

Edinburgh (cont.)
 entertainment **76–9**
 golf 189
 hotels 166–7
 map 54–5
 New Town 47, 53
 New Town: Street-by-Street map 64–5
 Old Town 53, 54, 59
 restaurants 176–8
 Royal Mile 53, **56–9**
 shopping **72–5**
Edinburgh Book Festival **79**
Edinburgh Castle 11, 53, **60–61**
Edinburgh Central Cycle Hire 195
Edinburgh Dental Hospital 203
Edinburgh Festival 13, 37, 53, **78–9**
Edinburgh Festival Theatre 77
Edinburgh Jazz & Blues Festival **79**
Edinburgh Military Tattoo 37, **79**
Edinburgh Playhouse 77
Edinburgh Royal Infirmary 203
Edinburgh's Hogmanay 39
Edward I, King of England 43, 90
Edwin, King 60
Eigg **136–7**
Eildon Hills **84**
Eilean Donan Castle 127, 151
Electricity 201
Elgin **145**
Elizabeth, Queen Mother 123
Elizabeth I, Queen of England 44
Elizabeth II, Queen of England 57, 66
Ellisland Farm 89
Email 207
Embassies 201
Emergencies 206
Enlightenment 22, 24, 47
Entertainment
 Edinburgh **76–9**
 Glasgow **108–9**
Episcopalian Church 44
Eriskay **161**
Escada (Edinburgh) 73
Eurocheques 204
Europcar/British Car Rental 215
Eurostar 213
Exchange (Edinburgh) **62**

F
Faed, Thomas, *The Last of the Clan* 150
Fair Isle 159
Fairlie, restaurants 181
Falkirk, Battle of (1746) 111
Falkirk Wheel 112, **125**
Falkland Palace **124**
Farrell, Terry 62
Farrer, Reginald 130
Fashion shops **106**
Fast food 175
Fergus 99
Ferguson, Adam 24
Ferguson, Robert 24
Ferrier, Susan 25
Ferries **212–13**
Festivals **36–9**
Fillan, St 124
Film
 Edinburgh **76**, 77
 Edinburgh International Film Festival **78–9**
 Glasgow **108**, 109
Filmhouse (Edinburgh) 77
Fingal's Cave 133
Finlaggan 131
FirstScotRail Telesales 211
Firth of Clyde **114**
Fishing **194**, 195
 Scottish Fisheries Museum 124
Five Sisters of Kintail 151
Fleming, Alexander 23, 47
Flodden, Battle of (1513) 44, 81
Floors Castle 84
Food and drink **32–3**
 Scotch whisky **30–31**
 shops **72–3**, **106–7**
 tours **184–5**
 vocabulary 224
 What to Buy **75**
 see also Restaurants
Forest Enterprise 195
Forestry Commission 191

Forests 17
Forsyth, Alan 62
Fort Augustus 149
Fort George **146**
Fort William **134**
Forth Bridges **69**
Fortrose 150
Foula 159
Fowke, Captain Francis 62
Fratelli Sarti (Glasgow) 107

G
Gaelic language 13, 224
Gaelic music 28
Gaelic studies **184**, 185
Galleries *see* Museums and galleries
Gallery of Modern Art (Glasgow) **98**
Galloway Forest Park **90–91**
Galt, John 25
Game Conservancy Scottish Fair 37
Gardens *see* Parks and gardens
Garioch, Robert 25
Geddes, Jenny 57
Genealogy **184**, 185
General Register Office for Scotland 185
Geology **14–15**
George II, King of England 45
George IV, King of England 63, 86, 138
George Square (Glasgow) **98**
Georgian House (Edinburgh)
 Street-by-Street map 65
Gibbon, Lewis Grassic 25
Gill's Bay (ferries) 158
Girvan, restaurants 181
Gladstone's Land (Edinburgh) **56**
Glamis, hotels 169
Glamis Castle **122–3**
Glasgow **95–109**
 airport 208
 Burrell Collection **104–5**
 entertainment **108–9**
 Glasgow Artists **101**
 golf 189
 history 46
 hotels 168–9
 map 96–7
 restaurants 178–80
 shopping **106–7**
Glasgow Art Fair 36, 107
Glasgow Boys 90, 98, **101**, 102
Glasgow Cathedral and Necropolis **99**
Glasgow Film Centre 109
Glasgow International Jazz Festival 37
Glasgow Print Studio 107
Glasgow Royal Concert Hall 109
Glasgow Royal Infirmary 203
Glasgow School of Art **100**
Glasgow Science Centre **102**
Glass & Thompson (Edinburgh) 73
Gledstanes, Thomas 56
Glen Nevis 135
Glen Shiel **151**
Glen Tanar Equestrian Centre 195
Glencoe 134
Glencoe Massacre (1692) 45, **134**
Glenfiddich Distillery 185
Glenfinnan Monument, Road to the Isles
 Tour 137
Glenmore Lodge 193
Glenshee, skiing 193
Glorious Twelfth 37
Goatfell ridge 111, 114
Golf 37, **188–9**
 The Birthplace of Golf **123**
 St Andrews 123
Graham, James Gillespie 64
Graham Tiso (Edinburgh) 73
Graham Tiso (Glasgow) 107
Gray, Alasdair 25
Great Cumbrae Island 114
Great Glen **148–9**
Greenock 114
Greyfriars Kirk (Edinburgh) **62**
Grass Roots (Glasgow) 107
Griffin (Glasgow) 109
Guesthouses 165
Gunn, Neil 25
Guthrie, Sir James 101

H
Haddington **70**

Hadrian's Wall 41, 125
Haggis 32
Haig, Field Marshal Earl 59
Hairth O'Knokrach Festival 38
Halt (Glasgow) 109
Hamilton, James, *The Massacre of Glencoe*
 102, **134**
Hamilton, Thomas 66
Hampden National Stadium (Glasgow) 109
Handa Island **157**, 186
Hardie, James Keir 47
Harris **160**
 ferries 213
 hotels 171
 restaurants 182
Harvey Nichols (Edinburgh) 72
Hawick Common Riding 37
Hawkcraig Point, hotels 169
Health care **202**
Heart of Midlothian 77
Hebrides *see* Highlands and Islands
Hector Russell (Edinburgh) 73
Hector Russell (Glasgow) 107
Henry, George, *Japanese Lady with a Fan* 102
Henry VIII, King of England 85, 86, 117
Henry's Jazz Joint (Edinburgh) 76
Henryson, Robert 24
Heritage House (Glasgow) 107
Hermanes National Nature Reserve 159
Hertz Rent A Car 215
Hibernian 77
Highland Boundary Fault 15, 111
Highland Feast 38
Highlands and Islands 111, **127–61**
 Aberdeen 142–3
 Cairngorms **140–41**
 Clearances 46, **150**, 152
 ferries **212–13**
 Great Glen **148–9**
 Highland music and games **28–9**
 hotels 170–73
 Isle of Skye **152–3**
 map 128–9
 Orkney Islands 158
 restaurants 181–3
 Road to the Isles tour 136–7
 Royal Deeside tour 144–5
 Shetland Islands 159
 Western Isles **160–61**
Hillphones 193
Hire for Lower 215
History **41–7**
Hogg, James 24–5
Hogmanay 39
Holidays, public 38
Holyrood Abbey 53
Holyrood Park (Edinburgh) **67**
Hopetoun House **70**
Hopkins, Sir Michael 67
Hornel, Edward 90
Horse riding **194**, 195
Horseshoe (Glasgow) 109
Hospitals **202**, 203
Hotels **164–73**
 bed-and-breakfasts and guesthouses 165
 Central Scotland 169–70
 coaching inns and shooting lodges 164–5
 country-house hotels and castles 164
 Edinburgh 166–7
 Glasgow 168–9
 Highlands and Islands 170–73
 Southern Scotland 167–8
 youth hostels 165
House for an Art Lover (Glasgow) **103**
House of Fraser (Edinburgh) 73
House of Fraser (Glasgow) 107
Hoy 158
Hume, David 24, 47, 66
Hunter, Dr William 102
Hunterian Art Gallery (Glasgow) **102–3**
Hunting **194**, 195

I
Iain Mellis (Edinburgh) 73
Iain Mellis (Glasgow) 107
Inchmahome Priory 117
Indigo Yard (Edinburgh) 77
Inhouse (Edinburgh) 73
Inhouse (Glasgow) 107
Insect bites 202
Insurance 198, 202
Intellectuals **24–5**

International Children's Festival 36
International Currency Exchange 204
International Directory Enquiries 206
International Newsagents (Edinburgh) 73
International Science Festival 36
International Youth Hostel Federation 201
Inventions **22–3**
Inveraray, restaurants 181
Inveraray Castle **130**
Inverawe Smokehouse 185
Inverewe Garden 20, **156**
Inverkip 114
Inverkirkaig, restaurants 182
Inverness **146–7**
  hotels 171
  restaurants 182
Inverness Music Festival 39
Inverness Raigmore 203
Iona 42, 133
  hotels 171
Islands *see* Highlands and Islands
Islay **131**
  ferries 213
Isle Ornsay, hotels 171

J
Jacobite movement 45, **147**
  Glenfinnan Monument 137
Jacobite Steam Train 134
James I, King 24, 44
James II, King 60, 89, 123
James II (Cooper) 147
James III, King 44
James IV, King 44, 53
  Battle of Flodden 81
  Falkland Palace 124
  Holyrood Palace 66
  Mons Meg 60
James V, King
  crown 60
  Falkland Palace 124
  Holyrood Palace 66, 67
  Linlithgow Palace 70
  Parliament House (Edinburgh) 57
James VI, King
  Act of Union 44, 45
  coronation 120
  Edinburgh Castle 61
  Falkland Palace 124
  statue of 122
James VII, King 45, 147
James VIII, the "Old Pretender" 147
James Thin (Edinburgh) 73
Jane Davidson (Edinburgh) 73
Japanese Lady with a Fan (Henry) 102
Jarlshof Prehistoric and Norse Settlement 159
Jazz
  Edinburgh **76**, 77
  Edinburgh Jazz & Blues Festival **79**
  Glasgow **108**, 109
Jedburgh **84**
  hotels 167
  restaurants 178
Jedburgh Abbey 84, 85
Jeffrey, Francis 24
Jenkins, Valentine 121
Jenners (Edinburgh) 73
John Knox's House (Edinburgh) **58**, 59
John Lewis (Edinburgh) 73
John Lewis (Glasgow) 107
John O'Groats 157
John O'Groats Ferries 213
Jura **130–31**
Justerini & Brooks (Edinburgh) 73

K
Kailzie Gardens 87
Kames Castle 115
Karen Millen (Glasgow) 107
Katrine, Loch 112, 116
Kay, Jackie 25
Kelman, James 25
Kelso **84**
  hotels 167
  restaurants 178
Kelso Abbey,
  Tour of the Border Abbeys 85
Kelvingrove Art Gallery and Museum
  (Glasgow) **102**

Kemp, George Meikle 63
Kennacraig, ferries 213
Kennedy, AL 25
Kennedy, William, *Stirling Station* 101
Kenneth MacAlpin, King 42
Kentallen of Appin, hotels 171
Kibble, John 103
Kilchoan, ferries 213
Kilchurn Castle 132
Kildrummy, hotels 172
Killiecrankie Pass
Killiecrankie Walk **138**
Kilmartin House 132
Kilmore, hotels 172
Kilt Rock 156
Kincardine on Forth, restaurants 181
Kinclaven, restaurants 181
Kincraig Highland Wildlife Park 140
King's (Glasgow) 109
King's College (Aberdeen) **142**
King's Theatre (Edinburgh) 77
Kinloch Anderson (Edinburgh) 73
Kinloch Castle 137
Kinross, golf 189
Kintyre **131**
Kippford, restaurants 178
Kirkcaldy, golf 189
Kirkcudbright **90**
  hotels 167
Kirkton of Glenisla, restaurants 182
Kirkwall 158
Kisimul Castle (Barra) 161
Knox, John 44, 45
  John Knox's House (Edinburgh) **58**
  Perth 122
  St Giles Cathedral (Edinburgh) 57
  statue of 99
Kyle of Lochalsh, restaurants 182
Kylesku, hotels 172

L
Laggan Bridge, restaurants 182
Lamlash, golf 189
Landscape **16–17**
Language 13, 224
Largs 114
  golf 189
  hotels 169
The Last of the Clan (Faed) 150
Lavery, Sir John, *A Star* 101
Ledaig, hotels 172
Leger, Fernand, *The Team at Rest* 69
Leith **68**
Lennoxlove House 70
Leonard, Tom 25
Lerwick 159
  ferries 213
Leuchars Air Show 38
Lewis **160**
  ferries 213
  hotels 172
Lindsay, Sir David 24
Lindsay, James Bowman 22
Linlithgow Palace **70**
Linn of Tummel, Killiecrankie Walk 138
Liquid Room (Edinburgh) 77
Lister, Joseph 23, 65
Literature **24–5**
  Edinburgh Book Festival **79**
Livingstone, David **88**
Loch Garten Nature Reserve 141
Loch Lomond and the Trossachs
  National Park 116
Loch Ness Monster **149**
Lochhead, Liz 25
Lochinver, restaurants 182
Lochmaddy 160
Lochy, Loch 148
Logan Botanic Garden 20, 91
Loganair 209
Lollius Urbicus 125
Lomond, Loch 50, **115**, 116
Lomond Shores 115
Long-distance walks 191
Lords of the Isles 43
Lost property 203, 211
Lowlands 111
Luib 153
Luss 115, 116
Luther, Martin 44

M
MacBean, Donald 138
Macbeth 146
MacCaig, Norman 25
MacColla, Fionn 25
MacCrimmon clan 100
MacDiarmid, Hugh 25, 47
Macdonald, Anne Maxwell 104
MacDonald, Flora 132, 153, 160
  grave of 152
Macdonald, Margaret 103
MacDonald clan 45, 134
MacDougal clan 132
MacGregor, Robert *see* Rob Roy
McGregor, Robert (artist) 101
Machrie 114
MacIlvanney, William 25
Mackenzie, Osgood 156
Mackintosh, Charles Rennie 95, **101**
  Glasgow School of Art **100**
  House for an Art Lover (Glasgow) **103**
  Hunterian Art Gallery 102
  Willow Tea Room (Glasgow) **100**
  A World in Miniature (Kilninver) 132
Maclean, Sorley 25
Maclean clan 133
McLean Museum and Art Gallery
  (Greenock) 114
McLellan Galleries (Glasgow) 102
MacLellan's Castle (Kirkcudbright) 90
MacLeod clan 100, 152
McManus Galleries (Dundee) 123
Macmillan, Kirkpatrick 22
Macpherson, James 24
MacSweens (Edinburgh) 73
McTaggart, William 103
Maes Howe 158
Magnus Barfud, King 131
Maid of the Forth Cruises 185
Mail services **207**
Malcolm III, King 42, 69, 124
Mallaig **137**
  ferries 213
  Road to the Isles Tour 136
Maps
  Aberdeen 143
  Ben Nevis 135
  Cairngorms 140–41
  Central Scotland 112–13
  East Lothian Coastal Walk 71
  Edinburgh 54–5
  Edinburgh: Further afield 68
  Edinburgh: New Town 64–5
  Europe 8
  Galloway Forest Park Walk 91
  Glasgow 96–7
  Great Glen 148–9
  Highlands and Islands 128–9
  Isle of Skye 152–3
  Killiecrankie Walk 138
  Orkney and Shetland Islands 9
  outdoor activities 186–7
  Rail Map of Scotland 210
  Road to the Isles Tour 136–7
  Royal Deeside tour 144–5
  Royal Mile (Edinburgh) 56–9
  Scotch whisky 30
  Scotland 8–9, 50–51
  Southern Scotland 82–3
  Tour of the Border Abbeys 85
  Touring Scotland by car 34–5
  Trossachs 116–17
Mar, 1st Earl of 120
Margaret, St, Queen 42
  Dunfermline 124
  Edinburgh Castle 61
  South Queensferry 69
Maritime Museum (Aberdeen) **142**
Markets, Glasgow **106**
Markinch, hotels 169
Marnoch, hotels 172
Mary, Queen of Scots 40, 44
  Abbotsford House 86
  Edinburgh Castle 61
  and golf 123
  Holyrood Palace 67
  Inchmahome Priory 117
  Jedburgh 84
  Kirkcudbright 90

Mary, Queen of Scots (cont.)
Linlithgow Palace 70
Provand's Lordship (Glasgow) 98
"Rough Wooing" 86
Scone Palace 122
Scottish National Portrait Gallery (Edinburgh) 63
Stirling 120
Traquair House **87**
Mary of Guise 66, 70
The Massacre of Glencoe (Hamilton) 102, **134**
Maxwell, James C 23
Maxwell, Sir John 104
Maxwell family 90, 104
May, Isle of 124
Meadowbank Stadium and Sports Centre 77
Medical insurance 198, 202
Medical treatment 202
Melrose, restaurants 178
Melrose Abbey 81, 82, **86**
Tour of the Border Abbeys 85
Memorial Arch, Killiecrankie Walk 138
Mercat Walking Tours 59
Meunier, Constantin, *The Blacksmith* 105
Midges 202
Mileage chart 9
Miller, Hugh 150
Millport, golf 189
Moffat, hotels 167
Money **204–5**
Mons Meg **60**, 89
Montrose, Duke of 117
Moorlands 17
Morar, Road to the Isles Tour 136
Moray Place (Edinburgh)
Street-by-Street map 64
Morgan, Edwin 25
Morris, Old Tom 22
Motte and bailey castles 18
Mount Stuart House 115
Mountain biking **194**, 195
Mountaineering Council of Scotland 191, 193
Mountains 17
outdoor activities **192–3**
Mousa Broch 159
Mr Ben (Glasgow) 107
Muck **136–7**
Muir, Edwin 25
Muir, Willa 25
Muir of Dinnet Nature Reserve, Royal Deeside tour 144
Muir of Ord, hotels 172
Mull **133**, 199
ferries 213
hotels 172
restaurants 183
Mungo, St 99, 125
"Munros", mountaineering 192–3
Murray, Patrick 58
Murrayfield Stadium 77
Museums and galleries (general)
admission charges 200
opening hours 200
Museums and galleries (individual)
Abbotsford House **86**
Annie McLeod Experience 88
Ardnamurchan Natural History Centre 136
Ardnamurchan Point Visitor Centre 136
Art Gallery (Aberdeen) **142**
Art Gallery and Museum (Perth) 122
Auchindrain Museum **130**
Balhousie Castle 122
Balnain House (Inverness) 147
Bannockburn Heritage Centre (Stirling) 120
Black House Museum (Arnol) 160
British Golf Museum (St Andrews) 123
Burns House (Dumfries) 89
Burns House and Museum (Mauchline) 89
Burrell Collection (Glasgow) 51, **104–5**
Canongate Tolbooth: The People's Story (Edinburgh) **58–9**
Carnegie Birthplace Museum 125
City Observatory (Edinburgh) 66
Combined Operations Museum (Inveraray) 130
Discovery (Dundee) 123
Dean Gallery (Edinburgh) **69**
Elgin Museum 145
Ellisland Farm 89
Gallery of Modern Art (Glasgow) **98**
Gladstone's Land (Edinburgh) **56**

Museums and galleries (cont.)
Glamis Castle **122–3**
Groam House Museum (Rosemarkie) 150
Hugh Miller Museum (Cromarty) 150
Hunterian Art Gallery (Glasgow) **102–3**
Inverness Museum and Art Gallery 147
Jedburgh Castle 84
Kelvingrove Art Gallery and Museum (Glasgow) **102**
Kilmartin House 132
McLean Museum and Art Gallery (Greenock) 114
McManus Galleries (Dundee) 123
Maritime Museum (Aberdeen) **142**
Mingarry Museum 136
Moray Motor Museum (Elgin) 145
Museum of Childhood (Edinburgh) **58**, 59
Museum of Edinburgh **59**
Museum of Islay Life (Port Charlotte) 131
Museum of Scotland (Edinburgh) **62–3**
Museum of Transport (Glasgow) **102**
National Gallery of Scotland (Edinburgh) **63**
National Museum of Piping (Glasgow) **100**
New Lanark **88**
Our Dynamic Earth (Edinburgh) **67**
People's Palace (Glasgow) **103**
Pollok House (Glasgow) **104**
Provand's Lordship (Glasgow) 98
Regimental Museum (Fort George) 146
Robert Burns Centre (Dumfries) 89
Royal Museum (Edinburgh) **62**
St Mungo Museum of Religious Life and Art (Glasgow) **99**
Sandaig Thatched House Museum (Tiree) 133
Scottish Exhibition Centre (Glasgow) **102**
Scottish Fisheries Museum 124
Scottish Museum of Ornamental Plasterwork 87
Scottish National Gallery of Modern Art 69
Scottish National Portrait Gallery (Edinburgh) **63**
Shetland Museum (Lerwick) 159
Skerryvore Lighthouse Museum (Tiree) 133
Strathnaver Museum (Bettyhill) 157
Tain Through Time 151
Tam O'Shanter Experience (Alloway) 89
Tenement House (Glasgow) **100**
Tolbooth Art Centre (Kirkcudbright) 90
Torridon Countryside Centre 151
Tweeddale Museum (Peebles) 87
Ullapool Museum 156
Unicorn, HMS (Dundee) 123
Whithorn: Cradle of Christianity 90
Writers' Museum (Edinburgh) **57**
Music
Celtic Connections 39
Edinburgh **76**, 77
Edinburgh Jazz & Blues Festival **79**
Glasgow **108**, 109
Glasgow International Jazz Festival 37
Highland music and games **28–9**
Inverness Music Festival 39
National Museum of Piping (Glasgow) **100**
Piping Centre (Glasgow) 100
Shetland Folk Festival 36
World Pipe Band Championships 37
World Piping Championships 38

N
Nairn
golf 189
hotels 172
Napier, John 22
Napoleon I, Emperor 93
Nasmyth, Alexander, *View of Culzean Castle* 92
National Car Rentals 215
National Express 211
National Gallery of Scotland (Edinburgh) **63**
National Museum of Piping (Glasgow) 100
National Trust for Scotland 191, **200**, 201
Canna 137
Culross 125
Georgian House (Edinburgh) 65
Inverewe Gardens 156
St Kilda 161
National Union of Students 201
Nature reserves *see* Wildlife
Neidpath Castle 18
Nelson Monument (Edinburgh) 66
Neptune's Staircase, Road to the Isles Tour 137
Ness, Loch 149

Neville's Cross, Battle of (1346) 8
Nevis Range, skiing 193
Nevis Range Gondola 135
New Lanark **88**
New Scottish Parliament (Edinburgh) **67**
New Zealand High Commission 201
Newmachar, golf 189
Newspapers 73, 201
Ninian, St 41, 90, 99
North Coast **157**
Noss 159

O
Oban **132**
ferries 213
OctopusTravel.com 211
Odeon Multiplex (Edinburgh) 77
Odeon at the Quay (Glasgow) 109
Old Fruitmarket (Glasgow) 109
Oliphant, Margaret 25
Onich, hotels 173
OMNI (Edinburgh) 77
Open Doors Day 38
Opening hours 200
Opera
Edinburgh **76**, 77
Glasgow **108**, 109
Orkney Islands **158**
ferries 213
hotels 173
map 9
restaurants 183
Orwell, George 130
Ottakar's 73, 107
Our Dynamic Earth (Edinburgh) **67**
Outdoor activities **184–95**
Outlook Tower (Edinburgh) **56**
Owen, Robert 88

P
P&O North Sea Ferries 213
Paisley patterns, textiles 89
Palace Keeper **124**
Palaces *see* Stately homes
Parking **214–15**
Parks and gardens **20–21**
Arduaine Garden 132
Botanic Gardens (Glasgow) 20, **103**
Crarae Gardens 20, **130**
Crathes Gardens 21, 145
Dawyck Botanic Garden 21
Drummond Castle Gardens 21
Holyrood Park (Edinburgh) **67**
Hydroponicum (Achiltibuie) 156
Inverewe Gardens 20, **156**
Kailzie Gardens 87
Logan Botanic Garden 20, 91
Pitmedden Garden 21
Royal Botanic Garden (Edinburgh) 21, **68**
Zen Garden (Glasgow) 99
Parliament 47
New Scottish Parliament (Edinburgh) **67**
Parliament House (Edinburgh) **57**
Passports 198
Peebles **87**
hotels 167
restaurants 178
Pentland Hills 83, **87**
Pentland Hills Icelandics 195
People's Palace (Glasgow) **103**
Personal security **202–3**
Perth **122**
restaurants 181
Perth Royal Infirmary 203
Peter Green (Edinburgh) 73
Petrol 215
Pharmacists 202
Phase Eight (Edinburgh) 73
Picts 41
Pied à Terre (Glasgow) 107
Piping Centre (Glasgow) **100**
Pitlochry **139**
restaurants 183
Pitmedden Garden 21
Plant badges, clans 27
Playfair, William 64, 66, 84
Po-Na-Na (Edinburgh) 77
Police 202, **203**
Pollok House (Glasgow) **104**
Pony trekking **194**, 195

Port Appin
  hotels 173
  restaurants 183
Port Edgar Marina 195
Port Ellen, ferries 213
Portpatrick
  hotels 168
  restaurants 178
Portree 153
  hotels 173
Postal services **207**
Poste restante 207
Presbyterian Church 44
Prestige Tours 211
Prestwick Airport 208
Prince's Cairn, Road to the Isles Tour 136
Princes Square (Glasgow) 107
Princes Street Gardens (Edinburgh)
  Street-by-Street map 65
Printmakers Workshop (Edinburgh) 73
Provand's Lordship (Glasgow) **98**
Provost Skene's House (Aberdeen) **143**
Public holidays 38
Pubs 175
Puppet and Annimation Festival 36

Q
Queen Elizabeth Forest Park 117
Queen's Gallery (Edinburgh) 67
Queen's Hall (Edinburgh) 77
Quiraing 153

R
Rabbie's Trail Burners 211
RAC 215
Racing, horse 36
Radio 201
Raeburn, Henry 130, 142
  Rev Robert Walker Skating on Duddington Loch 63
Ragamuffin (Edinburgh) 73
Rail Europe 211
Railways *see* Trains
Rainfall 38
Ramblers' Association Scotland 191
Ramsay, Allan 24, 63, 130
Rangers (Glasgow) 109
Rankin, Ian 25
Rare Breeds Park 132
Reformation 44, 57
Regional tourist boards 199
Reid, Robert 64
Reid Concert Hall (Edinburgh) 77
Rembrandt, *Self-portrait* 105
Renting cars 215
Restaurants **174–83**
  afternoon tea 174
  breakfast, lunch and dinner 174–5
  Central Scotland 180–81
  children in 175
  Edinburgh 176–8
  fast food 175
  Glasgow 178–80
  Highlands and Islands 181–3
  prices and booking 174
  pubs and wine bars 175
  seafood 175
  Southern Scotland 178
  vegetarian food 175
  see also Food and drink
The Return of Mary, Queen of Scots (Drummond) 40
Rev Robert Walker Skating on Duddington Loch (Raeburn) 63
Rhinns of Galloway **91**
Rhododendrons 20
Riding **194**, 195
Rights of way 190
Ring of Brodgar 158
Rivers 16
Rizzio, David 67
Road to the Isles Tour **136–7**
Road travel **214–15**
Rob Roy 86, 117
  The Trossachs 116
  Falkland Palace 124
Robert Adam (Willison) 92
Robert Burns Centre (Dumfries) 89
Robert the Bruce 81
  Arran 114
  Battle of Bannockburn 43, 120, 124
  Bruce's Stone 91

Robert the Bruce (cont.)
  Drum Castle 145
  heart 85, 89
  Loch Awe 132
  Melrose Abbey 85, 86
  Rathlin 131
  statue of 120
Robertson, William 24
Robin's Ghost and History Tour 59
Rock music
  Edinburgh **76**, 77
  Glasgow **108**, 109
Rocks **14–15**
Romans 41
  Antonine Wall **125**
Roots & Fruits (Glasgow) 107
Rossal 157
Rosslyn Chapel 87
Rothesay Castle 115
Rothiemurchus Estate 140
Rousay 158
Roxburgh, Graham 103
Royal Botanic Garden (Edinburgh) 21, **68**
Royal Deeside 51
  tour by car 144–5
Royal Highland Show 37
Royal Lyceum (Edinburgh) 77
Royal Mile (Edinburgh) 53, **56–9**
Royal Museum (Edinburgh) **62**
Royal National Mod 38
Royal Scottish Academy of Music and Drama (Glasgow) 109
Royal Yacht Britannia 68
RSAC Scottish Rally 37
Rugby 36
Rum **136–7**
Ryanair 209

S
Sabhal Mor Ostaig 185
Safety, mountain activities **192**, 193
Sailing **195**
St Abb's Head **84**
St Andrews **123**
  golf 189
  hotels 169
  restaurants 181
St Andrew's Cathedral (Aberdeen) **142**
St Andrew's Night 38
St Bride's (Edinburgh) 77
St Cecilia's Hall (Edinburgh) 77
St Fillan's Cave 124
St Giles Cathedral (Edinburgh) **57**, 77
St Kilda **161**
St Machar's Cathedral (Aberdeen) **142**
St Magnus Festival 37
St Mungo Museum of Religious Life and Art (Glasgow) **99**
St Nicholas (Aberdeen) **142**
Salisbury Crags (Edinburgh) 67
Salmon & Trout Association 195
Sandaig Thatched House Museum (Tiree) 133
Sanday 158
Sanquhar **88**
Seafood 175
Schuh (Edinburgh) 73
Schuh (Glasgow) 107
Scone
  golf 189
  hotels 169
Scone Palace 122
Scotch Malt Whisky Society 185
Scotline Tours 211
Scott, Sir Walter 24, 25, 47, **86**, 127
  Abbotsford House 81, **86**
  Castle Street 65
  Eildon Hills 84
  grave 85
  Loch Katrine 116
  Mons Meg 60
  Perth 122
  Scott Monument (Edinburgh) **63**
  statues of 63, 98
  tomb of 46
  Writers' Museum (Edinburgh) 57
Scottish Anglers National Association 195
Scottish Arts Council 13
Scottish Borders 85
  Tour of the Border Abbeys **85**
Scottish Citylink 211
Scottish Claymores 77

Scottish Cup Final 36
Scottish Cycling Holidays 195
Scottish Cyclists Union 195
Scottish Federation for Coarse Angling 195
Scottish Federation of Sea Anglers 195
Scottish Fisheries Museum 124
Scottish Gallery (Edinburgh) 73
Scottish Gallery of Modern Art 69
Scottish Genealogy Society 185
Scottish Grand National 36
Scottish Kiltmakers Visitor Centre 147
Scottish Labour Party 47
Scottish Museum of Ornamental Plasterwork 87
Scottish National Party (SNP) 12, 47
Scottish National Portrait Gallery (Edinburgh) **63**
Scottish National Watersports Centre 195
Scottish Natural Heritage 137, 191
Scottish Record Office 185
Scottish Rights of Way Society 191
Scottish Rugby Union Cup Final 36
Scottish Seabird Centre 71
Scottish Water Ski Centre 195
Scottish Youth Hostels Association 165, 201
Scott's View 84
  Tour of the Border Abbeys 85
Scrabster, ferries 213
Sea Life Cruises 185
Seabirds of the Orkney and Shetland Islands 158–9
Seabury, Samuel 142
Seacat 213
Seaforth, Countess of 150
Seil, Isle of 132
Self-catering accommodation 165
Selkirk, Alexander 124
Shakespeare, William 146
Shepherd, Nan 25
Shetland Folk Festival 36
Shetland Islands **159**
  ferries 213
  hotels 173
  map 9
  restaurants 183
Shieldaig, hotels 173
Shooting lodges 164–5
Shopping
  Edinburgh **72–5**
  Glasgow **106–7**
  opening hours 200
  What to Buy **74–5**
Sinclair, William 87
Skara Brae 41, 158
Skeabost 152
  golf 189
Skene, Sir George 143
Skerryvore Lighthouse Museum (Tiree) 133
Sketch for Annabel Lee (Whistler) 103
Skiing **193**
Skye, Isle of 11, 50, 128, **152–3**
  ferries 213
  hotels 173
  restaurants 183
Sleat, restaurants 183
Smith, Adam 24, 47
Smith, Sidney Goodsir 25
Smoking 201
Smollett, Tobias 24
Smoo Cave 157
Soldier's Leap, Killiecrankie Walk 138
Soutar, William 25
South Uist 161
Southern Scotland **81–93**
  Border Abbeys tour 85
  hotels 167–8
  map 82–3
  restaurants 178
Souvenirs **74–5**
Spark, Muriel 25
Spean Bridge 148
Speed limits 214
Speyside whiskies 30
  Speyside Malt Whisky Trail **144–5**
Sports
  Edinburgh 77
  Glasgow **109**.
  golf **188–9**
  Highland Games 29
  mountaineering **192–3**
  outdoor activities **194–5**
Staffa Island 15

Staffin, hotels 173
Stair, Elizabeth, Dowager Countess of 57
Standing Stones of Callanish 160
Standing Stones of Stenness 158
A Star (Lavery) 101
Starry Starry Night (Glasgow) 107
Stately homes
  Abbotsford House **86**
  Balmoral 144
  Culross Palace 125
  Falkland Palace **124**
  Hopetoun House **70**
  Lennoxlove House 70
  Linlithgow Palace **70**
  Mount Stuart House 115
  Palace of Holyroodhouse **66–7**
  Scone Palace 122
  Traquair House **87**
  see also Castles
Statues
  Alexander Selkirk 124
  Charles I 122
  James VI 122
  John Knox 99
  Robert the Bruce 120
  Sir Walter Scott 63, 98
Steall Waterfall 148
Stena Line 213
Stevenson, Robert Louis 24, 25
  Writer's Museum (Edinburgh) 57
Stewarton, hotels 169
Stirling **120**
  restaurants 181
Stirling Castle **120**
Stirling Castle in the Time of the Stuarts
  (Vorsterman) 120
Stirling Station (Kennedy) 101
Stone of Destiny 43, 47, 60, 122
Stonehaven
  golf 189
  restaurants 183
Stornoway 160
  ferries 213
Strachur, hotels 170
Strathnaver Museum (Bettyhill) 157
Strathpeffer **150**
Strathspey Steam Railway 140
Stromness, ferries 213
Stuart, Prince Charles Edward *see* Charlie,
  Bonnie Prince
Stuart dynasty 44–5, 63
Student travellers **200**, 201
Summer Isles 156
Superfast Ferries 213
Sunshine 37
Sutherland, Duke of 46
Sutherland, Earls of 150

T
T in the Park 37
Tacitus 41
Tain 150–51
Talisker distillery 152
Tam O'Shanter Experience (Alloway) 89
Tanaka, Yasutaro 99
Tantallon Castle 71
Tarbert (Harris), ferries 213
Tarbet (Strathclyde) 115
Tarbet (Sutherland), restaurants 183
Tartans 26–7
Tea 174
The Team at Rest (Leger) 69
Telephones **206**
Television 201
Telford, Thomas 47
  Caledonian Canal 147, 148, 149
  Dean Bridge (Edinburgh) 64, 69
  Neptune's Staircase 137
Temperatures 39
Tenement House (Glasgow) **100**
Textiles **89**
Theatre
  Edinburgh **76**, 77
  Edinburgh Festival **78**
  Glasgow **108–9**
Theatre Royal (Glasgow) 109
Theatre Workshop (Edinburgh) 77
Thomas Cook 204
Thomas Pink (Edinburgh) 73
Thomson, RW 22
Threave Castle **89**

Thurso 157
  hotels 173
  restaurants 183
Time zone 201
Tiree **133**
Tobermory 133, 199
  ferries 213
  hotels 172
Tolbooth (Sanquhar) 88
Tolbooth Art Centre (Kirkcudbright) 90
Tongue, restaurants 183
Torosay Castle 133
Torridon Countryside Centre 151
Torrylinn 114
Tourist information 199
Tours by car 34–5
  Border Abbeys **85**
  Road to the Isles **136–7**
  Royal Deeside 144–5
Toward, Agnes 100
Tower-houses 18–19
Traditional Boats Festival 37
Trains **210–11**
  Auto Shuttle Express 215
  Jacobite Steam Train 134
  Strathspey Steam Railway 140
Tramway (Glasgow) 109
Traquair Fair 37
Traquair House 19, **87**
Travel **208–15**
  air **208–9**
  cars **214–15**
  Central Scotland 112
  coaches **211**
  Edinburgh 55
  ferries **212–13**
  Glasgow 96
  Highlands and Islands 128
  Museum of Transport (Glasgow) **102**
  Southern Scotland 83
  trains **210–11**
Traveller's cheques 205
Treaty of Union (1707) 12
Trekking and Riding Society of Scotland
  (TRSS) 195
Treshnish Isles 133
Tron (Glasgow) 109
Tron Ceilidh House (Edinburgh) 77
Tron Kirk (Edinburgh) 58
Troon
  golf 189
  hotels 170
Trossach Trundler 211
Trossachs 50, **116–17**
Turnberry, hotels 170
Tweed, River 81
Tweeddale Museum (Peebles) 87
Tweedsmuir, restaurants 178

U
Ubiquitous Chip Wine Shop (Glasgow) 107
UCI (Edinburgh) 77
UGI (Edinburgh) 77
UGC (Glasgow) 109
Uig, ferries 213
Uists 160–61
Ullapool **156**
  ferries 213
  hotels 173
  restaurants 183
Unicorn, HMS 123
United States Consulate 201
Unst Heritage Centre and Boat Haven 159
Up Helly Aa 12, 39, 159

V
Value added tax (VAT) 200
  in hotels 164
  in restaurants 174
Valvona & Crolla (Edinburgh) 73
Van Dyck, Sir Anthony, *Princess Elizabeth
  and Princess Anne* 63
Vegetarian food 175
Victoria, Queen of England 46, 98
  Balmoral 127, 144
  Blair Castle 139
  Pitlochry 139
View of Culzean Castle (Nasmyth) 92
Vikings 42, 114
VisitScotland 191, 199
Vocabulary 224

Vorsterman, Johannes, *Stirling Castle in the
  Time of the Stuarts* 120

W
Wade, General 45, 138
Walkerburn, hotels 168
Walking **190–91**
  Climbing Ben Nevis **135**
  East Lothian Coastal Walk 71
  Galloway Forest Park Walk **91**
  Killiecrankie Walk 139
Wallace, William 43
  Wallace Monument (Abbey Craig) 121
Walls, hotels 173
Walton, Edward Arthur, *The Wayfarer* 101
Wars of Independence 81
Water of Leith (Edinburgh) 69
  Street-by-Street map 64
Waterfalls
  Eas Coul Aulin 157
  Steall Waterfall 148
Watersports **195**
Waterstone's (Edinburgh) 73
Waterstone's (Glasgow) 107
Watson-Watt, Robert 23
Watt, James 22, 46, 114
The Wayfarer (Walton) 101
Weather 36–9, 198
Weather forecasts 193
Welsh, Irvine 25
West Highland Way 186
West Register House (Edinburgh)
  Street-by-Street map 65
Wester Ross **151**
Western Isles **160–61**
  hotels 171
  restaurants 182
Western Union 204
Wheelchair access
  see Disabled travellers
Whisky **30–31**
  Blair Atholl Distillery 139
  Islay 131
  Mingarry Museum 136
  Speyside Malt Whisky Trail **144–5**
  Talisker distillery 152
Whisky Shop (Glasgow) 107
Whistler, James McNeill
  Sketch for Annabel Lee 103
White Corries, skiing 193
Whitebridge, hotels 173
Whithorn **90**
Wildlife **16–17**
  Ardnamurchan Natural History Centre 136
  Beinn Eighe National Nature Reserve 151
  Cairngorm Reindeer Centre 141
  Handa Island 157
  Hermaness National Nature Reserve 159
  Islay 131
  Kincraig Highland Wildlife Park 140
  Loch Garten Nature Reserve 141
  Muir of Dinnet Nature Reserve 144
  Rare Breeds Park 132
  St Abb's Head 84
  Seabirds of the Orkney and Shetland
    Islands 158–9
  viewing wildlife **185**
William III, King of England 134, 147
Willison, George, *Robert Adam* 92
Willow Tea Room (Glasgow) **100**
Wigtown Book Fair 36
Wine bars 175
Wine Basket (Edinburgh) 73
Winter in Scotland 39
Wishart, George 44
Women travellers 203
Woodlands 17
World Pipe Band Championships 37
Writers **24–5**
Writer's Museum (Edinburgh) **57**

Y
York, Duke of 60
Youth hostels 165

Acknowledgments

DORLING KINDERSLEY would like to thank the following people whose contributions and assistance have made the preparation of this book possible.

DESIGN AND EDITORIAL ASSISTANCE
Hilary Bird, Claire Folkard, Alrica Green, Kathleen Greig, Carolyn Hewitson, Jessica Hughes, Donnie Hutton, Marie Ingledew, Elly King, Kathryn Lane, Sue Megginson, Clare Pierotti, Tom Prentice, the Scottish Tourist Board (especially Vineet Lal), Pamela Shiels and Stewart Wild.

ADDITIONAL PHOTOGRAPHY
Joe Cornish, Andy Crawford, Philip Dowell, Chris Dyer, Andreas Einsiedel, Peter Gathercole, Steve Gorton, Paul Harris, Dave King, Cyril Laubscher, Brian D. Morgan, Ian O'Leary, Stephen Oliver, Tim Ridley, Kim Sayer, Karl Shore, Clive Streeter, Mathew Ward, Stephen Whitehorne.

PHOTOGRAPHIC AND ARTWORK REFERENCE
Aerographica: Patricia & Angus Macdonald; London Aerial Photo Library.

PHOTOGRAPHY PERMISSIONS
City of Edinburgh Council Heritage and Arts Marketing/People's Story Museum; Royal Botanic Garden, Edinburgh; House for an Art Lover, Glasgow; Glasgow School of Art; Glasgow Botanic Gardens.

PICTURE CREDITS
t = top; tl = top left; tlc = top left centre; tc = top centre; trc = top right centre; tr = top right; cla = centre left above; ca = centre above; cra = centre right above; cl = centre left; c = centre; cr = centre right; clb = centre left below; cb = centre below; crb = centre right below; bl = bottom left; b = bottom; bc = bottom centre; bcl = bottom centre left; br = bottom right; d = detail

The publisher would like to thank the following individuals, companies and picture libraries for their kind permission to reproduce their photographs:
ABERDEEN TOURIST BOARD: 51cra; ABERDEEN UNIVERSITY LIBRARY: George Washington Wilson Collection 161t; ACTION PLUS: 12t; AEROGRAPHICA: Patricia & Angus Macdonald 14t/b, 15tl, 16cra; ALLSPORT: Craig Prentis 36b; T & R ANNAN & SON (D): 101br. BANK OF SCOTLAND 204cb; BRIDGEMAN ART LIBRARY, London/New York: 25t, 146b, 147b (d); City of Edinburgh Museums & Galleries 26bl; Fine Art Society, London 101 clb; Robert Fleming Holdings Limited, London 43c; National Gallery of Scotland, Edinburgh 40; National Museet Copenhagen 42c; Collection of Andrew McIntosh Patrick, UK 101cla; Smith Art Gallery and Museum, Stirling 120b; South African National Gallery, Cape Town 101cra; Trinity College Library, Dublin 42t; BRITISH AIRWAYS: 208t; BT PAYPHONES: 206bl, 206tl. LAURIE CAMPBELL: 16clb/bl, 127b, 157t/c; BRUCE COLEMAN: 158br, 159bl/bcr/br; Peter Evans 140tl; Gordon Langsbury 141t; Hans Reinhard 116tl; Dr. Frieder Sauer 152t; COLLECTIONS: Michael St. Maur Sheil 159cr; DOUG CORRANCE: 10, 21br, 27b, 28c, 28bc, 29br, 32bl. 38t, 52, 90t, 108cl/b, 110, 133b, 139t, 144b, 146t, 147t, 186c, 187ca/cb/b, 190br, 192cl, 194tr/b, 198c, 212b; ERIC CRICHTON PHOTOS: 21cl/cr; CROWN COPYRIGHT: Historic Scotland 60 tr/c, 61bl, 121c; Ordnance Survey/Photo, Scotland in Focus 192tl.EDINBURGH FESTIVAL FRINGE SOCIETY: Andy Manzie, Royal Blind School, Edinburgh 36t; EMPICS: 109r; ET ARCHIVE: Bibliothèque Nationale, Paris 6–7; MARY EVANS PICTURE LIBRARY: 7 (inset), 24t/c/b, 44c, 45cr, 86bl, 88c, 123b, 153br, 163 (inset), 197 (inset). FALKIRK WHEEL: 125b; LOUIS FLOOD: 26br. GARDEN PICTURE LIBRARY: John Glover 20tr; GLASGOW MUSEUMS: Art Gallery

& Museum, Kelvingrove 102t, 134b, 150b; Burrell Collection 104–105 except 104tl; Saint Mungo Museum of Religious Life and Art 99b; Museum of Transport 22br, 23bl, 102c; RONALD GRANT ARCHIVE: 25c; V. K. GUY LTD: Mike Guy 16cla, 34cl, 133t, 3 (inset); Paul Guy 2–3; Vic Guy 118–119. ROBERT HARDING PICTURE LIBRARY: 130t, 193b; Van der Hars 142t; Michael Jenner 160c; Julia K. Thorne 18bl; Adina Tovy 18br; Andy Williams 126; Adam Woolfitt 140tr; DENNIS HARDLEY: 34cr, 35t/cb, 80, 82, 84c/b, 90b, 91t, 113, 114t/b, 115b, 136b, 137b, 156b, 161b, 199b; GORDON HENDERSON: 17cra, 34t, 35ca/b, 148c, 157b, 158t/cl, 159t, 160b, 213t; HOUSE OF LORDS RECORD OFFICE: Reproduced by permission of the Clerk of the Records 45t; HULTON GETTY COLLECTION: 23cra, 46t, 92tl, 117br, 149c; (c) HUNTERIAN ART GALLERY, UNIVERSITY OF GLASGOW: 103tl; Mackintosh Collection 94, 101crb; HUTCHISON LIBRARY: Bernard Gerard 13t. ANDREW LAWSON: 20bl, 21tl/tr, 156t. MUSEUM OF CHILDHOOD, Edinburgh: 58b. NATIONAL GALLERIES OF SCOTLAND: Scottish National Gallery of Modern Art *Study For Les Constructeurs: The Team At Rest* by Fernand Leger 1950 (c) ADAGP, Paris and DACS, London, 1999 69t; NATURAL HISTORY PHOTOGRAPHIC AGENCY: Bryan & Cherry Alexander 37tr; Laurie Campbell 11t, 17bla, 36c; Manfred Danegger 17br/bra; Scottish National Portrait Gallery 63t; NATIONAL MUSEUMS OF SCOTLAND: 62b; NATIONAL PHOTOGRAPHIC LIBRARY, London: 64b; NATIONAL TRUST FOR SCOTLAND: 50b, 56b, 92tr, 93tl/tr/br, 124b, 125c, 200cr; Lindsey Robertson 93bl; Glyn Satterley 100br; NATURE PHOTOGRAPHERS: William Paton 158bl; Paul Sterry 159bcl; NATWEST: 204br; NETWORK PHOTOGRAPHERS: Laurie Sparham 12b. ORTAK JEWELLERY, Edinburgh: 74ca, 106t. PA NEWS: 29t/bl; Chris Bacon 39c; Roslin Institute 23br; (c) 1996 POLYGRAM FILMED ENTERTAINMENT: 25b; THE POST OFFICE: 207tl, 207cla, 207clb; Glyn Satterley 211b; POWERSTOCK/ZEFA: 18c. REX FEATURES: J. Sutton Hibbert 47c; ROYAL AUTOMOBILE CLUB (RAC): 215b; ROYAL BANK OF SCOTLAND: 204bca; ROYAL BOTANIC GARDEN, Edinburgh: 21bl; ROYAL COLLECTION (c) 1999, HER MAJESTY QUEEN ELIZABETH II: 27tc; ROYAL PHOTOGRAPHIC SOCIETY: 23tl. SCIENCE PHOTO LIBRARY: M-SAT Ltd 8; SCIENCE & SOCIETY PICTURE LIBRARY: Science Museum 23crb; ALASTAIR SCOTT: 15b, 17cla, 29cb, 191b, 195l; SCOTTISH HIGHLAND PHOTO LIBRARY: 17tc, 135t; PHIL SHELDON GOLF PICTURE LIBRARY: 188tr; James Shuttleworth: 211c; STILL MOVING PICTURE COMPANY: Gordon Allison 28br; Marcus Brooke 15tr; Wade Cooper 47t; Doug Corrance 28t, 81b, 130b, 185cl, 190cl, 194c; Peter Davenport 16br; Distant Images 89t; Derek Lairs 41c; Robert Lees 39b, 186t, 191t; Paisley Museum 89b; Ken Paterson 65t; David Robertson 20cl, 149b; Glyn Satterley 187t; Colin Scott 29cl; Scottish Tourist Board 28bl, 140br, 141c, 184c, 185t; Paul Tomkins/STB 160t, 184b, 186b; Stephen J. Whitehorne 117t; Harvey Wood 139b. STRATHCLYDE PASSENGER TRANSPORT (SPT): Richard McPherson 96bl. TRON THEATRE: Keith Hunter 108cr. CHARLIE WAITE: 131t; DAVID WARD: 134t; STEPHEN J. WHITEHORNE: 1, 17tl, 29cra, 34b, 37c, 62tl, 63c, 66b, 83, 111b, 115t, 132t, 148b, 161c, 175c, 184t, 192b, 193t, 195r, 205t, 207cl, 213c. Front Endpaper: DOUG CORRANCE: cl, br; ROBERT HARDING PICTURE LIBRARY: Andy Williams tl; DENNIS HARDLEY: bl; HUNTERIAN ART GALLERY, UNIVERSITY OF GLASGOW: Mackintosh Collection tr.

JACKET Front - BRITSTOCK-IFA, Abraham main image; DOUG CORRANCE bl; DK PICTURE LIBRARY, Paul Harris crb; TRUSTEES OF THE NATIONAL MUSEUMS OF SCOTLAND clb. Back - DOUG CORRANCE t; GETTY IMAGES, Dave Jacobs b. Spine - BRITSTOCK-IFA, Abraham. All other images © Dorling Kindersley. For further information see www.dk.com

SPECIAL EDITIONS OF DK TRAVEL GUIDES

DK Travel Guides can be purchased in bulk quantities at discounted prices for use in promotions or as premiums. We are also able to offer special editions and personalized jackets, corporate imprints, and excerpts from all of our books, tailored specifically to meet your own needs.

To find out more, please contact:
(in the United States) **SpecialSales@dk.com**
(in the UK) **Sarah.Burgess@dk.com**
(in Canada) DK Special Sales at **general@tourmaline.ca**
(in Australia) **business.development@pearson.com.au**

Scottish Vocabulary

GAELIC IS A CELTIC LANGUAGE that is still spoken as a second language in the Highlands and Western Isles of Scotland. Estimates put the figure of Gaelic speakers throughout the country at around 80,000. The last decade has seen something of a revival of the language, due to the encouragement of both education and broadcasting authorities. However the majority of people are most likely to come across Gaelic today in the form of place names. Words such as glen, loch, eilean and kyle are all still very much in use. English remains the principal language of Scotland. However the country's very distinct education, religious,

political and judicial systems have given rise to a rich vocabulary that reflects Scottish culture. Many additional terms in current usage are colloquial. English as spoken by the Scots is commonly divided into four dialects. Central Scots can be heard across the Central Belt and the southwest of the country. As around a quarter of the population lives within 32 km (20 miles) of Glasgow, West Central Scots is one of the most frequently heard subdivisions of this dialect. Southern Scots is spoken in the east of Dumfries and Galloway and the Borders; Northern Scots in the northeast; and Island Scots in the Orkney and Shetland Islands.

PRONUNCIATION OF GAELIC WORDS

Letters	Example	Pronunciation
ao	craobh	this is pronounced similar to oo, as in cool
bh	dubh	"h" is silent unless at the beginning of a word in which case it is pronounced v, as in vet
ch	deich	this is pronounced as in the German composer Bach
cn	cnoc	this is pronounced cr, as in creek
ea	leabhar	this is pronounced e, as in get or a, as in cat
eu	sgeul	this is pronounced ay, as in say or ea, as in ear
gh	taigh-òsda	this is silent unless at the beginning of a word, in which case it is pronounced as in get
ia	fiadh	this is pronounced ea, as in ear
io	tiocaid	this is pronounced ee, as in deep or oo, as in took
rt	ceart	this is pronounced sht
th	theab	this is silent unless at the beginning of a word in which case it is pronounced h, as in house
ua	uaine	this is pronounced oo, as in poor

WORDS IN PLACE NAMES

ben	mountain
bothy	farm cottage
brae	hill
brig	bridge
burn	brook
cairn	mound of stones marking a place
close	block of flats (apartments) sharing a common entry and stairway
craig	steep peak
croft	small plot of farmland with dwellings in the Highlands
dubh	black
eilean	island
firth	estuary
gate/gait	street (in proper names)
glen	valley
howff	a regular meeting place, usually a pub
kirk	a Presbyterian church
kyle	a narrow strait of river
links	golf course by the sea
loaning	field
loch	lake
moss	moor
Munro	mountain over 914 m (3,000 ft) high
strath	valley/plain beside river
wynd	lane
yett	gate

FOOD AND DRINK

Arbroath smokie	small haddock that has been salted and then smoked
breid	bread
clapshot	mashed turnips and potatoes
clootie dumpling	rich fruit pudding
Cullen skink	fish soup made from smoked haddock
dram	a drink of whisky
haggis	sheep's offal, suet, oatmeal and seasonings, usually boiled in the animal's intestine
Irn-Bru	popular soft drink
neeps	turnips
oatcake	a savoury oatmeal biscuit
porridge	a hot breakfast dish made with oats, milk and water
shortie	shortbread
tattie	potato
tattie scone	type of savoury pancake made with potato

CULTURAL TERMS

Burns Night	25 January is the anniversary of the birth of the poet Robert Burns, celebrated with a meal of haggis
Caledonia	Scotland
ceilidh	an informal evening of traditional Scottish song and dance
clan	an extended family bearing the same surname (last name)
first foot	the first person to enter a house after midnight on New Year's Eve
Highland dress	Highland men's formal wear including the kilt
Hogmanay	New Year's Eve
kilt	knee-length pleated tartan skirt worn as traditional Highland dress
Ne'erday	New Year's Day
pibroch	type of bagpipe music
sgian-dubh	a small blade tucked into the outside of the sock on the right foot worn as part of the traditional Highland dress
sporran	pouch made of fur worn to the front of the kilt
tartan	chequered wool cloth, different colours being worn by each clan

COLLOQUIAL EXPRESSIONS

auld	old
auld lang syne	days of long ago
Auld Reekie	Edinburgh
aye	yes
bairn	child
barrie	excellent
blether	chat
bonnie	pretty
braw	excellent
dreich	wet (weather)
fae	from
fitba	football
hen	informal name used to address a woman or girl
ken	to know; to have knowledge
lassie	a young woman/girl
lumber	boyfriend/girlfriend
Nessie	legendary monster of Loch Ness
Old Firm	Celtic and Glasgow Rangers, Glasgow's main football teams
wean	child
wee	small

EYEWITNESS TRAVEL INSURANCE

FOR PEACE OF MIND ABROAD,
WE'VE GOT IT COVERED

DK INSURANCE PROVIDES YOU
WITH QUALITY WORLDWIDE
INSURANCE COVER

For an instant quote
go to **www.dk.com/travel-insurance**

Organised by Columbus Travel Insurance Services Ltd, 17 Devonshire Square, London EC2M 4SQ, UK.
Underwritten by certain underwriters at Lloyd's and Professional Travel Insurance Company Ltd.

Transport Map of Scotland

KEY

- 🛫 International Airport
- ☒ Domestic Airport
- ⛴ Major Ferry Services
- 🚉 Railway Terminus
- — Railway
- ▬ Motorway
- ▬ Major road
- ═ Minor road
- — National border

0 kilometres 50

0 miles 50

SCOTLAND

Cape Wrath

Durness
Scourie
Tongue
Altnaharra
Lochinver
Lairg
Achiltibuie
Ullapool
Loch Shin
Dingwall
Strathpeffer
Muir of Ord
INVERNESS
Nairn
Crom
Grantown-on-Spey
Poolewe
Gairloch
Loch Maree
Achnasheen
Torridon
Shieldaig
Lochcarron
Drumnadrochit
Loch Ness
Aviemore
Whitebridge
Fort Augustus
Kyle of Lochalsh
Kylerhea
Glen Shiel
Invergarry
Spean Bridge
Laggan
King

Port of Ness
Isle of Lewis
Callanish
Seisiadar
Stornoway
Harris
Tarbert
Scalpay
Leverburgh
Rodel
Berneray
North Uist
Lochmaddy
Staffin
Uig
Benbecula
Skeabost
Raasay
Dunvegan
Portree
South Uist
Sconser
Isle of Skye
Broadford
Lochboisdale
Canna
Barra
Castlebay
Armadale
Rum
Eigg
Arisaig
Muck
Ardnamurchan
Kilchoan
Corran
Strontian
Mallaig
Fort William
Onich
Glencoe
Ballachulish
Appin
Tobermory
Coll
Arinagour
Dervaig
Tiree
Scarinish
Lochaline
Fishnish
Ledaig
Craignure
Mull
Oban
Taynuilt
Tyndrum
Isle of Iona
Bunessan
Kilninver
Crianlarich
Kilmelford
Kilmartin
Arduaine
Inveraray
Balquhidder
Loch Lomond
Colonsay
Scalasaig
Jura
Crinan
Strachur
Ardlussa
Lochgilphead
Kilmartin
Tarbet
Aberfoyle
Helensburgh
Balloch
Dumbarton
Port Askaig
Feolin
Dunoon
Greenock
Paisley
GLASGOW
Portnahaven
Bowmore
Gigha
Rothesay
Largs
Bute
Millport
Johnstone
East Kilbride
Islay
Port Ellen
Brodick
Irvine
Prestwick
Troon
Kilmarnock
Campbeltown
Lamlash
Isle of Arran
Ayr
Mauchline
Turnberry
Girvan
New Galloway
Newton Stewart
Castle Douglas
Stranraer
Portpatrick
Port William
Kirkcudbright
Drummore
Whithorn

Scr

Dorr

Killiecrankie
Pitlochry
Aberfeldy
Dunk
Lochearnhead
Auchterarder
Callander
Dur
Stirl
Falk
Cum
M8

The Minch
The Minch
Little Minch
Inner Sound
Western Isles
Sound of Sleat
Summer only
Hebrides
Inner
Firth of Lorn
Sound of Jura
Firth of Clyde
North Channel
Solw
Whitehav
Isle of Man
Douglas

Belfast
Larne
Belfast
Belfast

A857
A859
A858
A865
A867
A855
A863
A851
A830
A861
A884
A849
A816
A846
A83
A82
A85
A87
A887
A886
A815
A819
A814
A811
A80
A71
A70
A713
A76
A75
A714
A77
A702
A7
A838
A836
A835
A832
A890
A831
A9
A97
A827
A823

Loch Shin
Loch Ness
Loch Lomond
Loch Maree
Glen Shiel